2,002
Surprising Things
about GOD
and the BIBLE

2,002
Surprising Things
about GOD
and the BIBLE

Jerry MacGregor & Marie Prys,
with Donna Wallace

BakerBooks
Grand Rapids, Michigan

Published by Baker Books
a division of Baker Publishing Group
P.O. Box 6287, Grand Rapids, MI 49516-6287

Previously published as two books: *1001 Surprising Things You Should Know about the Bible* (© 2002) and *1001 Surprising Things You Should Know about God* (© 2003).

Printed in the United States of America

Library of Congress Cataloging-in-Publication Data
MacGregor, Jerry.
    2002 surprising things about God and the Bible / Jerry MacGregor &
Marie Prys, with Donna Wallace.
        p.   cm.
    Includes bibliographical references and index.
    ISBN 0-8010-6617-4 (pbk.)
    1. God—Miscellanea. 2. Bible—Miscellanea. I. Title: Two thousand
two surprising things about God and the Bible. II. Title: Two thousand
and two surprising things about God and the Bible. III. Prys, Marie. IV.
Wallace, Donna K. V. Title.
BT103.M24 2006
230—dc22   2005024147

For Myra Grace MacGregor McGill, with fond memories.

For Kambiz Mirsepassi,
with thanks for your friendship.

Jerry

To Savannah Nelle, for keeping me company
as this book came together.

For my family—
immediate, extended, and inherited—
one of life's greatest gifts.

Marie

Contents

Part **1**

GOD

Introduction

"As fools long to play Shakespeare, so I have longed to write a book on God." These are the opening words of J. I. Packer's *Knowing God*. Of course, we wish we'd written them. The book you're holding in your hands probably won't take you down the same theological trail Packer does . . . but at least it should prove fun.

You see, we believe our God *is* fun. He is the creator of laughter, the originator of joy, and the God of surprises. It seems that everywhere you turn these days, people want to know God. We believe every individual was created with an innate desire to meet him. And the good news is that the Lord has *already* revealed himself to us clearly. Most of what we know about him is provided through his own words, as shared with us in the Bible. A careful reading of almost any passage of Scripture will reveal all sorts of insights into God—from his ancient plan to his present-day activities. All we have to do is open our eyes to the fact of God and we'll start to see him all around us. He has told us about his divine plan, his design for living, and his desire for our lives.

We therefore wrote this book in hopes of helping you know more about our God and about the Bible. Part 1 explores the character, actions, and events surrounding the one who authored life. This collection is not made up of the 1001 "most important" facts about God, the 1001 "best" facts, or even the 1001 "most necessary for a complete theological education" facts. Instead we have tried to pick the unique, the important, and the unfamiliar things we think every person ought to know . . . or at least consider. We've combined them into a volume that, while perhaps never being selected for a seminary course, will at least be read for enjoyment and enlightenment by those who want to know God better.

We recognize that no humanly authored book can offer a complete picture of the Lord of the universe. But we pray this book will be used in some little way to offer you a better understanding of God, a greater appreciation of the immense nature of our creator. Get to know him and see if your life doesn't change.

All about God

1. Theism is the belief in a supernatural power or supernatural powers, in one or many gods. This view includes all the various beliefs in a god or gods and is opposed only to atheism. Theism is also used to describe the belief in the existence of but one God, whether personal or impersonal, whether presently active in the universe or not. Some theists believe in a personal God, both transcendent and immanent, and existing only in one person. This includes Jewish, Islamic, and Unitarian concepts of God. A fourth view is the most discriminating and the one we hold throughout this book—the belief in one personal God, both immanent and transcendent, who exists in three personal distinctions, known as

Father, Son, and Holy Spirit. This is Christian theism and is opposed
to all the other views named.

2. The science of God and his works is called *theology.* This
word is derived from two Greek words, *theos* and *logos,* the former
meaning "God," and the latter, "word," "discourse," or "doctrine."
In a narrow sense, theology may be defined as "the doctrine of
God." However, in the broad and more usual sense, the term has
come to mean all Christian doctrines that deal with the relations
of God to the universe.

3. Theology has kept some pretty dry and dreary company,
according to Dallas Willard in his book *Spirit of the Disciplines.* "We
are tempted to leave it to the experts. But theology stands for
something far too important to each of our individual lives and
to the communities in which we live for us to shy away from it.
Theology is an integral part of our lives. We each have one—whether
thoughtless or carefully formed. Every Christian must strive to arrive at beliefs about God that faithfully reflect the realities of his
or her life and experience."

4. Theology versus philosophy. Both theology and philosophy
have the same basic objective—to seek a comprehensive worldview.
However, they differ greatly in their approach to attaining this
objective. While theology begins with the belief in the existence
of God and the idea that he is the cause of all things, philosophy
begins with the idea that it alone is sufficient to explain the existence of all other things. For some ancients, this explanation was
water, air, or fire; for others it has been the mind or ideas; for still
others, nature, personality, life, or some other thing. Theology
does not merely begin with the belief in the existence of God but
holds that he has graciously revealed himself. Philosophy denies
both these ideas.

5. Reflecting on God, pastor Charles Spurgeon once noted, "He
who often thinks of God, will have a larger mind than the man
who simply plods around this narrow globe. . . . The most excellent study for expanding the soul, is the science of Christ, and Him
crucified, and the knowledge of the Godhead in the glorious Trinity.
Nothing will so enlarge the intellect, nothing so magnify the whole

soul of man, as a devout, earnest, continued investigation of the great subject of the Deity."

6. The Christian God is omniscient, holy, loving, kind, and omnipotent. Being omniscient, he knows all about humanity's needs; since he is holy, he cannot excuse sin and take humanity in our fallen condition into fellowship with himself; because he is loving and kind, he may be moved to search for and put into operation a plan of salvation; and since he is omnipotent (all-powerful), he not only reveals himself but can also set forth in writing such revelations of himself as are needed for the experience of salvation.

7. *Deus Absconditus*. Blaise Pascal spoke of God as a *Deus Absconditus* (a hidden God), but he also held that this hidden God has revealed himself and therefore can be known.

8. The Bible and God. Because God is infinite, a comprehensive definition giving a complete and exhaustive portrayal of God is impossible. We can attempt to give a definition of God only as we know him and know *about* him as provided by Scripture.

9. The best summary of the doctrine of God as taught in the Bible is found in answer to question four of the *Westminster Shorter Catechism*, "What is God?" The answer: "God is a Spirit, infinite, eternal, and unchangeable, in his being, wisdom, power, holiness, justice, goodness, and truth." The great Charles Hodge described this statement as "the best definition of God ever penned by man."

10. Louis Berkhof's definition of God: "God is one, absolute, unchangeable and infinite in His knowledge and wisdom, His goodness and love, His grace and mercy, His righteousness and holiness."

11. In the Bible, life with God reads more like a mystery or a romance than a theology text. What is found in its pages differs markedly from what most people expect in getting to know God.

12. God is shy. The modern writer Philip Yancey describes God as shy, meaning not that he is bashful or timid, but rather that God shows incredible "self-restraint" even in things that displease him. After creating the world and the apex of his handiwork—humanity—God planned to enter into Sabbath rest when he and all his creatures would enjoy peace and harmony. Yet sin and history keep messing up his plan. Now God must set the pace of communication so we may know him when and how he wishes to make himself known.

13. God hides. Isaiah wrote, "Truly you are a God who hides himself" (45:15). Sometimes the Bible portrays God as the initiator, yet God sets a premium on his children living by faith, which can only be exercised in circumstances that allow for us to have doubts.

14. God is gentle. To describe God's gentle way of dealing with his children, contrast the possession of the Holy Spirit with that of an evil spirit described in the New Testament (Mark 9:18–21). Whenever the evil spirit seized the boy, he was thrown to the ground, his body rigid, teeth gnashing, and foaming at the mouth. God, on the other hand, humbles himself so deeply that he experiences emotional pain and suffering, so much that Paul has to warn his followers, "Quench not the Spirit" (1 Thess. 5:19 KJV) and "Grieve not the holy Spirit of God" (Eph. 4:30 KJV).

15. God is jealous. Jealousy is a strong emotion. The Song of Solomon likens it to love and compares its power to that of fire. Dan Allender and Tremper Longman set out to differentiate between godly jealousy and that which destroys. "Marriage is a mirror that reflects divine-human intimacy, and although this reflection is genuine, it is dim." As we may experience jealousy for our spouse, God feels it for his bride. But we must never lose sight of the difference between divine and human jealousy. God has the right to possess and protect. We do not possess our spouse, but *we do have the privilege of protecting* him or her.

16. God intends for us to feel righteous rage in order to mock the Evil One and destroy sin. Even though such rage appears to be the dark side of emotion, it bears the imprint of what God intended. As one modern writer puts it, "If we allow ourselves to join God's fury and then focus on what we are to hate—evil, sin, ugliness—our hearts may discover a new dimension of the character of God."

17. God has holy contempt. Contempt reflects something about the character of God that is often overlooked: God is a mocker. In fact, God does more than rage against arrogance; he plans on humiliating it. The psalmist writes, "The One enthroned in heaven laughs; the Lord scoffs at [those who rage against him]" (Ps. 2:4). "The wicked plot against the righteous and gnash their teeth at them; but the Lord laughs at the wicked, for he knows their day is coming" (Ps. 37:12–13).

18. The redemptive power of divine shame. Shame is an exposure of our idolatry because it reveals our foolish trust in ourselves. But it is also a great gift, because it is an invitation to grace. We encounter God's own humiliation in his Son's incarnation, earthly suffering, and crucifixion. Because God submitted to the shame of humility and lowliness, we are invited to enter into his humility by allowing our hearts to be grieved and broken through the exposure of sin.

19. He is a suffering God. "In all their affliction He was afflicted, and the angel of His presence saved them; in His love and in His mercy He redeemed them; and He lifted them and carried them all the days of old" (Isa. 63:9 NASB).

20. "The Lord longs to be gracious to you; he rises to show you compassion" (Isa. 30:18; cf. Gen. 21:15–17; 1 Samuel 1). Yet Scripture also says, "For it has been granted to you on behalf of Christ not only to believe on him, but also to suffer for him" (Phil. 1:29). Our call to suffer comes from a God tender beyond description.

21. Jesus' compassion drove him to open blind eyes and rouse lifeless limbs—he never glorified illness or eulogized pain and sorrow. But God's plan includes suffering. Despite Christ's compassionate death for our sins, God's plan calls for all Christians to suffer, sometimes intensely.

22. God is fully at peace. Only God is perfect in this. As a result, inner peace is not something we attain by eliminating pressure points or by the cessation of war or conflict. Rather, peace is allowing the perfectly integrated character of God to express himself through us.

23. The suffering God. When we read of Jeremiah mourning for his people, we see the heart of God through the words of his prophet: "Oh, that my head were a spring of water and my eyes a fountain of tears! I would weep day and night for . . . my people"

(Jer. 9:1). Hear the pain in God's heart when he pleads, "My people, what have I done to you? How have I burdened you?" (Micah 6:3). The pain described is that of a lover searching for the reason his people ignore his tender affection and protective love.

24. Frederick Buechner once wrote, "God puts Himself at our mercy not only in the sense of the suffering that we can cause Him by our blindness and coldness and cruelty, but the suffering that we can cause Him simply by suffering ourselves. Because that is the way love works, and when someone we love suffers, we suffer with him, and we would not have it otherwise because the suffering and the love are one, just as it is with God's love for us."

25. J. I. Packer challenges his readers to plug their ears to those who say there is no road to knowledge about God, and to travel a little way with him and see. "Anyone who is actually following a recognized road will not be too worried if he hears non-travelers telling each other that no such road exists."

26. We know God only through knowing Jesus Christ, who is himself God manifest in the flesh. Scripture makes this clear: "Hast thou not known me . . . ? he that hath seen me hath seen the Father." "No man cometh unto the Father, but by me" (John 14:9, 6 KJV). We must be clear in our minds as to what "knowing" Jesus Christ means.

What Is God Like?

2

27. Because God is infinite, a comprehensive definition providing a complete and exhaustive portrayal of God is impossible. However, we can give a definition of God insofar as we know him and know about him. The Bible reveals the attributes of God as revealed to humanity. We can say God is a being and then indicate the ways in which he is different from other beings.

28. God is with us. When considering the nature of God in relation to his created world, we usually speak of two concepts traditionally known as *transcendence* and *immanence*. Rather than exploring God's specific actions, these concepts regard his status in relationship to the world—the degree to which God is present and active within the universe.

29. Immanence. God is present and active within nature, human nature, and history. Jeremiah 23:24 emphasizes God's presence throughout the whole universe: "'Can anyone hide in secret places so that I cannot see him?' declares the LORD." The apostle Paul told the philosophers on Mars Hill, "Though he is not far from each one of us. 'For in him we live and move and have our being.' As some of your poets have said, 'We are his offspring'" (Acts 17:27–28).

30. Transcendence. The other aspect of the relationship of God to the world is the fact that he is separate from and independent of nature and humanity. God is not simply attached to or involved in his creation; he is superior in significant ways. "'For my thoughts are not your thoughts, neither are your ways my ways,' declares the LORD. 'As the heavens are higher than the earth, so are my ways higher than your ways and my thoughts than your thoughts'" (Isa. 55:8–9).

31. Kierkegaard once wrote, "The remarkable thing about the way in which people talk about God, or about their relation to God, is that it seems to escape them completely that God hears what they are saying. A man says, 'At the moment I have not the time or the necessary recollection to think about God, but later on perhaps.' Or better still a young man says, 'I am too young now; first of all I will enjoy life—and then.' Would it be possible to talk like that if one realized that God heard one?"

32. Philosophers and God. For Plato, God is the eternal mind, the cause of good in nature. Aristotle considered him to be "the first ground of all being." Benedict de Spinoza defined God as "the absolute, universal Substance, the real Cause of all and every existence: and not only the Cause of all being, but itself all being, of which every special existence is only a modification." Gottfried Leibniz said that the final reason of things is called God. Immanuel Kant defined God as a being who, by his understanding and will, is the cause of nature; a being who has all rights and no duties; the moral author of the world. For Johann Fichte, God was the moral

order of the universe, actually operative in life. Georg Wilhelm
Frederich Hegel considered God the absolute spirit, yet a spirit
without consciousness until it becomes conscious in the reason
and thoughts of man.

33. God is the infinite and perfect Spirit in whom all things have
their source, support, and end, according to Strong's definition.

34. The existence of God is automatically assumed by the
Scriptures. Because of this, the Bible does not attempt to prove his
existence, rather it is assumed. The Scriptures begin with the majestic statement, "In the beginning God." Such texts as Psalm 94:9–23
and Isaiah 40:12–31 are not proofs of God's existence, but rather
analytical accounts of all that is involved in the idea of God.

35. God is spirit. God is a substance. He is, however, not a material
substance but a spiritual substance. Jesus said, "God is spirit" (John
4:24). Christ also said, "A spirit does not have flesh and bones as
you see that I have" (Luke 24:39 NASB). The second commandment
of the Decalogue, which forbids the making of any graven image
or likeness of anything (Exod. 20:4), is based on the immaterial
nature of God. So are the numerous commands against idolatry
(see Lev. 26:1; Deut. 16:22).

36. God's body. What about the expressions that represent God as
having bodily parts, such as hands, feet, eyes, and ears? These are
anthropomorphic (assigning human form or character to God) and
symbolic representations that serve to make God understandable
and to express his various interests, powers, and activities.

37. God is infinite. God is spirit without beginning or end. Mankind
is spirit, too, but differs in that we have a *finite* spirit, which is able
to dwell in a material body (1 Cor. 2:11; 1 Thess. 5:23). God is
infinite spirit and as such is without form (Acts 7:48).

38. God is invisible. God told Moses that no man could see him
and live (Exod. 33:20). John says, "No one has seen God at any
time" (John 1:18 NASB). Paul calls him "the invisible God" (Col.
1:15 NASB) and declares that no man has seen him or can see
him (1 Tim. 6:16). Certain Scriptures, however, indicate that the
redeemed will one day see God (Ps. 17:15; Matt. 5:8; Heb. 12:14;
Rev. 22:4).

39. What about the Scriptures that say men saw God, such as
Genesis 32:30; Exodus 3:6; 24:9–11; Numbers 12:6–8; Deuteronomy
34:10; and Isaiah 6:1? When one looks in a mirror, he or she in a
sense sees oneself, yet does not literally see the true self. So men
saw the reflection of God's glory, but they did not see his essence
(Heb. 1:3). Then, too, spirit can be manifested in visible form (John
1:32). When Moses saw the "back" of God (Exod. 33:23), it was in
response to his request to see the glory of the Lord (v. 18). Rather
than literally and visibly seeing God, it is better understood that
Moses saw the aftereffects of God.

40. Theophanies are manifestations of deity in visible form.
After he had wrestled with the man, Jacob said, "I saw God face to
face" (Gen. 32:30). "The angel of the LORD" was a visible manifestation of deity (Gen. 16:7–14; 18:13–33; 22:11–18; Exod. 3:2–5; Judg.
6:11–23; 1 Kings 19:5–7; 2 Kings 19:35). In some of these passages,
"the angel of the LORD" is identified simply as "the LORD."

41. God is alive. The idea of spirit implies that God is not an inanimate substance but rather is alive. He is, therefore, called the
"living" God (Josh. 3:10; 1 Sam. 17:26; Ps. 84:2; Matt. 16:16; 1 Tim.
3:15; Rev. 7:2). Life implies feeling, power, and activity. God has
all of these (Ps. 115:3). He is also the source and support of all life:
plant, animal, human, spiritual, and eternal (Ps. 36:9; John 5:26).
The living God is always in contrast to dead idols (Ps. 115:3–9; Acts
14:15; 1 Thess. 1:9). Our God is alive. He sees, hears, and loves.

42. God is a person. The only way of determining what spirit is
like, apart from Scriptures, is by analogy with the human spirit.
Since the human spirit is personal, the Divine Spirit must be personal as well, for otherwise he is of a lower order of being than
humanity. What is the essence of personality? Self-consciousness
and self-determination.

43. God is self-conscious and self-determinative. As conscious
beings, we often think spontaneously but do not always think
about those thoughts. As *self*-conscious beings, however, we can
relate and reflect on our personal feelings, appetites, and thoughts.
Likewise, *self*-determination is more than determination. Humans
have the feeling of freedom, are able to make choices, and can
consider our motives and ends. The Scripture writers also ascribe

both self-consciousness (Exod. 3:14; Isa. 45:5; 1 Cor. 2:10) and self-determination (Job 23:13; Rom. 9:11; Eph. 1:9, 11; Heb. 6:17) to God.

44. God has personality. The Bible reveals that God has intellect (Gen. 18:19; Exod. 3:7; Acts 15:18), sensibility (Gen. 6:6; Ps. 103:8–14; John 3:16), and volition (Gen. 3:15; Ps. 115:3; John 6:38). Furthermore, it ascribes qualities and relations of personality to God. He is represented as speaking (Gen. 1:3), seeing (Gen. 11:5), hearing (Ps. 94:9), grieving (Gen. 6:6), and repenting (Gen. 6:6); and being angry (Deut. 1:37), jealous (Exod. 20:5), and compassionate (Ps. 111:4). He is said to be the creator (Acts 14:15), upholder (Neh. 9:6), ruler (Ps. 75:7; Dan. 4:32), and sustainer of all things (Ps. 104:27–30; Matt. 6:26–30).

45. The Bible calls him "the blessed God" (1 Tim. 1:11). Ancient Greeks used the word *blessed* to describe the rich and powerful—society's upper crust—and to label the gods, who could have whatever they wanted and do as they pleased.

46. God is self-existent. While humanity's ground of existence is outside ourselves, God's existence is not dependent upon anything outside himself. As Thomas Aquinas said, "He is the first cause, Himself uncaused." His self-existence is implied in his affirmation, "I AM WHO I AM" (Exod. 3:14).

47. God is immense. God is infinite in relation to space. He is not limited or bound by space; on the contrary, all finite space is dependent on him. He is, in fact, above space. Scripture clearly teaches God's immensity (1 Kings 8:27; 2 Chron. 2:6; Pss. 113:4–6; 139:7–12; Isa. 66:1; Jer. 23:24; Acts 17:24–28). Due to the spirituality of his nature and our inability to think in spaceless terms, God's immensity is a difficult doctrine to comprehend. God is both immanent and transcendent, and he is everywhere present in essence as well as in knowledge and power.

48. God is eternal. God is infinite in relation to time. He is without beginning or end, is free from all succession of time, and is the cause of time. He is called "the Everlasting God" (Gen. 21:33 NASB). The psalmists say, "From everlasting to everlasting, thou art God" (Ps. 90:2 KJV) and "Thou art the same, and thy years shall have no end" (Ps. 102:27 KJV). Isaiah represents God as "the high and exalted One Who lives forever" (Isa. 57:15 NASB). Paul says that God "alone possesses immortality" (1 Tim. 6:16 NASB).

49. Gregory the Great once said, "God is within all things, but not included; outside all things, but not excluded; above all things, but not beyond their reach."

50. Eternity for God is one "now," one eternal present. In Scripture this is referred to as "the day of eternity" (2 Peter 3:18 NASB) and "today" (Ps. 2:7). God sees the past and the future as vividly as he sees the present. In other words, a person may view a procession from the top of a high tower, seeing the whole procession at one glance, or he or she may view it from the street corner, where only one part can be seen at a time. God sees the whole as one unit, although he is aware of the sequence in the procession.

51. God is the cause of time. The reference to God in Isaiah 9:6 may be translated "Father of Eternity." Both time and space are among "all things" that "came into being through him" (John 1:3 NRSV). Time will someday merge into eternity (1 Cor. 15:28).

52. All contentment is a foretaste of eternity where "God himself will be with them and be their God. He will wipe every tear from their eyes. There will be no more death or mourning or crying or pain, for the old order of things has passed away" (Rev. 21:3–4).

53. God is unified. The unity of God means that there is one God and that the divine nature is undivided and indivisible. "Hear, O Israel! The LORD is our God, the LORD is one!" (Deut. 6:4 NASB). That there is but one God is the great truth of the Old Testament (Deut. 4:35, 39; 1 Kings 8:60; Isa. 45:5–6). The same truth is frequently taught in the New Testament (Mark 12:29–32; John 17:3). Unity implies that the three persons of the Trinity are not separate within the divine essence.

54. God is not merely one; he is the *only* God. Only one infinite and perfect being exists. The unity of God allows for personal distinctions in the divine nature, while at the same time recognizing that the divine nature is *numerically* and *eternally* One.

His Names

3

55. God in the plural. It is interesting that God used plural pronouns (Gen. 1:26; 3:22; 11:7; Isa. 6:8) and plural verbs (Gen. 1:26; 11:7) to refer to himself. The name for God (*Elohim*) is plural—though this form is most likely used for intensity.

56. Biblical names of persons and places carry great significance, a fact that is especially true with the names for deity. In biblical times, a name represented a person's character. God's name not only represents his character but his attributes and his nature as well. To know his name is *to know him*. To boast in his name is to have confidence in who he is (Ps. 20:7).

57. That I may know him. Jesus' prayer on our behalf just before he went to the cross was, "That they may know thee the only true God, and Jesus Christ whom thou hast sent" (John 17:3 KJV). Paul also states the ultimate goal in life, "That I may know him" (Phil. 3:10 KJV). Unfortunately, we often miss the multifaceted aspects of God's nature in translation.

58. Describing God. As it takes many rays to make up the pure light of the sun, it takes many varied descriptions to give us a true conception of the being and glory of God. No finite person is able to receive the whole revelation of his majesty at once. Only one part at a time can be comprehended. God carefully orchestrated ways to reveal himself with different names and titles describing his nature and purpose so that we may know him.

59. The Law of First Mention. In Bible study, it is important to keep in mind what Dr. A. T. Pierson calls *The Law of First Mention.* Often the first mention of a person, place, doctrine, or word is an "embryo of a feature or a fact that will develop further." This idea applies to almost all the divine names and titles in Scripture.

60. God. The fourth word in the opening of the Bible is the first mentioned name in the Bible—"In the beginning God . . ." (Gen. 1:1). This first verse is his signature, suggesting that the book holy men would write under his inspiration belonged to him.

El

61. *El,* **with its derivations** *Elim, Elohim,* **and** *Eloah,* is similar to the Greek *theos,* the Latin *Deus,* and the English *God.* This is one of the oldest and most widely distributed terms for deity known to the human race and is used to include all members of the class of deity. This short title is the most primitive Semitic name; its root meaning is most likely "to be strong," "might," or "power" (even when it's not used for God, it is still translated "might" or "power" [Gen. 31:29; Deut. 28:32]).

62. The poetical name. In classical Hebrew, *El* is mainly poetical. While found throughout the Old Testament, it is discovered more often in Job and the Psalms than in other books. *El* is also one of the names given to the promised Messiah, *El*, the mighty (Isa. 9:6–7).

63. *Eloi, Eloi*. In the New Testament crucifixion narrative, Jesus cried out in a loud voice, *"Eloi, Eloi"* (Mark 15:34). In his extreme weakness, he prayed "my strength, my strength," as he cried out for *El*, "the Strong One—the first and only cause of things." This moment was predicted hundreds of years earlier in Psalm 22 (called the Calvary Psalm). Christ pleads to *El* in his agony, "My God, my God, why have you forsaken me?"

64. *El* is found in ancient compound proper names such as Isra-*el*, Beth-*el*, *El*-elohe-*el*, meaning "House of Israel," Peni-*el*, face of *El*, Prince of *El*, *El* Shaddai. This two-letter name can also be found in all biblical names commencing with El, such as Eliakim, Elihu, Elimelech, Elisha, and Elizabeth.

65. Throughout the Bible, *Elohim* usually refers to God (found some three thousand times—over twenty-three hundred of which are applied to God). Though *Elohim* is the primary word translated "God" in the Old Testament, it can also be used of pagan deities or gods. For instance, it is used for idols (Exod. 34:17), men (Ps. 82:6; John 10:34–35), angels (Pss. 8:5; 97:7), god-men (Gen. 3:5), and judges (Exod. 22:8). In these instances, the idea of might and authority are communicated by the word. Deuteronomy 10:17 says, "For the LORD your God [*Elohim*] is God of gods. . . ."

66. *Elohim*—Creator. The name *Elohim* primarily designates God as God. The plural ending, *him*, is especially significant in Hebrew because it indicates three. *Elohim*, the name for God as creator, is used in Genesis 1:1 and thus could be translated, "In the beginning *Gods* created the heavens and the earth." (In the first two chapters of Genesis, *Elohim* occurs thirty-five times in connection with God's creative power.)

67. The plural *Elohim* does not mean there was more than one God. Rather, the Old Testament writers used the name with singular verbs and adjectives to denote a singular idea. "The LORD [Jehovah] our God [*Elohim*], the LORD is one" (Deut. 6:4). God the Father, God the Son, and God the Holy Spirit created the heavens and the earth. One in essence and in character; yet three persons united as one.

68. Each person in the Godhead had a part in creation. In various parts of Scripture, you can see the different persons of the Godhead participating in the work of creation. In Genesis 1:2–3 we read, "the Spirit of God was moving over the surface of the waters. Then God said, 'Let there be light'; and there was light" (NASB). God spoke, the Spirit moved, and Colossians 1:16 tells us that in him, Christ Jesus, the Son of God, "all things were created, both in the heavens and on earth." This is also seen in the creation of man. In Genesis 1:26, we read, "Then God [*Elohim*] said, 'Let us make man in our image.'"

69. The maker and keeper of covenant. The idea conveyed by *Elohim* is always that of one in a covenant relationship. In his words to Abram, *Elohim's* name pledges this relationship: "I am the Almighty God; walk before me, and be thou perfect. . . . And I will establish my covenant between me and thee and thy seed after thee in their generations . . . and I will be their" *Elohim*, that is, I will be with them in covenant relationship (Gen. 17:1–8 KJV).

70. "I am the LORD your God, . . . you are precious and honored in my sight, . . . everyone who is called by my name, whom I created for my glory, whom I formed and made" (Isa. 43:3–4, 7). The word for "glory" in Greek is *doxa,* and it means to give the correct opinion or estimate of. We have been created for God's glory—to give all of creation a correct opinion or estimate of who God is.

71. *Elah, Eloah*—the Adorable One. *Elah* is the Chaldee form of *Eloah*, which is known as a verbal noun, and is associated with the Hebrew verb *alah*, meaning to fear, to worship, to adore. The Adorable One. This distinctive divine name stands for the nature and expression of the only living and true God, the object of all testimony and worship. David asked, "Who is [*Eloah*] besides the LORD?" (2 Sam. 22:32). God asks, "Is there any [*Eloah*] besides me?" (Isa. 44:8).

72. One of the oldest names for God is "Redeemer." In faith Job proclaimed, "I know that my Redeemer lives, and that in the end he will stand upon the earth. And after my skin has been destroyed, yet in my flesh I will see God" (19:25–26). *Eloah*, the one we worship and adore.

73. *Eloah*—**Absolute Deity.** As in *Elohim* we have unity in the Trinity, so in *Eloah* we have absolute Deity. Both the Old and New Testaments emphasize, "The Lord our God is one Lord."

74. The first occurrence of *Elah* is in Ezra 4:24 where it is used in connection with the work of rebuilding "the house of God" (*Elah*). This divine title occurs some ninety times in the Old Testament—forty-three times in Ezra, forty-six times in Daniel, and once in Jeremiah 10:10. *Elah* indicates that the living and true God is identified with his people in captivity. The word *Elah* means an oak—the tree symbolizing durability—a virtue characteristic of him who is "the Everlasting God."

75. *El Elyon*—**the Most High God.** The compound *El-Elyon* designates God as the highest, the Most High (Ps. 78:35). He is the sovereign ruler over all the universe. It was *El Elyon*, "God Most High, who delivered" Abraham's enemies into his hand (Gen. 14:20). It was the Most High God who was and is the Redeemer of Israel (Ps. 78:35). And it is the Most High God who rules today over the affairs of men (Dan. 4:34–35). Although humanity has been given a free will, God still overrules so that no man, angel, demon, devil, or any circumstance of life can thwart his plan.

76. The Highest in Order. Several names for God are applied in Scripture to things and persons of the world. *Elyon*, for instance, was a name used by other nations than Israel. But wherever it is used, the person or thing it speaks of is the highest of a series or order of "like natures." When applied to God, *Elyon* or "Most High" reveals that though he is the highest, others below him are endowed with like natures, and are therefore in some way related to him.

77. *Theos.* In the New Testament, the term *theos* takes the place of *El, Elohim,* and *Elyon.* The names *Shaddai* and *El Shaddai* are rendered *pantokrator*, the almighty, and *theos pantokrator*, God almighty. Sometimes the Lord is called "the Alpha and the Omega" (Rev. 1:8), "who is, and who was, and who is to come" (Rev. 1:4), "the First and the Last" (Rev. 2:8), and "the Beginning and the End" (Rev. 21:6).

78. *El-Elohe-Israel*—**God of Israel.** Jacob gave this name to the altar he erected at Shalem (Gen. 33:18–20). Jacob's act of faith, allocating his new name, Israel, also claims *Elohim*. Only with God could Israel walk according to his new name. (When God's name is connected to human names, it communicates that the bearer of the name experienced a new revelation of God's character and purpose, such as the God of Abraham, the God of Isaac, the God of Jacob, etc.)

79. *El Olam*—God of Eternity. A rare title in Scripture, *El Olam* describes what extends beyond our farthest vision, whether looking forward or backward, to instill a sense of purpose. Such reason is found in the God of Eternity, or as the KJV translates it, "the Everlasting God." Any time this name occurs, a reference (sometimes more hidden) is made to the distinct stages of God's dealings with his people through his eternal wisdom.

80. The first occurrence of the name *El Olam* carries heavy spiritual significance. It is found in connection with Abraham's struggle with Abimelech over the right to use wells. God caused Abraham to wander for many years, until at last he felt as if he could settle in the pastures near the streams of Beersheba. But the men of Gerar wanted to oust him. It was at this time that *El Olam*, God the Everlasting, revealed himself to Abraham, reminding him of an everlasting purpose (Gen. 20:13).

81. *El Roi*—the God who sees. Have you ever been unjustly turned away or thrown out, perhaps abandoned? Perhaps you fulfilled someone's pleasure and then you weren't wanted anymore. Maybe you have a child who has run away. Deep in your heart you may wonder if you failed in some way or were inadequate. Divorces, company layoffs, affairs, thefts . . . where is God? Does he know what is going on? The omnipresent God is there with you, and he sees all. Healing begins with a God who saw it all. We can trust in righteous judgment because he is *El Roi*; he saw it all (2 Thess. 1:5–10).

82. The only occurrence of the title *El Roi* in Scripture is in connection with Hagar's flight from Sarah. Out in the wilderness of Shur, God spoke to Sarah's handmaid, instructing her to return. Hagar had borne the son of Sarah's husband, Abraham (Genesis 16), and then was terribly mistreated. *El Roi* accompanies us as we turn back and face our oppressors. Writes the psalmist, "Where can I go from your Spirit? Where can I flee from your presence?" (Ps. 139:7).

83. *El Shaddai*—the Almighty, All-Sufficient One. The translation of the Hebrew word *Shaddai* is not totally clear in its meaning because scholars are not absolutely sure of its root word, but many believe it is a designation of God as the All-Sufficient One.

84. The first mention of the all-sufficient nature of God comes during a solemn occasion when God appeared to Abram and opened his message to the patriarch with "I am the Almighty God" (Gen. 17:1 KJV). When the Lord appeared, ninety-nine-year-old Abram fell on his face before God (Gen. 17:1–3). *El Shaddai*, the All-Sufficient One, made a covenant with the new father of nations and changed his name to Abraham. The same title was used when God appeared to Jacob and Isaac to bless them. In God all fullness dwells, and out of his constant fullness, his own receive all things.

85. *Shaddai*. The thought expressed in this name for God describes power, not of violence but of all-bountifulness. *Shaddai* primarily means "breasted," being formed directly from the Hebrew word *shad*, that is, "the breast," or more precisely, a woman's breast. Lewis G. Parkhust explains the divine title or name *Shaddai* as "'The Pourer or Shedder forth,' One that Satisfies with blessings both physical and spiritual." "Can a woman forget her nursing child, and have no compassion [tenderness] on the son of her womb? Even these may forget, but I will not forget you" (Isa. 49:15 NASB).

86. *Sheddim*, the kindred name to *Shaddai*, refers to objects of idolatrous worship in other parts of Scripture and describes the many-breasted idols, representing the genial powers of nature, which were worshiped among the heathen as givers of rain and bounty. *El Shaddai* is the true Giver of Life—even of his own life, of whom these heathen *Sheddim* were the idolatrous perversion.

87. *Adonai*—Lord Master/Ruler is a title that appears frequently in the prophets, expressing humanity's dependence and submission, as of a servant to his master or a wife to her husband. The title, Lord of Hosts, appears frequently in the prophetical and postexilic literature (Isa. 1:9; 6:3 NRSV). Some take the term to refer to God's presence with the armies of Israel in the times of the monarchy

(1 Sam. 4:4; 17:45; 2 Sam. 6:2), but a more probable meaning is God's presence with the hosts of heaven, the angels (Ps. 89:6–8; cf. James 5:4).

88. *Adonai* is a title that heathen nations applied to their gods. The Greek word comes from the Phoenician word *adon*, which means "lord." In Scripture it is often compounded with Jehovah as a proper name as, for instance, in *Adoni-jah*, which means "Jehovah is LORD." *Baal* was also used, which implies master or owner.

89. *Baal*. While we think of *Baal* as the title of the Canaanite local gods, in earlier times it was actually used by worshipers of God. For this reason, one of Saul's sons was named Ish-baal. One of David's men of war was known as Baaliah, which means, "Jehovah is Baal." When this title came to have degrading associations, proper names were changed and *Baal* became *Bosheth*, which was substituted in names such as Ishbosheth.

JEHOVAH

90. The Name of God. "He that blasphemeth the name of the LORD, he shall surely be put to death" (Lev. 24:16 KJV). In response to the Old Testament law, every Jew became so alarmed at the danger connected with the pronouncing or writing of this wonderful name that they dared not give expression to it for fear that the stroke of God might come upon them for uttering, and possibly blaspheming, the incomprehensible, or what might be called, *the* name of God.

91. *Jehovah* or *Yahweh*—the Eternal, Ever-Loving One. This is the personal name par excellence of Israel's God. The term is connected with the Hebrew verb "to be," and means the "self-existent one," or the "one who causes to be." This name is often translated into the English version by the word "LORD," using capital and small capital letters.

92. *Jehovah* is the most frequently used of all the different names of God in the Old Testament (appearing about seven thousand times). Its meaning is "God of the covenant." The first usage occurs in Genesis, where *Jehovah* is compounded with *Elohim*.

93. Among all the divine names none is so solemn as *Jehovah*.
Rabbinical writings have distinguished *Jehovah* by such euphemistic
expressions as "*the* Name," "the Great and Terrible Name," "the
Peculiar Name," "the Separate Name," "the Unutterable Name," "the
Ineffable Name," "the Incommunicate Name," "the Holy Name,"
and "the Distinguished Name." It was also known as "the Name
of Four Letters" because when taken from the Hebrew it is spelled
YHVH in English. Such Jewish reverence remains today—so much
so that many refrain from writing it or pronouncing it.

94. At the time of the covenant, God gave something to Abram,
which at once changed him from Abram to Abraham. What God
adds is the letter *he,* the chief letter of his own name *Jehovah*—that
sound that can only be uttered by an out-breathing—thus giving
to the elect something of his own nature (remember, a name de-
notes nature).

95. The meaning of this ancient name, which is said to be whis-
pered only by the high priest in the Holy of Holies once a year, is
perhaps most adequately described in the Book of Revelation. The
absoluteness of the divine, who is independent and self-existent,
is found in the declaration "I am Alpha and Omega, the beginning
and the ending, saith the Lord [*Jehovah*] which is, and which was,
and which is to come, the Almighty" (Rev. 1:8 KJV).

96. *Jehovah* means "I AM WHO I AM." At the burning bush, Moses
"said to God, 'Behold, I am going to the sons of Israel, and I will
say to them, "The God of your fathers has sent me to you." Now
they may say to me, "What is His name?" What shall I say to
them?' God said to Moses, 'I AM WHO I AM;' and He said, 'Thus you
shall say to the sons of Israel, "I AM has sent me to you." ' . . . "The
LORD, the God of your fathers, the God of Abraham, the God of
Isaac, and the God of Jacob, has sent me to you." This is My name
forever, and this is My memorial-name to all generations'" (Exod.
3:13–15 NASB).

97. The name *Jehovah* is derived from the archaic *havah*,
which means "to be, to become." Jehovah speaks of God's being
or essence. When we read the name of Jehovah, or LORD in capital
and small capital letters in our Bible, we should think in terms of
being, or existence and life, and we must think of Jehovah as the

being who is absolutely self-existent, the one who in himself possesses essential life and permanent existence.

98. JAH—the Independent One. JAH, which is pronounced "ya," is a shortened form of *Jehovah*. This name signifies that *he is*, and can be made to correspond to I AM, just as *Jehovah* corresponds to the fuller expression I AM THAT I AM. The name first appears in the triumphal Song of Moses in Exodus 15. We also see the combination, "JAH Jehovah is my strength and my song," where both present and future deliverance are implied (Isa. 12:2).

99. JAH is the present tense of the verb "to be." It suggests Jehovah as the *present* living God—the presence of God in daily life, or his present activity. JAH is "an ever-*present* help in trouble" (Ps. 46:1, emphasis added). Most people miss the connection with the often-repeated exclamation, "Praise ye the Lord," also meaning, "Praise ye JAH," or "Hallelu*jah*."

100. JAH in human names. JAH, the shortened form of *Jehovah*, is interwoven like other divine names with human names, always with a particular purpose and meaning. Many more names contain JAH at the end than at the beginning, most likely to show reverence. For example, Abi*jah* means "whose father is Jehovah."

101. God's title, JAH, is found in Psalm 68:4: "Extol him that rideth upon the heavens by his name [JAH], and rejoice before him" (KJV). The same Hebrew word occurs over forty times in Isaiah, the Psalms, and Exodus but is translated "the Lord" in our English Bible. Regrettably, the various titles of God have not been given their Hebrew significance in translation.

102. Jehovah occurs in a number of powerful combinations. *Jehovah-Jireh,* the Lord will provide (Gen. 22:14); *Jehovah-Rapha,* the Lord that heals (Exod. 15:26); *Jehovah-Nissi,* the Lord is my banner (Exod. 17:15); *Jehovah-Shalom,* the Lord is peace (Judg. 6:24); *Jehovah-Raah,* the Lord is my shepherd (Ps. 23:1); *Jehovah-Tsidqenu,* the Lord our righteousness (Jer. 23:6); and *Jehovah-Shammah,* the Lord is present (Ezek. 48:35).

103. *Jehovah-Eloheenu*—the LORD *Our* God. Nineteen times this expression is given in the Book of Deuteronomy. It is a title suggesting the *commonwealth* of God's people in him (Ps. 99:5, 8–9).

From references in Deuteronomy, we learn what he is (6:4), where he is (4:7), what he said (1:6, 19; 2:37; 5:25, 27), what he did (2:33, 36; 3:3; 23:14), what he gave (1:20, 25), what he has (29:29), and what he shows (5:24).

104. *Jehovah-Eloheka*—**the Lord** *Thy* **God.** This title is closely related to *Jehovah-Eloheenu* (though it's more personal) and likewise occurs frequently in Deuteronomy, being found in chapter 16 twenty times. Often used in the Book of Exodus, this divine name describes Jehovah's relationship to his people and focuses more on their responsibility to him.

105. *Jehovah-Elohai*—**the Lord** *My* **God.** This name can be linked to *Adon* or *Adonai*, a personal name meaning *my Lord*, and likewise emphasizing divine sovereignty (Judg. 6:15; 13:8). *Elohai* specifically points to the personal pronoun "my" as being expressive of a personal faith in the God of power (Zech. 14:5). Though he is God of his people, we can know him—all that he is in himself and all his blessings on us personally.

106. *Jehovah-Hoseenu*—**the Lord Our Maker.** In Psalm 95:6, the writer invites us to join him in approaching the throne of God, "Come, let us bow down in worship, let us kneel before the LORD our Maker." The Hebrew word *asah* is used to speak about God in a variety of ways as our maker. When this term is applied to Jehovah as our maker, the reference is not to his work at creation when he spoke things into being, but rather to his ability to fashion something out of what already exists. Paul reminds us that "we are his workmanship."

107. *Jehovah-Jireh*—**the Lord Will Provide.** This name stands as a monument of a great discovery and a remarkable deliverance in Genesis 22. The story of Abraham and Isaac introduces the God who sees and provides. For death there is only one provider, *Jehovah-Jireh*. Jehovah, who in himself possesses essential life, is the only one who can make provision for sinful man to live, and he does it by providing the Lamb of God who takes away the sins of the world.

108. *Jehovah-Jireh*—**"Sees all of our needs."** The word for provide, *jireh*, in the Old Testament means literally to see. How do the words *see* and *provide* relate? Because of his omniscience and perfection of character, God not only sees, he foresees. And *Jehovah-Jireh* provides for, or supplies, whatever the foreseen need may be. The seeing or providing of the ram was what caused Abraham to name that place "The LORD Will Provide. And to this day it is said, 'On the mountain of the LORD it will be provided'" or "it will be seen" (Gen. 22:14).

109. *Jehovah-Jireh*—**The Provider of Our Salvation/Mount Moriah** (provides for both life and death). *Moriah*, in the Hebrew, is a kindred word to *Jireh*, taken from "Jehovah seeing," and can be translated "seen of JAH," or "the vision of Jehovah." Not only was Mount Moriah the location where Abraham offered Isaac, but it was also the site on which Solomon would build the house of the Lord in Jerusalem (2 Chron. 3:1). Down through the ages, at Mount Moriah every temple sacrifice for sin would echo Abraham's words, "The LORD Will Provide [*Jehovah-Jireh*]" (Gen. 22:14).

110. *Jehovah-Meqoddishkem* **(or** *M'Qaddesh***)—the Lord Who Sanctifies You.** God brought his people to Mount Sinai where he gave them the covenant of the law and the pattern of the tabernacle where they would worship their God. These commandments would set them apart for God's own possession. Here they would come to know Jehovah as *Jehovah-Meqoddishkem* through observing his Sabbaths (Exod. 31:12–18).

111. The words *sanctify, set apart, holy,* **and** *saint* **all come from a common root word,** *qadash* in the Hebrew and *hagios* in the Greek. For the first time in Scripture, at Mount Sinai the purpose of the command for the Sabbath is laid out before the children of Israel. The Sabbath is to be a sign between God and Israel throughout all their generations so "that you may know that I am the LORD who sanctifies you" (Exod. 31:13 NASB). As God made the Sabbath holy to the children of Israel, he made the children of Israel holy, or set apart, unto himself.

112. As God sanctified Israel, he sanctifies the church. Holiness is not an option for believers, rather it is part of a perpetual covenant . . . a sign between God and the sons of Israel forever. "By this will we have been sanctified through the offering of the body of Jesus Christ once for all" (Heb. 10:10 NASB; see also John 17:15–19; 1 Thess. 4:3–8; 5:23).

113. The correct pronunciation of JHWH, the original name of God, has been lost. After a certain time, no knowledge remained of the way in which Jehovah should be pronounced. When Jewish scribes were writing out the Scriptures and came to the name of Jehovah, the Awful One, they would in most cases not write it as originally given but would write the less awful name of *Adonai*, meaning, "*my Ruler.*"

THE BANNER

114. *Jehovah-Nissi*—the Lord My Banner first appears in Exodus 17 at verse 8 with this significant statement: "Then Amalek came and fought against Israel" (NASB). Amalek, the grandson of Esau, was the first and constant enemy of Israel. And there would be no white flag of surrender in this battle. Amalek was an enemy of God and had to be subdued. In this famous battle, God was first worshiped as *Jehovah-Nissi*, "The LORD is my Banner" (Exod. 17:15). When Moses held up his hands, Israel prevailed, but when his arms grew weak and fell, Amalek would begin to conquer.

115. A banner was an ensign or standard carried at the head of a military band to indicate the line of march or the rallying point. A banner in ancient times was not necessarily a flag such as we use today. Often it was a bare pole with a bright shining ornament that glittered in the sun. The word *nissi* has interesting implications: as a *standard* (Isa. 5:26), as a *sign* (Num. 26:10), and as a *pole* in connection with the brazen serpent lifted up upon it to give life to Israel. Our Savior was lifted up on the pole, and by all he accomplished, we have victory.

116. The fearless and courageous Joshua came to the front in God's war against Amalek. He had a name that in its Hebrew form means Jesus—"I will be salvation." Isaiah prophesied that "the Root of Jesse will stand as a banner for the peoples" and one around whom the Gentiles and Israel would rally (Isa. 11:10, 12).

117. A monument was built to celebrate this glorious deliverance from Amalek. Moses built an altar and called it *Jehovah-Nissi*, or Jehovah my Banner. Moses took care to give God the glory.

Although the name *Jehovah-Nissi* appears only here on the memorial altar, the truth it expresses runs throughout Scripture.

118. *Jehovah-Qanna.* When God gave the Ten Commandments, he said, "I am the LORD your God, who brought you out of Egypt, out of the land of slavery. You shall have no other gods before me. . . . You shall not bow down to them or worship them; for I, the LORD your God, am a jealous God" (Exod. 20:1–5). Again in Exodus 34:12–17, God tells his people not to make covenant with the inhabitants of the land into which they were going because "the LORD, whose name is Jealous, is a jealous God" (v. 14).

119. Holy jealousy. A holy and godly jealousy is rooted in divine love (2 Cor. 11:2), and God acts according to his name just as he has warned his people he will. His people acted like harlots in their worship of idols and other gods, and God kept his promise—his presence left Jerusalem (Ezra 8:3–6, 17–18; 9:9–10).

120. God's Word stands above and according to his name. Although God's presence withdrew from Jerusalem, God came back because he is a God of covenant (promise). God was jealous for his holy name, but his Word stands above or according to his name, so he would return in his glory to Jerusalem, though his children would have to wait approximately six hundred years. He returned as the Messiah, but most of Israel did not recognize him. He came to his own, but his own received him not (John 1:11).

HEALER AND SHEPHERD

121. *Jehovah-Rapha (Rophi)*—the Lord That Heals. "Is there no balm in Gilead? Is there no physician there?" (Jer. 8:22). *Rapha* means "to mend," as a garment is mended, "to repair" as a building is reconstructed, and "to cure" as a diseased person is restored to health. The psalmist wrote, "who . . . heals all your diseases" (Ps. 103:3). In Ezekiel, the Hebrew word for "heal" is translated as "physician" (30:21). *Jehovah-Rapha* also heals a distressed nation or person by restoring them to prosperous circumstances; healing in a moral sense, curing the mind and pardoning the soul.

122. The children of Israel needed a healer. Soon after God delivered Israel, they needed him as *Jehovah-Rapha*. As Moses led his people from the Red Sea into the wilderness of Shur, they found no water. When they came to Marah they couldn't drink because the water was bitter. The people grumbled. When Moses cried out to the Lord, God showed him a tree to throw into the waters and they became sweet. God then tested his people, saying, "If you will give earnest heed to the voice of the LORD your God, . . . I will put none of the diseases on you which I have put on the Egyptians; for I, the LORD, am your healer" (Exod. 15:26).

123. "Heal me, O Lord." Whether it is the illness of a nation or of a single human being, it is God who heals lands, pestilences, bodies, emotions, souls, and spirits. He may use other humans as his instruments, but they are useless without the Physician's power to heal. Whenever one needs healing, he or she must first consult *Jehovah-Rapha*. "Heal me, O LORD, and I shall be healed; save me, and I shall be saved: for thou art my praise" (Jer. 17:14 44 KJV).

124. The term *heal* is used:

- to express God's grace in restoring spiritual life—he heals all our diseases, spiritual as well as physical (Ps. 103:3).
- to heal the broken in heart (Ps. 147:3).
- to recover the faithless from backsliding (Jer. 3:22).
- to remove bodily sickness or disease (Gen. 20:17; 2 Kings 20:5).

125. *Jehovah-Raah (Rohi)*—the Lord My Shepherd. This name has several meanings, all suggesting the many aspects of Jehovah's care. For example, it can be translated "feeder, keeper" (Gen. 4:2), "companion" (Prov. 28:7), "friend" (Judg. 14:20), "pastor" (Jer. 17:16), "herdsman" (Gen. 13:7), and "shepherd" (Ps. 23:1).

126. Pastoral people of the Bible lands are familiar with the life and caring role of a shepherd and the utter dependence of sheep on their shepherd. Many have found great comfort knowing God thinks and cares for us as sheep. "We all, like sheep, have gone astray" (Isa. 53:6). "My sheep hear my voice" (John 10:27). "We are . . . sheep of his pasture" (Ps. 100:3 NRSV). "I . . . will search for My sheep and seek them out" (Ezek. 34:11 NASB). "Feed my sheep" (John 21:17). Many Scriptures refer to God as our shepherd and to us as his sheep (John 10:1–17, 26–30).

127. The Twenty-third Psalm opens by summarizing one of the greatest truths concerning what it means to be a child of God—to have him as our *Jehovah-Raah*. "The Lord is my shepherd; I shall not want" (KJV). The rest of the psalm describes why there is no want for those whose shepherd is Jehovah.

128. "He maketh me to lie down" (v. 2). Here the psalmist is not describing a shepherd who forces his sheep to rest, but rather he is saying that because the shepherd has met all the flock's needs, it can lie down. According to Phillip Keller, it is impossible for a sheep to lie down unless four things are true:

- First, sheep must be free from hunger. They cannot lie down as long as they feel a need for finding food. In the second verse of Psalm 23, the Shepherd has so satisfied the sheep's hunger that they can lie down in the midst of green pastures.
- Second, if sheep are to rest, they must be free of fear. Sheep are helpless, timid animals with little self-defense, and they are easily frightened.
- Third, sheep cannot rest unless they are free from friction. Tension with other sheep keeps them on their feet. They feel they must defend themselves.
- Fourth, sheep cannot rest unless they are free from pests like flies, parasites, or things that torment them.

The God of Peace

129. *Jehovah-Sabaoth* (also *Tsebaoth*)—the Lord of Hosts. The word *sabaoth* is *tsebaah* according to *Strong's Concordance* and is the word for "a mass," "a mass of people or things, such as an army." It is used to refer to a host of angels or heavenly bodies, a celestial army, or to all that the earth contains.

130. The name *Jehovah-Sabaoth* is not used in Scripture until the Book of 1 Samuel; following that, it is used in two out of three instances by individuals. At that time Israel did not apparently see her need to call upon God as Lord of Hosts. Yet when we read the prophets Isaiah, Jeremiah, Amos, Haggai, Zechariah, and Malachi, we find this name for God used over and over again. It appears fifty-two times in Zechariah's fourteen chapters, and eighty-three times in Jeremiah's fifty-two chapters.

131. God is repeatedly referred to as the Lord of Hosts in the Books of Isaiah and Jeremiah but not in Ezekiel. Why? Because this name belongs to a certain stage in the experience of God's people. This is a name for those who in the midst of a struggle find their own resources inadequate. In desperation they called on the name of *Jehovah-Sabaoth*. On the other hand, it is not a name used by those who have ceased to fight—such as those found in Ezekiel in the days when they were forced to settle into seventy years of captivity.

132. From God's perspective, Lord of Hosts is a name that reminds his people exactly who he is. Not only is he the one who delivers, he is also the one who judges. We see God in the Book of Malachi reminding his people over and over again of his name, *Jehovah-Sabaoth*. "'I am not pleased with you,' says the Lord of hosts. . . . 'For My name will be great among the nations,' says the Lord of hosts. . . . 'I am a great King,' says the Lord of hosts, 'and My name is feared among the nations'" (Mal. 1:10–11, 14 NASB).

133. *Jehovah-Shalom*—the Lord Is Peace. In the dark hours of Israel's history during the time of the judges, God revealed himself as *Jehovah-Shalom*, "the Lord is peace." The sons of Israel had done evil in the sight of the Lord, and he had given them into the hands of the Midianites for seven years. Things were bad for God's chosen people (Judg. 6:6). Midian prevailed against Israel, forcing them into mountain caves and dens. Judges 6 describes the Midianites coming up with the Amalekites to ravage and devastate the Israelites' crops and all their livestock. God's people were desperate for peace.

134. *Jehovah-Shalom* revealed true peace to Gideon. "When Gideon saw that he was the angel of the Lord, he said, 'Alas O Lord God! For now I have seen the angel of the Lord face to face.' The Lord said to him, 'Peace to you, do not fear; you shall not die.' Then Gideon built an altar there to the Lord and named it The Lord is

Peace" (Judg. 6:22–24 NASB). True peace cannot be found in any other place than in right relationship with God.

135. **The basic underlying meaning of the Hebrew word** *shalom* is "a harmony of relationship or a reconciliation"; therefore, the word is most often translated "peace" (approximately 170 times). The first time *shalom* appears in the Bible is in connection with "eternal peace." "Thou shalt go to thy fathers in peace" (Gen. 15:15 KJV).

136. **The uniqueness of the word** *shalom* **can be gathered from its alternative renderings:** "welfare" (Gen. 43:27); "good health" (Gen. 43:28); "all is well, safe" (2 Sam. 18:28–29); "prosperity" (Ps. 35:27); "favor" (Song of Sol. 8:10); "rest" (Ps. 38:3); "whole" (Deut. 27:6); "finished" (1 Kings 9:25; Dan. 5:26); "full" (Gen. 15:16); "make good" (Exod. 21:34); "restitution or repay, well or welfare" (Exod. 22: 5, 6); and "pay or perform in the sense of fulfilling or completing obligations" (Pss. 37:21; 50:14). Several times it is given as "perfect" (1 Chron. 29:19), the idea of wholeness or being in harmony with God.

THE GOD WHO IS THERE

137. *Jehovah-Shammah*—**the Lord Is There.** The children of Israel were in captivity and would be there for seventy years as a result of their sin (Jer. 29:10). They had heard from the prophet Ezekiel how the glory of the Lord had departed from the temple (Ezek. 10:18–19; 11:22–24). God had to judge his people for their adultery as a nation. "How I have been hurt by their adulterous hearts, which have turned away from me. . . . They will loathe themselves for the evil they have done. . . . And they will know that I am the LORD . . ." (Ezek. 6:9). God left them with a future hope.

138. *Jehovah-Shammah* **is found in the last verse** of the Book of Ezekiel where it is used in reference to the earthly Jerusalem, the city that the Lord Jesus Christ will inhabit when he returns to earth to reign as King of Kings and Lord of Lords. "The distance all around will be 18,000 cubits. And the name of the city from that time on will be: THE LORD IS THERE" (Ezek. 48:35).

139. The word *shammah* is simply the word for "there," but the fact that it is combined with Jehovah and the fact that the Spirit of God calls it a name makes it unique. When God named the futuristic city *Jehovah-Shammah*, he was assuring his people that he, Jehovah, would be there. It assured them of a future and gave them purpose.

140. God's presence did return to Jerusalem. Scripture tells us he came again to the temple when he was twelve, but although the Jews were impressed, they did not realize they were listening to *Jehovah-Shammah* (Luke 2:42–47). At the age of thirty, *Jehovah-Shammah* began his ministry among them (Luke 3:23). They saw his miracles and heard his words, but still they would not believe.

141. *Jehovah-Tsidqenu*—**the Lord Our Righteousness.** In a dark hour of judgment and failure, God revealed to his people another of his names—*Jehovah-Tsidqenu*. "This is the name by which he will be called: The LORD Our Righteousness" (Jer. 23:6). And with that revelation comes the promise of a new covenant, the covenant of grace and a new heart (Jer. 31:31–34; Matt. 26:26–28; Heb. 8:6–13).

142. To be right with God or to be *righteous* **means to be** "straight." It is more than goodness. It is to do what God says is right, to live according to his standards. To do so requires a new heart. "I will put my law in their minds and write it on their hearts. . . . For I will forgive their wickedness and will remember their sins no more" (Jer. 31:33–34). "I will give you a new heart and put a new spirit in you; I will remove from you your heart of stone and give you a heart of flesh. And I will put my Spirit in you and move you to follow my decrees and be careful to keep my laws" (Ezek. 36:26–27).

143. The Hebrew term *Tsedeq* **depicts a full weight or measure** toward God in the spiritual sense, as contrasted to justice, which is represented as a woman holding a pair of balanced scales in her hand. (See Job 31:6; Ps. 62:9.) *Jehovah-Tsidqenu* is like a river flowing throughout the whole of Scripture. Appearing well over a thousand times in Scripture, this word is translated as "right, righteous," and also as "just, justify," and "declared innocent."

144. The message of righteousness can be found on almost every page of the Bible. It is the chain of truth opening out in depth and force to grab our attention, not only because of its messianic nature but because of personal, practical implications. God wanted his children to recognize that goodness and character were of greater value than the wealth, wisdom, and ways of the world.

145. *Jehovah-Makkeh*—the Lord Shall Smite Thee. "I will recompense thee according to thy ways and thine abominations that are in the midst of thee; and ye shall know that I am the Lord that smiteth [*Jehovah-Makkeh*]" (Ezek. 7:9 KJV). The American Standard Version translates the passage, "Ye shall know that I, Jehovah, do smite." God had dealt graciously with his people, but they had despised his grace. They refused to walk in his statutes and to keep his judgments. Because of the gross sin of the people, he had to deal with them in judgment.

146. *Jehovah-Gmolah*—the God of Recompense or Vengeance (he will fully repay). While *Jehovah-Gmolah* may withhold his judgment, vengeance is ultimately meted to those who mock his authority. The weeping prophet, Jeremiah, wrote: "Babylon has been a golden cup in the hand of the Lord [Jehovah], intoxicating all the earth. The nations have drunk of her wine; therefore the nations are going mad" (NASB). As a result, "the destroyer is coming against her, against Babylon, and her mighty men will be captured, their bows are shattered; for the Lord is a God of recompense, He will fully repay" (Jer. 51:7, 56 NASB).

147. Vengeance belongs to God, not to us. "Recompense to no man evil for evil. . . . Avenge not yourselves, but rather give place unto wrath: for it is written, Vengeance is mine; I will repay, saith the Lord" (Rom. 12:17–19 KJV). Solomon, whose name means peaceful, also gave us this advice, "Do not say, 'I'll pay you back for this wrong!' Wait for the Lord, and he will deliver you" (Prov. 20:22). Our nature says that people must be paid back their just due whether for evil or good. But God instructs us to leave the matter to him; he will right our cause and deal with those who treat us unjustly.

THE LORD OUR GOD

148. *Jehovah* versus *Adonai*. When *Lord* is in capital and small capital letters the word is *Jehovah*; otherwise the word is *Adonai* or *Adon*. When you read the Old Testament and see LORD, you are reading what in Hebrew is *YHWH, Jehovah*.

149. The name *Adonai* brings clarity to Christ's Sermon on the Mount. Jesus said, "Why do you call me, 'Lord, Lord,' and do not do what I say?" (Luke 6:46). "Not everyone who says to me, 'Lord, Lord,' will enter the kingdom of heaven, but only he who does the will of my Father who is in heaven" (Matt. 7:21–23). *Lord* is more than a word; it indicates a relationship. As this Scripture clearly indicates, the lordship of God means his total possession of us and our total submission to him as Lord and Master.

150. As *Adonai*, God has a right to expect obedience. This is why God became angry with Moses when he called him to go before Pharaoh and tell the ruler to let God's people go (Exod. 4:10–14). "Then Moses said to [Jehovah], 'Please, [*Adonai*,] I have never been eloquent, neither recently nor in time past, nor since You have spoken to Your servant; for I am slow of speech and slow of tongue.' . . . Then the anger of the LORD burned against Moses" (NASB). Why did God's anger burn? Because Moses was saying, "Lord, Lord [*Adonai*]," but not trusting or submitting to God as his Master.

151. Jesus as Lord *(Adonai)*—If God the Father is Lord, it is true also of God the Son. Jesus once asked the Pharisees, "'What do you think about the Christ? Whose son is he?' 'The son of David,' they replied. He said to them, 'How is it then that David, speaking by the Spirit, calls him "Lord"? For he says, "The Lord said to my Lord: 'Sit at my right hand until I put your enemies under your feet.'" If then David calls him "Lord," how can he be his son?' No one could say a word in reply, and from that day on no one dared to ask him any more questions" (Matt. 22:42–46).

152. Jesus claimed to be *Adon*. He quoted Psalm 110:1 to prove to the Pharisees that he was the Son of God. As Jesus quoted the psalm, he also established the fact that he was *Adon*. The verse reads in Hebrew, "Jehovah says to my *Adon.*" In this passage, David was speaking prophetically of Christ, the Messiah.

153. "Lord" is a title translated from two words in the New Testament. *Kyrios* means supreme in authority, or controller. This is the most common word used in reference to Jesus Christ. The other is *despotes,* which means an absolute ruler, like a despot. "You call me 'Teacher' and 'Lord,' and rightly so, for that is what I am" (John 13:13; see Rom. 10:8–10). "Lord" is the one-word definition of God's sovereignty.

His Attributes

4

---

154. Perfectly balanced, perfectly integrated. In his book *The Knowledge of the Holy*, A. W. Tozer points out that there is no conflict between God's attributes within himself. He is perfectly integrated in his being; he is whole. This is what peace is. All of the expressions of God's character are perfectly balanced and perfectly manifested. What we call peace is the perfect, balanced expression of character that flows from a true and secure recognition of who God is.

155. Omnipresence. The first of the three compound words using the Latin prefix *omni*, meaning "all," is connected to the word "presence," meaning God is everywhere at once. God is present in all his creation but is in no way limited by it. Whereas immensity emphasizes the transcendence of God in that he transcends all space and is not subject to the limitations of space, omnipresence has special reference to his presence within the universe (1 Kings 8:27; Ps. 139:7–10; Isa. 66:1; Jer. 23:23–24; Acts 7:48–50; 17:24; Rom. 10:6–8).

156. The omnipresence of God means two things. The doctrine of the omnipresence of God is both comforting and subduing. It is a source of comfort, because God, the ever-present one, is always available to help us (Deut. 4:7; Pss. 46:1; 145:18; Matt. 28:20). But it is equally a source of warning and restraint. No matter how much we may try, the sinner cannot escape from God. Neither distance nor darkness hides us (Ps. 139:7–10). "And there is no creature hidden from His sight, but all things are open and laid bare to the eyes of Him with whom we have to do" (Heb. 4:13 NASB).

157. Omniscience. God is infinite in knowledge. He knows himself and all other things perfectly, whether they be past, present, or future. He knows things immediately, simultaneously, exhaustively, and truly. Scripture declares that God's understanding is infinite (Ps. 147:5; Isa. 46:10), that nothing is hidden from him (Heb. 4:13), and that even the hairs on our head are numbered (Matt. 10:30).

158. God knows himself perfectly. No created being has complete and perfect knowledge of self other than God. The Father, the Son, and the Holy Spirit know each other perfectly. The Trinity alone has intimate knowledge of each other. Jesus said, "No one knows the Son except the Father, and no one knows the Father except the Son and those to whom the Son chooses to reveal him" (Matt. 11:27). Paul wrote, "No one knows the thoughts of God except the Spirit of God" (1 Cor. 2:11).

159. God determines and knows all things. This includes inanimate creation (Ps. 147:4), all the beasts (Ps. 8:7), humanity and all their works (Ps. 33:13–15; Prov. 5:21), men's thoughts and hearts (Ps. 139:1–4; Prov. 15:3), and men's burdens and wants (Exod. 3:7; Matt. 6:8, 32).

160. God orders all things into being. God knew that Keilah would betray David to Saul if David remained in that vicinity (1 Sam. 23:11–12). Jesus knew that Tyre and Sidon would have repented had they seen the miracles that were done in Bethsaida and Chorazin (Matt. 11:21). He also knew the cities of Sodom and Gomorrah would have been spared had they seen the works that were done in Capernaum (Matt. 11:23–24).

161. God knows the future. From humanity's standpoint, God's knowledge of the future is foreknowledge, but from God's standpoint it is not, because he knows all things by one simultaneous intuition. He foreknew the future in general (Isa. 46:9–13; Daniel 2, 7; Matthew 24–25; Acts 15:18), the sinful course that Israel would take (Deut. 31:20–21), the rise of Cyrus (Isa. 44:26–45:7), the coming of Christ (Micah 5:2), and his crucifixion at the hands of wicked men (Acts 2:23; 3:18).

162. Omnipotence. God is all-powerful and able to do whatever he wills. Since his will is aligned with his nature, God can do everything that is in harmony with his perfections. Some things God cannot do because they are contrary to his nature as God. He cannot look with favor on iniquity (Hab. 1:13), deny himself (2 Tim. 2:13), lie (Titus 1:2; Heb. 6:18), or tempt or be tempted to sin (James 1:13).

163. God's possession of omnipotence does not demand the exercise of his power, and certainly not the exercise of *all* his power. In other words, God has power over his power. Omnipotence includes the power of self-limitation. God has limited himself to some extent by giving free will to his rational creatures.

164. The Bible clearly teaches the omnipotence of God. The Lord, who is called "Almighty" (Gen. 17:1; Rev. 4:8), is said to be able to do all things he purposes (Job 42:2), for with him all things are possible (Matt. 19:26) and nothing is too difficult (Jer. 32:17). He indeed reigns (Rev. 19:6).

165. Absolute versus ordinate power. A distinction can be made between God's absolute power, meaning that God may work directly, and his ordinate power, meaning he often uses second causes for divine intervention. Absolute power is used in creation, miracles, immediate revelation, inspiration, and regeneration.

166. To the Christian, the omnipotence of God is a source of great comfort and hope. The believer is urged to trust God in every walk of life with the knowledge of his creative, preserving, and providential power (Isa. 45:11–13; 46:4; Jer. 32:16–44; Acts 4:24–31). On the other hand, to the unbeliever, a God so mighty should be a source of fear (1 Peter 4:17; 2 Peter 3:10–12; Rev. 19:15). Even the demons shudder (James 2:19), knowing that God has power over them (Matt. 8:29). Someday even the strongest and greatest will seek to hide from God (Rev. 6:15–17), and every knee will bow at the name of Jesus (Phil. 2:10).

167. God is immutable and unchanging. All change is either for better or worse, but God cannot change to the better, because he is absolutely perfect; neither can he change for the worse, for the same reason. He can never be wiser, more holy, more just, more merciful, more truthful, or less so. Neither do his plans and purposes change. Scripture declares that there is no variation with God (James 1:17). He does not change with regard to his character (Ps. 102:26–27; Mal. 3:6; Heb. 1:12), his power (Rom. 4:20–21), his plans or purposes (Ps. 33:11; Isa. 46:10), his promises (1 Kings 8:56; 2 Cor. 1:20), his love and mercy (Ps. 103:17), or his justice (Gen. 18:25; Isa. 28:17).

168. Immutability is not to be confused with immobility. God is active and enters into relationships with changing people. In these relationships it is necessary for an unchangeable God to alter his dealings with changing humanity in order to remain constant in his character and purposes. For example, God deals differently with people before salvation than after (Prov. 11:20; 12:12; 1 Peter 3:12), and when his children change from evil to good, or from good to evil (Gen. 6:6; Exod. 32:14; Jer. 18:7–11; Joel 2:13; Jonah 3:10). God's immutability consists in always doing right.

GOD'S MORAL ATTRIBUTES

169. The holiness of God. God is absolutely separate from and exalted above all his creation, and he is equally separate from all evil and sin. God is perfect in all that he is. God's will is always the expression of his nature, which is holy.

170. Holiness in the Old Testament. Holiness is the attribute by which God wanted to be known in the Old Testament times.

It is emphasized by the boundaries set on Mount Sinai when God came down upon it (Exod. 19:12–25)—the division of the tabernacle and temple into the holy and most holy places (Exod. 26:33; 1 Kings 6:16, 19), the prescribed offerings (Leviticus 1–7), the special priesthood to mediate between God and the people, the many laws about impurity, the feasts of Israel, and the special position of Israel in Palestine. The Lord is called "the Holy One" some thirty times in Isaiah alone.

171. Holiness in the New Testament. In New Testament times, holiness is ascribed to God with less frequency than in the Old, but is still prevalent (John 17:11; Heb. 12:10; 1 Peter 1:15.). The angels around the throne of God sing "Holy, holy, holy" (Isa. 6:3; Rev. 4:8). The holiness of God, rather than the love, the power, or the will of God, should be given first place. Holiness is the regulative principle of the other three, for his throne is established on the basis of his holiness.

172. Righteousness and justice. Righteousness and justice are the aspects of God's holiness that are seen in his dealings with his creation. Abraham pondered, "Will not the Judge of all the earth do right?" (Gen. 18:25). The psalmist declares, "Righteousness and justice are the foundation of your throne" (Pss. 89:14; 97:2). (See *Jehovah-Tsidqenu*, chap. 3, no. 141.)

173. The goodness of God. In the larger sense of the term, the goodness of God includes many qualities such as God's holiness, righteousness, and truth. But in the narrower sense, God's goodness focuses on his love, benevolence, mercy, and grace.

174. The love of God is not a mere emotional impulse but a rational and voluntary affection, having its ground in truth and holiness. It exercises free choice. This does not deny feeling, for true love involves feeling. The fact that God grieves over the sins of his people implies that he loves his people with much feeling (Isa. 63:9; Eph. 4:30).

175. "God is love," the Scriptures declare (1 John 4:8, 16; 2 Cor. 13:11). It is his very nature to love. He initiates love (1 John 4:10). The Father loves the Son (Matt. 3:17), and the Son loves the Father (John 14:31). God loves the world (John 3:16; Eph. 2:4), his ancient people Israel (Deut. 7:6–8, 13; Jer. 31:3), and his true children

(John 14:23). He loves righteousness (Ps. 11:7) and justice (Isa. 61:8). The assurance of God's love is a source of comfort to the believer (Rom. 8:35–39).

176. The compassion of God. The Lamb of God turned his cheek to the smiters and pled clemency for his murderers—and we read of Jehovah: "The LORD is compassionate and gracious, slow to anger, abounding in love" (Ps. 103:8).

177. The benevolence of God. Because of his goodness, God deals bountifully, tenderly, and kindly with all his creatures. "The LORD is good to all and His mercies are over all His works. . . . The eyes of all look to You, and You give them their food in due time. You open Your hand and satisfy the desire of every living thing" (Ps. 145:9, 15–16 NASB). The benevolence of God is made known in his concern for the welfare of humanity and is suited to our needs and capacities (Job 38:41; Ps. 104:21). His benevolence is not restricted to believers, for "He causes his sun to rise on the evil and the good, and sends rain on the righteous and the unrighteous" (Matt. 5:45).

178. The mercy of God. God's mercy is his goodness shown to those who are *in misery or distress*. Compassion, pity, and loving-kindness are other terms in Scripture that communicate much the same thing. God is "rich in mercy" (Eph. 2:4) and "is full of compassion and mercy" (James 5:11). The term is often used in salutations and benedictions (Gal. 6:16; 1 Tim. 1:2; 2 Tim. 1:2; 2 John 3; Jude 2). Most important, God judges in mercy.

179. The grace of God. The grace of God is shown toward those who are *guilty*. Scripture speaks of "his glorious grace" (Eph. 1:6), "the incomparable riches of his grace" (Eph. 2:7), "abundant grace" (1 Peter 4:10), and "true grace" (1 Peter 5:12). The exercise of grace, like that of mercy, is optional with God.

180. Scriptures show the grace of God revealed to sinners through his long-suffering delay of the punishment of sin (Exod. 34:6; Rom. 2:4; 3:25; 1 Peter 3:20) and his showering of humanity with blessings instead of immediate judgment (Heb. 6:7). He made provision for our salvation (1 John 2:2), gave us the Word of God (Hosea 8:12), and made possible the convicting work of the Spirit (John 16:8–11) and common grace (Titus 2:11). God's special grace is also often mentioned in salutations and benedictions (1 Cor. 1:3; 16:23; Eph. 1:2; Phil. 1:2; Rev. 1:4; 22:21).

181. God is truth. The truth of God is not only the foundation of all religion but of all knowledge. God is the source of all truth. The conviction that the senses do not deceive, that consciousness is trustworthy, that things are what they appear to be, and that existence is not merely a dream rests ultimately upon the truth of God. Many like Pilate ask, "What is truth?" (John 18:38). Ultimate truth or reality is God.

182. Jesus affirmed God as "the only true God" (John 17:3). John wrote, "We are in him who is true" (1 John 5:20). His revelations of himself in nature, consciousness, and Scripture are true and trustworthy (Ps. 31:5; Heb. 6:17–18).

His Nature

5

---

183. The nature of God is generally described with the terms "essence" and "substance," meaning that which underlies all outward display—the reality itself, whether material or immaterial, the substratum of anything. To speak of God is to speak of an essence, a substance, not of a mere idea or the personification of an idea.

184. God has life. Science generally defines *life* as "having the powers of growth, reproduction or creation, and the ability to adapt or initiate change." In contrast to the pagan gods of other religions, God is alive. He hears, sees, feels, acts, and is a live being. "For as the Father has life in himself, so he has granted the Son to have life in himself" (John 5:26).

185. God has spirituality. God is invisible, without physical parts, and is therefore free from this world's limitations. John 4:24 tells us that "God is spirit," which opposes the false notion that everything in the world can be explained by material things or the laws of nature. He can make himself known to humanity, but he is in essence an invisible yet personal spirit.

186. Humanity was made in God's image, which means that humans are *personal* beings, have intellect, retain a sense of morality, and have the ability to *choose* between right and wrong.

187. Though it says in the Bible that no one can see God, some verses speak of God's "hands," and we also find the interesting story of Moses observing God's back as he walks by. Such expressions are *anthropomorphic*, describing an infinite God in human terms in order to help us better understand him.

188. God is personal. God has a personal existence, rather than being an impersonal force. He chooses people, reaches out to individuals, and develops relationships with them. Rather than the false notion of pantheism, which teaches that God is in everything and therefore has no distinct existence, our God has intellect, sensibility, and will. He chose to die personally on our behalf in order to restore our relationship with him.

189. God has personality. Psychology usually defines personality as "being self-conscious and having the powers of self-determination." God chose to create us, desires to know us, and explains himself to us in ways we can understand. All of these point to a God with personality.

190. God has names that reveal his nature. The name "I Am" reveals his own self-consciousness. The name "the Lord Will Provide" suggests his desire for personal provision. "The Lord Is Our Peace" reveals God's action on man's behalf. "The Lord Our Shepherd" demonstrates his personal guidance and goodness. And "the Lord of Hosts" reveals his headship over us.

191. God has emotions. If emotions help reveal the personhood of God, it should be noted that the Bible speaks of God grieving (Gen. 6:6), loving (Rev. 3:19), hating (Prov. 6:16), becoming angry

(1 Kings 11:9), and becoming jealous (Deut. 6:15). The fact that he possesses emotions reveals that he must be personal.

192. God is the Creator. The Book of Genesis says that God is the creator of all things. The fact that he simply spoke things into being means he has infinite power and chose to use it in a personal way by creating mankind. As the prophet Isaiah puts it in 45:18, "He created it not in vain" (KJV).

193. God is a God of order. A quick look at creation reveals that he balanced the land and the sea, designed the intricate workings of our bodies, and spoke mighty mountains into existence. Rather than the world being haphazard and a product of random sampling, creation reveals a God who has carefully planned and ordered all things.

194. God takes care of us. Not only does he provide for our immediate needs, he personally directs and controls the free actions of men so as to determine all things in accordance with his eternal purpose. As Wordsworth said, "God foresees evil deeds, but never forces them."

195. God has a hand in human history. As the preserver of all things, not just setting creation in motion but becoming actively involved with our lives, God sustains us and watches over us. Everything from the writing of Scripture to the resurrection of Jesus, to making sure *you* heard the Good News is evidence of his concern for our eternal destiny.

196. God is our Father. While this is largely a New Testament concept (the fatherhood of God could not be established until the appearing of his Son), it is clear that Christ's mission on earth was to make God known as "Father." Similarly, no one can experience God as Father except through the work of Jesus Christ, whose work on the cross makes us all brothers and sisters in the family of God.

197. God is unified. There is only one God, with one essence, existing in three persons. Though God has three distinct faces (the Father, Son, and Holy Spirit), he remains a single, uniform being. Many heresies have been battled over the course of history regarding this point.

198. God is one, according to Deuteronomy 6:4, which does not mean he has one personality, but that his three persons exist in one being. There is only one God, the maker and sustainer of all life.

199. God is triune. As stated in the Athanasian Creed, "We worship one God in trinity and trinity in unity, neither confounding the persons nor dividing the substance." The Trinity is three eternally interrelated, interexistent, inseparable persons within one being. He is one in being and substance, possessed of three personal distinctions revealed to us as the Father, the Son, and the Holy Spirit.

200. God is self-existent. He is absolutely independent of all else. As Christ says in John 5:26, "The Father has life in himself. . . ." The meaning is not that God *invented* himself but that he is self-sustaining and has been for all eternity.

201. God is eternal and is called "the Everlasting God" in Genesis 21:33 (KJV). He had no beginning and will have no end. The past, the present, and the future are equally known to him.

202. God is immutable. As an infinite being, he transcends all change. We can't add to him, increase his power, or watch him grow and change. His nature, attributes, and counsel are unchanging. "I the LORD do not change" (Mal. 3:6).

203. When the Bible says that God repents or changes (such as in Jonah 3:10 or Gen. 6:6), it doesn't mean that the Lord actually changed his *mind* . . . only that he changed his *method*. God remains the same in character, but as people change their attitude toward God, he in turn seems to change his attitude toward people. It's really the *people* who change!

204. God is omniscient. He has perfect and complete knowledge. In the words of John Calvin, "God knows Himself and all other things in one Eternal and most simple act." Or, as Paul put it, "Oh the depth of the riches of the wisdom and knowledge of God! How unsearchable his judgments, and his paths beyond tracing out!" (Rom. 11:33).

205. God knows all things, according to 1 John 3:20. He knows everything about the world—all actions throughout eternity, the entire plan of the ages, and each individual's part in it. "The eyes of the LORD are everywhere, keeping watch on the wicked and the good" (Prov. 15:3).

206. If God knows everything before it happens, why doesn't he stop evil from occurring? The point must be made that *he does!* The Bible refers to God as our protector and gives clear examples of God holding back evil. However, the fact that he knows everything before it occurs does not mean he is the *cause.* Sometimes in his wisdom he allows evil to take place as part of his divine plan.

207. God is omnipotent. His power is unlimited by anyone or anything outside himself. Nothing is too hard for him; he can bring anything to pass. As it says in Matthew 19:26, "With God all things are possible."

208. All nature is subject to God's control. He spoke light into being, calmed storms with his words, and raised the dead to life. Yet he will not do anything inconsistent with the nature of things—for example, he will not make past events to have not occurred. With the exception of miraculous events, God works *within* the realm of nature.

209. All human action is dependent on God's will and subject to divine control. When King Nebuchadnezzar became too proud, God compelled his humility (Dan. 4:19–37). When Jonah attempted to run away from God, the Lord arranged for him to repent. According to Daniel 4:35, "He does as he pleases with the powers of heaven and the peoples of the earth. No one can hold back his hand or say to him: 'What have you done?'"

210. Angels and demons are under divine control. As created beings, they have no power over God's people unless the Lord allows it (see Job 1:12; Luke 22:31–32; James 4:7; Rev. 20:2).

211. God is omnipresent. He is active everywhere, not meaning that he is there in bodily form, but that his personal, spiritual presence is present everywhere at all times. "Where can I go from your Spirit? Where can I flee from your presence?" asked the psalmist David. "If I go up to the heavens, you are there; if I make my bed in the depths, you are there. If I rise on the wings of the dawn, if

I settle on the far side of the sea, even there your hand will guide me, your right hand will hold me fast" (Ps. 139:7–10).

212. God is particularly manifest in heaven. He is not necessarily "everywhere" in the same sense. His throne and his dwelling place are in glory.

213. God is holy. The angels seen by the prophet Isaiah tell us he is "holy, holy, holy," which is his most emphasized characteristic. We are told in 1 John that "God is love," but we're never told he is "love, love, love." God is holy—Isaiah tells us his very *name* is holy.

214. God is separate from all evil. "Be holy, because I am holy," he says in Leviticus 11:44. He is perfect in character, he hates sin, and he desires for his followers to be holy. He delights in all that is righteous.

215. God is righteous and just. His holiness is revealed in the fact that he recognizes our sinful condition and offers atonement on our behalf. The holiness of God magnifies his redeeming love, which provides a means of escape to those who are dead in their sins.

216. The justice of God is evident in the fact that he punishes wickedness and rewards righteousness. Yet his justice is tempered by his love—forgiving the sins of repentant believers and delivering his people from eternal death.

217. God is love. He always seeks the highest good for us and desires a close relationship with each individual. He gave himself up for us through his substitutionary death on the cross. "This is love: not that we loved God, but that he loved us and sent his Son" (1 John 4:10).

218. The object of God's love is, first of all, his own Son, and second, all humankind. God loves each individual. He loves the world—even the worst sinner in it. As it says in John 3:16, "For God so loved the world that he gave his one and only Son, that whoever believes in him shall not perish but have eternal life."

219. God's love is shown through his sacrifice on the cross. The amazing part of Christ's death is not simply that he died for those who love him, but that he also died for those who *hate* him!

Jesus even died for those who were putting him to death, revealing a love with no boundaries.

220. God is merciful. The word translated "mercy" means, literally, "loving-kindness." While mercy in the Old Testament generally had a negative connotation (lightening the misery of the guilty), the New Testament gave it the more positive meaning of being nicer to someone than he or she truly deserves.

221. God is gracious. Unique from mercy, the word *grace* retains the meaning of unmerited favor. The Lord grants humankind his favor as a gift. Salvation is not something we can ever earn or demand—it comes only by God's grace.

222. The purpose of God is to create life, allow it to fall, provide a means of salvation, and thus demonstrate his grace and greatness. From eternity God has purposed to save those people who believe in him, making them the object of his favor.

What God
Really Said

6

---

223. "God helps those who help themselves." This quote is in fact from Benjamin Franklin, despite the fact that most people assume it comes from the Book of Proverbs. The words were made famous by President John F. Kennedy when he used them in one of his speeches.

224. "A land flowing with milk and honey" were the words God used to describe Palestine to Moses in Exodus 3:8. They are now generally used to describe a fine or pleasant place.

225. "An eye for an eye" first appears in Leviticus 24:20. Rather than being a vindictive call for revenge, it actually limited the damage one person could do to another when taking retribution. Human nature encourages an individual to hurt others, but the Old Testament law wanted to limit that hurt to equivalent damage.

226. "With God all things are possible." After explaining to the disciples how it would be easier for a camel to go through the eye of a needle than for a rich man to enter heaven, the disciples were understandably disillusioned with the concept of *anyone* getting into heaven. Jesus assured them that though it would be futile with men in charge, with God it was certainly possible to enter heaven (Matt. 19:25–26).

227. "The faith to move mountains." Although not currently used quite as often as it was in the twentieth century, the phrase refers to the power of belief. Jesus used this expression in Matthew 17:20 when talking to his disciples about healing the sick and the demon possessed.

228. "What God hath joined together . . ." Jesus spoke these words when he talked of marriage being a permanent covenant in Mark 10:9 (KJV). The words remain an important part of the traditional marriage ceremony even today.

229. "The salt of the earth." Many of the expressions we use in our culture come from the Lord Jesus. In describing his disciples with these words in Matthew 5:13, Christ emphasized their value—salt being the preferred method of payment in those days. The phrase is still used to describe people we find valuable or important.

230. "Holier than thou." God condemned those who considered themselves more self-righteous than their counterparts when he spoke against this attitude in Isaiah 65:2–5 (KJV). God mocked those who took such a position.

231. "Seek and ye shall find." These oft-quoted words of Jesus come from his Sermon on the Mount in Matthew 7:7 (KJV). It is still generally used as advice or encouragement to those who need to be seeking God's purpose and direction.

232. "The blind leading the blind . . ." Jesus spoke of false teachers when he used this expression. His point was that those teachers who are blind (do not know the real truth) cannot lead others anywhere that followers would want to go. Both the teacher and the followers will be lost and "fall into a ditch" as the verse goes on to say (Matt. 15:14 KJV).

233. "The spirit is willing, but the flesh is weak." Jesus spoke these words to his disciples the night of his betrayal. The disciples had fallen asleep after Jesus asked them to keep watch and pray with him. What is less quoted are the words Jesus quoted to the disciples before this phrase: "Watch and pray, that ye enter not into temptation" (Matt. 26:41 KJV). These words remind us why good intentions often lose out to weaknesses. Clearly Jesus suggested prayer and watchfulness to combat our weak flesh.

234. "The wolf in sheep's clothing." Jesus used this concept to describe false prophets who came to the people appearing as true teachers. He said, "Inwardly they are ferocious wolves" (Matt. 7:15), meaning that they were hypocrites and meant to lead people out of the safe "pasture" and into dangerous territory theologically.

235. "Cleanness of body was ever deemed to proceed from a due reverence to God," Francis Bacon (1561–1626) stated in his personal writings. Though Bacon might have wished it to be from the Bible, it is, in fact, not stated anywhere in that Book. From it many people have quoted, although the most popular version would be by John Wesley.

236. "Cleanliness is next to godliness." Stated by Wesley in 1772, the phrase "Certainly this is a duty, not a sin" preceded this now-famous quote. Though this might be a nice thought, it is hardly a biblical one and did not come from God.

237. "Do not throw pearls before swine." Jesus' words in Matthew 7:6 urge believers to take care with their message; it is not necessary to teach to those who are openly hostile to the gospel. A person wouldn't throw precious pearls to pigs, and Christians shouldn't throw the gift of salvation to those who will only turn around and attack them.

238. **"Eat, drink, and be merry"** was a phrase spoken by Jesus in Luke 12 while telling a cautionary tale about a rich fool thinking the rest of his life was set. The fool died that very night. The words are still generally used in a sarcastic or pejorative sense.

239. **"The straight and narrow."** Following the small, less traveled path leads to the narrow gate of life. In Matthew 7:14, Jesus cautioned people against following the more glamorous, broad, and well-traveled path that led to a wide gate full of destruction.

240. **"The apple of my eye"** is a phrase first used in Deuteronomy 32:10 to describe God's perspective of Israel. The Hebrew words literally mean "center" or "pupil" of the eye, but in the poetic sense the expression refers to someone or something highly valued by another. The poet David asks God in Psalm 17:8 to "keep me as the apple of your eye."

Surprising Symbols

241. Why symbols? One reason the Bible abounds in symbols is that it was written in the East where language was picturesque and people saw mirrors of spiritual truths in natural objects. Another more obvious reason may be that God, because of his infinity, had to express himself in speech that finite minds can understand in order to make clear and plain his being, revelation, and purpose.

242. Ancient of Days. Daniel repeats this name of grandeur three times to stress the importance of his vision (Dan. 7:9, 13, 22).

His narrative describes a central throne shaped like a chariot with wheels as burning fire upon which the Judge sat, whose name was the "Ancient of Days." The prophet had been outlining the nature of four succeeding empires and then presents Jehovah in contrast to earthly kings—not only as enduring but as Judge of the whole world. The Hebrew word used here for *ancient* means "advanced in age." Literally, the phrase "Ancient of Days" implies "a very old man"—the attribute of age expressing the majestic figure of the Judge. "God . . . abideth of old" (Ps. 55:19 KJV).

243. Ezekiel saw on a throne "the likeness as the appearance of a man" (1:26 KJV). This same prophet refers to "ancients of the house of Israel" (8:12 KJV; see also Jer. 19:1). Above the fleeting phases of life sits one who remains eternally the same (Pss. 90:1–3; 102:24–27). Hair as white and pure as wool symbolizes its owner as one who is holy and revered, and coincides with John's vision of the glorified Jesus whose head and hair was "white like wool, as white as snow" (Rev. 1:14).

244. Dazzling white raiment and beautiful white hair suggest the eternal being before whom an innumerable host stands in awe and adoration. These are characteristics of Christ, "the same yesterday, today, and forever." When Christ the Son of man appears crowned and with a sickle to reap the harvest of earth, he is depicted as one sitting on a cloud, and in this character he bears the attributes and moral glories of the Ancient of Days (Dan. 7:13; Rev. 1:13–14; 14:14).

245. The sun. God is the source of light and life. No more graphic symbol is used in Scripture to illustrate all that God is in himself. "For Jehovah God is a sun" (Ps. 84:11 ASV). "The sun of righteousness shall rise, with healing in its wings" (Mal. 4:2 RSV). If it were not for the sun, all the world would perish in darkness. Just as the natural sun is king of the planets, its creator is king over all humanity. Without his provision of heat and light, we could not exist.

246. Crown and diadem—God in his sovereignty and radiance. Isaiah says that "Jehovah of hosts (*Jehovah-Sabaoth*)" shall become "a crown of glory, and a diadem of beauty" unto the remnant of his people (28:5 ASV). Jehovah is known for his luster and loveliness. "How great is his beauty" (Zech. 9:17 KJV). A "crown of glory" is fitting for him who is the "King of Glory," and whose righteousness is "glorious" (2 Cor. 3:9–11). Truly he is incomparable! The wonder is that he waits to make us the recipients of all that he is in himself. Jesus prayed that his God-given glory might adorn our lives (John 17:22).

247. Wall of fire. The prophet Zechariah gives us the most forceful symbol of our God: "For I, saith the LORD, will be unto her a wall of fire round about, and will be the glory in the midst of her" (2:5 KJV). A "wall" is frequently used in Scripture as being symbolic of protective forces around us. Here the prophet presents the Lord as a "wall of fire" around his own. Many trials and tribulations threatened to overtake the children of Israel between the days of Zechariah and the coming of Christ. Even while Jerusalem is hemmed in on every side by enemies, God has not forgotten his promise to shield Jerusalem. With the surrounding fire of God's presence comes the promise "No weapon that is formed against thee shall prosper" (Isa. 54:17 KJV).

248. Refiner, purifier. "He will sit as a refiner and purifier of silver" (3:3), says Malachi of God's sanctifying work. God takes his time to make us holy. Patiently he sits at the crucible of our lives and separates out all that is alien to his holy mind and will. Note the double process of a silversmith. First, he is the *refiner*, tempering the heat so that all the impurities in the silver are forced to surface. Second, the refiner becomes the *purifier* as he skims the surface and removes all the dross. When does the silversmith know when his silver is thoroughly refined and purified? When he can see his own reflection on the surface.

249. The Rock. Symbols in Scripture were written by those who lived in Eastern lands, and they described God in terms of what was most familiar to them. Mountains surrounded Jerusalem with refreshing shade and shelter, offering travelers relief from the scorching heat of the desert sun. Prophets and psalmists, then, familiar with the protection of rocks, would know God as their Rock more so than Westerners.

250. An ancient Hebrew legend states that God had two bags of rocks when he made the world. He scattered the contents of one bag over the entire earth—but all the other rocks in the other bag he dropped on the small area of the Holy Land.

251. The Rock reveals God in his strength and stability. The original word for *rock* is also translated as "strength." "O LORD my strength" (Ps. 19:14 KJV). The Old Testament frequently refers to rock as a symbol of God's strength and stability. The psalmists especially loved this metaphor for God: "He is my Rock" (Ps. 92:15). This figure of speech reveals God in his permanence and unchangeable character.

252. Rock of Ages. Isaiah describes God as "the Rock eternal" (26:4). As Moses rebuked Israel for her idolatry, he spoke these words, "Of the Rock that begat thee thou are unmindful, and hast forgotten God that formed thee" (Deut. 32:18 KJV). In fact, in this chapter Moses speaks of the Rock four times:

- "The Rock of his salvation" (32:15 KJV)—the source of grace
- "The Rock that begat thee" (32:18 KJV)—the source of life
- "Their Rock had sold them" (32:30)—the source of ownership
- "Their rock is not like our Rock" (32:31)—the source of perfection

253. Cover/canopy—God as our protector and comforter. In 2 Kings 16:18, King Ahaz removed the "covert" (KJV) or "the covered way" (ASV). Opinions differ on the word's meaning. But possible explanations include a gallery belonging to the temple, the place where the king stood or sat during the Sabbath services, a public place for teaching, or the way by which the priest entered the sanctuary on the Sabbath. The word itself, from which we take *cover* or *canopy*, means a shelter of any kind (Isa. 4:6). It is used as a hiding place (Job 38:40); a place of secrecy (1 Sam. 25:20; Isa. 16:4); a den, or lair (Jer. 25:38). Applied to God, the symbol is a comforting picture of his protection and loving care of those who rest in his presence, "I long to . . . take refuge in the shelter of your wings" (Ps. 61:4).

254. City of Refuge—God is our haven from the enemy. The original Hebrew words for *refuge* are translated: "high tower," "shelter," and "hope" (Pss. 9:9 ASV; 61:3 KJV; Jer. 17:17 KJV). "The eternal God is thy refuge, and underneath are the everlasting arms"

(Deut. 33:27 KJV). This promise emphasizes a double safety for the saints. Not only is the everlasting God our refuge, but his everlasting arms are around us.

255. Refuge. The first reference to *refuge* in Scripture is in connection with the "six cities of refuge" that Joshua set up as places of asylum to protect those who had shed blood accidentally. These asylums of safety were appointed by God (Isa. 26:1). At every crossroad on the east and west of Jordan was marked an appointed protection (Isa. 30:21). "Then the LORD said to Moses: '. . . "When you cross the Jordan into Canaan, select some towns to be your cities of refuge, to which a person who has killed someone accidentally may flee"'" (Num. 35:9–11). Likewise God is our only safety from the avenger. In him we are secure from the judgment of the law.

256. Fortress—God as our defense against the foe. "Jehovah is my . . . fortress" (Ps. 18:2 ASV). In times of war and conflict, the image of a fortress, often high up and inaccessible, provided perfect safety from enemies and persecutors. The names *strong tower* and *high tower* as applied to God express a similar provision and purpose (Pss. 61:3; 144:2). Some thirteen times in the Psalms, God is exalted as our fortress or high tower. The writer exults in the protecting care and power of God: "I will love thee, O LORD, my strength. The LORD is my rock, and my fortress, . . . my high tower" (Ps. 18:1–2).

257. The shield is the most ancient and universal weapon of defense and was made in two varieties. The large shield, worn by heavily armed artillery, adapted to the form of the human body. It was made in an oval shape or in the shape of a door, hence the Greek name for *shield*, meaning "a door." Then there was the light, round buckler, like those the men of Benjamin carried (2 Chron. 14:8). The two kinds are often mentioned together (Ps. 35:2; Ezek. 23:24). Solomon boasted of having two hundred shields of beaten gold, and three hundred bucklers of beaten gold made to hang in the forest house at Lebanon (1 Kings 10:16–17).

258. Shield of faith. While instructing us to put on the whole armor of God, Paul spoke of faith as the large Greek-Roman shield, able to quench the fiery darts of hellish forces. A shield not only warded off sword thrusts or objects hurled at it but actually stood between the soldier and his foe. God is the preserver and protector of his children; our shield stands between the enemy and ourselves.

259. Husband. First, God is our maker. "All things were made by him." But Jehovah is also a husband. Hosea depicts Israel as the wife of Jehovah and illustrates her unfaithfulness as she went after other lovers. God is shown as the divine husband striving to win back his faithless wife by wooing her back from all her evil wanderings. Yet there is another side of God's role of husband spoken through Jeremiah: "Leave thy fatherless children, I will preserve them alive; and let thy widows trust in me" (49:11 KJV).

260. Governor. As we consider the worn, torn condition of our world today, it does not appear that God is ruling as its governor. Yet in the present tense, the psalmist writes about him who "doeth according to his will among the inhabitants of the earth." "For the kingdom is the LORD's: and he is the governor [ASV gives "ruler"] among the nations" (Ps. 22:28 KJV). The term *governor,* from the original meaning "to rule," is the same word used for Joseph whom Pharaoh appointed governor over all Egypt (Gen. 42:6). God alone is the perfect governor. He alone holds the divine right to govern the nations.

261. Redeemer. The word *redeem* first appears in Scripture in connection with Jacob's blessing of his son Joseph, where the verb is written in the present tense, "The angel who has redeemed me from all evil" (Gen. 48:16 NASB). *Goel,* the Hebrew term for "redeem," came to be used as the nearest blood relative, whose duty it was to avenge a murder. Jacob, however, used it in a broader sense as a deliverer or savior (see Exod. 6:6; Isa. 59:20).

262. "Redemption" implies freedom and an entire change of state or condition and therefore differs from "purchase," which describes a simple exchange of owners. Though a slave may be purchased, it does not necessarily mean he or she is delivered from slavery. When God speaks of his redemption of Israel, however, he makes possible both a change of masters *and* condition. "In your unfailing love you will lead the people you have redeemed" (Exod. 15:13).

263. King. Kings and kingdoms dominate the Bible as is seen by the fact that the term *king* occurs some 2,400 times, and *kingdom* some 350 times. Fascinated by the pomp and splendor of surrounding kings with their courts and palaces, Israel became dissatisfied with serving and obeying an invisible deity. She wanted a visible, authoritative human king to lead her (1 Sam. 8:6). The Israelites' request (or demand) meant that the people had not actually rejected Samuel, who acted as God's representative, but as Jehovah said, "They have rejected me as their king" (1 Sam. 8:7).

264. "Earthly kings come and go, but God is 'an everlasting king'" (Jer. 10:10). He is "the King eternal, immortal, invisible, the only God," worthy of "honor and glory for ever and ever. Amen" (1 Tim. 1:17).

265. A symbol of Christ in the Old Testament. God said to Moses, "Thou shalt smite the rock, and there shall come water out of it, that the people may drink" (Exod. 17:6 KJV). At the cross, the Rock of Ages was smitten, and at Pentecost, water flowed out of it through the giving of the Holy Spirit (1 Cor. 10:4).

SALT, OIL, AND WINE

266. Salt. Ancient Hebrews had an unlimited supply of salt. They formed brine pits called "salt pans" along the Dead Sea's flat coastal area. The sun evaporated the water in the pits, leaving behind an abundant supply of mineral salts. Salt was the chief economic product of the ancient world, and the Hebrews used it in a variety of ways: for flavoring foods, preserving fish, curing meat, and pickling olives and vegetables.

267. Jesus used salt to give flavor and preserve other substances (Matt. 5:13; Mark 9:50). All who have accepted the Holy Spirit through salvation are to be used by him to preserve the earth from corruption, to season its blandness, to heal, and to freshen. We are the salt of the earth because of the Spirit's indwelling.

268. Salt for seasoning/flavor. From ancient times, salt has been recognized as one of the most important elements in the seasoning of food. Job was asked by Eliphaz, "Is tasteless food eaten without salt?" (Job 6:6). May even our "conversation be always full of grace, seasoned with salt" (Col. 4:6). The role of the Holy Spirit within our lives is to keep the gospel message savory.

269. Salt for healing. In Bible lands, infants were rubbed with salt to ensure good health before swaddling. And salt was believed to have been an antidote for tooth decay. Salt was an ingredient in the sacred anointing oil and ritual sacrifices symbolizing God's perpetual covenant with Israel (Num. 18:19). Salt purifies as does the work of the Holy Spirit. Here it serves as a symbol for inner healing as well as physical healing.

270. Salt for preservation. Without refrigeration, people of ancient Bible lands relied on salt to preserve their meats from rotting. Likewise all who are born again by the Holy Spirit are to be used by him to preserve the earth from corruption. We are the salt of the earth, because the Holy Spirit dwelling in us is holy.

271. Oil was a main item in every Jewish household. The olive, native only to the lands bordering the Mediterranean Sea, was the most important tree cultivated in the Holy Land. A single large olive tree in biblical times provided an entire family with all of the oil it needed—as much as half a ton a year.

272. The use of oil for anointing is beautifully symbolic of the manifold ministry of the Holy Spirit. Many accounts of anointing are presented in the Bible, each carrying different meanings of the custom as a way of showing courtesy, respect, even devotion; for healing purposes; and as a symbol of the pouring out of God's Spirit. "God anointed Jesus of Nazareth with the Holy Spirit and power" that he might do good and heal all those under the power of evil (Acts 10:38).

273. Oil for healing. "Is any one of you sick? He should call the elders of the church to pray over him and anoint him with oil in the name of the Lord" (James 5:14). Oil not only acts as a healing agent for the body, it also symbolizes the quiet work of the Spirit who alone can heal our bruised hearts.

274. Oil for illumination. Jesus called his disciples "lights," or lamps. The indwelling Spirit as oil enabled them to shine and maintain an effective witness in dark days. Light comes from within, as does spiritual illumination made possible by the Spirit. This is not to be confused with what men call "the light of reason," which can keep them in darkness as far as spiritual truth is concerned (see Ps. 119:105).

275. Wine. When the Holy Spirit came at Pentecost, a crowd gathered, and some made fun of the apostles, thinking they were drunk. But Peter stood up and addressed the crowd, saying, "These men are not drunk, as you suppose. It's only nine in the morning!" (Acts 2:15). Such was the effect of the Holy Spirit. Their spiritual exhilaration and joy and their amazing display of linguistic power was mistaken for drunkenness. "Do not get drunk on wine. . . . Instead, be filled with the Spirit" (Eph. 5:18). The more deeply and repeatedly we drink of him, the more capacity we have and the more we will desire.

276. Seed (1 John 3:9). In the fullness of time, Jesus came as the seed of a woman—the seed implanted within her by the Holy Spirit when he overshadowed her, making her the mother of our Lord (Luke 1:31, 35): "to thy seed, which is Christ" (Gal. 3:16 KJV). The Scripture, which reveals him, is also likened unto a seed (Luke 8:5). Peter calls it imperishable seed (1 Peter 1:23).

277. Seal. Like his Master, Jesus, Paul knew how to use what was around him to illustrate divine truth. His numerous military metaphors, for example, reflect his long and close association with the Roman army. While at Ephesus, a prosperous maritime city in the apostle's day, Paul came to know of its extensive timber trade and noticed that when the great logs and planks were brought in and sold, they were then sealed with burned-in marks indicating ownership.

278. A seal for the completion of a transaction. Under ancient Jewish law, when an agreement was completed and the price paid, a seal was applied to the contract to make it definite and binding (Jer. 32:9–10). The moment a person is reborn in the Spirit, he or she is sealed with the Spirit, and because he is the Seal, he cannot be broken. With this Seal, we are no longer our own. We now have the divine stamp upon us, which marks us as divine property until the day of final redemption (Rom. 8:23).

279. A seal communicated the image of its originator. In ages past, an imprinted design of a seal would be pressed into melted wax (such as a monogram or recognized symbol) and often implied a finished transaction when applied to documents. It is said of Jesus, "him hath God the Father sealed" (John 6:27 KJV), and he was "the express image of his person" (Heb. 1:3 KJV), just as the wax bore the image of the seal.

280. Earnest or deposit (2 Cor. 1:22; 5:5; Eph. 1:13–14). *Earnest* generally means a deposit paid by a purchaser to give validity to a contract. Paul used the symbol in this sense: "Who hath . . . given the earnest of the Spirit in our hearts" (2 Cor. 1:22 KJV). The Spirit is our pledge, the deposit on our complete inheritance. The symbol of the earnest, relative to the Holy Spirit, is used by Paul three times in connection with the believer's redemption-inheritance.

281. Our English word *earnest.* "*Arrabon,* originally meant earnest—money deposited by the purchaser and forfeited if the purchase was not complete, and was probably a Phoenician word, introduced into Greece. In general, the word came to mean a pledge of any sort. In the New Testament it is used only of that which is assured by God to believers: It is said that the Holy Spirit is the Divine pledge of all their future blessedness, particularly of their eternal inheritance. (See Gen. 38:17, 20, 25.) In modern Greek, *Arrabona* is an engagement ring."—W. E. Vine

282. Clothing. The phrase "came upon" literally means, "the Spirit of Jehovah clothed himself with Gideon" (Judg. 6:34 ASV margin). Clothing as a verb is frequently used in a figurative sense (see Isa. 61:10). *Endued* implies "clothed with power from on high" (Luke 24:49). The Spirit's empowerment is likened to an act of clothing or covering. Often the Spirit cast himself like a mantle around those he sought to use for a specific purpose. Acting in free sovereignty, he came upon men. "He came upon [clothed himself with] Gideon" (Judg. 6:34). "He came upon [clothed himself with] Amasai" (1 Chron. 12:18). "He came upon [clothed himself with] Zechariah" (2 Chron. 24:20).

283. Some symbols are drawn from natural life. What a perfect reflection of the spiritual is the natural! How gracious of God it is to convey heavenly truth through the media of natural elements we are accustomed to. In this way infinity enlightens our finite understanding. The emblems used to convey the Spirit's attributes and activities are as windows allowing light to reach our minds so that we can more readily understand the things of the Spirit.

284. Wind. In the original text, *spirit* means wind or breath. That the Holy Spirit is the secret of all life and vitality is evident from this forceful symbol describing his activity. As the natural wind is air in motion, so in the spiritual realm, the Spirit is God in action.

285. Breath. Just as God breathed upon Adam and he became a living soul (Gen. 2:7), the new creation in Christ is birthed by the breath of the Holy Spirit. "And with that he [Jesus] breathed on them and said, 'Receive the Holy Spirit'"(John 20:22). Job emphasizes this same truth in the phrase, "The breath [wind] of the Almighty . . . gives him understanding" (Job 32:8; see also 33:4). In his prophecy of Israel, Ezekiel also prayed to the Spirit, "Come from the four winds, O breath, and breathe into these slain, that they may live" (37:9).

286. Just as the wind is invisible, unpredictable, and out of human control, yet powerful in its effects, it is a fitting symbol of the mysterious work of the Holy Spirit. While speaking to Nicodemus, Jesus said, "The wind blows wherever it pleases. You hear its sound, but you cannot tell where it comes from or where it is going. So it is with everyone born of the Spirit" (John 3:8).

287. The wind's forces. At times wind comes with hurricane force, yet it can become as soft as a whisper upon one's cheek. The hard, cruel jailer in the Book of Acts needed the Spirit's power in great magnitude (Acts 16:25–31). But no cyclone experience was necessary for Lydia, whose heart silently opened to the Lord in Acts 16:14.

288. A mighty wind. Luke describes the coming of the Spirit on the Day of Pentecost "as of a rushing mighty wind" (Acts 2:2 KJV). *Rushing* suggests the irresistible action of the Spirit and *mighty* speaks of power. The Spirit who came to impart power to witness (Acts 1:8) is all-powerful in himself (Micah 3:8).

289. Acting as a sudden and mighty wind, the Spirit can control and do as he deems best with those he desires to use. "God's ways are as mysterious as the pathway of the wind [Spirit]," says Solomon (Eccles. 11:5 TLB). "The Wind of God," the Spirit, is often found in vehement action, as is illustrated in the following passages:

- "The Spirit lifted me up between earth and heaven" (Ezek. 8:3).

- "Then the Spirit lifted me up and brought me to the gate of the house of the LORD" (Ezek. 11:1).
- "Then the Spirit of the LORD came upon me" (Ezek. 11:5).
- "The Spirit of the Lord caught away Philip . . . was found at Azotus" (Acts 8:39–40 ASV).

290. Water is one of the most common symbols used to describe not only the varied ministry of the Holy Spirit but also the Holy Scriptures. The symbol of water is easy to understand and was used in several passages of Scripture for cleansing (Ezek. 36:25–27); life, fertility, beauty (Ezek. 47:1–12); and joy (Isa. 12:3). We could not live without water or rain. "Whoever drinks the water I give him will never thirst" (John 4:14).

291. Living Water. Clean water is one of the necessities of life, and in his conversation with the woman at the well, Jesus sought to show her how the Holy Spirit, as a well of water within her, provided not only clean water but Living Water. He was her only source of spiritual life and refreshment. As Living Water, the presence of the Spirit in the heart quenches thirst and produces life. He alone satisfies the soul's deepest thirst.

292. Rivers or streams. Rivers or "streams of living water. . . . By this he meant the Spirit, whom those who believed in him were later to receive" (John 7:37–39). Written in plural form—rivers, streams—our Lord's prophecy indicates the variety and abundance of the Spirit's activities. Consider the diversity of his dealings with us. Many rivers and streams cover the earth, yet no two are alike.

293. Floods. Just as water flooded the earth with judgment in Noah's day, a deluge of the Spirit is just as able to engulf the earth with blessing. The flood not only symbolized destruction, but it can stand for the lavish and bountiful supply of the Spirit.

294. Rain. "May he come down like rain"(Ps. 72:6 NASB). Absence of rain means famine, scarcity, and ruin as many arid countries experience. The church is certainly suffering from spiritual famine and is in need of the abundance of rain. May he send upon her the latter rains of the Spirit for he alone can transform the desert, causing it to blossom as the rose (Isa. 35:1; Joel 2:23).

295. Springs. "Indeed, the water I give him will become in him a spring of water welling up to eternal life" (John 4:14). Springs are not only reservoirs of pure, fresh water, but the *source* of great rivers. Said the psalmist, "All my springs are in thee" (Ps. 87:7 KJV), and this is true of the Spirit, who is our "secret source of every precious thing." In Christ we have an unending source of supply—a Spring that never ceases to flow.

296. Dew. "I will be like the dew" (Hosea 14:5). The Anglican *Book of Common Prayer* has a request for "the continual dew of Thy blessing," and this is what the Spirit waits to bestow upon every believer. Shakespeare has a phrase about "morning roses newly washed with dew." Secretly, unnoticed through the night and early morning, the dew descends upon the earth. So also the Holy Spirit comes quietly and rests upon us.

297. The Spirit's fire (Isa. 4:4; Acts 2:3). Twice John the Baptist said of Jesus, "He will baptize you with the Holy Spirit and with fire" (Matt. 3:11; Luke 3:16). The Spirit is the fire, as symbolized when he came upon the disciples at Pentecost as "cloven tongues like as of fire" (Acts 2:3 KJV; see also Luke 12:49; Rev. 4:5). The symbol of fire is also used to portray the holy presence and character of God (Deut. 4:24; Heb. 12:29) and also of the Word itself (Jer. 5:14; 20:9; 23:29).

298. Fire consumes what is combustible and tests what is not. It cleanses that which neither air nor water can cleanse.

299. Fire gives light. As fire, the Spirit is the source of spiritual illumination and knowledge. He enlightens the eyes of our understanding (Eph. 1:17–18; Heb. 6:4).

300. Fire purifies. As fire, the Spirit exercises his power to purify, to judge and consume all impurity, and burn within us all that is not in conformity with his holy will (Lev. 10:2; Mal. 3:2–3).

301. Fire gives heat. "I am warm; I see the fire," said the writer of Isaiah (44:16). How quickly fire can warm—symbolizing the Spirit's power to shed God's love that warms cold hearts (Rom. 5:5). Fire gives life and warmth. Somehow the church at Ephesus had lost this warmth (Rev. 2:4).

302. Fire gives power. In the life and service of the believer, the Holy Spirit is a driving power. He is the fire in the boiler, the energizing influence in our witness (see Lev. 9:24; 10:2; Acts 2:3–4).

303. "Came mightily upon." Akin to clothing is the strong verbiage about the Spirit who "came mightily upon" certain leaders. Literally the phrase implies that he attacked men, and as a greater force, compelled those he arrested to accomplish his task. As the Omnipotent One, he "came mightily upon" Samson (Judg. 14:6, 19; 15:14 KJV), "came mightily upon [Saul]" (1 Sam. 10:6, 10 ASV), and "came mightily upon David" (1 Sam. 16:13 ASV).

304. "Upon." Further, there is the softer, milder term *upon*, expressing a temporary divine covering. Many illustrations of this action of the Spirit can be found in Scripture (e.g., Num. 11:17; 24:2; 1 Sam. 19:20, 23; Isa. 59:21; 60:1). Another gentle term is that of *rest*, used in connection with the mantling of the Spirit, and is associated with his dovelike character. The Spirit "rested on" the seventy elders (Num. 11:25–26), rested upon Elisha (2 Kings 2:15), and rested upon the Messiah (Isa. 11:2).

305. Seven. Representing perfection, the number seven is symbolic of the Holy Spirit in the perfection of deity, and also in the perfection of his mission. He is spoken of as having:

- "seven eyes" (Zech. 3:9; 4:10; Rev. 5:6), symbolizing possession of perfect insight, knowledge, and understanding.
- "seven horns" (Rev. 5:6). Horns symbolize power, and the Spirit is perfect in power and authority.
- "seven spirits" (Rev. 1:4). We see here perfection of manifestation, as well as perfect obedience to the divine will.
- "seven lamps of fire" (Rev. 1:12–13). Symbolic of divine holiness, these lamps suggest the Spirit's holiness.

306. As the sevenfold Spirit, he is intimately associated with the seven churches, and is revealed as having a separate message and ministry for each of the churches (Revelation 2–3).

307. A dove represents the Spirit's gentleness, tenderness, peace, beauty, innocence, patience, and sincerity. When Jesus was initiated into his public ministry, "the Holy Spirit descended on him in bodily form like a dove" (Luke 3:22). Such semblance proclaimed two things, namely, the Spirit's own nature and the loving, quiet, gentle, mission Jesus was to undertake—one of sacrifice. Six characteristics of the dove given in the Bible are applicable to the Spirit.

- Swift in flight—wings like a dove (Ps. 55:6)
- Beautiful—wings of a dove covered with silver (Ps. 68:13)
- Constant in love—the eyes of doves (Song of Sol. 5:12)
- Mournful—mourn like doves (Isa. 59:11)
- Gentle—harmless as doves (Matt. 10:16)
- Particular—"The dove found no rest for the sole of her foot" (Gen. 8:9 KJV)

308. Porter/doorkeeper. Scripture is rich in many direct, evident, and unmistakable symbols of God the Father, God the Son, and God the Holy Spirit. There are also *implied* symbols. The occupation of the porter is one of these implied designations of the Spirit. The Greek word our Lord used for porter was *thyroros*, the one who opens doors. Some scholars believe the porter Jesus spoke of was a reference to John the Baptist, who as Christ's forerunner came opening the door of the ministry of Jesus, or in other words, prepared his way (Mark 1:1–8). The Holy Spirit, however, was the divine forerunner of Jesus, and opened the door for his entrance into the world.

309. Paraclete/counselor. As a favorite designation for the Spirit, Christ used this symbol at least four times. As a paraclete, the Holy Spirit is an abiding counselor (John 14:16); he came as the gift of the Father (John 14:26); he is represented as the gift of the Son (John 15:26); and he came as Christ's gift at the time of ascension (John 16:7). Because the Greek language is pliable and gives one word several meanings, we have three words for *paraclete*: *comforter*, *advocate*, and *helper*.

310. Comforter. As such the Spirit is present and involved with our trials and sufferings. "Then the church throughout Judea, Galilee and Samaria enjoyed a time of peace. It was strengthened; and encouraged by the Holy Spirit" (Acts 9:31). The New American Standard Bible translates the rest of this verse "going on in the fear of the Lord and in the comfort of the Holy Spirit, it continued to increase."

311. Augustine once wrote, "The Holy Spirit on the Day of Pentecost descended into the temple of His Apostles, which He had prepared for Himself, as a shower of sanctification and a perpetual Comforter. . . . He is our sweetest Comforter."

312. Advocate/intercessor. "We have an advocate with the Father" (1 John 2:1 KJV). This term, which John applied to Jesus as our intercessor in heaven, and which Jesus himself used while on earth (Luke 22:31–32), is the same word translated "paraclete." It is a term representing a pleader who comes forward in favor of, and as the representative of, another. This idea is present in our two advocates. The Holy Spirit advocates, Christ pleads his cause for the believer (Rom. 8:26–27), and in heaven Christ intercedes for the believer (Heb. 7:25).

313. Helper. "In the same way, the Spirit helps us in our weakness" (Rom. 8:26). *Helper* is another word resident in the original "paraclete." Among the gifts of the Spirit is the help of the Helper himself. Paul obtained help from the Holy Spirit to continue his arduous labors (Acts 26:22). All believers can find in the Spirit the "grace to help us in our time of need" (Heb. 4:16).

314. Witness. Our Lord said of the Spirit, "He will testify about me" (John 15:26), and *testify* is the same word for *witness* in the original text. Throughout Scripture the Spirit is before us as a true and faithful witness for God the Father and the Son. Witness is related to an old English word, *witan,* meaning "to know." Paul proved the Holy Spirit to be a perfect witness in such passages as: "The Spirit Himself bears witness" (Rom. 8:16 NASB) and "My conscience bearing witness with me in the Holy Spirit" (Rom. 9:1 NRSV). As a witness, the Spirit's testimony is always in harmony with his own just and righteous nature. He witnesses in and to the believer in at least three ways: to our pardon, to our adoption, and to our sanctification.

315. Witness to our pardon. As sinners we are lost, and in the court of divine justice we are guilty of breaking the laws of God. But by pleading the saving grace of Jesus Christ, we are forgiven of our crime. The Spirit enters and stands as the witness of our divine pardon, assuring us that we are no longer under condemnation (Rom. 5:1; 8:1).

316. Witness to our adoption. The Holy Spirit witnesses with our spirits that we are the sons of God. From the court of justice, we have been pardoned and acquitted. We can now be adopted into the family of God. The Holy Spirit acts as our continued witness to our adoption as children and heirs of an eternal inheritance (Rom. 8:14–17; Gal. 4:6).

317. Witness to our sanctification. The indwelling Spirit is not only the evidence of our sonship, he is also the source of our holiness. Pardoned in court, we become children in the Father's house, and then holy ones serving in his temple. One reason why the Spirit is called holy is because it is his mission to empower us to live in holiness (2 Tim. 1:14).

318. Finger. Early church fathers spoke of the Holy Spirit as "the Finger of the Hand Divine." In Scripture, "the finger of God" and "the hand of God" are symbolic of his omnipotence and of divine authorship, visible in all God's works. The finger of God has five uses: as the Spirit of God, for writing the law of God, as the judgment of God, as the power of God, and on the saints of God.

319. Finger—the Spirit of God. Combining what Matthew and Luke have to say about our Lord's miracle of casting out demons, we discover that the Holy Spirit is the finger of God: "I drive out demons by the Spirit of God" (Matt. 12:28). "I with the finger of God cast out devils" (Luke 11:20 KJV). "Finger," as Christ's title for the Spirit of Power, describes him accomplishing the purpose of God.

320. Finger—writing the law of God. "Written with the finger of God" upon the two tablets of stone were etched the Ten Commandments (Exod. 31:18; Deut. 9:10). Jesus named the Spirit "the finger of God," hence the implication that he was associated with God in the framing and writing of divine truth. Also, while human fingers actually penned the Scriptures as a whole, they were under the direct control of the divine finger (2 Peter 1:21; 1 Peter 1:11).

321. Finger—the judgment of God. Two references to the divine finger are associated with judgment. First, when the magicians, in spite of their impressive enchantments, could no longer produce the same plagues with which God smote the Egyptians, they confessed to Pharaoh, "This is the finger of God" (Exod. 8:19). The second illustration of divine fingers being connected with judgment is found during the feast of Belshazzar, who shrank with fear as he saw "the fingers of a human hand" write out on the palace wall the drunken king's condemnation (Dan. 5:5, 24).

322. Finger—the power of God. Our first glimpse of the Spirit in Scripture is that of the Creator-Spirit (Gen. 1:2). David, a great lover of nature, considered the brilliant heavens God's masterpiece. He exclaimed, "O LORD, Our Lord, how majestic is your name in all the earth! . . . When I consider your heavens, the work of your fingers" (Ps. 8:1, 3a). The creative power of the Holy Spirit, the finger of God, still writes on the hearts of humanity as we are transformed into new creations in Christ Jesus (John 3:6–8; 2 Cor. 5:17; Gal. 6:15).

323. Finger—on the saints of God. To ancient Orientals, fingers were essential in conversation because they could indicate what their mouths dared not utter in respect to concern or grave insult. Referring to a wicked person who plots evil, Solomon wrote, "motions with his fingers" (Prov. 6:13). Isaiah also speaks of "the pointing finger and malicious talk" (Isa. 58:9). But Paul writes to the Corinthians in his second letter, reminding them that as a Christian church they were "a letter from Christ . . . written not with ink but with the Spirit of the living God" (2 Cor. 3:3). The Spirit writes upon the hearts of believers the laws of God (Heb. 8:10; 10:16).

324. Circumcision. God made a covenant with Abraham that brought with it a promise of unparalleled blessing. The sign of the covenant was circumcision. Every male of Abraham's descendants was to enter the covenant with the outward sign of circumcision. This rite was the key to releasing God's blessing to each subsequent generation, foreshadowing the "circumcision of the heart," when a person submits his or her life to the Lord Jesus Christ and receives the indwelling power of the Holy Spirit.

Famous Quotes

8

---

325. A philosopher once asked, "Where is God?" The Christian answered, "Let me first ask you, where is He not?"—John Arrowsmith

326. "The human mind, being created, has an understandable uneasiness about the Uncreated. We do not find it comfortable to allow for the presence of One who is wholly outside of the circle of our familiar knowledge. We tend to be disquieted by the thought of One who does not account to us for his being, who is responsible to no one, who is self-existent, self-dependent, and self-sufficient."—A. W. Tozer

327. "A sense of deity is inscribed on every heart."—John Calvin

328. "To say with all that we have, think, feel, and are 'God exists' is the most world-shattering statement that a human being can make. When we make that statement, all the distinctions between the intellectual, emotional, affective, and spiritual understanding fall away and there is only one truth left to acclaim: God exists."—Henri J. M. Nouwen

329. "The whole law of human existence lies in this: that man be able to bow down before the infinitely great."—Fyodor Dostoyevski

330. "Poetry is God's invitation to glimpse the unseen—His very character. The psalms were composed in poetic form, reaching beyond the world of sight and sound to reveal what our senses long to see and hear. In a voice that disrupts, invites, and reveals, the psalmist draws us to the voice of God."—Dan Allender and Tremper Longman

331. "Long, long before matter existed, before the cosmos took its first breath, before the first angel opened his eyes, when there was nothing—God had already lived forever. He had not just lived forever. He had been contented forever. And whatever God was, He still is and always will be."—Steven Estes

332. "God made man in his own image and man returned the compliment."—Blaise Pascal

333. "God so invested his image in our humanity that it is inescapably in operation. . . . We are pre-programmed to 'be,' to relate to other people, to comfort the grieving, to rescue the dying, and to reach out to touch the lonely and the sick. All of that is 'image of God' representation. And if we choose to save ourselves, to withdraw from the impulses to help, to rescue, to touch, then we are denying the image of God in us."—Donald and Robbie Joy

334. "The God of power, as he did ride/In his majestick robes of glorie / Resolv'd to light; and so one day / He did descend, undressing all the way."—George Herbert

335. "If we cannot find God in your house or in mine, upon the roadside or the margin of the sea; in the bursting seed or opening flower; in the day duty or the night musing; in the general laugh or the secret grief; in the procession of life, ever entering afresh, and solemnly passing by and dropping off; I do not think we should discern him any more on the grass of Eden, or beneath the moonlight of Gethsemane."—James Martineau

336. **"God is an utterable sigh,** planted in the depths of the soul."—Johann Paul Friedrich Richter

337. **"Joy is that deep settled confidence** that God is in control in every area of my life."—Paul Sailhamer

338. **"Omnipotence** which can lay its hand so heavily upon the world can also make its touch so light that the creature receives independence."—Søren Kierkegaard

339. **"Although power can force obedience,** only love can summon a response of love, which is the one thing God wants from us and the reason he created us. . . . Love has its own power, the only power ultimately capable of conquering the human heart."—Philip Yancey

340. **"God permits** what He hates to achieve what He loves."— Steven Estes

341. **"When I describe my children to people I meet,** I describe them by their attributes. These are words describing a quality or their inherent characteristics. For example, my older son Josh is creative and artistic. My daughter is dramatic, followed by her younger brother, the loud and boisterous adventurer. At first glance, these words can be confused with skills or abilities. But I use them to describe my children's inner nature. They have these qualities by nature and through the makeup of their character. As they age, these qualities will never change. God's attributes can be understood in the same way."—Doug Herman

342. **"'God is love,'** says the apostle John. 'Whoever lives in love lives in God, and God in him' (1 John 4:16). It would be difficult to get more personal than this."—Philip Yancey

343. **"If God forgives us,** we must forgive ourselves. Otherwise it is almost like setting up ourselves as a higher tribunal than him."— C. S. Lewis

344. **"Once I 'know' God,** that is, once I experience God's love as the love in which all my human experiences are anchored, I can only desire one thing: to be in that love."—Henri J. M. Nouwen

345. **"The Holy Spirit is the bond of tenderness** between the Father and the Son. Thus, the indwelling Spirit bears the indelible stamp of the compassion of God."—Brennan Manning

346. **"The presence of God's glory** is in heaven; the presence of his power on earth; the presence of his justice in hell; and the presence of his grace with his people. If he deny us his powerful presence, we fall into nothing; if he deny us his gracious presence, we fall into sin; if he deny us his merciful presence, we fall into hell."—John Mason

347. **"The most costly sins** I have committed came at a time when I briefly suspended my reverence for God. In such a moment I quietly (and insanely) concluded that God didn't care and most likely wouldn't intervene were I to risk the violation of one of His commandments."—Gordon MacDonald

348. **"The first great commandment** requires us to love God, which we do best through awareness of His great love for us. The 'remembering' of God, of which we sing in the Psalms, is simply the rediscovery, in deep compunction of heart, that God remembers us."—Thomas Merton

349. **"Human language is at best insufficient** to convey the full comprehension of the ideas of righteousness and justification contained in this word [*tsidqenu*]. It is only as we see it exhibited in God's character and acts that we see it clearly."—Dr. Nathan Stone

350. **"The God who came to earth** came not in a raging whirl-wind nor in a devouring fire. Unimaginably, the Maker of all things shrank down, down, down, so small as to become an ovum, a single fertilized egg barely visible to the naked eye, an egg that would divide and redivide until a fetus took shape, enlarging cell by cell inside a nervous teenager."—Philip Yancey

351. **"Man's maker was made man** that He, Ruler of the stars, might nurse at His mother's breast; that the Bread might hunger, the Fountain thirst, the Light sleep, the Way be tired on its journey; that Truth might be accused of false witnesses, the Teacher be beaten with whips, the Foundation be suspended on wood; that Strength might grow weak; that the Healer might be wounded; that Life might die."—Augustine

352. "My identity as Abba's child is not an abstraction or a tap dance into religiosity. It is the core truth of my existence. Living in the wisdom of accepted tenderness profoundly affects my perception of reality, the way I respond to people and their life situations."—Brennan Manning

353. "Joy is the most infallible sign of the presence of God."—Léon Henri Marie Bloy

354. "Were I a preacher, I should preach above all other things the practice of the presence of God. Were I a teacher, I should advise all the world to it; so necessary do I think it, and so easy."—Brother Lawrence of the Resurrection

355. "When, by the reception of the Holy Spirit, I begin to realize that God knows all the deepest possibilities there are in me, knows all the eccentricities of my being, I find that the mystery of myself is solved by this besetting God."—Oswald Chambers

356. "I have concluded that the evident existence of God, and that my existence depends entirely on God in all the moments of my life, that I do not think that the human spirit may know anything with greater evidence and certitude."—René Descartes

357. "Is God all-wise? Then the darkest providences have meaning. We will set ourselves as God's interpreters, and because we cannot make straight lines out of our crooked lot, we think that God has turned our life into inextricable confusion. The darkest hours in our life have some intent, and it is really not needful that we should know all at once what that intent is. Let us keep within our own little sphere, and live a day at a time, and breathe a breath at a time, and be content with one pulsation at a time, and interpretation will come when God pleases, and as he pleases."—Joseph Parker

358. "Prayer is essentially the expression of our heart longing for love. It is not so much the listing of our requests but the breathing of our own deepest request, to be united with God as fully as possible."—Jeffery D. Imbach

359. "'**Repent and believe in the gospel,**' Jesus says. Turn around and believe that the good news that we are loved is better than we ever dared hope, and that to believe in that good news, to live out of it and toward it, to be in love with that good news, is of all glad things in this world the gladdest thing of all."—Frederick Buechner

360. "**After an exhaustive study** was conducted on the great men and women of God throughout the centuries, one thing was found in common: They are marked by 'a holy leisure'—a sense of divinely ordered relaxation, an inner serenity that cultivates the wisdom to prioritize one's time and energy, and a productive leisure that kindles relationships and fires inspiration."—Gail MacDonald

361. "**Love is giving someone else power to change.** God knows that we can only change in the context of freedom. That is why he has lavished his favor on us: so that we could be cut free from every insecurity, healed of rejection's residue, and released from every sense of abandonment that would keep us from truly changing."—Steve Fry

362. "**The first step to be taken by the soul** who desires to draw near to God, is to learn to know God in very truth, and not only outwardly as though by the color of the writing. *For as we know, so do we love;* therefore if we know but little and darkly, if we reflect and meditate on Him only superficially and pleadingly, we shall in consequence love Him but little."—Angelina Foligna, a disciple of St. Francis of Assisi

363. "**How can we pray to thee,** thou holy and hidden God, whose ways are not our ways, who reignest in awful mystery beyond the realm of space and time? Yet how can we not pray to thee, Heavenly Father, who knowest what it is to be a man because thou hast walked among us as a man, breaking the bread of our affliction and drinking deep of the cup of our despair? How can we not pray to thee when it is thy very Spirit alive within us that moves our lips in prayer?"—Frederick Buechner

364. "**The Bible** sometimes portrays God as the initiator, yet just when we think we have God we suddenly feel like Isaiah searching for the One who absconds, *Deus absconditus.*"—Philip Yancey

365. "**The Bible knows** of God's hiding His face, of time when the contact between heaven and earth seems to be interrupted. God seems to withdraw himself utterly from the earth and no longer to participate in its existence. The space of history is then full of noise, but as it were, empty of divine breath."—Martin Buber

366. "**If you find God with great ease,** perhaps it is not God that you have found."—Thomas Merton

367. "**God is** like a person who clears his throat while hiding and so gives himself away."—Meister Eckhart

368. "**An 'impersonal God'**—well and good. A subjective God of beauty, truth and goodness, inside our own heads—better still. A formless life-force surging through us, a vast power which we can tap—best of all. But God Himself, alive, pulling at the other end of the cord, perhaps approaching at an infinite speed, the hunter, king, husband—that is quite another matter."—C. S. Lewis

369. "**The sensation of silence** cannot be helped: a loud and evident God would be a bully, an insecure tyrant, an all-crushing datum instead of, as He is, a bottomless encouragement to our faltering and frightened being."—John Updike

370. "**I envision the Spirit** not so much as touching our mundane lives with a supernatural wand as bringing the Recognition (Dorothy Sayer's word) of God's presence into places we may have overlooked. The Spirit may bring that jolt of Recognition to the most ordinary things: a baby's grin, snow falling on a frozen lake, a field of lavender in morning dew, a worship ritual that unexpectedly becomes more than ritual. Suddenly we see these momentary pleasures as gifts from God who is worthy of praise."—Philip Yancey

371. "**The soul must long for God** in order to be set aflame by God's love; but if the soul cannot yet feel this longing, then it must long for the longing. To long for the longing is also from God."—Meister Eckhart

372. **"We must flee to God** in our many tribulations whatever they may be—domestic worries, ill health, danger to those dear to us. The Christian can have no other refuge but his Saviour, his God. He will have not strength in himself, but in Him in whom he has taken refuge."—Augustine

373. **"'Joy,' said one of the martyrs, 'is the most infallible proof** of the presence of God.' . . . The presence of Jesus evokes a sense of joy. We will from time to time trust in the presence of Jesus. We will from time to time weep in the presence of Jesus. But when he is with us, and he always is, laughter will mark our lives. Joy is indeed the most infallible proof that his indwelling Spirit is in us."—Calvin Miller

374. **"How astonishing** that God chooses to give us a glimpse of Himself—however tarnished or imperfect the picture is to us— through allowing us to grapple with difficult emotions. As we seek a deeper grasp of our own emotions, the struggle opens our vision to see in fresh ways the heart of God."—Dan Allender

375. **"The reason** the mass of men fear God, and at the bottom dislike Him, is because they rather distrust His heart, and fancy Him all brain like a watch."—Herman Melville

376. **"Not many of us,** I think, would ever naturally say that we have known God. . . . We claim, perhaps, to have a testimony, and can rattle off our conversion story with the best of them; we say that we *know* God—this, after all, is what evangelicals are expected to say; but would it occur to us to say, without hesitation, that we *have known* God?"—J. I. Packer

377. **"God himself is present,** not in weakness that permits men to suffer without hope and perspective, but in the sovereignty of His love."—Karl Barth

378. **"There is only one question** which is really serious, and that is the question concerning the being and nature of God. From this all other questions derive their significance."—Emil Brunner

379. **"One can know a great deal** about godliness without much knowledge of God. There is no shortage of books on the church, or sermons from the pulpits, on how to pray, how to witness, how to read our Bibles, how to tithe our money, how to be a young Christian, how to be an old Christian, how to be a happy Christian, how to get consecrated, how to lead men to Christ, how to receive the baptism of the Holy Spirit (or, in some cases, how to avoid receiving it), how to speak in tongues (or, how to explain away Pentecostal manifestations), and generally how to go through all the various motions which the teachers in question associate with being a Christian believer . . . it is possible to learn a great deal at second-hand about the practice of Christianity. . . . Yet one can have all this and hardly know God at all."—J. I. Packer

380. **"That God is love** is certainly universally true, but it is not necessary truth, for He does not have to love us, nor does He owe it to Himself or to us to love us."—Thomas Torrance

381. **"Even the unbeliever encounters God,** but he does not penetrate through to the truth of God that is hidden from him."—Karl Barth

382. **"They that deny** a God destroy man's nobility; for certainly man is of kin to the beasts in his body; and, if he be not of kin to God by his spirit, he is a base and ignoble creature."—Francis Bacon

383. **"Over time,** both through personal experience and my study of the Bible, I have come to know certain qualities of God. God's style often baffles me: He moves at a slow pace, prefers rebels and prodigals, restrains his power, and speaks in whispers and silence. Yet even in these qualities I see evidence of his longsuffering, mercy, and desire to woo rather than compel. When in doubt, I focus on Jesus, the most unfiltered revelation of God's own self."—Philip Yancey

384. **"The fact that God reveals Himself** through His Word presupposes that man is a being who has been created for this kind of communication, for communication through speech."—Emil Brunner

385. **"Thou art the true,** eternal, blessed, unchangeable light of all time and space. Thy wisdom apprehends thousands and still thousands of laws, and yet Thou ever actest of Thy free will, and to Thy honor. Thou wast before all that we worship. To Thee is due praise and adoration."—Ludwig van Beethoven

9

Prayers
and Petitions

---

386. "Prayer is the contact of a living soul with God. In prayer, God stoops to kiss man, to bless man, and to aid in everything God can devise or man can need."—E. M. Bounds

387. "The discussion of prayer is so great that it requires the Father to reveal it, his firstborn Word to teach it, and the Spirit to enable us to think and speak rightly of so great a subject."—Origen

388. "For everyone who asks receives; he who seeks finds; and to him who knocks, the door will be opened" (Matt. 7:8).

389. "**In him and through faith in him** [Christ] we may approach God with freedom and confidence" (Eph. 3:12).

390. "**Oh highest heavenly Father,** pour into our hearts, through Thy son, Jesus Christ, such a light, that by it we may know what messenger we are bound to obey, so that with good conscience we may lay aside the burdens of others and serve Thee, eternal, heavenly Father with happy and joyful hearts."—Albrecht Dürer

391. "**My dear Lord,** only You I call and supplicate / About the vain and blind torment: / You only can renew me within and without."—Michelangelo Buonarroti

392. "**I obey Thee, Lord,** first for the love I, in all reason, owe Thee; secondly, because Thou can shorten or prolong the lives of men."—Leonardo daVinci

393. "**Lord!** That lends me life, lend me a heart replete with thankfulness."—William Shakespeare

394. "**Hear, O Israel:** The Lord is our God, the Lord alone [or, "the Lord our God is one"]. You shall love the Lord your God with all your heart, and with all your soul, and with all your might" (Deut. 6:4–5 NRSV). This is the Shema, the most commonly spoken prayer in Judaism, also traditionally called the "Great Commandment." Many Christians know it in the form that Jesus used in Mark 12:29.

395. "**May it be our lot,** by the grace of the true Son, pure and immaculate, to learn from Him, with all other truths, that which we are now seeking."—Galileo Galilei

396. "**For me, prayer means launching out of the heart towards God;** it means lifting up one's eyes, quite simply, to Heaven, a cry of grateful love from the crest of joy or the trough of despair; it is a vast, supernatural force which opens out my heart, and binds me close to Jesus."—Thérèse de Lisieux

397. "**Have mercy on me, O God,** according to your unfailing love; according to your great compassion blot out my transgressions. Wash away all my iniquity and cleanse me from my sin" (Ps. 51:1).

398. "I thank the Lord Jesus Christ . . . [and beseech him] to send me grace to bewail my guilts and to study to the salvation of my soul, and grant me grace of true repentance . . . through the benign grace of Him that is King of kings and Priest over all priests, that bought us with the precious blood of His heart."—Geoffrey Chaucer

399. "In the name of God, I William Shakespeare . . . God be praised, do make and ordain this, my last will and testament in manner and form following. That is to say, first I commend my soul into the hands of God my Creator, hoping and assuredly believing, through the only merits of Jesus Christ, my saviour, to be made partaker of eternal life, and my body to the earth whereof it is made."—William Shakespeare

400. "How easy it is for me to live with Thee Lord! How easy to believe in Thee! When my thoughts pull back in puzzlement or go soft, when the brightest people see no further than this evening and know not what to do tomorrow, Thou sendest down to me clear confidence that Thou art, and will make sure that not all the ways of the good are closed."—Aleksander Solzhenitsyn

401. "I tell you the truth, if anyone says to this mountain, 'Go, throw yourself into the sea,' and does not doubt in his heart but believes that what he says will happen, it will be done for him. Therefore I tell you, whatever you ask for in prayer, believe that you have received it, and it will be yours" (Mark 11:23–24).

402. "The house of my soul is too small for You to come to it. May it be enlarged by You. It is in ruins: restore it. In Your eyes it has offensive features. I admit it, I know it; but who will clean it up? Or to whom shall I cry other than You? 'Cleanse me from my secret faults, Lord, and spare Your servant from sins to which I am tempted by others' (Ps. 31:5)."—Augustine

403. "O people of Zion, who live in Jerusalem, you will weep no more. How gracious he will be when you cry for help! As soon as he hears, he will answer you" (Isa. 30:19).

404. "Father in heaven, now that another cloud the road / Effectively hides, and wrong ways I take / With uncertain walk among this unstable field / Of the worldly and marshy valley, / Sustain with Your holy hand, keep from failing / My erring way, and by Your mercy the light / Sweet over me shine, and for an escape / Show me the path that I had left behind."—Torquato Tasso

405. "Oh God, God inconceivable . . . I have erred . . . I knew that I was going astray . . . but I never forgot Thee. I always felt Thy presence even in the very moment of my sins. I all but lost Thee, but Thou hast . . . saved me!"—Leo Tolstoy

406. "Let us pray for ourselves, that we may not lose the word 'concern' out of our Christian vocabulary. Let us pray for our nation. Let us pray for those who have never known Jesus Christ and redeeming love, for moral forces everywhere, for our national leaders. Let prayer be our passion. Let prayer be our practice."—Robert E. Lee

407. "O sad estate / Of human wretchedness; so / weak is man, / So ignorant and blind, that / did not God / Sometimes withhold in mercy / what we ask / We should be ruined at our own request."—Hannah More

408. "This, then, is how you should pray: 'Our Father in heaven, hallowed be your name, your kingdom come, your will be done on earth as it is in heaven. Give us today our daily bread. Forgive us our debts, as we also have forgiven our debtors. And lead us not into temptation, but deliver us from the evil one'" (Matt. 6:9–13).

409. "I am convinced that when a Christian rightly prays the Lord's Prayer at any time . . . his praying is more than adequate."—Martin Luther

410. "Come, Lord, and speak to my heart. Communicate to it Your holy will, and mercifully work within it both to will and to do according to Your good pleasure."—Thomas à Kempis

411. "God grant us the serenity to accept the things we cannot change, the courage to change the things we can, and the wisdom to know the difference. Amen."—Reinhold Niebuhr

412. "I ask You, Lord Jesus, to develop in me, Your lover, an immeasurable urge towards You, an affection that is unbounded, a longing that is unrestrained, a fervor that throws discretion to the winds! The more worthwhile our love for You, all the more pressing does it become. Reason cannot hold it in check, fear does not make it tremble, wise judgment does not temper it."—Richard Rolle

413. "I do need Thee, Lord. I need Thee now. I know that I can do without many things that once I thought were necessities, but without Thee I cannot live, and I dare not die. . . . I ask of Thee no easy way, but just Thy grace that is sufficient for every need, so that no matter how hard the way, how challenging the hour, how dark the sky, I may be enabled to overcome. In Thy strength, who hast overcome the world, I make this prayer. Amen."—Peter Marshall

414. "Teach me, Lord, to sing of Your mercies. Turn my soul into a garden, where the flowers dance in the gentle breeze, praising You with their beauty. Let my soul be filled with beautiful virtues; let me be inspired by Your Holy Spirit; let me praise You always."—Teresa of Avila

415. "I have been driven many times to my knees by the overwhelming conviction that I had nowhere else to go. My own wisdom, and that of all about me seemed insufficient for the day."—Abraham Lincoln

416. "God be in my head, and in my understanding; God be in my eyes, and in my looking; God be in my mouth, and in my speaking; God be in my heart, and in my thinking; God be at my end, and at my departing."—Traditional Irish prayer

417. "Now I lay me down to sleep, I pray Thee, Lord, my soul to keep; if I should die before I wake, I pray Thee, Lord, my soul to take."—*New England Primer*

418. "Blessed are Your saints, O Lord, who have traveled over the rough sea of this life, and have reached the harbor of eternal peace and joy. Watch over us who are still on the dangerous voyage. Our ship is frail, and the ocean is wide. But in Your mercy You have set us on Your course with Your son as our pilot, guiding us towards the everlasting shore of peace, the quiet haven of our hectic desire."—Augustine

419. "You, O Eternal Trinity, are a deep sea into which, the more I enter, the more I find, and the more I find, the more I seek. O abyss, O eternal Godhead, O sea profound, what more could You give me than Yourself? Amen."—Catherine of Siena

The Creator

420. God began it all. "In the beginning God . . ." is how the first verse of the first chapter of the first book of the Bible begins. The beginning of the history of the world is chronicled with those words!

421. When creation began. Relying on biblical sources such as the chronologies and genealogies in Genesis, numerous people have attempted to pinpoint a time and date for the precise moment of creation. Ancient Hebrew scholars placed the moment at 3761 BC. Perhaps the most famous creation date was the one produced by Irish bishop James Ussher (1581–1656). Using Genesis, Ussher dated the moment of creation to the early morning of the twenty-

third of October in 4004 BC (Ussher actually used the Julian calendar year of 710). Ussher's calculation was widely accepted by
European Christians for centuries and was included in the margins
of many editions of the King James Bible, giving it nearly divine
"authority."

422. Genesis 1:1 begins the summary of creation. "In the beginning God created the heavens and the earth." This first verse is
considered a summary of what is to come in the following six days
of creation (Gen. 1:3–31).

423. God's creation followed a specific order. Of the six days
of creation, there is a parallel structure between God's creating
work in days one through three and four through six. The first segment of creation can be considered the forming of the structure of
creation. The second segment includes the filling of that structure
with every type of life.

424. On the first day, God created light. The light was separated
from the darkness that had previously covered the earth. "Day" and
"night" are introduced; the first day ends with "there was evening,
and there was morning—the first day" (Gen. 1:5).

425. On the second day, God took a watery world and gave it
definition. Whereas at the end of the first day, there was only water
to see in the light, at the end of the second day there was sky present, separated from the waters.

426. On the third day, the waters under the sky were put in their
place as dry ground appeared. God named the dry places "land" and
the gathered waters "seas" (Gen. 1:9–10). The third day is also the
first time when we read that "God saw that it was good" (v. 10).

427. During the second part of the third day, God made the
land productive with fruit-producing trees and seed-bearing plants.
Every imaginable seed-bearing plant and tree, every green living
type of vegetation, was created at this time. God again stated that
what he saw was "good."

428. On the fourth day, God began the second phase of his creation. Paralleling the creation of "light" and "day" from the first day,
God creates two "great lights—the greater light to govern the day

and the lesser light to govern the night" (Gen. 1:16). These great lights were put in the sky to serve as signs of the seasons as well as to separate the day from the night. The stars were also created on the fourth day. God again "saw that it was good" (v. 18).

429. On the fifth day, God filled the water and the air with every imaginable living creature. On the second day, he created the two expanses of sky and water; on this fifth day he filled those two portions of the earth. The "great creatures of the sea" and "every winged bird" were created, blessed, and given a command to increase their numbers. Showing his continuing pleasure with the creation, God saw it was good.

430. On the sixth day, God's creation had two parts. In the first part, God told the land to produce living creatures that will live on the land. This parallels the creation account of God creating "dry ground" on the third day. Also created on this day was man. God said, "Let us make man in our image, in our likeness" (v. 26). Man was told to rule over the living creatures in the sky, sea, and on the land. God told his two image-bearers (a male and a female) to increase their numbers too.

431. "Let us make man in our image . . ." Here God is speaking to those who are in heaven and watching what God is doing, his angels and the like. God mentions "us" again after the fall occurs, saying, "The man has now become like one of us, knowing good and evil" (3:22).

432. The second part of God's creative work on the sixth day involves what God gave man and the animals to live on. God gave man every "seed-bearing plant . . . and every tree that has fruit with seed in it" to eat (1:29). To every animal he gave the remaining vegetation—every green plant. This too parallels God's work on the third day; God had made vegetation during the latter half of the second day. On day six, he gave that vegetation over to his image-bearer and every living creature in order to eat and live.

433. Day six ends with God seeing everything he had done. On this final day, God saw that "it was very good" (v. 31). Chapter 2 opens with a final thought on the creation: "Thus the heavens and the earth were completed in all their vast array."

434. Eden, which means "a place of delight," is believed by some scholars to have been located at the eastern end of the Fertile Crescent, near where the Tigris and Euphrates rivers meet the Persian Gulf.

435. The term *create* **is used in two senses in Scripture:** in the sense of immediate creation and in the sense of mediate creation. *Immediate* creation is that free act of the triune God in the beginning. Without the use of preexisting materials or secondary causes, he brought into being, immediately and instantaneously, the whole visible and invisible universe. *Mediate* creation, on the other hand, is those acts of God that are also called creation, but do not originate things. Instead they shape, adapt, combine, or transform existing materials.

436. Proof of creation. From ancient times humanity has been trying to solve the "riddle" of the universe. Humankind asks, "Did it always exist, or was there a beginning? If it did have a beginning, how and when did it come into being?" Science seeks to find an answer but is limited to empirical knowledge. Philosophy has not been able to arrive at an adequate solution either. The answer to our origin must ultimately come from Scripture and be accepted by faith (Heb. 11:3). Scripture declares both the how and why of physical and spiritual existence.

437. Creation was immediate, mediate, or a combination of both. Some limit immediate creation to the act described in Genesis 1:1 and regard the rest of the chapter as mediate creation. Others see a combination of both through the entire chapter. For example, the sun may have been included in the original creation, and the light (vv. 3–5) may have come from the sun. However, God most likely created light apart from the sun.

438. What was included in the immediate creation of God? Certainly not only the heavens, but also the angelic inhabitants of heaven (Job 38:7; Neh. 9:6); and not only the earth, but also all the waters and gases of the earth (Isa. 42:5; Col. 1:16; Rev. 4:11).

439. The restoration theory, or "gap" theory, of creation proposes that after the original creation (Gen. 1:1), Satan fell, resulting in divine judgment upon the earth (v. 2). What follows are six days of re-creating the earth. This view holds that "was" (v. 2) should be better translated "became." It further argues that the picture of formlessness, emptiness, and darkness (v. 2) is chiefly a picture of divine judgment, for God would not have created the earth this way (Isa. 34:11; 45:18; Jer. 4:23; 1 John 1:5). Further, this position provides a framework in which the fall of Satan may have taken place (Isa. 14:9–14; Ezek. 28:12–19).

440. Many philosophies deny the doctrine of creation and postulate other origins for the universe. Atheism, which denies the existence of God, must either make matter eternal or find some other natural cause. Dualism argues for two eternal principles, one good and one evil, or two eternal beings, God and Satan or God and matter. Pantheism makes creation a part of God. Agnosticism says no one can know about God or his creation.

441. Christianity affirms that creation came through God's sovereign will. God, though immanent in his creation, also transcends his creation. The universe is God's handiwork and is intended to display his glory.

442. The God of nature was once described by theologian J. I. Packer this way: "We are cruel to ourselves if we try to live in this world without knowing about the God whose world it is and who runs it. The world becomes a strange, mad, painful place, and life in it a disappointing and unpleasant business, for those who do not know about God. Disregard the study of God, and you sentence yourself to stumble and blunder through life blindfolded, as it were, with no sense of direction and no understanding of what surrounds you."

443. Adam and Eve were the first humans. We know God caused a deep sleep to fall upon Adam, and while he slept, God took one of Adam's ribs and closed up his flesh. Woman was then formed from the extracted rib. When the Old Testament was translated into Greek, the Hebrew word *tsela* in Genesis 2 became *pleura*. Only in its plural form does *pleura* refer to a set of ribs, but its more common translation is "side," "side of man," even the membranes that line the thoracic cavity. The term may even possibly refer to "wife," as the Hebrew *tsela* sometimes signifies a bosom friend or a person who is at one's side.

444. The word translated "rib" is not translated as such any-where else in the Old Testament. Its most frequent use seems to be related to construction, and in references dealing with the build-ing of the tabernacle, the word is translated "beam," "chamber," "plank," "corner," "side chamber," and "side" (Exod. 25:12, 14; 26:27, 35; 27:8; 36:25–30).

445. God's sovereign rule. God, as creator of all things visible and invisible and the owner of all, has an absolute right to rule over all (Matt. 20:15; Rom. 9:20–21). He exercises his author-ity in the universe (Eph. 1:11). "Indeed everything that is in the heavens and the earth; Yours is the dominion, O LORD" (1 Chron. 29:11 NASB); "Woe to the one who quarrels with his Maker—an earthenware vessel among the vessels of earth! Will the clay say to the potter, 'What are you doing?' Or the thing you are making say, 'He has no hands'?" (Isa. 45:9 NASB); "Behold, all souls are mine; as the soul of the father, so also the soul of the son is mine" (Ezek. 18:4 KJV).

446. Humans were made in God's image, which means that we are *personal* beings, have intellect, retain a sense of morality, and have the ability to *choose* between right and wrong.

447. Genesis tells us that humans were created "in the image of God." This refers to the spirit and character that universally and unfailingly belong to humans only. Because God is spirit, we are created with the capacity for eternity and for valuing the self beyond our bodies.

448. *Imago Dei*. Only humanity is created in "the image of God." Though we share the same day of creation with all the animal king-dom and though we are made of the same stuff as the animals—the dust of the earth—only we are the *Imago Dei*.

449. Male or female? God is spirit and is therefore without body parts. Knowing that we, in our finite understanding, would need something tangible, God gave us symbols to bring us understand-ing of the great love offered to us. For example, the imagery of *parent—Father*—is one for us to grasp.

450. One flesh. The original "one flesh" union of the first man and woman forms a picture of the full spectrum "image of God."

Differentiated as they were by the scalpel of God and formed into two distinct models—male and female—their first and almost involuntary response was to reach out and reattach to the other half, thus displaying God's personal and intimate nature.

451. God created them male and female *(Ish* and *Ishah)*. In the creation of his most glorious reflection, the image of God is multifaceted, is specific and individual, but is also general and communal.

452. Adam and Eve's firstborn son, Cain, is remembered as the first murderer for killing his brother, Abel. When God sentenced Cain to wander the earth, Cain begged for mercy and, in fear, thought that someone would kill him. So God marked him. Widely viewed as a sign of guilt, the so-called mark of Cain is actually a symbol of divine mercy. Opponents of the death penalty point to this first murder and God's merciful sentence on the murderer as a biblical rejection of capital punishment. For his crime, Cain received a life sentence of hard labor.

His People

453. God's chosen people. One of the most significant lines in Amos is the prophet's message to Israel from God: "You only have I chosen of all the families of the earth; therefore I will punish you for all your sins" (3:2). This is the essence of the Jews' designation as the "chosen people." God's covenant with the people did not entitle them to special favors, but rather being chosen increased their responsibility.

454. Origin of the term "Jews." In the year 587 BC, the holy city lay in ruins, and its people were led off to captivity in Babylon after the armies of King Nebuchadnezzar of Babylonia overran Judah and conquered Jerusalem. Their name changed to "Jews" (from the Hebrew *Yehudi,* which means "belonging to the tribe of Judah"). They kept alive their faith and their way of life during their years of exile.

455. *Habiru* (or "Hebrew") was a word of disparagement, probably meaning "the dusty ones." It did not refer to the Hebrew people in particular but rather to all the land-hungry Semites who led a nomadic life. In the Book of Genesis (14:13), Abraham is called "the Hebrew," and so this general name was finally limited to his descendants.

456. The history of the Israelites. Through God's revelation of himself to the children of Israel, humanity first conceived of how they were originally created in the image of God but fell from this high position after sinning. They learned of God's purpose of redemption through sacrifice, of deliverance through the death of a Messiah, of salvation for all nations, and of a final reign in righteousness and peace.

457. Abram was given his new name, Abraham, when God came to him in his ninety-ninth year. At that time he had one son, Ishmael. Abraham's new name meant "father of many nations." Abraham must have been puzzled how God would bring him into a full understanding of his new name with but one child when he was already quite old.

458. Throughout God's early conversations with Abraham, a covenant child was promised to continue this special man's line. God's promises are eternal; his words surpass logic and our plans of timing, and include a strong dose of miracles as well. Abraham and Sarah were unsure how this promise would come to be, as Sarah had been barren for many, many years. Though Abraham trusted God, he and Sarah also took matters into their own hands. Abraham made Sarah's maid, Hagar, pregnant, and though Abraham loved Ishmael and hoped God would make him the covenant son, God's will was already set. The Hebrews were told to trust God, to obey God, to follow him in all their ways, even when they didn't see exactly where that path was leading.

459. Abraham's covenant son, Isaac, was promised to Abraham first by God and then by the three angels who visited and prophesied of the event to Abraham shortly before Sarah discovered she was pregnant. Though Sarah laughed at their proclamation and Abraham was undoubtedly skeptical, God's message carried his promise, something not to doubt. Sarah delivered a healthy infant son within a year of that proclamation, and they called this special baby Isaac. He was truly a miraculous sign of God's covenant with Abraham—Isaac's parents were in their nineties!

460. The sacrifice of Isaac. God called Abraham to follow him to a far land. God promised to make his family a great nation. Yet when Abraham finally had a son in his old age, the Lord asked him to sacrifice the boy on Mount Moriah. Instead of a pagan practice, it was a test of faith—God intervened to stop the sacrifice and provided a ram to sacrifice in the boy's place. Then, praising Abraham's faith, God promised to bless all nations through his offspring.

461. The story of Abraham's unshakable faith while offering Isaac is a central moment in the Bible. To many people it seems an unnecessarily cruel test of faith. Abraham doesn't even make the arguments for his own son that he made for the citizens of Sodom. His wife, Sarah, is silent in this episode, and Isaac's thoughts are not available to us either.

462. When God stays Abraham's hand. The passage says that Abraham "fears" God (Gen. 22:12). The "fear of God" is a commonly used expression today. The Hebrew verb for "fear" can be understood two ways. Occasionally it meant being afraid, but very often the biblical "fear" meant awe or reverence for someone of exalted position. Abraham was not necessarily "afraid" of God as much as he held God in profound respect.

463. Isaac was a godly patriarch and followed in his father's footsteps. He married Rebekah after Abraham sent Eliezer to find a wife for him. Eliezer's method of finding a wife was truly a testimony to his faith in God. Eliezer's prayer to God asked for a very specific sign to show him whom Isaac was to marry. He asked that the girl would be the one who, when Eliezer asked for water for himself, would say, "Drink, and I'll water your camels too." That very scenario occurred, and Eliezer confidently brought Rebekah to Isaac!

464. Isaac and Rebekah suffered some of the same difficulties as their parents—they were unable to have children too. It must have seemed impossible to imagine God's original covenant to Abraham of a people being greater "than the sands of the seashore" with both father and son being unable to have children on their own. Yet Isaac prayed to God for his wife, and she did become pregnant. Her twins represented two different nations; Jacob's family line would continue the covenant. Esau and Jacob were constantly at odds and only made peace many years after Jacob received the covenant blessing from his father, Isaac.

465. Jacob married two sisters, Rachel and Leah. Through deceit on the girls' father's part, Jacob was tricked on his wedding night. Jacob served Laban for seven years for Laban's younger daughter, Rachel. The morning after the wedding, Jacob found he had married Leah, Laban's older daughter, instead! Jacob agreed to serve Laban another seven years in exchange for Rachel.

466. Jacob was continually blessed. He experienced a dream early on that demonstrated God's faithful promise to be with him (Genesis 28). In addition to the blessing of his father, Isaac, God told him: "I will give you and your descendants the land on which you are lying. Your descendants will be like the dust of the earth, and you will spread out to the west and to the east, to the north and to the south. All peoples on earth will be blessed through you and your offspring. I am with you and will watch over you wherever you go" (vv. 13–15).

467. Wrestling with God. The life of Jacob contains a number of interesting stories that make him appear more a scoundrel than a patriarch. He cheated his brother, Esau, manipulated for a wife, and tricked his father. However, one of the strangest stories occurs in Genesis 32. While running from Esau, Jacob met God (appearing as a man) and wrestled with him all night. After having his hip torn from its socket, Jacob told the man that he would continue wrestling until he was blessed. With that God changed Jacob's name to *Israel*, which means, "wrestles with God."

468. Jacob had twelve sons by his two wives and their respective maids. These twelve sons would become the twelve seeds of the twelve tribes of Israel. The two sisters, Rachel and Leah, were bitter toward one another throughout their childbearing years. Rachel, Jacob's true love, could not produce children and was truly bitter toward Leah, who produced six sons. When God heard Jacob's pleas, as well as Rachel's, for children, God blessed them with the birth of a son, Joseph, and later Benjamin.

469. Joseph, though one of the youngest children of Jacob, was God's choice to continue his blessing. God consistently picked a son other than the firstborn and normal choice to be blessed and lead the family on. Joseph had many gifts, including the gift of interpreting dreams. He was continually blessed throughout his life.

470. The story of Joseph's "coat of many colors" remains a favorite of many people. His father gave him a special coat to wear that distinguished him from his brothers. Joseph was his father's favorite son, much to the chagrin of most of the other brothers. Jacob made Joseph his heir, even though he was the second to the youngest! Joseph's brothers eventually sold him into slavery in Egypt and joyfully took the coat, tore it up, and told Jacob his beloved son was dead.

471. God never forgot Joseph. Eventually this young man who saw visions and could interpret dreams made himself useful to Pharaoh! He became a chief minister of Egypt and was reunited with his family in their time of need during a drought spreading throughout the whole land. They all then settled in Egypt.

472. The twelve brothers and their father all remained in Egypt and lived happily there until the whole generation of Joseph and his brothers passed away. Then their people became oppressed by the Egyptians and were used as slaves. The Egyptians feared the great numbers of Hebrew people being born and even demanded that the midwives kill the newborn males. The oppression lasted over four hundred years!

473. Moses—or *Moshe* **in Hebrew—**is the central human figure in the Hebrew Bible, the great law bringer, and for Christians, the symbolic model for Jesus. God had a special plan for Moses. When the Egyptian pharaoh ordered all the Jewish babies killed, Moses was saved. His was a parallel experience to Jesus'—the Messiah was saved after a king ordered Jewish babies to be killed when Jesus was around two years old. His family ironically took the baby back to Egypt. Other instances of Moses foreshadowing Jesus: Moses parted the waters; Jesus walked on the waters. Moses spent forty years in the wilderness; Jesus spent forty days in the wilderness. Moses went to a mountain and gave a sermon; Jesus gave the Sermon on the Mount. Moses delivered the covenant; Jesus delivered the new covenant.

474. The escape from Egypt. Moses went before Pharaoh and demanded that his people be set free. The story of Moses, who was miraculously saved and raised as royalty, then lost his position due to immature violence only to be called by God to greatness, is a wonderful riches-to-rags-to-riches story. The plagues, the escape, and the parting of the Red Sea make it one of the most-told stories of all time.

475. The "Aaronic benediction" was given by God to Aaron, Moses' brother and the Israelites' priest. This extremely ancient blessing is still widely used in temples and churches today among both Jews and Christians: "The Lord bless you and keep you; the Lord make his face to shine upon you, and be gracious to you; the Lord lift up his countenance upon you, and give you peace" (Num. 6:24–26 NRSV).

476. God brought his people out of Egypt and they settled in the desert. The Israelites, as they had come to be called, didn't always trust God as they should have. They constantly forgot what a miracle their escape from Egypt was. Their disregard for this miracle led them to worship other gods and even to be angry at God. As a result, God put off taking them to Canaan until they had lived in the desert for forty years and a whole generation had died off.

477. Freed at last, the Israelites set about making a place in which to worship God. The tabernacle was their first place of worship. Very explicit instructions were given for how it was to be built (Exodus 26). Inside the tabernacle, which was a giant tent, were several rooms, including the Most Holy Place and the curtain separating that section from the Holy Place. The tabernacle was 75 feet by 150 feet in diameter.

478. The tent of the tabernacle was covered with badger skins. These skins are mentioned several times in the Old Testament. They were highly valued and listed along with gold, jewels, and other precious objects as materials for the tabernacle. Most badger pelts were extremely durable and tough, making excellent waterproofing for the tabernacle.

479. Some of the Israelites continued to disobey God in spite of the intensity of his miracles. Achan was one such case. During the battle of Jericho, he took some of the prized gold and other precious items that belonged to God and kept them for himself. As a result, the Israelites lost their next battle. God punished his people repeatedly for disobeying his commands, ever the faithful Father, yet a righteous God who demanded obedience.

480. Once the Israelites were established in Canaan, they were governed by judges, leaders who normally had first been warriors. God gave his people strong leaders to follow, but they didn't always do so. The Book of Judges tells of the difficulties the Israelites suffered when they did not obey God.

481. The ark of the covenant was the single most important object in the history of ancient Israel, though it eventually disappeared from the Bible without further mention. It was first housed in the tabernacle. It was a huge chest that contained the stone tables of the Ten Commandments. Above the chest hovered the wings of two cherubim. After Jerusalem was destroyed in 586 BC, the fate of the ark was never discussed.

482. Saul was the first king of Israel. He was anointed by the prophet Samuel. Saul was known to be very tall and majestic of frame. God blessed Saul as long as he was obedient to God and listened to Samuel. But Saul fell away from God and suffered an unhappy ending. He became proud and jealous of David, a young man who was loyal to him and served him both personally and in battle. God did not allow Saul's sins to go unpunished. During a battle, Saul and many of his family were lost; Saul killed himself in order to avoid being captured.

483. David, the youngest son of Jesse, was anointed to be the second king of Israel when he was only a shepherd boy. He was a faithful witness to God's amazing love and found much joy and happiness as both a warrior and a king. Yet he too sinned and was punished. But he came back to God and was forgiven. David was also a famous poet—many of the Psalms were written by him.

484. Solomon became king in the year 961 BC and reigned for thirty-nine years. The name *Solomon* is derived from the Hebrew word for "peace," and Solomon indeed lived up to his name. Under Solomon's reign, Jerusalem became one of the most important cities in the Near East.

12

The Battle
Belongs to the Lord

---

485. **"If you [LORD] will deliver these people into our hands,** we will totally destroy their cities" (Num. 21:2). Several Israelites were captured by the Canaanite king of Arad while the Israelites were traveling. God's people responded by making a vow to the Lord that they would destroy the cities if God would deliver the Canaanites into their hands. God listened to their plea and the Canaanites were defeated and their cities destroyed.

486. God remained the general of his people so long as the people deferred to him. When the two kings Sihon and Og opted to battle the Israelites rather than let them pass, God handed these forces into Israel's hands and allowed his people to kill everyone, capture their cities, and occupy their land.

487. At times God demanded vengeance of the Israelites, such as when they were ordered to attack the Midianites (Num. 31:1). Yet when God called his people to battle and they obeyed, they were blessed. At that particular battle, God delivered into Israel's hands the five kings of Midian as well as all their cities, flocks, people, and goods. Not a single Israelite fell in that battle!

488. The battle of Jericho is one of the most miraculous demonstrations of God's power to the Israelites as they became a new nation. The Israelites were instructed to march around Jericho one time each day for six days. The priests were to carry rams' horns at the front of the army. On the seventh day, the priests were instructed to blow the trumpets, then the people were all to shout. God promised Joshua that the walls would then collapse, and the men would be able to go inside the city walls and take the city. And it happened just as the angel promised Joshua it would.

489. The battle of Ai is a reminder of what happens when all Israel is not united in their obedience to the Lord. Achan, one of the Hebrew warriors, took for himself some of the plunder from Jericho instead of turning it all over to God. As a result, God did not give Ai into the Israelites' hands; instead, three thousand of their men were routed, some of them dying as a result of the disobedient Achan. God was angry with all Israel for this indiscretion, and his anger did not turn until Achan and all his household were destroyed. Again, God's actions are based on his complete righteousness. If the people obeyed, he blessed them. If not, he punished them.

490. God did eventually deliver Ai into the Israelites' hands. Joshua gave the soldiers strict orders on how to ambush the city. The Israelites were to pretend to flee as they had in the first battle; then their opponents would chase them. The battle worked out handily, with the entire city of Ai emptying out in order to chase the running Israelites. The city was left behind with no one to defend it. Some of the Israelite army then captured the city easily and set it on fire. The fleeing Israelites turned around to fight, with those in the city coming from behind. The Ai soldiers were struck down easily, and not one remained alive, not even their king. Then the Israelites took the livestock and plundered the city as God had instructed them to.

491. Enemies didn't stand a chance against the Israelites when the Lord was on their side! When the five kings of the Amorites joined forces against Israel, Joshua was assured by God that not a single one of their enemies would stand. God threw the Amorites into a confused state and made them flee. Then God pursued them by making big hailstones fall from the sky, an act that actually killed more Amorites than Israel did by the sword.

492. The sun stood still. While battling the Amorites, Joshua asked the Lord to allow the sun to stand in the sky until "the nation avenged itself on its enemies" (Josh. 10:12). The Bible account says that the "sun stopped in the middle of the sky and delayed going down about a full day. There has never been a day like it before or since, a day when the LORD listened to a man. Surely the LORD was fighting for Israel!" (Josh. 10:13–14).

493. "The LORD, the God of Israel, fought for Israel" (Josh. 10:42). Thanks to their God, the Israelites gained control of an entire region that had previously been ruled by peoples who were much stronger on a military front, had more riches and resources, and made alliances among others in their region. Yet those whom Israel defeated were idol worshipers, and they could not stand against God's power and righteousness. The Israelites left no survivors in their battles; they wiped out entire peoples as God had commanded them to.

494. Once the Southern region had been taken, the Northern kings became fearful and united in order to wage war on Israel. The Bible says they "came out with all their troops and a large number of horses and chariots—a huge army, as numerous as the sand on the seashore" (Josh. 11:4). God reminded Joshua that they were not to fear them, for he would hand over the entire lot to Israel. Joshua brought this message to the people and they attacked, without leaving a single survivor. The enemies' chariots were burned and their horses crippled.

495. Why were they warring? God had blessed his people with plenty of land and resources at this point, but the Israelites continued to battle. Why? God wanted the entire land taken as an inheritance for Israel; the Israelites didn't rest until they had done this. When they finished, they lived peacefully.

496. The time of the judges came after the death of Joshua. The judges were godly men and followed God. But after one judge would die, the people would revert to worshiping false gods and living as the people around them. Then God's anger would return, and the people would suffer oppression from those same people. All of the work of Joshua and his generation was undone in between the various judges. Many battles were lost in this time period as a result of Israel's disobedience.

497. Ehud was one such judge whom God used to deliver the people. The Moabites ruled over Israel for eighteen years before God allowed Ehud to deliver them. The Bible tells us Ehud was a left-handed man; this one characteristic is important to how the battle began. Ehud killed the king of Moab by tricking him. He met privately with the king and drew his sword from his right thigh with his left hand. He plunged it into the king and was able to get away without anyone even knowing what had happened. Afterward he sounded a trumpet and the other Israelites joined him to do battle against Moab. The Israelites won the battle and successfully ruled over Moab for eighty years.

498. The two most famous military heroines mentioned in the Old Testament are Deborah and Jael, judges who both had a hand in the same victory. God spoke through Deborah to tell the general Barak how to defeat the Canaanites, including their king, Jabin. Barak agreed to attack, but he wanted Deborah to go with him into the battle. She did and the enemies were defeated.

499. Gideon was called by God to "save Israel out of Midian's hand" (Judg. 6:14). At first Gideon led an army of thirty-two thousand men, but God told Gideon to send home all but three hundred! With trumpets, glass jars, torches, and faith in God's promise, the small Israelite army followed Gideon's lead and watched in amazement as they scared the Midianites awake. Then God caused the enemy soldiers to turn on one another with their swords before the whole bunch fled and were tracked down and killed.

500. During one particular battle, the ark of the covenant was taken by the Philistines. The Israelites were defeated on the battlefield and had lost four thousand of their men (1 Sam. 4:2). The people were fearful of why they had been defeated and requested that the ark be brought. When the Philistines realized that the Israelites' ark was in their midst, they descended on the Israelites' camp, killed thirty thousand more foot soldiers, and took the ark. This all happened in order to fulfill the prophecy of God given in 1 Samuel 2:30–35.

501. Samuel served as the last judge of the Israelites before Saul was made king. One particular battle demonstrated God's continuing faithfulness to Israel and involved this special judge. Samuel had assembled all the Israelites at Mizpah (1 Sam. 7:6–8). The Philistines heard that Israel was all in one place and hurried to wage war against them. Samuel took a lamb and offered it as a sacrifice to God and pleaded to him for his people. The Lord promised to take care of Israel, and he caused loud thunder to come around the Philistines, which caused them to panic. Israel then rushed in and pursued the Philistines, slaughtering them all.

502. Saul was the first king of the Israelites. The Lord worked in his heart and made him a true leader of the people. Before Saul was officially made king, yet after he had been anointed, God showed the people he was with Saul. The Ammonites besieged Jabesh Gilead, an Israelite stronghold, and the people were fearful and cried out for deliverance. They would not assemble to fight, however, choosing instead to send messages to the rest of Israel, asking for warriors to be delivered within seven days. When Saul heard about this plan, "the Spirit of God came upon him in power, and he burned with anger" (1 Sam. 11:6). He demanded that every able Israelite fight, and he raised 330,000 men total. They slaughtered the Ammonites and, as the Bible relays, "Those who survived were scattered, so that no two of them were left together" (1 Sam. 11:11).

503. Jonathan, the son of King Saul, also was successful in battle. He and his armor bearer climbed over a cliff to meet their Philistine enemies after Jonathan declared that "the LORD has given them [Philistines] into the hand of Israel" (1 Sam. 14:12). Together with his armor bearer, they killed twenty men in a space no larger than half an acre. Their attack spawned another attack after God caused a great panic among the Philistines. The enemy forces were so confused they were striking each other with their swords! Once again God demonstrated his faithfulness to Israel by winning the battle for them.

504. David fought Goliath because the Philistine giant had "defied the armies of the living God" (1 Sam. 17:36). David declared that God would deliver the Philistine into Israel's hands because God was with his people. With five smooth stones and only his sling as a weapon, the young shepherd boy defeated Goliath easily, assured that this was God's battle. Israel consistently found that if they trusted in God and sought his will, their enemies would not stand.

505. David lost favor with Saul and had to flee for his life. While he was living in caves and fleeing from one town to another, he heard that the Philistines were attacking an Israelite place called Keilah. Though it wasn't David's responsibility to go, and he had very few men with him, he inquired of God whether he should go and fight the Philistines. God answered by promising to "give the Philistines into your hand" (1 Sam. 23:5). David and his men saved the people of Keilah, took the Philistines' livestock, and killed many Philistines. They were successful because they consistently sought the Lord's will and obeyed his call.

506. David eventually went to live in the land of the Philistines in order to avoid Saul's attempts to kill him. During one occasion, while David and his men were intent on fighting Israel with the Philistines, the Amalekites came and raided David's own refuge, stealing all the women and children and plundering the place before burning it. David and his men were distraught, but they again sought God's leading. God assured David of the victory and so the warrior pursued the Amalekites. God gave the group into their hand, and the Israelites recovered everything—no single person or thing was missing from the Israelites' recovered belongings! (1 Sam. 30:19).

507. The Philistines were finally routed completely when King David sought God's leading and overtook them in battle with

God leading the first assault against the Philistines. This was shortly after the Israelites overtook Jerusalem and the Jebusites and made that city David's city.

508. One of the most interesting motivations for a battle can be found in 2 Samuel 10:4. King David had sent a group of men to express Israel's sympathy over the death of the king of the Ammonites, a group that had lived in peace with Israel. The men were humiliated via this method: Half of each of their beards were shaved and their garments were cut around the buttocks (a sign saved for degrading prisoners of war). The shaving of the beards was considered an insult of the deepest kind. Beards were only shaved as signs of deep mourning. The Ammonites knew David would not accept such an action, and so they hired more soldiers to fight against Israel, but God delivered his people and made those other nations subject to Israel and at peace with God's people.

509. Battles naturally took many lives on both sides of the fighting. Such losses couldn't always be avoided, and the kings who waged wars knew it. David was one such king. He purposefully had Uriah, the husband of Bathsheba, put at the front of the battle in order that this innocent man might be killed and David's adultery with Bathsheba hidden. Uriah was a loyal soldier and went where he was directed. God knew what David had done and didn't let this offense go unpunished (the child born to David and Bathsheba died as a result). God consistently demonstrated his awareness of Israel's spiritual state.

510. "Twenty-four in all." One of those who fell against Israel was said to have twelve fingers and twelve toes. Four descendants of Rapha, all giants perhaps, also fell against Israel (2 Sam. 21:20–22). These were Philistines whom God delivered into Israel's hands.

511. Prayers to God for deliverance often preceded battles. David's psalms lament his pain and sorrow over enemies coming after him. Psalm 54 is one such plea: "Save me, O God, by your name; vindicate me by your might. Hear my prayer, O God; listen to the words of my mouth. Strangers are attacking me; ruthless men seek my life—men without regard for God. Surely God is my help; the LORD is the one who sustains me" (vv. 1–4).

13

Through Poetry, Song, and Lament

512. The books of poetry. Job, Psalms, Proverbs, Ecclesiastes, and Song of Solomon make up the Bible's books of poetry. Sometimes these are also called the "wisdom writings." All demonstrate Israel's need to commune with God through prayer and worship. Though they were supremely blessed, the Hebrews suffered through many difficulties and often called out to God for mercy. Their prayers were answered and they would then praise God for his faithfulness.

513. Hebrew poetry is picturesque and vivid. The rhythm or cadence to Hebrew poetry is lost to some degree in the translation, but it is filled with concrete images and deep emotion. These five books of poetry aren't just a change in style from previous books; the subject matter shifts as well. Wisdom takes center stage with these five books, therefore they are called the "wisdom literature" of the Bible.

514. Job is a book of both lament and praise. Whenever the troubling question of "Why do bad things happen to good people?" comes up, Job is the first to come to mind. Satan uses Job to try and prove a point to God that without God's protective covering over his people, they would fall away. Satan ultimately failed in his efforts. Though many ills happened to Job, he did not curse God or turn from the difficulties. As he states in Job 2:10, "Shall we accept good from God, and not trouble?"

515. Job is never identified as a Jew, and he wasn't a king, but his book fits with the poetic books of both King David and King Solomon. Job is thought to have lived in the Arabian Desert somewhere between Babylon and the Holy Land during the years of exile. So the Book of Job might fit more easily near Exodus!

516. God valued Job's faithfulness greatly, and though the heavenly Father did give Satan permission to harm what belonged to Job and eventually to harm his very person, he did not give Satan everything. Job's eternal life was already signed and sealed—God said, "There is no one on earth like [Job]; he is blameless and upright, a man who fears God and shuns evil" (Job 1:8). It can be difficult to resolve why God would put one of his children into such a predicament, and, like us, Job had the same questions.

517. Why did God allow Satan such opportunity? Satan accused God of being foolish; the great deceiver claimed that Job was only righteous and "faithful" because it helped him receive great blessing. In essence, Satan undermined the godliness of a redeemed man. If Satan could prove that Job's godliness was truthfully a self-serving sin, then redemption would be an impossibility. Satan wanted to show that this was indeed the case, and that ultimately, God's system is flawed. God allowed Satan to trouble

Job because it was necessary in order to silence Satan. However, God is in control—he puts limits on how far Satan may go.

518. Job remained faithful to God. Job's friends told him that his sin was causing the problems, that God would not allow such suffering if he had been faithful. His wife told him to curse God and die. Job was left alone with his thoughts but would not turn his back on God. He cried out because he felt alienated from God, chided God for being unjust, and cursed the day of his birth, but he would not curse God. What pained Job most was God's apparent alienation from him—a sign that it is not earthly pain or misery we should fear, but the spiritual pain of separation from our heavenly Father.

519. Job won an audience with God. It is truly magnificent what God has to say to his child in chapters 38–42. God's sovereignty is firmly established, as is his faithfulness. Job's friends are chastised for their lack of faith, Job and God's relationship is completely restored, and Job is blessed even more in the second part of his life than he had been in the first.

520. Psalms. While Jews and Christians share the entire Hebrew Scriptures, or Old Testament, Psalms is the most emotionally and intensely shared book of Hebrew Scripture. Jews know many of the Psalms and individual verses by heart. Jesus often quoted or referred to the Psalms. Martin Luther called the Book of Psalms "a Bible in miniature." The 150 "rosaries" later instituted by the Roman Catholic Church are in honor of the 150 Psalms.

521. The Psalms chronicle both the joys and sorrows of God's people. They are timeless and demonstrate even today what it is to be a child of God: "Sing to the Lord, you saints of his; praise his holy name. For his anger lasts only a moment, but his favor lasts a lifetime; weeping may remain for a night, but rejoicing comes in the morning" (Ps. 30:4–5).

522. David was more than a great warrior. He was a musician who played the eight-stringed harplike instrument known as the lyre. He was also a great poet who composed about half of the Psalms. David used many descriptions of animals, birds, and plant life in the Psalms to portray poetic images. His songs were full of lament as well as praise. They were his prayers to the Lord.

523. "Oh, that I had the wings of a dove! I would fly away and be at rest." David, weighed down by his duties, must have wished he could take flight from his tasks. He might have selected almost any bird to express this wish in Psalm 55, yet he chose the dove for a particular reason. The former shepherd knew that while most birds can fly, only doves can take off with a sudden burst of speed and sustain their powerful flight for a long distance.

524. The shortest psalm (117) has just two verses, and the longest psalm is just two chapters later (119). It is also the longest chapter in the Bible, and longer than some whole Bible books—such as Obadiah, Philemon, and Jude.

525. The Book of Psalms is really five different books of songs and poems, all connecting our relationship to God.

Book 1   Psalms 1–41
Book 2   Psalms 42–72
Book 3   Psalms 73–89
Book 4   Psalms 90–106
Book 5   Psalms 107–150

526. It appears that this collection was begun as something of a hymnbook for temple worship in Jerusalem. Words such as *selah*, *maskil*, and *miktam* are found throughout the book to give direction to those who would speak or chant these psalms in public worship.

527. The Penitential Psalms is the title given to seven psalms that express deep repentance over sin: Psalms 7, 32, 38, 51, 102, 130, and 143. All but two are attributed to King David—most notably Psalm 51, which is his lament over committing adultery with Bathsheba.

528. The Messianic Psalms are Old Testament psalms that relate information about the coming Messiah, and were generally quoted by the Lord Jesus or the New Testament writers in reference to him. These include Psalms 22, 40, 41, 45, 69, 72, and 118.

529. The Psalms of Ascent were sung by Jewish pilgrims as they traveled upward from the surrounding areas of Palestine to the city of Jerusalem for festivals. The songs tell of looking up to the hills, seeing the walls of Jerusalem, and observing the many people gathering together to worship, and they end with a joyous shout of praise as the pilgrims finally arrive at the gates of the temple.

530. Acrostic poems are found throughout Jewish literature. Psalm 119, the longest chapter in the Bible, is an acrostic poem—every new stanza begins with the successive letter of the Hebrew alphabet. Psalm 112 is similar, each line beginning with the next letter of the alphabet. This was not only poetic but also aided in the memorization of the psalm.

531. Knowing it all. Solomon spoke over three thousand proverbs and wrote more than a thousand songs, some of which come down to us in the Books of Proverbs and the Song of Solomon. This son of David found favor with God and was given great wisdom, yet he too fell away from God. Different stages of his personal walk can be seen throughout his writings.

532. Proverbs. Some proverbs are strung together in a meaningful sequence, while others are independent of each other and need to be "unpacked" by the reader. The opening chapters of Proverbs contain extended proverbs progressing with each verse. Shorter bits of wisdom form chapters 10 and following. Proverbs leaves no ambiguity over the contrast between the righteous and the wicked.

533. The call of wisdom is made throughout the first ten chapters of Proverbs. Solomon, who was given great wisdom from God, says in Proverbs 8:22 that wisdom was the first creation of God. Solomon always refers to wisdom in the feminine sense: "She calls out . . ."

534. Solomon was the wisest man who ever lived; he was "wiser than all men" (1 Kings 4:31). God had asked him what he wanted more than anything, and Solomon asked for wisdom in order to better rule the people of Israel. His wisdom was unsurpassed, and the people lived very well under his rule. A beautiful temple was even built, but sadly, many of the Israelites, including Solomon, eventually began sacrificing to other gods. God raised up armies to fight against him and his people, but he made a decision not to take the nation from Solomon's rule. He would spare Solomon for his father, David's, sake. Instead Israel would be lost during the reign of Solomon's son, Rehoboam.

535. Ecclesiastes. If Job reads like a play, and Psalms like poetry, and Proverbs like a book of maxims, then Ecclesiastes reads like an essay or the musings of an old man. Its subject is the vanity of life. The book approaches Job's question from the opposite side: If this universe is governed by a moral God, why doesn't everything make sense?

536. It is believed that Solomon wrote Ecclesiastes. Solomon's struggle through this book to understand the purpose behind everything comes to a very strong conclusion. Essentially, God has ordered life for his own purpose, not man's. As a result, the worry and desire that cause people to constantly seek more in life—money, peace, happiness—are best served by turning to God. God controls everything, and man should know his limitations.

537. "To the man who pleases him, God gives wisdom, knowledge and happiness, but to the sinner he gives the task of gathering and storing up wealth to hand it over to the one who pleases God" (Eccles. 2:26). Striving after things is not where meaning is to be found, concludes Solomon. He calls it "a chasing after the wind."

538. Ecclesiastes's conclusion? "Fear God and keep his commandments, for this is the whole duty of man" (Eccles. 12:13). We should enjoy what God has given us, live in the Word, work hard and well, strive for righteousness, and enjoy God and the relationship we have with him!

539. Song of Solomon. Plain and simple, this book is an erotic love poem. The writing resembles Egyptian love poetry and Arabic wedding songs that praise the charm and beauty of the bride. The traditional interpretation, in both Judaism and Christianity, is that these love poems represent Yahweh's love for Israel as well as establishing God's high regard for male-female love and sexuality.

540. Some of the images are so mature that Jewish boys were not allowed to read Song of Solomon until they attained adulthood. Many people have questioned its place in Scripture, but Jewish leaders decided in ancient times that the book is allegorical—the man chasing a woman is a depiction of God pursuing sinful Israel. In medieval times, Christian scholars suggested that the book also represented Christ pursuing the church.

541. "Song of Songs" means "the greatest of songs" and is about the "God of gods and Lord of lords." It is believed Solomon wrote this book; however, others maintain that there were multiple authors for this unique book of Scripture.

542. Though it is a relatively short book, Song of Songs is a full and complete book. The voice of the beloved character (the one who is loved, such as Israel) is the one most heard from throughout. Through five meetings with the beloved, the lover is asked for first a kiss and ultimately for complete intimacy.

His Mouthpieces

543. The books of prophecy. This section of the Bible is composed of seventeen books beginning with Isaiah and ending with Malachi, closing out the Old Testament. Like the books of poetry, these books don't extend the time line of Israel's history; rather, they fill in the one laid down by the books of history. Apart from Job, most of the books of poetry were associated with the kings of Israel's glory days. By contrast, the books of prophecy were associated mainly with the period of Israel's decline and fall.

544. Prophets and priests played an important role in early Israel, though many of the prophets do not have books named after them. These godly men served as messengers from God to the people.

The prophets and priests received orders from God and acted on them.

545. Prophecy in the Old Testament was not so much a telling of the future as it was an urgent statement made on behalf of God to his people. Certain elements of Hebrew prophecy spoke of the future in terms that human behavior could not change, but most of it offered God's people a choice and often stated the harsh consequences if the Israelites chose to disobey. Biblical prophecy emphasizes the kind of living that secures a happy future and warns against behavior that clouds the future.

546. Both the Major Prophets (Isaiah, Jeremiah, Ezekiel, and Daniel) and the Minor Prophets ("the twelve") are organized in historical order. However, this doesn't mean the minor prophets follow the major ones in history; they coexisted. Hosea, for example, was a contemporary of Isaiah. Since the fall of Jerusalem is dated by historians at 586 BC, all the books of prophecy—major and minor—can be dated within a century or two of that date.

547. Moses said God would raise up prophets like him in the generations to follow. And God did. Generally keeping a low profile, the prophets did not possess administrative power like the kings. They didn't have a place in the tabernacle or temple rituals like the priests. They simply spoke the mind of God as it was given to them. Unlike the kingship and the priesthood, the position of prophet could not be passed on to one's descendants. God individually chose each one.

548. Elijah trusted God completely, so much so that when King Ahab, a later king, appointed prophets to worship the false god Baal, Elijah told him no more rain would fall. Three years after the drought began, when Israel was literally starving, Elijah had a contest with the Baal prophets to see which entity would answer their prayers—God or the false god Baal. The people were brought to their senses by the sign of a soaked altar bursting into flames, and they came back to God.

549. As one of only two men who never died, Elijah was truly a special prophet of God. Enoch, a man who walked with God, was the other man who didn't die. Elijah was taken up to heaven in a chariot of fire, but before he was taken he appointed Elisha, his servant, to succeed him.

550. Not a popular group. Israel's prophets were not the type of people to include on your party invitation list. The Hebrew prophets denounced evil, corruption, and immorality. They brought "bad" news, and people steered clear of them for the most part.

551. At the forefront. In the period of the divided kingdom, the focus of the Bible books moved away from the kings to the exploits of a series of "prophets," those who spoke on the behalf of God after receiving divine messages through dreams or visions. Prophets tried to counsel—usually with little success—the rulers and people of Israel and Judah. The prophets became crucial biblical characters who overshadowed the kings and took their message to the entire nation.

552. In Jewish history, law, and theology, Ezra is a character of great significance. Some Hebrew scholars rank him second only to Moses as a law giver and prophet, and he's considered by many as the second founder (after Moses) of the Jewish nation. Not only did Ezra reinstate the Law and temple worship practices, he required that all Jewish men get rid of their foreign wives and children. Ezra ends poignantly with the words, "All these had married foreign women, and some of them had children by these wives" (10:44).

553. Hosea is considered the first in the line of minor prophets. This is largely because his and the other minor prophets' books are short in length compared to Isaiah, Jeremiah, or Ezekiel. According to the recorded dates in Hosea, his ministry began shortly after that of Amos, and both of them were active before the fall of Jerusalem in 586 BC.

554. Gomer, Hosea's adulterous wife, is a symbol of God's wayward people. God told Hosea to marry this wayward wife in order to further drive home the point of his message to Israel given through Hosea. Israel was rebellious and wicked, and worshiped other gods. God's nation was not to do these things under any circumstances, and though he was angered, God continued to love his people. Hosea was told to behave in a similar manner with Gomer. Each time she strayed, God's prophet was to bring her back home.

555. The message of Hosea to the Israelites used even the names of the three children Gomer bore. Hosea gave them names representative of how God felt about Israel. The children are a symbol of the results of the sin reaped by Israel for falling away from God—Gomer was unfaithful and the children were the fruit of her adultery. God told Hosea to name the children accordingly: Jezreel, meaning "God scatters"; Lo-Ruhamah, meaning "not loved"; and Lo-Ammi, meaning something similar to "not my people, and I am not your God."

556. God wants his people to repent. God wants to claim Israel for his own. He wants to call these children "his," "loved," and "my people." Through all of Gomer's waywardness, Hosea is not told to seek a divorce. Always he is instructed to reconcile with her, to bring her home, to love her. Hosea's life example is a symbol of what God continually did for his people. It would take exile for Israel to finally listen and repent, but God never forgot about them or stopped loving them.

557. The prophet Amos was the first prophet to have his words written down. His ministry occurred sometime during the years of 793–740 BC. It is thought that most of his main prophesying occurred between 760 and 750 BC. Where Hosea spoke of God's mercy, love, and forgiveness for his people, Amos spoke of God's justice and righteousness.

558. Israel worshiped God in a pagan manner—sacred altars and even the temple were given touches of the pagans. God's people went through the motions and did the rituals God required of them and then lived exactly as they wanted to. The result was an immoral society far from what God's people were called to be. As a result, Amos preached about true piety and social justice.

559. Micah lived after Amos and Hosea. He prophesied of a future king who would be born in Bethlehem. He looked forward to that time as the current kings he suffered with consistently led the people toward idol worship and other forms of sin.

560. Nahum's name means "comfort." His book was written for Judah and served to comfort them with a prophecy of Nineveh's future destruction. Nineveh was the capital city of Assyria, which had already taken possession of the Northern kingdom of Israel.

Judah feared they were next. The Assyrians were a brutal people known for their ferocious wars.

561. Nahum's book demonstrates that God is sovereign over all nations, not just his own. The destinies of Assyria, Babylon, Rome, and Israel and Judah were all under God's control. That God had Judah carried off by Babylon and Israel carried off by Assyria was all part of his plan for his people.

562. The longest prophetic book in Hebrew Scripture, Isaiah has played a central role for Christians and has even been called "the fifth Gospel" because so many of the book's prophecies were fulfilled in the life of Jesus. This book has also had an impact on our language.

563. Many well-worn phrases were born in the Book of Isaiah. Besides providing Handel with wonderful lyrics, Isaiah has yielded phrases commonly used even today:

"White as snow"
"Neither shall they learn war anymore"
"The people that walked in darkness"
"And a little child shall lead them"
"They shall mount up with wings as eagles"
"Be of good courage"
"Like a lamb to the slaughter"

564. The Servant Songs are the passages of Scripture describing an innocent man who endures great pain (Isaiah 42, 49, 50, 52, and 53). Many Jewish scholars did not know what to do with these passages and could not reconcile them to the images of the Messiah coming as a mighty king. But Christians from earliest times have applied them to Jesus Christ, who suffered greatly for the sins of all mankind.

565. Jeremiah is the longest book in the Bible, containing more words than any other Bible book. This prophet was unpopular largely because his messages of Judah's coming destruction were different from what the false prophets were telling the people—that all was well, God was pleased with them, and peace would reign. Through Jeremiah God demonstrated that judgment would come for disobedience, but that even judgment has boundaries. Israel would be subject to Babylon, but only for a time—seventy years. God would not abandon them.

566. **Also known as the "weeping prophet,"** Jeremiah's out-pourings to God reveal that even prophets had difficulties with their relationship with God. In chapter 4 of the book that bears his name, he cries out to God: "Oh, my anguish, my anguish! I writhe in pain. Oh, the agony of my heart!" (v. 19). Jeremiah was honest with God when he was frustrated—on several occasions he questioned God's plan for himself, God's plan for his people, and ultimately God's faithfulness. Yet God used him and made him a great prophet.

567. **Habakkuk** is thought to have been a prophet around the time of Jeremiah. He struggled with how God would want his people, despite how badly they were behaving, to come under the influence of an even more ungodly people—the Babylonians. God was faithful to his prophet and assured Habakkuk to trust him for the answer.

568. **The Book of Lamentations** may have been written by the prophet Jeremiah, but this fact is not certain. Interestingly the Hebrew title for the book is *eykah*, which means "How . . . !" Simply put, Lamentations describes the horrendous loss of Jerusalem, the temple, and the exile of Judah's inhabitants to Babylon. As Jerusalem was destroyed in 586 BC, this book was likely written shortly after.

569. **Lamentations** is a grievous statement of all the ills that befell this people as a result of their turning away from God. It is the only book of the Bible that consists *solely* of laments. Though the book begins with lament, it ends with heartfelt repentance, as it should. The author is very clear that though Babylon is the enemy carrying out the destruction, God has truly destroyed his people's city and allowed them to be carried off.

570. **The final verses of Lamentations** demonstrate exactly how Israel responded to God's judgment: "Restore us to yourself, O LORD, that we may return; renew our days as of old unless you have utterly rejected us and are angry with us beyond measure" (Lam. 5:21–22).

571. Ezekiel was living in exile in Babylon when Jerusalem fell. His prophetic work was to a people who had been exiled with him since 596 BC. Ezekiel was served some truly bitter news that directly affected his work as well. God told his prophet that Ezekiel's wife was going to die, and soon. The prophet was instructed not to mourn openly for his wife, just as Israel was not to grieve openly for the temple that they had lost as a nation.

572. God's prophets were tested with difficulty like all of Israel was during this period of loss. They were God's voices and stayed with the people to tell them what their Lord had to say, even in the midst of grief, exile, and personal pain. They also passed judgments from the Lord on to others. Ezekiel pronounced God's judgment on seven different nations while he was in Babylon.

573. Ezekiel's message is filled with the theme of Israel as "the holy people," a people set apart. With Israel's departure from worshiping God, the nation became unclean and defiled the temple, city, and land. God responded by withdrawing from his people and allowing national destruction of all that he had given them. God had no choice but to destroy that which had become unclean.

574. Daniel is considered a book more of a statesman than a prophet. As a result, Jewish scholars do not place this book among the prophetic books. However, since Daniel had the gift of prediction, the New Testament calls him a "prophet" (Matt. 24:15). Daniel saw many symbols in his prophetic visions, and he often recorded them without attempting to interpret what they meant.

575. Daniel contains a fair amount of apocalyptic material. Whether it is to be interpreted literally or symbolically, it served as an encouragement to Israel. God's prophets were the closest thing the people had to a direct line to God. Through Daniel God told the people that there would be an end to their exile; there would be good times again. Daniel's prophetic themes are largely about God's sovereignty and appear in Revelation: "The kingdom of the world has become the kingdom of our Lord and of his Christ, and he will reign for ever and ever" (Rev. 11:15; see Dan. 2:44; 7:27).

Pointing to Christ 15

576. Jesus can be seen in the Old Testament through many characters in the Bible who are pictures of Christ. Long before Jesus' birth in Bethlehem, God's plan for his Son was in place. The Old Testament patriarchs, prophets, and heroic figures are all linked to Christ and point to the Messiah.

577. Another word used to describe these "pictures" is the word *type*. Though this word isn't in the Bible, it comes from the study of types, or typology. *Type* comes from the Greek word *typos*, which is translated as "figure" or "shadow." These original types are historically accurate, but they also foreshadow another person, incident, or event to happen in the future.

578. "**Although the Bible contains no visual picture or portrait** in the generally accepted sense of the word, it is filled with word pictures, and all these have as their central figure a Person, and that Person is the Lord Jesus Christ, the Son of God and Son of Man, the Savior of Sinners."—Dr. M. R. DeHaan

579. "**And beginning with Moses and all the Prophets,** [Jesus] explained to them [the disciples] what was said in all the Scriptures concerning himself" (Luke 24:27).

580. Adam is the first picture of Christ that Genesis reveals. Paul speaks of this portrait of Christ in Ephesians 5. When Adam was in a deep sleep, God took one of his ribs and created Eve. The apostle Paul speaks of Christians being members of Jesus' body and his bones. Paul quotes how a man shall leave his family and be joined to his wife. Paul says "this is a profound mystery—but I am talking about Christ and the church" (Eph. 5:32). The apostle is alluding to the fact that Jesus left God's house to be joined to his bride, the church, and that he too was put to sleep, only his three-day sleep would result in resurrection. As Adam suffered a wound to his side, Christ's side too was wounded, but his blood is our redemption.

581. Abel, the son of Adam and Eve, is also a picture of Jesus Christ. Abel was obedient and followed God's instructions regarding sacrifice. His gift of the best lambs in his flock was the exact opposite of Cain's sacrifice—essentially a poor gift of his own hands as a gardener, a picture of selfishness and an attempt to gain favor through a personal work rather than a wholehearted sacrifice. Abel foreshadowed the coming Messiah, who would do everything according to God's commandments yet still be rejected and ultimately killed by his own people because of his personal faithfulness to God. As Cain slew Abel, so the Jews would demand Jesus' death.

582. Another demonstration of Abel's foreshadowing has to do with his profession. Abel was a shepherd, the very first the world had ever seen. Jesus called himself the good shepherd who "lays down his life for the sheep" (John 10:11).

583. The story of Noah and the ark yields some interesting analysis as a type of Christ. The ark itself is a type of Christ! God gave Noah every detail of how it was to be built, from its dimensions to its purpose in protecting Noah and his family from the judgment that awaited the rest of the world. Likewise God planned every minute detail of how Jesus would redeem God's people; not a single detail was left to man. As the big boat brought earthly salvation for Noah, so Christ brings eternal salvation for all who believe in him. As the ark had but one door, so Christ is the door to God—he is the only way we may gain forgiveness for our sins and come to the Father.

584. We have a responsibility just as Noah did. As Noah was safe in the ark, God had given him duties and responsibilities. Noah was to care for the animals and keep things orderly. God had protected him within the ark, just as we are protected (redeemed) within Christ. God has responsibilities for us too; we are to care for one another.

585. Isaac, the son of the patriarch Abraham, is perhaps one of the most vivid foreshadows of Jesus Christ. Just as Jesus was miraculously conceived by the Holy Spirit through Mary, Isaac was a miracle given to Abraham and Sarah in their old age. Both were the "child of promise." Abraham had been told his offspring would be great in number, yet Sarah was barren into her nineties. As Isaac was a miracle, he also points to the miraculous virgin birth of our Savior.

586. The call for Abraham to sacrifice Isaac is another fore-shadowing of Christ's earthly existence. God commanded Abraham to sacrifice his only son as a sign of obedience to God's commands, as all sacrifices were. Christ was the supreme atoning sacrifice, putting an end to the need to make sacrifices to God. As Isaac carried the wood for the altar he was to be sacrificed on, Christ carried the cross he was to be crucified on. Yet Isaac did not serve as a sacrifice as Jesus did, because only Christ can redeem us. God provided a ram for the sacrifice in Isaac's stead, causing Isaac to be saved from death.

587. Jacob is the next patriarch and type of Christ. The fa-mous story of the "stealing of the birthright" is a foreshadowing of the first and second Adams' experience. As Adam was given dominion first, before any other, so also was Esau given dominion by his birthright. Yet just as Adam forfeited his right, so also did

Esau. Those rights passed on to the second Adam, Christ, and to Esau's brother, Jacob, who was to carry on the covenant with God as a patriarch of Israel.

588. Joseph, Jacob's favorite son, is another figure whose foreshadowing is very vivid. Joseph was well known for his ability to foretell the future. Though his brothers found his dreams offensive, Joseph did have the ability to correctly interpret dreams. Jesus told of his own future too, and he consistently angered those who heard him do it. The Pharisees were constantly angry at what they considered blasphemy. Joseph's brothers and those who were offended by Jesus' prophecies are the same image.

589. Just as Joseph came to his own people (his brothers) and was rejected, so Jesus was rejected by his own people. Just as the brothers of Joseph were jealous of his beautiful coat and stripped it off of him before they sold him to the peddlers heading to Egypt, Jesus was stripped of the robe he wore before he was crucified. Soldiers cast lots for it because it was a specially woven item and too expensive to be cut into parts.

590. Joseph is also the deliverer; he is an early picture of what Christ will be for all people. Joseph delivered his brothers from starvation. As a high-ranking official of Egypt, he saved them. Christ also saved us, but just as Joseph's brothers had to go about it in a specific manner, humbly, seeking favor, so also we must be humble and approach what Christ has done for us in a specific manner. We do not save ourselves, because only Christ can save us. Joseph saved his brothers from starvation, because he was the only one who could.

591. Moses was also a deliverer. God called him to lead the Israelites out of Egypt in a mass exodus. Pointing to Jesus, Moses is a great man, but he is not the supreme deliverer. From our fallen state, Jesus redeems us and makes us forgiven, bringing us into a new and ultimately heavenly relationship with the Father. Moses brought enslaved Israel out of a foreign land. As God called Moses, God called Jesus.

592. "When Israel was a child, I loved him, and out of Egypt I called my son" (Hosea 11:1). "So he [Joseph, Jesus' earthly father] got up, took the child and his mother during the night and left for

Egypt, where he stayed until the death of Herod. And so was fulfilled what the Lord had said through the prophet: 'Out of Egypt
I called my son'" (Matt. 2:14–15). Matthew was under the divine
inspiration of the Holy Spirit and saw the history of Israel being
replayed in the life of Jesus. As Israel went to Egypt in its infancy,
so Jesus went to Egypt in his own infancy.

593. David was the Lord's anointed and suffered because of it.
He and his greater Son, Jesus, demonstrate how David is a type of
Christ figure (Matt. 1:1; Rev. 22:16). Jesus' ministry was plagued
by difficulties, as was David's role both before and after he became
king. The common theme is of the servant of the Lord enduring
scorn and suffering trials in the name of the Lord.

594. Psalm 69 demonstrates this point as David cries out to
God: "For I endure scorn for your sake, and shame covers my
face. I am a stranger to my brothers, an alien to my own mother's
sons; for zeal for your house consumes me, and the insults of those
who insult you fall on me" (Ps. 69:7–9). The Gospel of John makes
reference to these verses.

595. "The Bible is a collection of portraits of one supreme Person
who overshadows all the rest of the pictures. The central object of
this Bible Album is Jesus Christ. . . . He is the central figure on every
page, and the other pictures grouped about Him are added only to
bring into bolder relief the loveliness, the superlative beauty, the
infinite perfection of the Man of the Book, the Lord Jesus."—Dr.
M. R. DeHaan

New Times

16

596. "To him give all the prophets witness." Truly, God had been telling his people about the coming Savior long before Jesus was ever born. Micah foretells Jesus' birth; Zechariah tells of how he will eventually reign as King over all the earth. Joel describes the day of judgment and what part Jesus will play in it.

597. The four Gospels follow closely in the tradition of the books of history we saw in the Old Testament—words are spoken and deeds are done. Little is told of the inward thoughts and motivations of the various people in the stories. The Gospels tell how Jesus was born as a descendant of David, an essential requirement of the Messiah according to the prophecies of Scripture.

598. The Gospel of Matthew was written by a former tax collector named Matthew. His book covers the lineage of Jesus and also tells the story of much of his ministry, including the Beatitudes.

599. Mark details Jesus' service to those he called and preached to. Jesus' portrayal as the great servant can be found in this Gospel, written by someone about whom we know very little.

600. Luke opens his Gospel by saying that "many" had attempted to write an account of Jesus' life and ministry, but that he himself is doing so because God has given him "perfect understanding of all things from the very first" (Luke 1:3 KJV). God not only gave the Gospel writers firsthand exposure as eyewitnesses to the events of Jesus' ministry but also perfect understanding. Luke is especially forthright about Christ the man.

601. John, perhaps the most famous book of the whole Bible in terms of its saving message, is a description of both Christ's deity and his redeeming work for sinners. The Gospel was written by the "disciple whom Jesus loved," John.

602. The four Gospels therefore tell of all aspects of Jesus: Matthew of his right to be called "King," Mark of his title as "Greatest Servant," Luke of his completely human nature, and John of his being the Savior of the World—God's only Son.

603. Jesus Christ, more than any other figure or historical happening mentioned, is the most important figure in the Bible. The Old Testament prophesies about his coming and his death, and the New Testament sees him born, establish a ministry, and eventually sacrifice himself for all who believe in him.

604. Many incidents in the Old Testament point to Christ: Abel's lamb was a type of Christ. So was Abraham's willing offering of his son, Isaac, for sacrifice. The Passover lamb in Egypt was a type of Christ. Even the scarlet cord the prostitute Rahab hung in her window is a symbol of Christ!

605. Jesus met all manner of people—and accepted them all if they repented of their sins. Harlots, tax collectors, liars, cheats, the infirm, the diseased all received kind words, healing, and a message of hope.

606. Obedience to laws without a sense of mercy is empty of spiritual value. Several times Jesus quoted the prophets who had said, "God desires mercy more than sacrifice." He reserved a special anger for those he called the "scribes and Pharisees," a group that might be loosely called "lawyers." Matthew's term for Pharisees is "hypocrites," a term in Greek that applied to actors or people who were pretenders, people who said one thing but did another.

607. **The Beatitudes** is the well-known portion of Scripture from Christ's Sermon on the Mount in which he blesses certain types of people. Matthew 5 records that Jesus blessed the poor in spirit, those who mourn, the meek, those who hunger and thirst for righteousness, the merciful, the pure in heart, the peacemakers, and those who are persecuted for righteousness' sake—all of which describe the people who would populate the kingdom of God. However, the actual word *beatitude* doesn't appear in Scripture. It's from the Latin word for "blessed," and was made popular by the Vulgate.

608. Parables are stories Jesus used to convey spiritual truth. They were essentially comparisons: "The kingdom of heaven is like a treasure hidden in a field" or "Everyone who hears these words and puts them into practice is like a wise man who built a house." While Jesus' concrete images made the parables memorable, they also puzzled people who could not always follow Christ's meaning.

609. Biblical miracles are found in both the Old and New Testaments. Many show God's power over nature, while others are a sign of his mercy and love for those who fear him. These events are supernatural and can only be the work of God.

610. Miracles demonstrate God's hand intervening in earthly affairs in extraordinary ways. But New Testament miracles tend to be "personal" miracles, as opposed to miracles affecting the entire nation, such as the plagues on Egypt or the crossing of the Red Sea. Apart from his own miraculous birth, resurrection, and transfiguration, Jesus performed more than thirty-five miracles in the Gospels.

611. The parable of the sower, found in Matthew 13, likens sharing the gospel to a farmer scattering seed. Seed sown on the path is eaten by birds—which the Lord explains is similar to what occurs when a hearer doesn't understand the message. Satan snatches it away so that it cannot have an impact on the hearer's life. Seed scattered on rocky soil sprouts but dies because it cannot set its roots—this is likened to someone who initially believes the gospel but falls away from the faith due to persecution. Some seed grows but is choked out by thorns—a depiction of the person whose belief is undermined by worldly concerns. But the good seed that grows is like the individual who hears the gospel, understands it, and chooses to follow Christ.

612. Water into wine. The first recorded miracle of Jesus occurs in John 2, when Christ was attending a wedding in the city of Cana and the hosts ran out of wine. Jesus had the servants fill six large jars with water, which miraculously turned into fine wine. As John records, "He thus revealed his glory, and his disciples put their faith in him" (2:11).

613. The parable of the mustard seed likens the kingdom of heaven to the smallest seed known in that part of the world. Though the seed is tiny, the plant grows to a great height. In the same way, though the church started small, it would grow rapidly and become a worldwide force throughout the rest of history.

614. The centurion's servant. Since Roman conquerors were hated by most Jewish citizens, it was generally forbidden for a Jew to enter a Roman's home. Thus when a God-fearing Roman centurion told Jesus that his servant was ill, he informed the Lord that Jesus didn't have to enter his home to perform the healing. Instead Christ could do it from a distance. Marveling at the man's faith, Jesus replied, "I have not found anyone in Israel with such great faith." Before the centurion could get home, his servant was healed.

615. The parable of the sheep and the goats is a picture of what will happen when Christ returns. Sheep symbolize believers; goats symbolize unbelievers. The sheep will be parted from the goats with a final destination of heaven. The goats will be sent to hell, the place of eternal punishment.

616. The transfiguration. A few days before his death, Jesus took Peter, James, and John up to a high mountain. There he was "transfigured" before them; his face "shone like the sun, and his clothes became as white as the light." Moses and Elijah, two of the handful of miracle workers in Scripture, then appeared with Jesus, and the voice of God announced, "This is my Son, whom I love; with him I am well pleased" (Matt. 17:5).

617. The parable of the lost sheep, in Matthew 18, is one of the sweetest stories of Jesus. In it he tells of a loving shepherd caring for a hundred sheep. If one gets lost, he will leave the ninety-nine to go find the one that is missing. In the same way, God is concerned about each person. He doesn't want anyone to be lost.

618. Jesus was well received by the people as long as he was performing miracles and teaching, but they did not look to him as the King of Kings. Sadly they were looking for an earthly king instead of a heavenly one. As a result, their love for Jesus was short-lived.

619. Satan tempted Christ and tried to weaken the Savior's resolve, but Jesus stood firm in his mission. Christ's ministry would ultimately lead to his death, and though Satan's temptations would have saved him great pain, he was faithful to his heavenly Father.

620. Jesus called special helpers to his aid in order to preach and teach and minister to the people. There were twelve disciples in all—Simon Peter, Andrew, James, John, Philip, Bartholomew, Thomas, Matthew, James, Thaddaeus, Simon the Zealot, and Judas Iscariot.

621. The Last Supper was a preparation for Jesus himself as he readied himself for the end, which he knew was near. He even confronted Judas Iscariot at the table. The Lord celebrated a final supper with his disciples, his most trusted companions. This special dinner was given to Christians in order to remember the sacrifice Jesus made for his people.

622. The words "Take and eat, this is my body," and "This is my blood of the covenant, which is poured out for many for the forgiveness of sins" originated with the Last Supper. Communion recalls the Last Supper and serves as one of two main ordinances, or sacraments, in the Christian church to this day.

623. Many first-century Jews died, just like Jesus, on a cross. Some estimates for the number of Jews crucified during this time for a variety of crimes run as high as one hundred thousand. But these crucifixions were not at the hand of other Jews. Crucifixion was exclusive to the Romans, and it was an extreme penalty generally reserved for cases of runaway slaves or rebellion against Rome.

624. The Seven Last Utterances are the final words spoken by Christ while on the cross. The four Gospels reveal different phrases, but grouped together they include: (1) "Today you will be with me in paradise" (spoken to the thief next to him). (2) "My God, my God, why have you forsaken me?" (3) "Father, forgive them, for they know not what they do." (4) "I thirst." (5) "Woman, behold your son. Son, behold your mother" (spoken to Mary and the disciple John). (6) "It is finished." (7) "Into your hands I commit my spirit."

625. Jesus commissioned his followers to preach the gospel to all people. His call to them brought the disciples and other faithful followers to begin the church. And through a history of almost two thousand years, the church has experienced persecution, misery, and separation. Yet never has it died and never will it fall, despite what might happen, for Christ is the head of his church. And his kingdom cannot fail!

626. The resurrection. The greatest of all miracles in the Christian faith is the fact that Jesus rose from the dead, conquering death and sin. The evidence for the resurrection as a historical fact (the empty tomb, the Roman guard, the eyewitness reports of those who were there, the lack of any other explanation) is overwhelming.

627. The resurrection of Jesus is the central story of all Christianity. After dying on the cross and being wrapped in a burial shroud and interred in a sealed tomb, Jesus rose from the dead—conquering death and offering the hope of eternal life to all who believe in him.

628. Christ ascended into heaven, on a cloud, to be with the Father until the time of his second coming and to "sit at the right hand of God." He will come again at "the last days" as the Bible writers prophesied. His message remains today for all who will believe in him and trust him as their personal Savior.

629. The apostles' letters are sometimes called epistles. The word *epistle* conveys a formal or public element to these letters. These last twenty-two books of the Bible were personal letters often specifying the names of both the sender and the recipients. The fact that no point is made of the authors' identities implies how unimportant the issue is. The apostles were charged with the responsibility of spreading Jesus' message faithfully, and that in and of itself gave the writings authority in the eyes of Christ's followers.

God's Church

17

630. Until the Book of Acts, the Bible primarily belonged to the Jewish people. Of the many radical elements of Jesus' message, one of the most radical was that he meant for it to apply to Gentiles (non-Jews) as well as Jews. When Jesus told his apostles to go to the ends of the world, he really meant it. This brisk narrative begins in Jerusalem and ends in Rome, symbolizing how Jesus took the faith of ancient Israel and opened it up to the whole world.

631. The lists of disciples differ slightly from one book to another. The Gospel of Matthew lists Simon, Andrew (Simon's brother), James and John (the sons of Zebedee), Philip, Bartholomew, Thomas, Matthew the tax collector, James the son of Alphaeus, Thaddaeus, Simon the Cananite, and Judas Iscariot. Luke refers to Simon as "the zealot" (a brand of political protestors) and mentions

"Judas son of James" instead of Thaddaeus. Many of these men were pillars of the early church.

632. Peter was called Simon before Jesus renamed him and was prominent in the early church. Peter had a long history with the Lord; he denied Christ before the cock crowed three times but went on in faith following Christ's death and resurrection to become exactly what his new name meant: "the rock."

633. James and John, both sons of Zebedee, were brothers. They both were active in the early church. Both had been especially close to Jesus, being present at the transfiguration. It is strongly believed that John went on to write the Gospel of John.

634. Acts introduces the New Testament's second most influential figure (Jesus was the first!), an educated, pious Jew and tent maker named Saul. Born in what is now Turkey, Saul went to Jerusalem to learn from the esteemed rabbi Gamaliel, grandson of the legendary rabbi Hillel, the most prominent Pharisaic rabbi of the first century. Given authority by the high priest to arrest followers of Christ in Damascus for blasphemy, Saul vigorously persecuted early Christians. His name was changed to Paul after he experienced a transforming vision and conversion.

635. Paul developed a strategy for his traveling ministry that he followed through all his journeys. He generally moved farther westward from Israel with each mission. When he entered a city for the first time, he would look for a synagogue or other place where he could find the Jews of the city. In the first century AD, Jews were dispersed throughout the world. Rarely did a city not have Jews who met together regularly. Sometimes synagogues were receptive to his message; at other times hearers were extremely hostile.

636. When Paul was arrested in Jerusalem for his "heretical" views, he demanded a trial in Rome before the emperor, his right as a Roman citizen.

637. Many other missionaries preached the gospel in the early years of the church. Their mission was to spread the word of Christ to all parts of the known earth, as they had been commissioned to do by Jesus before he returned to heaven. Thanks to their efforts,

Christianity gained a foothold quickly in nearly every part of the known world.

638. Barnabas was one of the earliest converts to Christianity and a close friend of Paul's. A Greek-speaking Jew from Cyprus, his real name was Joseph, but because he was an excellent teacher, his friends called him Barnabas, which means "son of encouragement." He accompanied Paul on the first missionary journey through Asia Minor.

639. Timothy was one of Paul's main helpers. Paul mentored the younger man through two letters (1 and 2 Timothy) and called him "my true son in the faith." Timothy also traveled on his own.

640. Philip became a missionary and was the first to preach the gospel to those living in Samaria. He is especially remembered for how he helped an Ethiopian read a passage from Isaiah. An angel directed him to go to the Ethiopian. Upon his arrival, they read the passage together. The foreigner asked to be baptized and became the first Ethiopian Christian.

641. Silas traveled as a missionary with Paul and Peter. He sang hymns joyously to Christ while imprisoned with Paul during the earthquake in Philippi. The jailer became a Christian because he was so moved by their display of faith. Silas was to Paul a "faithful brother."

642. Phoebe is one of the few women missionary figures of the New Testament. History indicates that it was not uncommon for women to be in leadership roles in the early church, though it was certainly not typical in Jewish synagogues. Phoebe traveled to Rome, most likely to bring Paul's letter to the Christians in that city.

643. Apollos was a Jew from Alexandria. He was actually a missionary before he met Paul. John the Baptist had mentored him and helped Apollos become a powerful preacher. He found help for his questions about Jesus in Corinth when he spoke with Priscilla and Aquila.

644. Roman subjects incorporated emperor worship into the local religion throughout the empire. In the provinces, leading citizens became priests in the imperial cult to cement their ties with

Rome. (Augustus, however, exempted the Jews from the imperial cult.) Emperor worship continued as the official pagan religion of the empire until Christianity was recognized under the Emperor Constantine (AD 306–337).

645. Paul stayed longer in some cities than others. Some larger cities, such as Ephesus, became teaching centers through which he could reach the surrounding regions. Paul's goal was to teach his followers well enough so they could teach others. Those who were able to accept this role were called elders, overseers, and pastors. The focus, however, was not on building an organization, but on preaching the Word.

646. The excellent highway system constructed throughout the Mediterranean world by the Romans was traveled frequently by Paul. Built so Roman armies could move swiftly and their traders could deliver goods efficiently, the Roman roads also contributed to the spread of the Christian message.

647. Corinth was the main city of the Roman province of Greece. It held a large community of Christians, thanks in large part to the missionary work of the apostle Paul. Corinth was an immoral and highly cosmopolitan city. Calling someone a "Corinthian" was for many people another way of saying "prostitute." The Christians faced moral dilemmas and difficulties and were counseled by Paul in 1 and 2 Corinthians regarding these issues.

648. When the New Testament writers speak of "Asia," they are not referring to the whole continent of Asia as we know it. Rather they are speaking of the province of the Roman Empire known as "Asia," a piece of land in the vicinity of modern-day Turkey. This province's capital was Ephesus. This city received one of Paul's epistles, which we know as Ephesians. John makes note of the seven churches of the province of Asia when he writes the Book of Revelation.

649. Since many Jews traveled to Jerusalem for annual feasts, and since many apostles were on the road with Christ's message, Paul sometimes found that the gospel message had reached a town before he did. This was the case with Rome, the center of the world in its day. There were many disciples in this metropolis long before Paul reached it.

650. The gospel of Christ spread primarily by word of mouth. Sometimes the apostles would move on to another city only to receive a request for more teaching from the city they had recently left. So they would write letters to be read aloud to groups of individuals who met for teaching and encouragement. They also wrote letters while confined in prison.

651. The Agrapha is a phrase meaning "things not written." It was used in the early church to refer to sayings of Jesus that his followers remembered, but which were not written down in any of the Gospels. For example, in Acts 20:35, Paul quotes the Lord Jesus as saying, "It is more blessed to give than to receive." Those words can't be found in any of the Gospels, so apparently that is one of the things the Lord's followers remembered him saying, and they would cite him as the source even though it was never written down as such.

652. How do you tell the world the Good News if you don't speak their language? The disciples were gathered in an upper room when all of a sudden "tongues of fire" touched the followers. And they began to speak in other languages. Some people who saw them thought they were drunk. This was the arrival of the Holy Spirit whom Jesus had promised. The disciples could now go and spread the Word everywhere.

653. The early church grew as a "communistic" society in which everyone shared, according to the reports in Acts. A utopian state of harmony is depicted in these first days of the Christian community, although they were not yet called "Christians." A young man named Matthias was elected to replace Judas as one of the Twelve, and the group prospered and made collective decisions and enjoyed common ownership of goods, making the early Christians in Jerusalem a practical model for the kibbutz.

654. Seven young men were appointed in Acts 6 to see to the needs of the church people in order to free up the time of the disciples and eventual apostles. Stephen, a gifted speaker, was one of these men. He was a skilled debater and angered many who could not argue well with him or win him over. Eventually these men became so angry that Stephen was arrested and tried before the Sanhedrin.

655. Stephen was the first martyr of the church. A young Pharisee named Saul was present. Eventually Saul would be converted and receive the name Paul. His conversion is a sign of the wondrous grace God has in store for those who believe in him. Stephen died with a vision of Jesus in sight. He was at peace and thus incensed his captors even more. Before he died, Stephen said, "Lord, do not hold this sin against them."

656. The early church was not a perfect organization. Christians were as sinful then as they can be now. One of the earliest instances of this appears in Acts 5. Ananias and his wife, Sapphira, lied about the amount of compensation they received after selling a field. Had they not pretended to sell it for less, it wouldn't have mattered, but since they did lie in order to keep back money for themselves, God took them both. As Peter told them, "You have lied to the Holy Spirit!"

657. Another famous Ananias was Ananias of Damascus. When Paul was converted, he became blinded. Ananias was told to go to the house where Paul was staying. He did so, though he knew that the man Saul was coming to arrest Christians. He went as he was called, however. He prayed, and the newly converted Paul received his sight back.

658. Dorcas, who was also called Tabitha, received a miracle during the early days of the church. She lived in Joppa. She fell ill and then died. Her distressed friends sent for Peter, the "rock" of the church. He prayed for her even as she was dead! She was given her life back and sat up. Many of her friends became believers as a result of this miracle.

659. Cornelius was a Roman soldier stationed at Caesarea. He was a Gentile who had joined a synagogue in order to seek God. He was a "God fearer." An angel appeared to Cornelius one day and told him to send for Peter. When Peter came, Cornelius and his entire family learned about Jesus. They were baptized immediately and praised God.

660. Eutychus was named well. His name means "lucky." While he was listening to Paul preach, he fell out of a third-story window (he fell asleep) and was lying still and believed to be dead when they reached him. Paul embraced him and he was healed. He had been blessed, not lucky, but his name seems appropriate!

661. Philemon had an interesting conversion experience.
He was a wealthy Christian from Colossae and was converted by
his slave, Onesimus. Onesimus had run away and eventually met
the apostle Paul and became a believer. Paul sent him back to his
master, Philemon, and urged Philemon to receive him as a "beloved
brother." Philemon did so and was also saved!

662. Lydia is one of the few women mentioned in the early
church. She was a seller of purple cloth and a Gentile, but she
sought God by going to a Jewish prayer center. She then met Paul
and his fellow missionaries. She became converted and eventually
she and her family and even their workers were baptized. Paul and
his friends stayed in her house.

663. Stephanas and his entire household were the first Christians
to convert during Paul's ministry in Achaia. As the church grew in
that area, Stephanas took a more active role in caring for other new
Christians. Paul was fond of him and his family and he especially
enjoyed when Stephanas visited him in Ephesus.

664. Aquila and Priscilla were a tent-making couple from Corinth.
They became Christians after listening to Paul preach. Dear friends
of Paul, they supported him to the very end, even risking their
lives for him. They were loved and known in many churches in
Greece and Asia Minor.

665. Acts closes with Paul incarcerated and under house arrest in the imperial capital. He continued preaching the gospel
and writing letters to the churches he had established. Acts says
nothing more about Paul's appeal or ultimate fate, or that of Peter.
Both eventually disappeared from the biblical account without any
specific word of what happened to them. According to well-established tradition, both apostles were martyred during Emperor Nero's
persecution of Christians after the great fire in Rome in AD 64.

666. Early Christians used the "holy kiss" as a sign of their
concern and love for one another. Paul ends several of his epistles
with reminders to "Greet one another with a holy kiss" (Rom.
16:16). The holy kiss was most likely a peck on the cheek, much
as might be used today to greet visiting family or friends.

18

The End—
Revelation

667. Revelation. The longest of all the New Testament letters, "The Revelation to John" was addressed to seven specific communities, all located in Asia. There is overwhelming evidence that this book was written by the apostle John, the son of Zebedee. Like Hebrews, this book is built upon quotations and allusions to Old Testament passages (hundreds of references).

668. Patmos is where John wrote this final book. This small island is located off the coast of Turkey and is thought to have held a Roman penal colony. John was exiled there for his activities as a missionary of Christ.

669. Revelation was written just as Christians were entering an intense period of persecution. The second half of Nero's reign (AD 54–68) and the late years of Domitian's reign (AD 81–96) are mentioned several times. Most scholars date Revelation around AD 95.

670. John wrote mainly in response to the continuing growth of emperor worship being enforced by the Romans. Christians were naturally being pressured to proclaim Caesar as Lord, but John wrote to encourage them to resist such demands since they were signed and sealed in Christ and would be vindicated when Christ returned, an event John expected was imminent. He could not visit the churches in Asia Minor, as he had been exiled to the island of Patmos, so he wrote them a letter instead.

671. Revelation's theme. Perhaps a story of goodness and evil waging a cataclysmic battle in which goodness wins the decisive victory, Revelation is more often seen as a prophecy of end times. The use of bizarre, conflicting images was a practiced style in ancient times. It was called "apocalyptic," so the book is sometimes called the Apocalypse instead of Revelation. The meaning is actually the same, only "apocalypse" comes from a Greek root while "revelation" comes from a Latin root word.

672. There are four interpretations of Revelation. *Preterists* believe Revelation's events have already taken place; they understand Revelation exclusively in terms of its first-century settings. *Futurists* see John's visions primarily coming to fruition in the end times. *Historicists* believe it is a book meant to describe history from John's time in Patmos to the end times. *Idealists* view Revelation as a symbolic story of timeless truths, especially of good conquering evil.

673. "Apocalyptic" writing is very symbolic. As a result, it is important that readers understand Revelation as a distinct book of the Bible. To understand what is being said, readers must recognize symbols: stars are angels, "the great prostitute" is Babylon (possibly Rome?), lampstands are churches, and the heavenly Jerusalem is the wife of the Lamb, Christ.

674. A unique feature of Revelation is the frequent use of the number *seven*. This happens fifty-two times! The number seven is a symbol for completeness; there are references to the seven churches, seven seals, seven signs, seven crowns, and many other items numbering seven.

675. The extraordinary prophetic vision of the second coming of Jesus and the last judgment were given while John was exiled on Patmos, an Aegean island, used as a Roman penal colony. The author had been banished there for his preaching most likely during the reign of Roman emperor Domitian (AD 81–96).

676. Apocalypse is the Greek name for the Book of Revelation. The word literally means "to unveil" or "to reveal something that has been hidden." The early church had numerous books claiming to reveal future events, and it wasn't until the fourth century that John's apocalypse was recognized as the one inspired version.

677. John heard a voice telling him what to do before he viewed the speaker (1:10–12). The voice told John to write down what he saw and then to send it to the seven churches. When John turned around, he viewed "someone 'like a son of man'" speaking to him. The person, Jesus Christ, is described as having hair that was white like wool and even snow, with eyes blazing fire. The speaker was dressed in a robe with a gold sash around his chest.

678. John was given direct instruction as to whom to address his account: the seven churches in Ephesus, Smyrna, Pergamum, Thyatira, Sardis, Philadelphia, and Laodicea. Each of the seven receives individual instructions tailored to their particular problems and weaknesses.

679. The pattern for these individual instructions is generally the same for all seven churches: commendation for their current efforts, expressions of disappointment for weakness or sin, and straightforward direction on how to correct the situation.

680. The churches are chastised and warned for forgetting to show love to Christ and one another, for failing to stand strong in the face of persecution, for allowing dissidents and religious heresy to exist in their churches, for being "dead" in their faith and refusing to repent, and for being lukewarm in their faith and not taking a solid stance within their surroundings.

681. Interestingly, all seven churches are given a promise if they will "overcome" the current situation. The promises all include being one with Christ through salvation, yet there is also mention of eternal reward, having authority over other nations, and being seated with Christ on his heavenly throne.

682. John discusses the throne in heaven where God sits. There is lightning, thunder, and great light. Brilliant color surrounds the Lord, his light reflected in gemlike beams. Surrounding the throne are twenty-four other smaller thrones with an elder seated in each one. The elders are in a constant state of worship of the Almighty.

683. The four living creatures behind the throne are truly monstrous visions. They too worship the Lord. They are covered with eyes, in order to see every detail. They each have six wings, though their images are all different—a figure like a lion, one like an ox, another with a face like a man, and the last resembling an eagle. Their job is to guard the heavenly throne as well as lead the others in worship. Revelation says that "day and night they never stop saying: 'Holy, holy, holy is the Lord God Almighty, who was, and is, and is to come'" (4:8).

684. A scroll bearing seven seals is held by Christ, but there is no one worthy to open it anywhere on earth. John says he weeps at the sight because he desperately wants to see what the scroll has to say. Yet there is one worthy to open the scroll. A Lamb that was slain appears, bearing seven horns and seven eyes (symbols of the seven spirits God had sent out into all the earth [5:6]). The lamb is a symbol of Christ—the righteous figure who was the atoning sacrifice for all people.

685. The Lamb is the only figure worthy to open the scroll. All in heaven fall down to worship him. It is undeniable that God and the Lamb are the Father and the Son and deserve equal reverence and awe.

686. As the Lamb opens the seals, many terrible things happen on earth. John speaks openly, understanding that such things are inescapable for those who have not turned to the Lamb in repentance. Each seal represents a source of destructive power that is unleashed on the earth. The fourth seal unleashes Death and Hades, who are given power over one quarter of the earth to kill, whether with a sword, by famine and plague, or with wild beasts (6:8).

687. Mention is made of the 144,000 believers who are sealed. Though Revelation says they were from the twelve tribes of Israel (7:4), it is uncertain if this is a symbolic number of those who withstood the last days of tribulation as Christians. Whoever they are, they are given seals on their foreheads to claim them as Christ's own so they are not harmed.

688. Those who have believed are sealed in the Lamb and joyfully present in heaven. John says they were dressed in white robes and were waving palm branches and praising God and the Lamb. Their numbers are too great to count, according to John, and they are from every corner of the earth and speak every tongue imaginable.

689. Those remaining on earth are tortured violently for five months by plagues, natural disasters, and warfare. Revelation 9:6 says, "During those days men will seek death, but will not find it; they will long to die, but death will elude them." It is a terrible picture, and though there will be a third of mankind who will die, the remaining people will still be unrepentant. The Bible states that this is the period of the first woe, and that two more will follow, correlating to the angels blowing their trumpets.

690. Two witnesses are mentioned in Revelation 11. It is unknown exactly who these two figures are. It is believed they are modeled after Moses and Elijah, two major prophets of the Old Testament. However, it is possible that these are actual believers who testify in the last days before the return of Christ. Another possibility is that these two witnesses will suffer martyrdom for their testimony. In any case, they are eventually overcome by a beast, and their deaths are heralded as a victory for those still on earth. But God will raise the two witnesses, and they will come to heaven.

691. A terrible earthquake occurs after the witnesses are raised. Revelation 11:13 says seven thousand people are killed. The survivors are terrified and recognize that this is Christ acting against them. They are terrified and yet do not repent. This is the end of the second woe.

692. The turning point of the Book of Revelation comes in chapter 11. It is loudly proclaimed that the kingdom is Christ's, and he will reign forever. Yet the war is not over between good and evil. A battle is to be waged in heaven. Chapter 12 opens with a woman giving birth in heaven, and all eagerly looking on at this wondrous sign—she will birth the Messiah. But then a red dragon appears, and he tries to eat her child. However, he is not successful. The male infant is brought to God, who is on his throne. The woman is taken to a place of spiritual protection for a period of 1,260 days.

693. A battle is then waged in heaven. Christ's angels, who are led by Michael, and the devil (the red dragon) and his angels wage a brutal war. The dragon is not strong enough to succeed. Satan is thrown to earth with his angels following. The dragon is so enraged at his loss that he goes after the woman who birthed the Messiah.

694. The devil is unsuccessful in his pursuit of the woman, so he turns to her children who remain on earth: those who love and obey God. He is determined to kill them all or turn them from their God. He calls upon a beast to help him.

695. This beast, though he is powerful, has a limited amount of time to reign: forty-two months. This beast comes out of the sea and is given all the power that Satan has. He will take over the earth, subject God's people to tyranny, and gather the worship of all those who are not signed and sealed with Christ's blood. Most consider this figure to be the true and final antichrist.

696. Interestingly, forty-two months is considered a symbolic length of time—three-and-a-half years. The period of forty-two months is also mentioned in Revelation 11:2. Many people believe the premise for this belief comes from a time when Jews were suffering persecution under Antiochus Epiphanes around 175 BC. Others say this is a natural division of the number seven into two equal parts, each being equally good and evil.

697. Another beast emerges from the earth. This beast makes everyone on earth worship the antichrist. This beast has great power and is able to kill all who do not worship the antichrist. The earthly beast's greater claim to fame, however, is that he forces everyone to have a mark on his or her forehead or right hand. Those who refuse the mark are not allowed to buy or sell anything from anyone and will presumably suffer greatly. The beast is known by his number: 666.

698. The identity and meaning of the mystical beast numbered 666 has deeply concerned Christians throughout history. Its symbolism has been assigned to Satanism in popular culture and to such notorious figures as Napoleon and Hitler. Some scholars believe that while Satan is a major player in Revelation, the meaning of 666 was clear to the people of the time of its writing. In both Greek and Hebrew, letters doubled as numerals.

699. One solution to the 666 puzzle. The number is produced by adding up the Hebrew letters of "Kaisar Neron," or Emperor Nero, which reaches an equivalent of the number 666. Other possibilities have been other persecuting leaders, such as Euanthas and Lateinos. Still others believe 666 is significant as a symbol of triune evil, as each of the three digits are one number short of the perfect number seven.

700. Those who have the mark of the beast suffer great misery in the end times. The beast is felled and they are left on their own. Seven plagues are waged on them by seven different angels. These plagues are also referred to as the "seven bowls of God's wrath." Through these dreadful days, the people still refuse to repent. They curse God and continue to follow the beast.

701. Kings are gathered from all corners of the world to gather at the place called Armageddon (a Hebrew word), presumably for the final battle. John then sees a vision of a woman riding a beast—Babylon is her name; the beast is the antichrist. Babylon will fall, much to the fear and sadness of those people who associated with her. Those with the mark of the beast had worshiped her, even adored her.

702. God's army will do battle under the leadership of a rider on a white horse. Revelation 19:13 says, "his name is the Word of God." The rider leads victoriously forward, and eventually the beast and his false prophet (presumed to be the beast numbered 666) are cast into the fiery lake of sulfur.

703. Satan is then bound for a thousand years. He will be allowed out for a time following this period, according to Revelation 20. Those who suffered during the reign of the beast as Christians and did not succumb and did not receive the beast's mark are raised and seated with Christ for the thousand-year time period. This is called the first resurrection, since only those recently killed are raised from the dead; the rest will wait until the final resurrection.

704. The final judgment is covered in Revelation 20. God sits on his throne with the Book of Life and judges all who have died. All the dead, from the earth and the sea and Hades, are judged by what they had done (v. 12). All whose names are not in the book are thrown into the lake of fire, as are death and Hades.

705. God proclaims the old order completed and promises an end to "death or mourning or crying or pain" (Rev. 21:4). Everything will be new, perfect, and forever, because God has conquered death and Christ has vanquished sin.

706. The New Jerusalem, according to some interpreters, is another name for the holy city and has a mixture of elements from Jerusalem, the temple, and the Garden of Eden. John describes in vivid detail its gold and precious stones, and the beauty of this holy place. He even measures the city with a gold measuring rod! Others believe this term is a metaphorical allusion to heaven in general, connoting the place where God and his people reside in holy communion.

The Trinity Triangle

19

---

707. The doctrine of the Trinity is more clearly defined in the New Testament than in the Old. Several times the three persons of the Trinity are shown together and seemingly are equal to one another. At the baptism of Jesus, the Spirit descended on him and a voice from God out of heaven identified Jesus as his beloved Son (Matt. 3:16–17). Jesus prayed that the Father would send another Comforter (John 14:16). The disciples were told to baptize in the name (singular) of the Father, Son, and the Holy Spirit (Matt. 28:19). The three persons of the Trinity are also associated together in their work (1 Cor. 12:4–6; Eph. 1:3–14; 1 Peter 1:2; 3:18; Rev. 1:4–6).

708. The fact of the Trinity is taught in the Old Testament. The very name for God is *Elohim*—a plural word. Plural pronouns were often used for God (see Gen. 1:26), and even the Hebrew word used to refer to "one God" was the word *echad,* which connotes a compound unity. There are also references to both "the Son" and "the Spirit of God" throughout the Old Testament, clearly referring to the Trinity.

709. The Trinity of God. Though the term *trinity* does not occur in the Bible, it had very early usage in the church. Its Greek form, *trias,* seems to have been first used by Theophilus of Antioch (AD 181), and its Latin form, *trinitas,* by Tertullian (AD 220). In Christian theology, the term *Trinity* means that there are three eternal distinctions in the one divine essence, known respectively as Father, Son, and Holy Spirit. These three distinctions are three persons, and one may speak of the tri-personality of God. The doctrine of the Trinity *is* a great mystery. However, it was not birthed by speculation but was given as revelation in Scripture.

710. "You deserted the Rock, who fathered you; you forgot the God who gave you birth" (Deut. 32:18). Not only is God the father of Jesus Christ; God is our father and our creator.

711. "Jesus said, 'Do not hold on to me, for I have not yet returned to the Father. Go instead to my brothers and tell them, "I am returning to my Father and your Father, to my God and your God"'" (John 20:17). After Christ's resurrection, he appeared to Mary Magdalene. His instructions to her demonstrate God is fully heavenly Father and God to both himself and to all who believe.

712. "For to us a child is born, to us a son is given, and the government will be on his shoulders. And he will be called Wonderful Counselor, Mighty God, Everlasting Father, Prince of Peace" (Isa. 9:6). The prophet Isaiah's words remained a testimony to God's people of the promised Messiah throughout many generations. That the people believed a Messiah would come is unquestionable. However, they were looking for an earthly king who would bring Israel to great heights rather than a Savior who would redeem the world and be their heavenly King first.

713. "As Jesus was coming up out of the water, he saw heaven being torn open and the Spirit descending on him like a dove. And a voice came from heaven: 'You are my Son, whom I love; with you I am well pleased'" (Mark 1:10–11). God himself, visible through the person of the Holy Spirit, spoke to Jesus as John the Baptist baptized Jesus in the Jordan River.

714. "Now the earth was formless and empty, darkness was over the surface of the deep, and the Spirit of God was hovering over the waters" (Gen. 1:2). The Spirit was present at the creation of the world and remains just as present today.

715. "But you will receive power when the Holy Spirit comes on you; and you will be my witnesses in Jerusalem, and in all Judea and Samaria, and to the ends of the earth" (Acts 1:8). Jesus made this promise to his disciples before ascending into heaven. The Book of Acts studies the early church; chapter 2 tells of the Holy Spirit's coming at Pentecost.

716. Trinitarian belief as expressed by the Athanasian Creed. "We worship one God in the Trinity, and the Trinity in unity; we distinguish among the persons, but we do not divide the substance." It goes on to say, "The entire three persons are coeternal and coequal with one another. . . ." "The heart of Christian faith in God is the revealed mystery of the Trinity. *Trinitas* is a Latin word meaning three-ness. Christianity rests on the doctrinal truths of the *trinitas*, the tri-personality, of God. Each person in the Godhead played not only a significant role in our creation but also our redemption."—J. I. Packer

717. Perfect harmony. The persons of the Godhead relate one to another in perfect harmony and intimacy—a perfect society. One theologian explains, "If there were no trinity, there could be no incarnation, no objective redemption, and therefore no salvation; for there would be no one capable of acting as mediator between God and man." The Trinity allows for eternal love. Love was before creation, yet love needs an object. Love is always flowing among the persons of the Trinity.

718. The three persons of the Trinity act in cooperation with one another. No one person in the Godhead acts free of the connection of the other two. They are anchored—the Spirit and Son do not act in opposition to the Father. Were they to do so, we could not speak of the Trinity as "one God, with three distinct persons."

719. The Father is "the God of Peace," the Son is "our Peace," and the Holy Spirit is "the Spirit of Peace" and produces "the fruit of . . . peace." Peace expresses the deepest desire and need of the human heart. It represents the greatest measure of contentment and satisfaction in life.

720. There are seven different views on the makeup of the Trinity in regards to subordination and equality between the three distinct persons of the Godhead. Some of these views place more emphasis on power and "line of command" than others; all respect and revere the Trinity as biblical and historically faithful to the beliefs of the church.

721. The first model posits both the Son and the Spirit proceeding from the Father. The Son and Spirit are on the same level yet independent of one another. The Father is the source of the latter two, yet all three are equally God.

722. Another model states that the Father again is the beginning point from which the Son proceeds. The Spirit, however, proceeds from both the Father and the Son. The Spirit does not have any impact, in essence, on the other two.

723. A third model places the Father and the Son on an equal plane, making them equal in glory. However, the Spirit proceeds from the two at a lower level, acting as a mediator between the divine Father and Son and the earthly world below.

724. Another model shows less of a triangle effect and instead posits that all things originate with the Father, are then passed to the Son, and then through the Son to the Holy Spirit. The Father, Son, and Holy Spirit are all on the same plane of deity, but all things originate with the Father. This view is deeply rooted in both the Eastern and Western churches.

725. The fifth model comes from a more mystical view within the church. The Father is the head, and the rest—the Son, Spirit, and the world—emanate from him. However, the model also holds a place for a return to the Father. It is believed that the Spirit prepares the world for the Son, and the Son (along with the Holy Spirit) leads us back to the Father. This model definitely loses the equality of all three persons within the Godhead.

726. Augustine's model represents a much more fluid relationship between the three persons of the Godhead. The Father, Son, and Spirit are all on the same level (negating a triangle view such as models one and two), but the Spirit is actually in between the Father and the Son. The Spirit proceeds from the Father and the Son. David N. Bell suggests the relationship is similar to that of the workings of an electric battery where the Father is the "positive" and the Son is the "negative"—the Spirit is "the current flowing and flashing between them." He goes on to explain that there is only one substance, one current, but the battery will not function without both the positive and negative ends as well as a route for the current between them. A weakness of this view is that it tends to put the Spirit in a subordinate role as a conduit of the currents flowing from Father to Son and vice versa.

727. The seventh and final model takes more of a give-and-take approach between the three persons. Father, Son, and Spirit are points on a circle with no end and no beginning. As the Father influences the Son, the Son influences the Spirit, and the Spirit influences the Father. It is less a picture of two or one being subordinate to the other and more a picture of interdependence between all three. Though the Father might be the starting point from which the Son and Spirit proceed, the Son and Spirit proceed *to* the Father with their own response.

728. Various analogies have been made in order to explain the mystery of the Trinity. Augustine proposed that the three persons may be likened to "proposed lover, beloved, and love itself." Another is that of the components of an apple: the core, flesh, and peel representing God, the Son, and the Holy Spirit as the "visible," "tangible" peel that wraps the flesh of the Son and the core of the Father into one thing, an apple.

729. Tertullian and Anselm, both church fathers, had views with a more subordinationist approach. Tertullian likened the persons of the Trinity to the root, tree, and fruit. Anselm offered a picture of a spring, stream, and lake to demonstrate how the Trinity flowed and existed.

730. Others prefer to speak of the Trinity in more equal terms. For example, one space with three dimensions: height, length, and depth. Or the three phases of matter: solid, liquid, and gas. All may exist at the same time, with the temperature being the determining factor.

731. The Nicene Creed is a statement of the orthodox faith of the early Christian church. Written in response to heresies that included the doctrine of the Trinity, among others, its words remain a testimony of the church's belief in this respect. The creed was used by both Western and Eastern churches, although the Western church insisted on the inclusion of the phrase "and the Son" (known as the *Filioque*) in the article on the procession of the Holy Spirit. The Eastern church remains steadfast in leaving this phrase out. The creed covers the three persons of the Trinity separately.

732. "I believe in one God, the Father Almighty, Maker of heaven and earth, and of all things visible and invisible."—Nicene Creed, First Article

733. "And in one Lord Jesus Christ, the only-begotten Son of God, begotten of the Father before all worlds; God of God, Light of Light, very God of very God; begotten, not made, being of one substance with the Father, by whom all things were made."—Nicene Creed, Second Article

734. "And I believe in the Holy Spirit, the Lord and Giver of life; who proceedeth from the Father and the Son; who with the Father and the Son together is worshipped and glorified; who spoke by the prophets."—Nicene Creed, Fourth Article

735. Denial of the Trinity leads to dangerous theology. Without a view of an active, dynamic God who performs as the Trinity does, it's easy to fall into heresy—deism, pantheism, and agnosticism to name a few. Deism views God as one who is unattached and uninvolved, a God who put the world in motion but doesn't monitor it. Pantheism believes God is inseparable from the world, and many parts of the world are worshiped as God. In agnosticism, God cannot be known—he is a mystery that is impossible to even know. When the Trinity is denied, often Christ's deity is questioned, and the story of the Bible, God's Word, is in effect lost.

The Names of the Members of the Trinity

20

THE NAMES OF GOD THE FATHER

736. The names of God in Scripture describe his character . . .

a faithful God who does no wrong
a forgiving God
God of grace
God of hope
God of love and peace
God of peace
a jealous and avenging God

737. The names of God describe him as our protector . . .

a refuge for his people
a refuge for the needy in his distress
a refuge for the oppressed
a refuge for the poor
a sanctuary
a shade from the heat
a shelter from the storm
a stronghold in times of trouble
a fortress of salvation
an ever-present help in trouble
defender of widows
our dwelling place

738. God's names reveal his leadership . . .

a Master in heaven
commander of the Lord's army
God our strength
helper of the fatherless
the great King above all gods
the only God
the just and mighty One Shepherd

739. God's name reveals his royalty . . .

a glorious crown
a source of strength
eternal King
God of Glory
Most High
the Exalted God
Sovereign Lord
the Glorious Father
the Majestic Glory
the Majesty in heaven

your glory
your praise
the Glory of Israel
God of gods

740. The names of God reveal his creativity . . .

architect and builder
builder of everything
Creator of heaven and earth
he who reveals his thoughts to man
the potter
the gardener (husbandman)
only wise God
him who is able to do immeasurably more than all we ask or
   imagine

741. His names reveal his fatherhood . . .

Father
Father of compassion
Father of our spirits
Father of the heavenly lights
Father to the fatherless
God and Father of our Lord Jesus Christ
God of Abraham, Isaac, and Jacob
God of all mankind
God our Father

742. The names of God reveal his majesty . . .

God
God of the Sabbath (*El Sabaoth*)
God Almighty (*El Shaddai*)
God Most High
God my Maker
King of Glory
God over all the kingdoms of the earth
King of heaven

743. God's names reveal his strength . . .

God my rock
God my Savior
God my stronghold
one to be feared
he who raised Christ from the dead
him who is able to keep you from falling
Lord who strikes the blow
our Mighty One
the one who sustains me
the strength of my heart
the rock in whom I take refuge
Rock of our salvation
our refuge and strength

744. His names reveal his actions on our behalf . . .

God of all comfort
God of retribution
God who avenges me
God who gives endurance and encouragement
God who relents from sending calamity
he who blots out your transgressions
he who comforts you

745. The names of God reveal his greatness . . .

great and awesome God
great and powerful God
great, mighty, and awesome God
Lord will provide
the Almighty
the consuming fire
the everlasting God
your very great reward

746. His names reveal his nature . . .

God of truth
living and true God
jealous
the spring of living water
love
you who keep your covenant of love with your servants
you who love the people
the faithful God
the God who saves me
you who hear prayer
the Eternal God

747. His names reveal his eternity . . .

I Am
the living Father
God of the living

748. The names of God reveal his judgeship . . .

Judge of all the earth
him who is ready to judge the living and the dead
our judge
our lawgiver
the true God
you who judge righteously and test the heart and mind
Righteous Father
the compassionate and gracious God
Righteous Judge
our redeemer

749. The names of God reveal his holiness . . .

Holy Father
Holy One
Holy One among you
Lord who makes you holy

750. His names reveal his lordship . . .

Adonai (Lord)
Lord Almighty
Lord God
Lord our Peace
Lord (Jehovah)
Lord Most High
Lord my Banner
Lord my Rock
Lord of all the earth
Lord of heaven and earth
Lord of lords
Lord our God
Lord our Maker
Lord our shield
Lord who heals you
Lord who is there

751. His names reveal that he is our Maker . . .

God our Maker
Maker of all things
Maker of heaven and earth
he who forms the hearts of all
the God who sees me
the God of the spirits of all mankind

752. The names of God reveal that he is personal . . .

my advocate
my comforter in sorrow
my confidence
my help
my helper
my hiding place
my hope
my light

my mighty rock
my refuge in the day of disaster
my refuge in times of trouble
my song
my strong deliverer
my support

THE NAMES OF GOD THE SON

753. Jesus is the Son . . .

Branch of the Lord
Son of Mary
Heir of Salvation
Son of the Living God
heir of all things
his one and only Son
Son of the Most High God
Holy One of God
Lion of the Tribe of Judah
Son of the Blessed One

754. Jesus is Eternal . . .

Emmanuel (God with us)
Eternal Life
the Beginning and the End
the Amen
the First and the Last
the last Adam
the Living One
the Living Stone

755. Jesus is the Messiah . . .

Christ
Anointed One

Bread of Life
Hope of Glory
Horn of Salvation
one who makes men holy
one who speaks to the Father in our defense
Passover Lamb
Prince of Peace
Redeemer
the man from heaven
Savior of the world
the stone the builders rejected

756. Christ's character is revealed in his names . . .

Lord
our hope
faithful and true
our peace
fragrant offering and sacrifice to God
our righteousness, holiness, and redemption
Great Physician
Righteous Judge
sure foundation

757. Christ's actions are revealed in his names . . .

author and perfecter of our faith
author of our salvation
Bridegroom
chief cornerstone
consolation of Israel
friend of tax collectors and sinners
covenant for the people
he who comes down from heaven and gives life to the world
he who searches hearts and minds
him who died and came to life again
him who loves us and has freed us from our sins

Lamb of God
mediator of a new covenant

758. Christ's humanity is revealed in his names . . .

the Son of Man
firstborn among the dead
a Nazarene
firstborn over all creation
Man of sorrows
Root of David
the Son

759. Christ's divinity is revealed in his names . . .

Alpha and Omega
Ancient of Days
author of life
God of all the earth
Son of God
Light
image of the invisible God
Immanuel (God with us)
Judge of the living and the dead
Messiah
our God and Savior Jesus Christ
Sovereign and Lord
Word of God

760. The priesthood of Jesus is revealed in his names . . .

apostle and high priest
Great High Priest
merciful and faithful high priest
Rabbi
Teacher
the Head
the atoning sacrifice for our sins
Servant

761. Christ's beauty is revealed in his names . . .

Beloved
Holy and Righteous One
Rose of Sharon
the Lord our Righteousness
Fountain
True Vine
Shiloh

762. Christ's majesty and kingship are revealed in his names . . .

blessed and only Ruler
Bright and Morning Star
chosen and precious cornerstone
Crown of Splendor
Desire of Nations
Master
head of every man
head of the body, the church
head over every power and authority
King of Kings
King of the ages
King of the Jews
Ruler over the nations
Ruler of God's creation
Ruler of the kings of the earth

763. The protection of Christ is revealed in his names . . .

a banner for the peoples
Deliverer
Good Shepherd
ransom for all men
Shepherd and Overseer of your souls
the gate (door)
Refiner and Purifier
Great Shepherd of the sheep

764. The lordship of Jesus is revealed in his names . . .

Lord (Kurios)
Lord and Savior Jesus Christ
Lord of Glory
Lord of lords
Lord of peace
Lord of the harvest
Lord of the Sabbath
Lord (Rabboni)

765. The illumination of Jesus is revealed in his names . . .

Light of Life
Light of Men
Light of the World
Light of the Gentiles
Morning Star
the true light
the radiance of God's glory
the truth

766. The blessing of Jesus is revealed in his names . . .

indescribable gift
Dayspring
guarantee of a better covenant
Resurrection and the Life
Wonderful Counselor
the Bright and Morning Star

THE NAMES OF GOD THE HOLY SPIRIT

767. The names for the Spirit reveal his actions . . .

Counselor
a deposit guaranteeing what is to come

Spirit of judgment
Spirit of life
Spirit of sonship (adoption)
the gift

768. The names for the Spirit reveal his character . . .

Breath of the Almighty
Spirit of counsel and of power
Spirit of grace and supplication
Spirit of holiness
Spirit of truth
Spirit of justice
Spirit of wisdom and of understanding
Spirit of wisdom and revelation
Spirit of faith
Spirit of fire

769. The names for the Spirit reveal his divinity . . .

Holy Spirit
Holy One
Spirit of Christ
Spirit of the living God
Spirit of the Lord
Spirit of the Sovereign Lord
Voice of the Lord

770. The names for the Spirit reveal his greatness . . .

Spirit of God
the promised Holy Spirit
Spirit of Glory
God's seal

A Heavenly Father

21

---

771. The Father is recognized as God. A brief scan of the New Testament reveals the numerous times and roles in which the Father is identified as God. "Paul, an apostle—not from men nor through man, but through Jesus Christ and God the Father, who raised him from the dead" (Gal. 1:1 NRSV; see also John 6:27; Rom. 1:7).

772. Father—a distinguishing title of the New Testament. To Israel, he was revealed as *Jehovah*, and the patriarchs reveled in such triumphant names as *God Almighty* and *Lord of Heaven and Earth*. But in all the divine names or titles disclosed in Scripture, there is no revelation of the fatherhood of God until his beloved Son taught his disciples to pray, "Our Father which art in heaven, Hallowed be thy name" (Matt. 6:9).

773. Old Testament references to the Father are figurative. Only a few references to God's fatherhood are mentioned in Old

Testament Scriptures and they are mainly figurative and used as illustrations. "Like as a father pitieth his children, so the LORD pitieth them that fear him" (Ps. 103:13 KJV). It is in this way that he also likens himself to a mother. "As one whom his mother comforteth, so will I comfort you" (Isa. 66:13 KJV).

774. God reserved his role of Father. We see glimpses of God's relationship to his redeemed people as in the song of Moses where we find the question, "Is not he thy father that hath bought thee?" (Deut. 32:6 KJV). He also speaks of himself as "Israel's father" in Jeremiah (31:9) and refers to Israel as his "firstborn" (Exod. 4:22; Hosea 11:1). But scholars hold that God reserved his role of Father to express his unique relationship founded only on the accomplished redemption of the coming Messiah. Jesus said, "No man cometh unto the Father, *but by me*" (John 14:6 KJV, emphasis added).

775. A tender name. Of all the divine names, none is more full of comfort or more touching to the heart than that of *Father*. In the Gospels alone, we find that Matthew mentions "the Father" 44 times; Mark, 5 times; Luke, 17 times; and John, 122 times. John's is especially the Gospel revealing the Father, and a definite aspect of God's role is emphasized in each chapter where this name is mentioned.

776. Aspects of Father. The identifying terms used by the Son of God in the New Testament Scriptures are: *the Father, Father, my Father, your Father, our Father, Holy Father, Righteous Father, Abba Father.* Added to these are several relative expressions in the Epistles that, along with those found in the Gospels, emphasize the many-sided character inherent in the fatherhood of God:

- a Father
- God the Father
- God our Father
- God and Father of our Lord Jesus Christ
- Father of mercies
- Father of spirits
- Father of lights
- Father of glory

777. "Jesus said to them, 'If God were your Father, you would love me, for I came from God and now am here. I have not come on my own; but he sent me'" (John 8:42). God is the Father of those who believe in him; he is the Creator of all, but the Father of the elect.

778. "'You do not know me or my Father,' Jesus replied. 'If you knew me, you would know my Father also'" (John 8:19). The Father cannot be known unless it is through the Son. You cannot know the one without the other.

779. "If you [believers] then, though you are evil, know how to give good gifts to your children, how much more will your Father in heaven give the Holy Spirit to those who ask him!" (Luke 11:13). The heavenly Father's greatest gift to his redeemed people who have experienced Christ's atonement is the Holy Spirit.

780. *The* Father. As *the* is emphasized in this title, God's own personal glory as Father is conveyed wherever it is used. The exclusiveness of his being and behavior as our heavenly Father is prominent here. In the Gospel of John, this title is used several times to illustrate the Father as the one above all other fathers, as the source of all things. "He that hath seen me hath seen the Father" (John 14:9 KJV; see also 1:14; 3:35; 4:21; 6:44; 12:49; 14:24, 26; 16:27).

781. Father. While Jesus often spoke about God, he only addressed him once as such: "My God, my God" (Matt. 27:46). Apart from this exception, Christ addressed him as Father—the single most intimate term for the relationship existing between the Father and the Son. His first recorded use of *Father* was when at age twelve Jesus spoke to Joseph and Mary about being in the temple (Luke 2:49). And the last occasion was on the cross, where his final prayer was, "Father, into your hands I commit my spirit" (Luke 23:46).

782. The mystery of the incarnation is that Jesus was "conceived of the Holy Spirit, and born of the virgin Mary." He came as the Son of Man, but not as *a* son of man. Though he was foster parented by Joseph, he was God's only begotten Son. He had only one Father.

783. *My* Father. Spoken only by Jesus, the pronoun of personal possession—*my*—expresses not only an eternal relationship between him and God the Father, but also in the fellowship of mutual love and action on behalf of the believers. "Neither shall any man pluck them out of my hand. . . . No man is able to pluck them out of my Father's hand. I and my Father are one" (John 10:28–30).

784. *Your* Father. Fourteen times in Matthew's Gospel alone does this particular combination occur, bringing with it responsibility to the Lord and to others. The privilege of being God's children through the finished work of Christ brings a certain obligation. "Let your light so shine before men, that they may see your good works, and glorify *your Father* which is in heaven" (5:16 KJV, emphasis added).

785. *Our* Father. In response to the request of his disciples, "Lord, teach us to pray," Jesus guided them with a model to follow, opening with "*Our Father* which art in heaven" (Matt. 6:9 KJV, emphasis added). But this was not the language of Jesus *and* his disciples, meaning joint relationship. This prayer was intended for the family of the redeemed rather than a prayer that Jesus himself prayed. Why? Jesus had no evil to be delivered from and no trespasses to be forgiven.

786. *Holy* Father. In the prayer recorded in John 17, Jesus used the title of Father different ways. First, he repeated the single name, *Father*, four times (vv. 1, 5, 21, 24), while speaking to God about his past glory, present life, approaching sacrifice, and future glory. But in verse 9, he begins to pray for the believers, "I pray not for the world, but for them which thou hast given me; for they are thine" (KJV). His burden was that his redeemed ones might be kept from evil in the world. He interceded for their sanctification, so the term *Holy Father* was most fitting.

787. *Righteous* Father. Why did Jesus use "Righteous Father" in John 17:25 and not "Holy Father"? In the last verse of this most remarkable prayer, Jesus said, "I have declared unto them thy name, and will declare it" (17:26 KJV). With his approaching death, Jesus knew divine righteousness would be manifested. Here he cries out to his Father who knows his ultimate purpose.

788. *Abba* Father. *Abba* is an Aramaic word that describes simple affection for the Father (Mark 14:36; Rom. 8:15; Gal. 4:6). In Jewish and old Christian prayers, it was a name by which God was addressed. *Abba* is the name a child would use and *Father* expresses an intelligent realization of the relationship. The two combined express the confident love and growing intelligence of a child.

The Son, a Savior   22

789. The Son is recognized as God. The doctrine of the deity of Christ is crucial to the Christian faith. "What think you of Christ?" is the paramount question of life (see Matt. 16:15; 22:42). Jesus Christ is the greatest of all men, but he is infinitely more than mere man. He is Immanuel, God with us. Matthew explicitly applies the passage from Isaiah 7:14 to Jesus (Matt. 1:22–23).

790. Jesus reflects God. Christ was moved at the sight of the straining, clueless crowds—but a millennium earlier it was written of Jehovah: "As a father has compassion on his children, so the LORD has compassion on those who fear him; for he knows how we are formed, he remembers that we are dust" (Ps. 103:13–14). We know Jesus took pity on orphans, but Hosea said of the Father, "In you the fatherless find compassion" (Hosea 14:3). Yes, Jesus wept at the tomb of Lazarus, but of the Father we learn, "Precious in the sight of the LORD is the death of his saints" (Ps. 116:15).

791. The "Angel of the Lord" is a recurring phrase in the Old Testament and has special reference to the preincarnate Second Person of the Trinity. His appearances in the Old Testament foreshadowed his coming in the flesh. The Angel of the Lord is identified with the Lord and yet distinguished from him. He appeared to Hagar, Abraham, Jacob, Moses, Israel, Balaam, Gideon, Manoah, Elijah, and David. The Angel of the Lord slew 185,000 Assyrians, stood among the myrtle trees in Zechariah's vision, defended Joshua the high priest against Satan, and was one of the three men who appeared to Abraham.

792. The Christmas story reveals the depth of God's love to us. Matthew's and Luke's Gospels tell the story of the virgin birth, the humble beginnings of Jesus, and the joyous celebration set off in heaven when Christ was born. Though missed by many, God allowed both great (the magi) and humble (the shepherds) to join in the celebration.

793. The baby Jesus was like any other baby—he was human and had the same needs as babies do today. He cried to be held and fed, needed his diapers changed, and learned to talk as any other baby does.

794. Jesus did not receive his name, which means "the Messiah" or "the Christ," until his eighth day when he was circumcised. The name had been given to Mary by the angel before she conceived, but the practice was to officially name the child when he was circumcised.

795. At twelve years of age, Jesus already demonstrated that he was aware of his lifework. His parents had taken him to the Passover feast in Jerusalem. When they left, they thought he was with them, but he had stayed behind in order to speak with the teachers at the temple.

796. His ministry began when he was in his late twenties. John the Baptist was serving as a "voice in the wilderness" and calling the people to remember that their Savior was coming, that the time had come to repent.

797. The demons never failed to recognize Jesus as the "holy one of God" or "son of the Most High"; only human beings questioned his identity.

798. The Lord's preaching took him all over the area for three years. He traveled throughout Galilee, Judea, and Samaria. He healed the sick and brought hope to many through miracles. He often spoke in parables to the people to help them better understand what his ministry was all about.

799. Jesus spent much of his ministry life in and around the Sea of Galilee. Galileans in Bible times were considered country hicks by the more cosmopolitan residents of Jerusalem. Jesus spoke primarily to the humble people who labored on the land and were familiar with the animals and plants around them. His parables are filled with images of the natural world.

800. To the devout Jews who accepted Jesus, he was the promised Savior who fulfilled the promise expressed in their Scriptures of a coming "Messiah" or "anointed one" from the line of David who would deliver the children of Israel and usher in a new age of peace under God's rule. Though he was later called the "Christ," this is not a name but a title. *Christos* comes from the Greek, meaning "anointed one" or "Messiah."

801. As Christ rode a donkey into Jerusalem, he was hailed by the people with palm leaves and shouts of "Hosanna!" The people celebrated him as their king. They did not want the greatest gift that Christ offered and that they needed most. They wanted freedom from the Romans and a nation of their own instead, and thought that was what Christ brought, despite the many warnings and explanations given of his ministry.

802. Satan provoked Judas to betray Jesus, as it is stated in the Gospel of John. The treachery of Judas has provoked some speculation over motives, including the notion that he might have been an anti-Roman zealot who was disappointed that Jesus had not proved to be the rebel leader many were expecting. In Mark, Judas went to the chief priests to betray Jesus before being offered a bribe, suggesting that he had some other motive besides money. Matthew specifically states that Judas asked how much he would be given, and he was paid "thirty pieces of silver" in fulfillment of ancient Hebrew prophecy.

803. After the Last Supper, Jesus spent his last night of freedom in the Garden of Gethsemane on the slopes of the Mount of Olives. The name means "olive presses." In Jesus' time, the Mount of Olives was covered with a luxuriant growth of these trees, and the inhabitants of Jerusalem often rested there to seek relief from the sun.

804. "This day, even in this night, before the cock crows twice, you will deny me three times" (Mark 14:30). On the way to Gethsemane, Jesus told his disciple Peter this prophecy. The roosters first crowed about midnight, and they were so punctual that Roman soldiers used the sound as a signal for changing the guard. The roosters crowed a second time about three o'clock in the morning, which awakened the second watch of soldiers.

805. After Jesus was resurrected, he appeared several times to various disciples. His resurrection fulfilled every prophecy he and all the Old Testament prophets had made concerning the Savior of the world. Though some doubted, many believed and were brought to a saving understanding that Jesus was truly their Savior and the King of Kings.

A Spirit Was Sent

23

---

806. The study of the Holy Spirit is called "pneumatology," which comes from the Greek words *pneuma* (meaning "spirit") and *logos* (meaning "doctrine").

807. The Hebrew word that is commonly translated "Spirit" literally means "wind" or "breath." Thus the "Spirit of God" is literally the invisible, active presence of God. You can hear the wind and see its result as it moves the branches of a tree, but you cannot see the wind itself. Similarly the actions of the Holy Spirit are evident in the lives of believers, even though we cannot see him directly.

808. The Spirit is a person. Before it can be decided that the Holy Spirit is God, it must first be established that he is a person, not a mere influence or divine power. And he truly is. Though the Greek term for spirit is neuter, Jesus in John 14:26 and 16:13–14 used the masculine pronoun "he" when speaking of the Holy Spirit. He also has the three essential elements of personality: intellect (1 Cor. 2:11), sensibilities (Rom. 8:27; 15:30), and will (1 Cor. 12:11). He can be tempted (Acts 5:9), lied to (Acts 5:3), grieved (Eph. 4:30), resisted (Acts 7:51), insulted (Heb. 10:29), and blasphemed (Matt. 12:31–32).

809. The Holy Spirit is recognized as God. He is a divine person as can be shown by his attributes of deity: He is eternal (Heb. 9:14), omniscient (1 Cor. 2:10–11), omnipotent (Luke 1:35), and omnipresent (Ps. 139:7–10). Works of deity are also ascribed to him such as creation, regeneration, inspiration of the Scriptures, and raising of the dead.

810. Some groups (for example, the Jehovah's Witness cult) view the Holy Spirit as a "force" or "power," rather than as a person. However, that heresy grew largely from the translators of the King James Bible, who referred to the Spirit as "it."

811. The Holy Spirit has personality, as revealed by the fact that he has a will (1 Cor. 12:11), a mind (Rom. 8:27), knowledge (John 14:26), the ability to communicate (Acts 1:16), and emotions (Eph. 4:30). His personality is also demonstrated in the fact that he has a job: to teach, guide, restrain, comfort, and intercede on behalf of believers.

812. The New Testament reveals that the Spirit can be grieved, quenched, resisted, blasphemed, and insulted.

813. The Holy Spirit is referred to as "God" in Acts 5:3–4, as "Lord" in 2 Corinthians 3:18, and as being equal to the Father and the Son in Matthew 28:19.

814. Scripture reveals the divine attributes of the Holy Spirit, referring to him as eternal (Heb. 9:14), omniscient (John 14:26), omnipotent (Job 26:13), all-wise (Isa. 40:13), sovereign (1 Cor. 12:11), and the giver of life (Rom. 8:2).

815. One of the most common descriptors for the Holy Spirit is the name "Comforter." This comes from the Greek word *paracletos*, which literally means "one who comes alongside." The Holy Spirit is God's way of personally coming alongside each believer (see John 15:26).

816. The Holy Spirit is referred to as our "guide" in several New Testament passages. This reveals the Spirit's job of leading believers into maturity in Christ. As John 16:13 puts it, "The Spirit of truth . . . will guide you . . ."

817. Romans 8:26–27 describes the Holy Spirit as our *intercessor*. In that role he will reveal the Father's will, pray with us, and connect us to the Father.

818. The work of the Holy Spirit is evident in creation (see Gen. 1:2, 26), in the inspiration of Scripture (see 2 Tim. 3:16 and 2 Peter 1:21), and in the salvation of humankind (see John 7:38–39).

819. The Holy Spirit was active in the Old Testament. He empowered Gideon in Judges 6:34, Samson in Judges 14:6, and David in 1 Samuel 16:13.

820. "Quenching the Spirit" is referred to in several passages of Scripture, including 1 Thessalonians 5:19, Psalm 51, and 1 Samuel 16:14. Sin, particularly secret sin in the life of a believer, will prevent the Spirit from working in one's life.

821. The Holy Spirit became manifest in the lives of believers on the day of Pentecost, when he came upon the members of the early church and allowed them to speak in other tongues so that everyone in the crowd heard their own language (see Acts 2).

822. "And be not drunk with wine . . . but be filled with the Spirit," Paul wrote in Ephesians 5:18. The "filling of the Spirit" is likened to being drunk, since control of our lives is turned over to something else—in this case, God. Some charismatic and Pentecostal groups believe this is a regular event in the lives of believers, while most other believers see the filling of the Spirit as a onetime event, occurring at the moment of salvation.

823. One of the activities of the Holy Spirit is to provide believers with spiritual gifts. Romans 12 and 1 Corinthians 12 both describe a number of gifts the Spirit gives to believers, including wisdom, knowledge, faith, healing, miracles, prophecy, tongues, interpretation, serving, teaching, discerning, and encouraging. While each believer has been given at least one spiritual gift, no one has a right to *ask* for a particular gift. These gifts blend together in a church to bring unity to the body of Christ.

824. The Holy Spirit also produces "fruit" in the lives of believers. Galatians 5:22–23 details some of the fruit that is produced: love, joy, peace, patience, kindness, goodness, faithfulness, gentleness, and self-control.

825. "Blasphemy against the Holy Spirit" is sometimes referred to as "the unpardonable sin." According to Matthew 12:22–32, Mark 3:22–30, and Luke 12:10, blasphemy against the Holy Spirit refers to examining the clear, supernatural work of God and ascribing it to Satan.

826. The Spirit was active all along from the beginning of time, hovering over the waters at creation and inspiring God's messengers throughout the Old Testament history—378 passages in the Hebrew Bible mention the Spirit.

24

The Word

827. The Bible is not only special revelation but also the final authority on God. It is the embodiment of a divine revelation. The records containing this revelation are genuine, credible, and supernaturally inspired.

828. The Canon of Scripture is the supreme and only infallible source of theology. We do not forget the importance of reason, intuition, and the creeds and confessions of the church, but we understand these to be aids in the understanding of the revelation of God, particularly as contained in the Scriptures.

829. The Bible. Christians believe this book to be the true Word of God. From the creation account of Genesis to the end-time visions of Revelation, the story of Israel to Jesus' ministry, it is the source for what Christians believe and how they try to live.

830. The word *Bible* comes from the Greek word *biblia*, which means "books," which comes from another word, *byblos*, meaning papyrus, a material books were made from in ancient times.

831. The ancient Greeks obtained their supplies of paper from the port of Byblos, in what is now Lebanon. Their word for book—*biblion*—was derived from the name of this port, and from this we get our English word *Bible*, meaning the Book of books.

832. The word *Bible* **is not in the Bible.** The term came long after all the writings were completed and assembled.

833. The Bible is the world's best-selling book as well as the world's most shoplifted book!

834. The Bible is the most bought, yet least understood book. Nine out of ten Americans own a Bible, but fewer than half ever read it. Worldwide sales of the Bible are uncountable.

835. Just how big is the Bible? Stack ten average-sized non-fiction books printed today. That pile will contain the same number of words that are found in one Bible. That's close to one million words, not counting the number of words added—footnotes, verse numbers, concordances, etc.

836. The Bible looks like one book, but it is actually an anthology, a collection of many smaller books. In an even broader sense, it is not just an anthology of shorter works but an entire library.

837. Some Bible books are as short as half a page. One of the longest books—Jeremiah—is roughly the length of today's short novel. This makes the Bible's longest book a hundred times longer than its shortest book.

838. Though the Bible as a whole is much longer than nearly any other book we'd like to read, its individual books are mostly shorter than any other book we consider reading.

839. The Bible is an extraordinary gathering of many books of law, wisdom, poetry, philosophy, and history. The number of books in this portable library depends on which Bible you are holding. The Bible of a Jew is different from the Bible of a Roman Catholic, which in turn is different from the Bible of a Protestant.

840. The Bible is both ancient and contemporary as it deals with the unchanging issues of human existence: life, death, joy, sorrow, achievement, and failure. Yet these issues are couched in the language and correspondence of ancient times.

841. "The Bible is in my opinion the most sublime of all books; when all others will bore me, I will always go back to it with new pleasure; and when all human consolations will be lacking, never have I vainly turned to its own."—Jean Jacques Rousseau

842. "Testament" was another word for "covenant"—meaning an agreement, contract, or pact. For Christians, the Old Testament represents the ancient covenant made between God and his people. In the New Testament, Christians believe in a new covenant with God made through the life, death, and resurrection of Jesus.

843. Written over the course of a thousand years, primarily in ancient Hebrew, the Jewish Bible is the equivalent of Christianity's Old Testament. For Jews, there is no New Testament.

844. At least half as much time elapsed between the Bible's first book and its last (with well over a thousand years between the first writing and the time of the last), as has elapsed between its last book and now. This means that you can expect writing styles to vary not just between modern books and the Bible but between the Bible books themselves.

845. The terms "Old Testament" and "New Testament" originated with the prophet Jeremiah. When he spoke about the glorious future for Israel that the prophets often spoke of, he said that God would "make a new covenant with the house of Israel." *Testament* means "covenant," and Jesus of Nazareth, the long-awaited Messiah, made a new covenant with God's people. The books of the New Testament provide the fulfillment of the promises made throughout the Old Testament books.

846. The translation of the Hebrew Scriptures into the *koine* Greek dialect was an outstanding literary accomplishment under the Ptolemies. This translation was called the *Septuagint*. The translation project is said to have been sponsored by Ptolemy II Philadelphus around the third century BC. According to tradition, seventy-two Jewish scholars (six from each tribe) were summoned for the project. The work was finished in seventy-two days; the Jewish scholars were then sent away with many gifts.

847. The Septuagint provided a bridge between the thoughts and vocabulary of the Old and New Testaments. The language of the New Testament is not the *koine* of the everyday Greek but the *koine* of the Jew living in Greek surroundings. By the New Testament era, it was the most widely used edition of the Old Testament.

848. Most Jews of Jesus' day spoke Aramaic, a Syrian language similar to Hebrew that was commonly used at the time. Jesus surely studied the formal Hebrew of the Torah, Prophets, and Writings. Whether he could also speak Greek is unknown. Jesus left no personal writings.

849. Both the Jewish Bible and Christian Old Testament contain the same thirty-nine books, although they are arranged and numbered in a slightly different order. In Jewish traditions, their Bible is called the *Tanakh*, an acronym of the Hebrew words *Torah* (for "law" or "teaching"), *Nevi'im* ("the Prophets"), and *Kethuvim* ("the Writings").

850. The Canon of Scripture is the complete and divine revelation of God, authoritative and binding in relation to the Christian faith and its practice. Since the Canon was closed (that is, all the inspired books were written for our edification), no books are to be added to it or taken away from it.

851. The word *canon* is an English version of the Greek word *kanon*, which in turn was borrowed from the Hebrew word *qaneh*, which means "measuring rod." The word came to mean "norm" or "rule," and evolved into the catalog or list of books we consider sacred.

852. It is sometimes assumed that the "canonization" of a book of Scripture meant that the Jewish nation or the Christian church "gave" authority to it. Instead, to canonize a book meant that Israel or the church recognized the authority of a book was already evident and ought to be recognized as such.

853. The two qualities of canonicity, as defined by the early church, were (1) that the teaching of a book was, in some unique sense, clearly divine; and (2) that the leadership of the church ascribed authority to it for all members.

854. The fact that the Books of the Law were recognized as being part of the Old Testament Canon is evident in that the tables of the Law were preserved in the ark of the covenant; the Book of the Law was kept by the side of the ark as a witness for God (see Deut. 31:24–26); and when the temple was renewed in the days of Josiah, the Scriptures were found hidden in the house of the Lord.

855. Moses commanded the people that the Books of the Law were to be read aloud to the people every seven years. The entire nation of Israel was to gather together so that every man, woman, and child would hear the Scriptures and be reminded of all God had done for them. (For details, see Deut. 31:10–13.)

856. The importance of the Old Testament law is made clear in 2 Chronicles 17:9, when the people were all urged to "obey" them. The king was to keep a copy by his side, to help guide his decisions. The Scriptures make it clear that the capture of Israel and Judah was caused by the people disobeying God's plain Word.

857. The New Testament Canon was formally recognized at the Third Council of Carthage in AD 397, but Christian churches had long before realized that some books stood on a plane of authority not shared by other books. The people were given spiritual discernment to enable them to determine the false books from the true.

858. The credibility of the Scriptures is evidenced by a comparison of facts. Nothing in the Bible is clearly contradictory to well-established facts of science. Archaeology has proven that the people, places, and events described in the Bible are found exactly where Scripture locates them. Facts about history, chronology, and ethnology are in complete harmony with the evidence of archaeology and historical records.

859. The Old Testament's first five books, the Pentateuch, were already considered authoritative Scripture by the time of Ezra in the fifth century BC. The other books were recognized into the Old Testament at later times.

860. Jesus himself knew the "old covenant." As a Jewish boy, he diligently studied the Torah, Prophets, and Writings. He could cite them by heart when he was twelve. Because there was no Bible as we know it, he would have learned by rote from scrolls kept by local teachers or "rabbis."

861. The earliest references to the Old Testament were "the Law of Moses," "the Law of the Lord," or simply "Moses." Since the additional writings were considered the work of prophets, the common term came to be "Moses and the Prophets" or something similar. Note: wherever the word "law" is seen, the Jewish reference would be "torah." By New Testament times, "Scripture" or "the Scriptures" became common. The simplest generic term for the collection was Writings, often with "sacred" or "holy" added.

862. The uniformity of Bible printing sometimes obscures the scope of variety within the Bible's writings. If Bible printers laid out the print with all the different styles accounted for, a wheelbarrow would be needed to move a Bible from the den to the bedroom.

863. No Bible writer whom we know of ever drew a map to accompany his writing—at least not one that managed to get preserved. Maps are drawn from facts discovered through historical and archaeological research.

25

Interesting Ideas

864. The followers of the Astara religion teach that the Holy Spirit is the *Nahd*, or "holy sound current." In this role, they claim the Spirit presents "no creeds, dogmas, nor precepts which bind the mind in any way." In other words, every religion is right, no matter what dumb thing they proclaim!

865. Baha'i reject God as completely unknowable, regardless of what he has done in history. However, their founder, a man who called himself "Baha'u'llah," is more or less a divine figure. He once wrote, "Verily if I declare the right to be left, or the south to be north, it is true and there is no doubt therein." He also decreed, in his "secret" writings, that he discovered "the Greatest name is Baha'u'llah."

866. The religion of Buddhism is interesting in that it was originally atheistic, rejecting the reality of God, but later became polytheistic, claiming there are thousands of gods. Rejecting Jesus because they do not believe in a Savior (or even a need for salvation), they claim that this world is nothing more than an illusion, created in the minds of individuals.

867. Edgar Cayce, an influential mystic of the early 1900s, claimed to go into trances in which he received "the akashic records"—which is to say, purported wisdom from otherworldly beings. One of those tidbits of information was that the members of the Trinity are actually "Time, Space, and Patience."

868. The Christadelphian church got started the way most cults do—a man went into his barn with a Bible and came out six months later, claiming to have found the "new truth." Christadelphians superficially reject the Trinity because "the word does not appear in the Bible." However, *many* words that are true don't appear in Scripture (including "monotheism").

869. Mary Baker Eddy, a spirit medium who founded the Christian Science church, wrote, "We have no more proof of human sin . . . than we have that the earth's surface is flat and her motions imaginary." Claiming that man is god, death nonexistent, and Satan a myth, Baker (who loved wordplay) thought it significant that "God" and "good" contained the same letters. She said nothing about the fact that "God" and "dog" do also.

870. The Free Communion Church follows the writings of Franklin Jones, who refers to himself as "Da Free John," and claims to disseminate "the Way of Divine Ignorance." He is on record as calling himself God, arguing that all existence is garbage, and for sayings such as, "True wisdom is the capacity for madness."

871. The Divine Life Society is the official name of Swami Satchidananda's yoga organizations. The swami once claimed, "I am a true Christian, a true Muslim, a true Hindu, a true Buddhist, a true Sikh, and a true Parsi"—apparently unaware that at least *some* of those things are mutually exclusive. To yoga proponents, God is not a person but a state of "bliss."

872. Maharaj Ji, who broke away to start his own yoga outfit and is most famous for being pudgy and smoking marijuana with the Beatles, once quoted Scripture by saying, "Be still and know that I am God," and then adding his own flavoring: "Be still and know that *you* are god . . . for in stilling the mind is found salvation." Ji claims that "sin is forgiven by meditation."

873. Eckankar is a religion founded by Paul Twitchell, Darwin Gross, and Harold Klemp—three guys who claim to be the most recent in a six-million-year line of "living ECK masters." Depicting God as impersonal, amoral, and pantheistic, and likewise Jesus as a "son of the devil," they nevertheless claim themselves to be divine.

874. David Berg, who started the "Children of God" and refers to himself as everything from "Moses" to "King David," claimed that everything he wrote—even his papers for a business correspondence course—were inspired by God. Rejecting the Christian God as immoral, Berg once asked, "Where are God's witches? Where are His wizards? . . . They're here. It's *you!*"

875. The Holy Order of Mans, which uses everything from Tarot cards to psychic readings in order to find "wisdom," claims that Jesus Christ was an extremely advanced mystic who must have attained perfection. In recent years, one group has broken away and embraced biblical Christianity; another has moved into the Eastern Orthodox Church, renamed themselves "Christ the Savior Brotherhood," and made claims that the increasing interest in psychic stuff will herald the second coming.

876. Est, the Forum, Lifespring, Actualizations, and Silva Mind Control are all "human potential" seminars, claiming to present secrets of unlocking your inner power. They present the typical range of quasireligious thinking (God is within you; sin is a myth; you need to develop your psychic powers). But in recent years, one former follower, Daniel Tocchini, has molded this training into a "Christian" version he calls "Momentus." It's proven popular in churches throughout (surprise!) California.

877. The Jehovah's Witnesses is a cult that teaches the second coming occurred in 1874 (later changed to 1914), but that its arrival was "invisible." They believe Jesus is a created angel who first appeared as Michael the Archangel, later morphed into Jesus of Nazareth, and now exists as an exalted Michael. Their teaching also claims that Jesus wasn't born the Christ—instead he "became" the Christ when he got baptized.

878. The Lucis Trust views God as indefinable energy, ever evolving into some sort of advanced cosmic being. Like most cults, they base their beliefs on the unique interpretations of one person (in this case, Alice Bailey), subscribe to psychic development, believe that man can become God, view sin as nothing more than ignorance, and believe that Jesus was some sort of enlightened occult initiate.

879. Mormons believe that God is nothing more than an exalted man—in fact, they claim that the God of the Old Testament was created by the sexual union of a divine mother and father, and that he is merely the God of this earth, since there are potentially an infinite number of other gods. Early Mormonism taught that God was originally Adam who fell in the Garden of Eden (which, by the way, was located in Missouri, in case you hadn't heard).

880. The Mighty I AM, a small "Christian" cult, believes that God is "Saint Germain." They also list "Guy Ballard" as equal to Jesus in being an ascended master . . . Guy Ballard being the pen name of Godfre Ray King, who started the group.

881. Like most New Age groups, the New Thought Church rejects the personal God of the Bible in order to proclaim an impersonal "Universal Law" that is the essence of God. They view Jesus as a great man who realized his potential and oneness with God, and point to that as their hope that all men have a piece of the Almighty residing within them.

882. The "Jesus only" groups, particularly the members of the United Pentecostal Church, deny the Trinity as a "doctrine of demons." They baptize and pray "in the name of Jesus only," claiming that Matthew 28:19 demands believers to do so in "one name" (and conveniently ignoring the words of Christ himself). They reject the biblical account of Christ's preexistence and incarnation, insist on interpreting the Bible only through their own literature, and deny the personality and deity of the Holy Spirit.

883. Bhagwan Shree Rajneesh wrote that "obedience to God is the greatest sin," insisted that "Jesus is a mental case. . . . He carries the same mind as Adolf Hitler . . ." and declared that "my ashram makes no difference between the devil and the divine."

884. Richard Alpert, who started the Hanuman Foundation and went by the religious-sounding name "Ram Dass," claimed that "God came to the United States in the form of LSD." In one of his popular books about Eastern mysticism, he noted that "Krishna, Christ, Durga, Kali—all of them [are] the same." Then he offered this insightful analysis: "Different strokes for different folks."

885. "Who is Christ? He is *not* the only begotten Son of God"—the words of Ernest Holmes, founder of Religious Science. Rather than seeing Jesus as God, Holmes claimed Jesus expertly understood secret principles and thereby "became Christ conscious."

886. Rosicrucians offer a unique take on the Holy Spirit—they view him as "the Race god," who started Western thinking by pitting one race against another.

887. Those in the Ruhani Satsang hold to one of the strangest views of God in existence: they believe God is "sound" and refer to him as "the Divine Vibration."

888. The followers of Sai Baba believe him to be divine—literally the embodiment of "the second coming of Christ." This despite the fact that Baba, while claiming to make objects appear from nowhere, has been caught on tape relying on simple magic tricks to try and deceive his disciples into believing he has magical powers.

889. Scientology, trendy in Hollywood circles, was founded by science fiction writer L. Ron Hubbard. They believe people's souls have existed for eternity, that they are constantly being reincarnated, and that God is merely the term we use to refer to all life.

890. The Self-Realization Fellowship, another Buddhist-based cult, came up with a new take on the Trinity—they claim that the Father is "bliss," the Son is "universal consciousness," and the Spirit is "cosmic vibration." To get in touch with him, they use everything from mantras and yoga to channeling and divination.

891. Sikh, a form of the Hindu faith, rejects the divinity of Jesus, but at the same time claims that "god" is simply "knowing yourself." In the words of their guru, "To know thyself is to know God."

892. The Sufi Order claims to be the "original religion of God" (why God would *need* a religion isn't exactly clear). Their belief system argues that *everything* is God—every person, every action, every word, every animal, every plant. That's why one of their leaders, Meher Baba, can humbly declare, "I am God."

893. Emanuel Swedenborg (1688–1772) claimed to re-create the "one true Christian religion" when he started a church based on spiritism and talking to the dead. A brilliant scientist and inventor (Swedenborg designed airplanes and submarines more than one hundred years before their invention), he rejected orthodox teaching about God, encouraged occultic activity, and claimed humankind is "the symbol for God."

894. Helene Petrovna Blavatsky (1831–1891), the founder of Theosophy, claimed to have psychic powers and ancient wisdom given her by the gods. Her most famous spectacle was occasionally having letters flutter down from the ceiling of her home, suddenly appearing as though from another dimension. Unfortunately, the housekeeper, Emma Coulomb, later admitted to writing the letters and dropping them through a crack in the ceiling. The *Society for Psychical Research* examined Blavatsky's claims in 1884 and produced a two-hundred-page report that concluded she was a blatant fraud.

895. While the media has made a big deal about the Dalai Llama and his purported deep spirituality, the theology of Tibetan Buddhism is nontheistic—that is to say, they don't believe God exists, except as an undifferentiated and impersonal "universal mind."

896. UFOlogists (those who believe in UFOs) have generally formed their own unique theology in recent years. According to their belief system, visitors from other planets are abducting people and (even though these visitors are supposedly extremely creative and intelligent) drawing designs in crop fields. The theology is almost always the same: an impersonal God exists; Jesus was a great man but isn't God; humankind is basically good and has limitless potential; and creatures from space need to bring us wisdom and salvation because current religion doesn't contain the truth.

897. Sun Moon, the founder of the Unification Church, is famous for saying inanities such as, "As soon as a person believes in Jesus, Satan can invade his body" and "Your green bills are crying; if you want to make them happy, give them to the Father" (i.e., "hand over your money to me"). He views God as a being who has trouble controlling his own emotions, and who is dependent on man for his well-being. However, one of his most unique ideas is that the Holy Spirit is a woman.

898. The Unitarian Universalist Church is probably best known for allowing its members to accept (or reject) almost any belief system. But Jack Mendelsohn, an influential UU writer in the 1960s, noted that the God of the Bible is "a brutal deity . . . a monstrous being" and referred to the Lord as "demented."

899. Victor Paul Wierwille, who founded "the Way International" and takes out advertisements in college newspapers promising "personal power, success, health, and happiness" to those who join his cult, not only argues that Jesus was merely a man, but denies the virgin birth and claims that Christ was sent as the "replacement" for Lucifer!

Concepts and Doctrine

26

900. The Heidelberg Catechism was written in Germany at the request of the pious Christian Prince Frederick III, who ruled Heidelberg from 1559 to 1576. The prince asked two men, Zacharius Ursinus and Caspar Olevianus, to prepare a document that would instruct the youth and guide pastors and teachers as to the teachings of the Christian faith. Both men were under thirty years of age when the request was made, yet both were well versed in theology, Ursinus serving as a professor of theology at Heidelberg University and Olevianus acting as the prince's pastor.

901. A catechism is a summary of the principles of Christianity given in a question-and-answer format. The statements use Bible texts as proof of their truth. The idea was (and remains) that listeners were to take to heart and memory the statements of their faith and beliefs. The Heidelberg Catechism was first published in 1563 but went on to be published again (in German and Latin) with new additions that same year. The entire document was divided into fifty-two individual sections shortly after publication in order that one section of the catechism could be explained each week of the year, enabling a church to cover the catechism consistently.

902. Perhaps one of the most poignant statements of God's existence can be found in the first question of the Heidelberg Catechism: "What is your only comfort in life and in death?" The answer: "That I am not my own, but belong—body and soul, in life and in death—to my faithful Savior Jesus Christ. He has fully paid for all my sins with his precious blood, and has set me free from the tyranny of the devil. He also watches over me in such a way that not a hair can fall from my head without the will of my Father in heaven: in fact, all things must work together for my salvation. Because I belong to him, Christ, by his Holy Spirit, assures me of eternal life and makes me whole-heartedly willing and ready from now on to live for him."

903. Another catechism, the Westminster Catechism, came out of the request of the Westminster Assembly, which was assembled by the English parliament in 1643. The purpose was very similar to that of the Heidelberg Catechism—to educate the people sitting in the churches in a forthright manner about the principles of their faith. Two versions of this document emerged, the first in 1647 and the longer version a year later—a larger form for pulpit exposition. The first one remains in use today in many churches. It is loved by many for its direct focus and the ease in memorizing it over the larger form. The larger one has fallen into disuse.

904. The Westminster Catechism is structured on a two-part system: (1) What we are to believe concerning God, and (2) what duty God requires of us. The first part explains the basic teaching on God's nature as well as his creative and redemptive work. The second section covers the Ten Commandments, the doctrines of faith and repentance, the means of grace (reading the Word, celebrating the sacraments, prayer), and an explanation of the Lord's Supper.

905. The first question of the Westminster Shorter Catechism reads: "What is the chief end of man?" The answer: "The chief end of man is to glorify God and to enjoy Him forever."

906. Salvation is by grace. The most unique concept in the Christian faith is the fact that we do not *earn* our salvation by our good works. In fact, our good works contribute nothing to our standing with God. Instead salvation is a free gift from God, given to those who choose to follow him.

907. "Original sin" means "sinful from one's origin." Essentially Christians believe that we are born sinful and therefore incapable of becoming cleansed from our sins of our own abilities. Though this phrase is not mentioned in the Bible, Paul speaks of it somewhat in Romans. Original sin is a part of our human condition that can only be helped by the intercessory work of Jesus Christ. This idea originated with the first person ever placed on earth—Adam. Adam disobeyed God, an act that alienated him from God and caused all of his offspring to inherit his spiritual condition.

908. We were made in the "image of God." Even though we are all bound by original sin, we were made spiritually to resemble God. Through Christ's atoning work, a person can have a restored relationship with God, and through the Holy Spirit, we can put on the new person God has made us to be, resembling God more than ever before.

909. The idea of election is clear in Matthew 22, John 6, and Ephesians 1, as well as other places in the Bible. The Scripture teaches that certain individuals are given an inward experience through the Holy Spirit, imparting a sense of personal sin and inclining them toward repentance and faith in Jesus Christ. At the same time, *everyone* is invited to participate in the life of God, and his mercy is demonstrated to all. We are condemned as sinners, but the sovereign Lord shows leniency to some.

910. Atonement means to bring two distinct, individual things together in order to make them connect into one. In the Old Testament, the Israelites constantly offered sacrifices in order to "reconnect" with

God as a result of their sins. In the New Testament, Christ came in order to be the final sacrifice for all people's sins. His death on the cross is often referred to as "*the* atonement" since it is the only sacrifice that completely and finally reconciles humanity with God.

911. Justification means "to make valid" or "to right," bringing righteousness. Because Jesus was a perfect man and completely without sin, those who believe in him and repent of their sins can be made righteous in God's sight. Becoming righteous is a free gift of God; with it a person is covered with Christ's atoning work so that the penalty for their sins is removed.

912. Sanctification means to "make holy." This is a work of the Holy Spirit within us after a Christian has been justified. Sanctification is the putting on of the new person that a believer has become as a result of believing in Jesus Christ and having faith in his atoning work. Sincere Christians want to stop sinning, to become more like Christ in their daily work and life. The Holy Spirit who now lives in them helps new believers to do this.

913. Covenants are a very important aspect to keep in mind when reading the Bible. A covenant is an "agreement between two or more parties." The Bible is especially about those covenants made between God and man. The agreements were formal and were a demonstration of God's continued faithfulness to those with whom he made the agreements.

914. The rainbow was a sign of the first covenant God made with his people. Noah and his family were the only ones to survive the flood; God told them he would never again cause such a flood to happen. The sign of his promise was the rainbow. Man wasn't required to do anything—it was a promise of God to all creation that he would spare humankind from a worldwide flood.

915. The circumcision covenant made between Abraham and God directly affected all the male descendants of Abraham, who was considered the father of the Israelites (Genesis 17). All were required to undergo the surgical procedure. Those males who did not become circumcised were considered outsiders of the covenant and were banished from their people. Circumcision was a sign that the Israelites were God's special people, "the people of the covenant."

916. When the Israelites reached Mount Sinai on their way to Canaan (after leaving Egypt), Moses gave them the laws that had been given to him by God. The people were brought into the Sinai Covenant at this time: If they would obey the laws of God, he would bless them and settle his people in the land of Canaan. However, if they disobeyed, they would suffer the consequences. The law Moses gave the people included a system of sacrifices they were to use in order to show their repentance of sins. God did not expect perfection of his people, only obedient hearts who were willing to follow him.

917. Another covenant was made with the Israelites after they were carried into exile in Babylon as a result of breaking the Sinai Covenant. This new covenant was prophesied by Jeremiah and stated that God would put his law into the people's hearts and minds so that they would want to serve him. The people thus would obey God and want to please him, and God would continue to love the Israelites and take care of them (Jer. 31:33).

918. The New Covenant was made when Christ died and became the atoning sacrifice for all who choose to repent and believe. As Jesus himself states, the old covenant was no longer applicable: "This is my blood of the new covenant, which is shed for many" (Mark 14:24 NKJV). Christ's death was the ultimate sacrifice and did away with the old system of law God had given to his people at Sinai.

919. Baptism is one of two sacraments or ordinances of the Christian church. It is the act of using water to demonstrate a person's cleansing from sin by Jesus Christ's atoning work. It is a symbol of one's being "signed and sealed" in the forgiveness of Jesus Christ and follows God's covenant of the Old Testament regarding circumcision. As baptized Christians, we are designated God's people. Some people believe in infant baptism, while others believe a person should be old enough to make a conscious decision about this practice. Baptism is purely a symbol—people are not made into Christians by its practice.

920. The Lord's Supper, or communion, is the other sacrament of the Christian church. Christians come together in their church services and celebrate communion as a reminder of Jesus' Last

Supper. Partaking of the wine and bread, which is what Jesus partook of in the upper room with his disciples the night he was betrayed, is a symbol of our sharing in Christ's suffering. Jesus told his disciples when he ate those elements, "This is my body (my blood), which is given for you, do this in remembrance of me." Jesus' atoning work on the cross as a sacrifice for our sins is the reason we may have forgiveness; the church celebrates the Lord's Supper in memory of it.

921. The body of Christ is the earthly church. The idea behind this metaphor is that a fellowship of believers is a living, tangible being with all different parts (people) working together to function as one unit. The apostle Paul states that Christ is the head of the body and leads it, and that "each member belongs to all the others" (Rom. 12:5).

922. Evangelism means "good news" and comes from the New Testament word *euangelion*. The "Good News" is a reference to the message of Christ's redemptive work for our sins. Sharing this message with others was a direct result of Christ's instruction to his disciples: the Great Commission. The universal church is to share this message with those who have not heard about what Jesus did for them.

923. Excommunication is a biblical and Christian concept for dealing with those who are unrepentant, heretical, or living in a state of sin while also maintaining a profession of being a Christian. It is not a tool to be used quickly or taken lightly. Those in the church who are leaders use it as the final step in dealing with an unrepentant Christian. After an initial path of going to the person privately with the matter to seek understanding, then taking the case to the church authorities, who will also try to pray, counsel, and reason with the person, the Bible says, if they continue in unrepentance, to refuse them a place to worship. Excommunication is not an end all either. People who have been excommunicated have also come to repentance and been welcomed back with open arms by those in the church who originally cast them out. It is also not a method of shunning. Christians are not called to ignore the person should they see her or him, and all in the church are generally encouraged to pray for the person.

924. The tribulation is a period during the end times when evil will be running wild, before God triumphs over Satan. Jesus spoke of this time in the Book of Matthew: "For then shall be great tribulation, such as was not since the beginning of the world to this time, no, nor ever shall be" (24:21 KJV). This time of persecution that is spoken of in Revelation 7:14 is called the "great tribulation." Christians have taken that word and used it as a reference to this time. Some theorize that the tribulation is already underway, citing those many Christians who have died of persecution since the beginning of the church.

925. The millennium is a time period of a thousand years. In Revelation 20, the Bible speaks of a thousand-year reign of Christ on earth. During this time, Satan will be bound and unable to do any evil on earth. However, Satan will be released at some point, but then he will be defeated forever. Three main views are held by Christians regarding this time period.

926. Postmillennialism is the belief that the Christian faith is expanding, thus continually improving the world. Throughout the eighteenth and nineteenth centuries, theologians posited that the "church era" would eventually bring all things under the headship of Christ, ushering in an era of peace that would last for a thousand years.

927. Premillennialism isn't a new invention. Manuel de Lacunza, a Chilean monk in the mid-1700s, was the first modern scholar to suggest a premillennial return of Christ. Lacunza said the world would head toward destruction, but that Christ would appear and remove his faithful from the worst of it (the tribulation), before returning to establish his one-thousand-year reign. Written during a time of almost universal postmillennialism, Lacunza's words were ignored for almost two centuries.

928. Amillennialism has been around longer than either of its counterparts. The Book of Revelation is read as symbolic rather than literal, and the coming of the kingdom of God is a two-part event. The first part began when Christ came to earth and continues even now; for the amillennialist, the final things are essentially accomplished already, though not by sight but by faith. The second part will begin at his second coming. Christ is ruling on high in the present age, which is seen as being symbolic of the thousand-year reign discussed in Revelation. Evil is fully present (note Christ's parable of the wheat and the tares growing next to each other), but Christ is dominant. The kingdom of God is present through the church, but this is not a presence that is moving toward fulfillment because fulfillment will come with the glory of heaven, not with the earthly church.

929. Dispensationalism is a method of viewing the history of how God has dealt with his people, beginning with Adam in the Garden of Eden. In this theory, there are seven time periods (dispensations) in history. The seventh dispensation includes the return of Christ. Dispensationalists believe God has used varying methods to deal with humans, depending on the dispensation currently being experienced. The current time period would be the sixth dispensation, which is the age of the church. With this method comes a tendency to disregard the Old Testament (and sometimes parts of the New Testament) as being out-of-date or unapplicable as those were different periods of time and required a different approach.

930. The second coming refers to when Christ will return to earth to be with his people. Though this phrase is not used in the Bible, Jesus spoke of his return in the Gospels of Matthew and John. The New Testament authors all spoke of staying alert, of being prepared as no one knows "the day or the hour" when Christ will return.

An Eternal Purpose

27

931. The decrees of God may be defined as God's eternal purpose (in a real sense, all things are embraced in one purpose) or purposes, based on his most wise and holy counsel, whereby he ordained (appointed or predetermined) all that comes to pass. With infinite power and infinite wisdom, God has from all eternity past decided and chosen and determined the course of all events.

932. His decrees . . .

reveal God's eternal purpose;
are based on his most wise and holy counsel;

originate in his freedom;
are a result of his omnipotent desires;
have as their end his glory; and
embrace all that comes to pass.

933. The two kinds of decrees. There are things that God purposes through his power to bring about; there are other things that he merely determines to permit (Rom. 8:28). But even in the case of the permissive decrees, God rules over all things for his glory (Matt. 18:7; Acts 2:23).

934. Proof of the decrees. The events in the universe are neither a surprise nor a disappointment to God, nor the result of his impulsive or random will. Instead they are the outworking of a definite purpose and plan of God as taught in Scripture: The Lord of hosts has sworn, saying, "Surely, just as I have intended so it has happened, and just as I have planned so it will stand, . . . For the LORD of hosts has planned, and who can frustrate it? And as for His stretched-out hand, who can turn it back?" (Isa. 14:24, 27 NASB).

935. Reasons for God's actions. Why was God not content to confine his fellowship and activity to the Trinity? We are assured that God always has reasons for his actions (Deut. 29:29). "Later you will understand" (John 13:7) is encouraging in that we will someday understand the meaning of certain puzzling Scriptures and the mysteries of certain perplexing acts of God.

936. The highest aim of the decrees is the glory of God. Creation glorifies him. David says, "The heavens declare the glory of God; the skies proclaim the work of his hands" (Ps. 19:1). When God declares that he will refine Israel in the furnace of affliction, he adds, "For my own sake, for my own sake, I do this. How can I let myself be defamed? I will not yield my glory to another" (Isa. 48:11).

937. Seeking glory. For humanity to seek glory would be selfishness, but that is because we are sinful and imperfect. To seek for such glory would be to seek to glorify sinfulness and imperfection. But this is not the case with God. He is absolutely sinless and perfect in holiness. For him to aim at his own glory is, therefore, merely to seek the glory of absolute holiness and sinless perfection. There is no one and nothing higher to glorify. We must aim in everything to glorify him who is the manifestation of all goodness, purity, wisdom, and truth.

938. God has decreed all that has come to pass in the material and physical realm, in the moral and spiritual realm, and in the social and political realm.

939. God decreed to create the universe and humankind. He decreed to establish the earth. He also decreed never again to destroy the population of the earth by means of a universal flood. He distributed the nations, appointed their seasons, and set the bounds of their habitation. He also decreed the length of human life and the manner of our exit from this life. All the other events in the material and physical realm have likewise been decreed and are in God's plan and purpose.

940. God's decrees in the moral and spiritual realm leave us with two basic problems: the existence of evil in the world and the freedom of humanity. How can a holy God allow moral evil, and how can a sovereign God permit man to be free?

941. God determined to permit sin. Though God is not the author of sin (James 1:13–14), and didn't necessitate it, he did, on the basis of his wise and holy counsel, decree to permit the fall and sin to come. God did this in light of what he knew would be the nature of sin, of what he knew sin would do to his creation. And he knew all that would have to be done to redeem humanity from their sin. God could have prevented it, but he chose instead to gift his creatures—angels and mankind—with a free will. "In the generations gone by He permitted all the nations to go their own ways" (Acts 14:16 NASB).

942. He determined to overrule sin for good. This determination is inseparable from the one to permit sin. But God is sovereign, holy, and wise and he cannot permit sin to thwart his purposes. It must be overruled for good. Joseph said to his brothers, "You meant evil against me, but God meant it for good in order to bring about this present result, to preserve many people alive" (Gen. 50:20 NASB). The psalmist said, "The Lord foils the plans of the nations; he thwarts the purposes of the peoples. But the plans of the L ORD stand firm forever, the purposes of his heart through all generations" (Ps. 33:10–11).

943. God determined to save mankind from sin. All Christians are agreed that God has decreed to save humanity, but not all are agreed as to *how* he does so. We must remember that (1) God must take the initiative in salvation, (2) humanity, even in our present helpless state, is responsible, and (3) God's decrees are not based on random or arbitrary decisions but rather on his wise and holy counsel. Some see election as dependent upon divine foreknowledge; others see election and foreknowledge, as they relate to saving faith, as essentially inseparable.

944. The "plan of God" or the "will of God" refers not only to all events in history, but all human actions, all the affairs of nations, and even the period of human life. Each man's and woman's birth, death, and salvation are part of God's plan.

945. God "calls" or "invites" all to know him. Some believe that God has called only the elect to know him. Others believe there is a general invitation for all people to be saved, and it is given through the Word of God. That said, it is understood that not all people will be saved.

946. God determined to reward his servants and to punish the disobedient. Although God is active and demonstrates grace to both believers and unbelievers, he does promise to care for his children and to never forget them. That cannot be said for the disobedient who do not follow him.

947. A severe love is what distinguishes the difference between the Father giving Christ over for execution, Jesus delivering himself, and Judas betraying Christ to the authorities for thirty pieces of silver. As Augustine of Hippo once said, "What the Father and the Son did in love, Judas did in treacherous betrayal. . . . God had in mind our redemption, Judas had in mind the price for which he sold Jesus. Jesus himself, had in mind the price He gave for us. . . . Love must sometimes show itself severe."

948. God's decrees in the social and political realm include the family and the home. In the very beginning, God said, "It is not good for the man to be alone; I will make him a helper suitable for him" (Gen. 2:18). By the fact that God made one man and only one woman, he indicated that marriage was to be monogamous and indissoluble (Matt. 19:3–9). All through the Scriptures, the sanctity of marriage is recognized. The decree of marriage implies the decree to have and to establish a home.

949. The decree of human government is closely related to that of the family. God has by decree determined the location, season, and boundaries of the nations. He has likewise ordained the rulers of the nations (Dan. 4:34–37; Rom. 13:1–7). All rulers are to recognize the sovereign rule of God and to seek to carry out his will (Ps. 2:10–12). If the ruler chooses not to and makes laws contrary to the commandments of God, the subjects are to obey God rather than the human ruler (Acts 4:19; 5:29).

950. The call and mission of Israel began when God chose Abraham to be the leader of his chosen people (Gen. 12:1–3). God then limited the bloodline after Abraham to Isaac, Jacob, and the twelve sons of Jacob. God chose Israel for himself, to make them a kingdom of priests, and a holy nation (Exod. 19:4–6). When Israel miserably failed God, the natural branches were broken off and the Gentiles, signified by branches of a wild olive tree, were grafted into the stem (Rom. 11:11–22). Someday God will graft in again the natural branches (Rom. 11:23–27).

951. The founding and mission of the church came about when Jesus declared that he would build his church (Matt. 16:18), indicating that it was not yet in existence at that time. Paul declared that while the church was included in God's eternal purpose, the nature of it was not fully revealed until Jesus' day (Eph. 3:1–13).

952. The final triumph of God will occur when the Father gives all the kingdoms of the world to Christ (Ps. 2:6–9; Dan. 7:13–14; Luke 1:31–33; Rev. 11:15–17; 19:11–20:6). In connection with his taking over these kingdoms, there will be the "regeneration" of nature (Matt. 19:27–30; Rom. 8:19–22). His rule will be characterized by peace and righteousness (Ps. 2:8–12; Isa. 9:6–7). This first phase of God's triumph on the earth will last for a period of a thousand years (Rev. 20:1–6). After Satan's final revolt and the great white throne judgment (Rev. 20:7–15) will come the new heavens, new earth, and the New Jerusalem (Rev. 21:1–22:5). Then Christ will deliver up the kingdom of God, even the Father; and the Triune God—Father, Son, and Holy Spirit—will reign forever and ever (1 Cor. 15:23–28). All of these things were decreed by God and will come to pass.

953. The core of God's plan is to rescue us from sin. Our pain, poverty, and broken hearts are not his ultimate focus. . . . God cares most about teaching us to hate our sins, grow up spiritually, and love him. People's illnesses weren't Jesus' focus—the gospel was. His miracles were a backdrop, a visual aid, to his urgent message. Jesus' message was: Sin will kill you, hell is real, God is merciful, his kingdom will change you, and I am your passport.

How Can We Find Him?

28

954. Having faith in God is the first step to understanding him. We must believe he exists before we can go any further. The first four words of Genesis make it clear that God was in the beginning: "In the beginning God. . . ."

955. There must also be a belief that God can be known—that he can be found—in order to have faith in him. As described later, two kinds of revelation make this possible, general and special revelation. Romans 1:19–20 says, "What may be known about God is plain to them, because God has made it plain to them. For since the creation of the world God's invisible qualities—his eternal power and divine nature—have been clearly seen, being understood from what has been made, so that men are without excuse."

956. There must be a belief in the rationality of God. This is not to say that we believe it is possible to understand exactly why God does things the way he does; God is a deity and far beyond the knowledge of man. However, from the Bible and from God's promises, we can know that he acts for our greater good and honors his covenants. He is an orderly God, a knowledgeable God, a God of reason.

957. A final necessity for finding faith in God is the need to believe in the character of God. A biblical faith rests on the philosophy that God is sovereign, omnipresent, loving, just, righteous, and unchanging from age to age. We know God to be faithful to us by his continual care for his people and by how he has accepted us after we repent of our sins.

958. Revelation is the act of God whereby he discloses himself, or communicates truth to the mind, of things that could not be known in any other way. Theologians often refer to two different types of God's revelation: general and special.

959. God is revealed in nature. The earth reveals that there is a God and that he has such attributes as power, glory, divinity, and goodness. General revelation draws humanity to search for a fuller revelation of God and his plan of salvation. The psalmists, prophets, and apostles expressed the revelation of God through nature (Job 12:7–9; Ps. 8:1–3; 19:1–3; Isa. 40:12–14, 26; Acts 14:15–17; Rom. 1:19–20).

960. God is revealed in conscience. The human conscience judges whether an action or attitude is in harmony with our moral standard, and urges us to make the right choice. The presence in humanity of this sense of right and wrong reveals the existence of God. The conscience is the reflection of God in the soul. Just as a mirror or the smooth surface of a lake reflects the sun and reveals not only its existence but also to some extent its nature, so conscience in man reveals both the existence of God and, to some extent, the nature of God.

961. God is revealed in history. The Christian finds a revelation of God's power and providence throughout ancient and recent history. The apostle Paul declares that God has "made from one man every nation of mankind to live on all the face of the earth, having determined their appointed times and the boundaries of their habitation, that they would seek God, if perhaps they might grope for Him and find Him" (Acts 17:26–27 NASB). History became, in Bonhoeffer's phrase, "the womb of the birth of God."

962. God personally appeared to the patriarchs, making himself and his will known in dreams and visions, and communicating his message directly to them. At a time when the whole world had sunk into polytheism and pantheism, Abraham, Isaac, Jacob, and their descendants came to know God as a personal, infinite, holy, and self-revealing God (see Josh. 24:2).

963. General revelation is the term used to describe the evidence of God as seen in the world. According to Psalm 19, "The heavens declare the glory of God; the skies proclaim the work of his hands. Day after day they pour forth speech; night after night they display knowledge. There is no speech or language where their voice is not heard" (vv. 1–3). In other words, God's presence is evident in nature.

964. In Acts 17:22–29, the apostle Paul argues that since God made the world, he is therefore bigger than the world. Furthermore, if mankind is truly his creation, then it is obvious God is personal rather than inanimate. A personal Creator would certainly not make an impersonal being. This is the type of "general revelation" that declares the reality of God.

965. The concept of general revelation is most obvious in nature (see Rom. 1:20). John Calvin once wrote that God has so manifested "his perfections in the whole structure of the universe . . . we cannot open our eyes without being compelled to behold him" (*Institutes of the Christian Religion,* 1.5.1).

966. The concept of general revelation also takes place *within* mankind. Since man is made in God's image, being personal and having a capacity for love, creativity, and history means we cannot escape the notion that man was created by a loving, creative God. And since man has a built-in ethical inclination, the theistic implication is that man holds the truth of his origin within himself, but continually attempts to suppress this indicator of the divine so that he can become his own God. Augustine, in *Confessions* 1.1.1, wrote, "Thou has formed us for Thyself, and our hearts are restless until they find rest in Thee."

967. The result of general revelation is that man is left without excuse before God. He cannot claim he was unaware of the reality of God, since the Lord is present both within and without man. No individual can escape the knowledge of God's reality unless he or she chooses to suppress or avoid the revelation of God in creation.

968. Special revelation is the term used to describe the unique ways God has chosen to reveal himself in history. Remember that God is transcendent—he exists beyond human comprehension. If he is to be known, it must happen outside the normal path of human understanding. God, in his divine will, *chooses* to make himself known to man. The methods that he uses are termed "special revelation."

969. Special revelation includes those acts of God whereby he makes himself and his truth known at special times and to specific peoples. Yet the revelation is not necessarily intended for that time and people only. The special revelation is a treasure to be shared with the whole world, according to Matthew 28:19–20. It is given to humanity in various ways: in the form of miracles, in prophecy, in the person and life of Jesus Christ, in the Scriptures, and in personal experience.

970. Since special revelation is given to save mankind from sin, the content of special revelation is the story of our salvation. Thus the most well-known means of special revelation—the Bible—details the relationship between God and humans.

971. Sometimes special revelation occurs as historical events. For example, the salvation of the Israelites from Egypt, their survival in the wilderness, and their capture of Jericho are all examples of special revelation. Miracles are demonstrations of God's power and point to his presence in the midst of humankind.

972. Another form of special revelation is the Bible. In it, God's very words reveal the truth of history, offering descriptions of God's redemptive acts throughout the ages. The Scriptures were given in order to help mankind recognize God, better understand him, and know how to develop a healthy relationship with him.

973. The Bible uses pictures and analogies to express the relationship in the manner of a son knowing his father, a wife knowing her husband, a subject knowing his king, and a sheep knowing its shepherd. This is the biblical concept of knowing God: Those to whom he allows himself to be known are loved and cared for by him.

974. The term "inspiration," when applied to the Bible, means that the writers of each book were empowered and controlled by the Holy Spirit in the production of the Scriptures. The hand of God is evident in the fact that each book has a divine, infallible authority.

975. "Internal proof" is the term used to describe the Bible's divine origin. The fact that forty different authors from several different countries, sharing almost no mutual acquaintance, wrote sixty-six books in three different languages over the course of two thousand years, yet produced essentially one book with one clear message is strong evidence that God was behind the writing of Scripture. Though some books were historical, others prophetical, some devotional, and still others ethical, yet the writers created one unified text. Its shared thoughts about God, man, sin, eternal punishment, and the mode of salvation are all strong proofs that the book is a revelation from God.

976. Sometimes the Word of God arrives *before* events occur, declaring that something will come to pass in the future. This is prophecy—an example of God being all-knowing by revealing the truth in advance. Prophecy is generally given to declare God's glory, to warn about future events, or to point people toward the Lord.

977. The New Testament in particular is the perpetuation of God's story. The words of the Gospels reveal Jesus Christ as the only avenue to God and the perfect extension of God's spoken word.

978. Jesus Christ is the epitome of special revelation. He is the supreme event in the revelation of God's will, God's love, and God's desire to redeem humanity. Jesus is the supreme expression of special revelation as historical event, since he is the center of all history.

979. "Soteriology" is the study of salvation. The word comes from the Greek word *soteria*, which means "salvation." Someone studying salvation would explore topics such as faith, repentance, justification, and regeneration.

980. Adam's sin makes salvation by God necessary. Sin brought death to the human race, and corrupted the entire universe. As a result, man is in need of redemption. Since man cannot save himself, a special act of God was necessary in order to bring about salvation.

981. We are saved by grace through faith in Jesus Christ, according to Ephesians 2:8–9. In Old Testament times, salvation was also offered as a gracious gift of God to those who had faith—as Genesis 15:6 puts it, "Abram believed the LORD, and he credited it to him as righteousness" (see also Gal. 3:8; Titus 2:11; Heb. 4:2; and 1 Peter 1:10–11).

982. The Hebrew word for "salvation" can also be translated "health" or "rescue," so the saving work of God *rescues* us from eternal punishment.

983. Christ paid the penalty for our sins when he died on the cross. As Romans 8:1 puts it, "Therefore, there is now no condemnation for those who are in Christ Jesus."

984. The word *salvation* refers not only to the moment an individual believes in Jesus, but also to the *process* of being sanctified. That's why Paul encourages believers to "continue to work out your salvation in fear and trembling" (Phil. 2:12).

985. Salvation has a future aspect, at which time we will be permanently changed, losing our old sin nature and becoming like Jesus (Rom. 8:22–23).

986. While salvation is given by faith, rather than by our works (see Rom. 3:28), our new life should manifest itself through good works (see James 2:22–24). As Paul put it in Ephesians 2:8–10, "For it is by grace you have been saved, through faith—and this not from yourselves, it is the gift of God—not by works, so that no one can boast. For we are God's workmanship, created in Christ Jesus to do good works."

987. Some critics have argued that Paul and James disagree with each other, since Paul focused on salvation by grace and James writes about the importance of works. However, a careful reading reveals that the two authors are exploring two different aspects of the faith. Paul presents God's view: we are saved by grace through faith. James presents the view from our perspective: true faith will demonstrate itself through good works.

988. The word *repentance* means literally "to change directions." Believers in Christ were once headed their own way but are now headed toward the Lord.

989. The word *justification* is a judicial term in which an individual is declared innocent by a judge. Since man is the sinner, God is the Judge. Although man is sinful and therefore guilty before God, in the case of the believer Christ's death on the cross is presented as the full payment for sin—thereby allowing the Judge to declare those under Christ's control as innocent.

990. *Sanctification* means to be "set apart" for something sacred. Believers in Jesus are *sanctified*—that is, they have been set apart from the evil in the world, for the purpose of having their lives point others to God (John 17:19–21).

991. Believers in Jesus are "adopted" into the family of God. That's why Jesus could call his disciples "brothers," and why the apostle John could declare, "How great is the love the Father has lavished on us, that we should be called children of God! And that is what we are!" (1 John 3:1).

992. Adoption was a Jewish custom that occurred when a child reached the age of twelve. At that time, the father would publicly declare he was "adopting" his natural-born son. In doing so, the father was declaring that the son was responsible for his own actions. God's "adoption" of believers is therefore a way of noting that his children are responsible to demonstrate their Father's character—in the words of Romans 8:29, "to be conformed to the likeness of his Son."

993. The blessings of salvation include forgiveness of sin, adoption as God's child, access to God, victory over sin, peace in our current world, and the future promise of eternity in heaven. Becoming a child of God is a process laid out in the Bible that remains true today.

994. A. W. Tozer gives seven steps for coming to a saving knowledge of God in his book *The Knowledge of the Holy*. As he says in preface to these, "As sunlight falls free on the open field, so the knowledge of the holy God is a free gift to men who are open to receive it. But this knowledge is difficult because there are conditions to be met and the obstinate nature of fallen man does not take kindly to them."

995. Step 1: Becoming a child of God requires us to forsake our sins. Our sin keeps us from a relationship with a holy, perfect God who is without sin. Jesus made reference to the need to be free of sin in order to be closer to God when he said, "Blessed are the pure in heart; for they will see God" (Matt. 5:8). There must be repentance and an acknowledgment of our complete inability to save ourselves. We must be "justified."

996. Step 2: After we have turned from our sins, there is a need to make a complete committal of our lives to Christ. Through a faith in him, we must "believe in Christ." Such a commitment requires both a personal, spiritual attachment to our Savior as well as an active intent to obey God in all matters.

997. Step 3: We must undergo this turning from our sin to the point that we die to sin and become alive to Jesus Christ. Furthermore, we must open our heart, soul, mind, and strength to the Holy Spirit, who will uphold us and comfort us as we begin growing in our faith. This process is called "sanctification."

998. Step 4: As we turn from sin, we must also turn from the fallen world that used to be our comfort. We must live lives dedicated to God that are absent of idolatry for what the world has to offer. Our lives should reflect a new commitment—a new focus.

999. Step 5: We must spend time in prayer and worship of God. God can be known in greater detail through communion with him, through study of his Word, and through reflection on his creation. Our personal relationship with God requires us to want to seek to know him more and more in order to continue to grow in him. The more we know him, the more we are likely to seek his will for our lives.

1000. Step 6: As we grow in our knowledge of God, we should have a greater desire to serve others as Christ taught us to. A natural response to God revealing himself to us includes demonstrating that knowledge in the way we live. Through greater knowledge of his abundant love and mercy, believers will automatically share that which has been given freely to them to others through kindness and love to our fellowmen. As Tozer states: "The God who gave all *to* us will continue to give all *through* us as we come to know Him better."

1001. Step 7: The final step breaks away from the pattern of the previous six. These dealt more with the personal relationship we have with God; the last step involves purposefully sharing this wonderful gift of God through active involvement in his church. Our light should be evident to all, but especially to our fellow believers in the Christian community.

Part **2**

THE
BIBLE

Introduction

It's the best-selling book of all time—a volume that has changed the course of history, affected the lives of millions, and made all of us stop and think. Christian martyrs have died for reading this precious volume. It's been hidden, suppressed, and exalted through the ages. Though the authors lived thousands of years apart and included kings, shepherds, prophets, humble fishermen, and well-educated apostles, this book speaks to *every* person.

The Bible also holds the key to the most famous person the world has ever seen or known—Jesus Christ. It tells us where we came from and directs us where we may ultimately go. Why do we read this book? *To know God.* To meet him, commune with him, and find peace with him. Along the way, we discover amazing prophecies, inspiring stories, and truly horrible happenings that changed history forever.

Part 2 of this book illuminates the many characters, events, and exciting facts about the most influential book ever written in the history of the world. This collection is not made up of the 1001 "most important" facts, the 1001 "best" facts, or even the 1001 "most necessary for a complete education" facts. Rather we have picked what is unique, unfamiliar, and might not be included in a scholarly examination of the Bible . . . yet what is indeed still a part of it. All 1001 facts were checked and considered, but this isn't what you might consider a "researched" volume. Instead it's fun. And true.

No book about the Bible will ever be a substitute for the original, inspired Word of God. So we pray *this* book will be used and enjoyed for its information, but that the Bible's authority will always remain primary in your life.

About the Bible

29

1002. The Bible. Christians believe this book to be the true Word of God. From the creation account of Genesis to the end-time visions of Revelation, from the story of Israel to Jesus' ministry, it is the source for what Christians believe and how they try to live.

1003. The word *Bible* comes from the Greek word *biblia*, which means "books," which comes from another word, *byblos*, meaning papyrus, a material books were made from in ancient times.

1004. The ancient Greeks obtained their supplies of paper from the port of Byblos, in what is now Lebanon. Their word for book—*biblion* (the singular form of *biblia*)—was derived from the name of this port, and from this we get our English word Bible, meaning the Book of books.

1005. The word *Bible* **is not in the Bible.** The term came long after all the writings were completed and assembled.

1006. The Bible is the world's best-selling book as well as the world's most shoplifted book!

1007. The Bible is the most bought yet least understood book. Nine out of ten Americans own a Bible, but fewer than half ever read it. Worldwide sales of the Bible are uncountable.

1008. Just how big is the Bible? Stack ten average-sized nonfiction books printed today. That pile will contain the same number of words that are found in one Bible—close to one million words not counting the number of words in features like footnotes, verse numbers, and concordances.

1009. The Bible looks like one book, but it is actually an anthology, a collection of many smaller books. In an even broader sense, it is not just an anthology of shorter works but an entire library.

1010. Some Bible books are as short as half a page. One of the longest books—Jeremiah—is roughly the length of today's short novel. This makes the Bible's longest book one hundred times longer than its shortest book.

1011. Though the Bible as a whole is much longer than most any other book we'd like to read, its individual books are mostly shorter than any other book we consider reading.

1012. The Bible is an extraordinary gathering of many books of law, wisdom, poetry, philosophy, and history. The number of books in this portable library depends on which Bible you are holding. The Bible of a Jew is different from the Bible of a Roman Catholic, which in turn is different from the Bible of a Protestant.

1013. The Bible is both ancient and contemporary as it deals with the unchanging issues of human existence: life, death, joy, sorrow, achievement, and failure. Yet these issues are couched in the language and correspondence of ancient times.

1014. *Testament* was another word for "covenant"—meaning an agreement, contract, or pact. For Christians, the Old Testament represents the ancient covenant made between God and his people. In the New Testament, Christians believe in a new covenant with God made through the life, death, and resurrection of Jesus.

1015. Written over the course of a thousand years, primarily in ancient Hebrew, the Jewish Bible is the equivalent of Christianity's Old Testament. For Jews there is no New Testament.

1016. At least half as much time elapsed between the Bible's first book and its last (with well over a thousand years between the first writing and the time of the last), as has elapsed between its last book and now. This means that writing styles vary not just between modern books and the Bible but among the Bible books themselves.

1017. The terms *Old Testament* **and** *New Testament* originated with the prophet Jeremiah. When he spoke about the glorious future for Israel of which the prophets often spoke, he said that God would "make a new covenant with the house of Israel." Testament means "covenant," and Jesus of Nazareth, the long-awaited Messiah, made a new covenant with God's people. The books of the New Testament provide the fulfillment of the promises made throughout the Old Testament books.

1018. The translation of the Hebrew Scriptures into the *koine* Greek dialect was an outstanding literary accomplishment under the Ptolemies. This translation was called the *Septuagint*. The translation project is said to have been sponsored by Ptolemy II Philadelphus around the third century BC. According to tradition, seventy-two Jewish scholars (six from each of the twelve tribes) were summoned for the project. The work was finished in seventy-two days; the Jewish scholars were then sent away with many gifts.

1019. The Septuagint provided a bridge between the thoughts and vocabulary of the Old and New Testaments. The language of the New Testament is not the *koine* of the everyday Greek, but the *koine* of the Jew living in Greek surroundings. By the New Testament era, it was the most widely used edition of the Old Testament.

1020. Most Jews of Jesus' day spoke Aramaic, a Syrian language similar to Hebrew that was commonly used at the time.

Jesus surely studied the formal Hebrew of the Torah, Prophets, and Writings. Whether he could also speak Greek is unknown. Jesus left no personal writings.

1021. Both the Jewish Bible and Christian Old Testament contain the same thirty-nine books, although they are arranged and numbered in a slightly different order. In Jewish traditions the Bible is called the *Tanakh*, an acronym of the Hebrew words Torah (for "law" or "teaching"), *Nevi'im* ("the Prophets"), and *Kethuvim* ("the Writings").

1022. The Old Testament's first five books, the Pentateuch, were already considered authoritative Scripture by the time of Ezra in the fifth century BC. The other books were recognized as part of the Old Testament at later times.

1023. Jesus himself knew the "old covenant." As a Jewish boy, he diligently studied the Torah, Prophets, and Writings. He could recite them by heart when he was twelve. Because there was no Bible as we know it, he would have learned by rote from scrolls kept by local teachers or rabbis.

1024. The earliest references to the Old Testament were "the law of Moses," "the law of the Lord," or simply "Moses." Since the additional writings were considered the work of prophets, the common term became "Moses and the Prophets" or something similar. *Note: Wherever the word "law" is seen, the Jewish reference would be "Torah."* By New Testament times, "Scripture" or "the Scriptures" became common. The simplest generic term for the collection was "writings," often with "sacred" or "holy" added.

1025. The uniformity of Bible printing sometimes obscures the scope of variety within the Bible's writings. If Bible printers laid out the print with all the different styles and languages accounted for, including prose, poetry, and songs, a wheelbarrow would be needed to move a Bible from the den to the bedroom.

1026. No Bible writer we know of ever drew a map to accompany his writing—at least not one that was preserved. Maps are generally drawn from facts discovered through historical and archaeological research.

Nuts and Bolts

30

1027. Jerome (340–420) began his ascetic lifestyle as a hermit but found he needed something to occupy his mind. He took up Hebrew and eventually began teaching classes in biblical interpretation. In AD 382 he would translate the Old and New Testaments from their original languages (Hebrew and Greek) into Latin—what we call the "Vulgate."

1028. The tests of canonicity included: (1) the book had to have a history of being used in Christian worship; (2) the book had to be written by an apostle, or associated with an apostle; and (3) the book had to have evidenced power in the lives of believers.

1029. No New Testament. During the entire first century and much of the second century, there was no concept of a New Testament canon. Church fathers often quoted from sources that were familiar in tone yet different in the names of the sources. Paul's writings were the most well known and were quoted often, but they were not thought of as scriptural.

1030. The term *New Testament* was created by Tertullian around the year 200. In an attempt to move the church away from Greek and toward Latin, which had become the preferred language of scholars, Tertullian referred to the writings of the Christian church as *Novum Testamentum*—a phrase we still employ today. Interestingly Tertullian also coined the term *Trinity* to refer to the Father, Son, and Holy Spirit.

1031. A New Testament Canon was not looked upon favorably at first. In fact it was through heretical movements that the New Testament came into being as a legitimate part of the Holy Bible. Marcion was a teacher who broke away from the church in Rome. Around AD 150 he rejected the Old Testament and instead chose to accept only ten letters from Paul along with the Gospel of Luke as authoritative Christian Scripture.

1032. The Muratorian Canon is named for its discoverer, L. A. Muratori, who first published it in 1740. A fascinating look into the early church, it reveals that by the year 190, Christians had developed their own New Testament and put it alongside the Jewish Scriptures—the former the fulfillment of the latter. It contains in order: Matthew, Mark, Luke, John, Acts, 1 and 2 Corinthians, Ephesians, Philippians, Colossians, Galatians, 1 and 2 Thessalonians, Romans, Philemon, Titus, 1 and 2 Timothy, the Apocalypse of John (Revelation), the Apocalypse of Peter, and the Wisdom of Solomon.

1033. Some books of Scripture faced challenges. Christians in the West didn't like Hebrews, while those in the East opposed Revelation. Church historian Eusebius, writing in the fourth century, noted that James, 2 Peter, 2 and 3 John, Jude, and Revelation were the only books "spoken against." Martin Luther would challenge the Book of James in the sixteenth century, calling it "an epistle of straw."

1034. Accepted at last. The Eastern church accepted the New Testament as we know it in AD 367 with the 39th Paschal Letter of Athanasius, and the Western church followed suit after Pope Damascus called a synod together in Rome in 382.

1035. The allegorical method of interpretation went to extreme lengths to try to make the Old Testament into a Christian book. Origen, one of the first Christian theologians, believed that "the Scriptures were composed through the Spirit of God, and have both a meaning which is obvious and another which is hidden." He then proceeded to create all sorts of allegorical meanings to the Word of God—infuriating his critics, who felt that Origen was crafting theological implications out of thin air.

1036. We get our word *paper* from the papyrus plant—a tall weed that could be cut into strips, flattened, then woven together and dried to form sheets of paper. It is incredibly resilient, and scraps of paper with Scripture on them date back to the early second century. Writing done on sheepskin was known as "parchment."

1037. In ancient times when parchment was too expensive to possess, peasants would use fragments of pottery to write (scratch) memoranda of business transactions. Many of these have been uncovered by archaeologists, and they reveal much about ancient history. These fragments are called ostraca.

1038. The word translated "book" in your Bible is really the word for "scroll." The words of Scripture were written onto pieces of parchment or papyrus; then those pieces were glued together to form scrolls. It wasn't until the second century that the notion of "pages" was invented, when a "codex" was created by gluing several flat sheets to a wooden spine.

1039. The Bible wasn't translated into English until the seventh century AD. The translations weren't precise at that point—they read more as a paraphrasing of the original manuscripts. The copies were known as "manuscript Bibles," and few have survived.

1040. Florilegia were popular with the masses before the invention of movable type. Artists would create a collection of Bible verses and pictures, often on one particular topic, and produce them in quantities. These small booklets (which get their name from the

Latin phrase "to gather flowers") were then used to teach basic Christian doctrine to groups of people.

1041. The Glosses were Latin Bibles in which a scholar had taken a pen and written a translation into another language. This was generally done in secret because the Roman Catholic Church had banned Bibles in any language but Latin. By writing a literal translation of each word, those who did it were "glossing" or "explaining" foreign words to future readers. Their notes, written above each line of Latin type, gave rise to the expression "reading between the lines."

1042. The Lindisfarne Gospels are one such manuscript Bible that has survived. It was written in Latin around AD 700, but it has an English interlinear translation that was added into the original 250 years later.

1043. The earliest known *fragment* **of a New Testament papyrus manuscript** was recovered from the ruins of a Greek town in ancient Egypt. A mere 2-1/2 inches by 3-1/4 inches, the fragment dates from about AD 115 or 125 and contains a portion of John 18:31–33, 37–38. It is commonly called the Rylands Fragment because it is housed in the John Rylands Library of Manchester, England.

1044. The Codex Sinaiticus is the oldest copy of the complete New Testament. Housed in the British Museum in London, it contains handwritten pages bound to a spine on one side. Written in Greek, it dates from about the year AD 350.

1045. Count Constantine von Tischendorf discovered the Codex Sinaiticus at the Monastery of Saint Catherine on Mount Sinai in 1859. It was written in large Greek letters (uncials) on vellum sheets that measured fifteen by thirteen inches wide. It had been copied in the fourth century AD, making it the earliest complete copy of the New Testament in existence. Many other manuscripts were written earlier, but they were not complete copies.

1046. The Book of Kells is an illuminated manuscript—that is, a lavishly decorated, handwritten copy—of the four Gospels in Latin. Produced in Ireland, it is generally regarded as the most beautiful handcrafted book of all time.

How the Bible Reads

31

1047. More than three thousand versions of the entire Bible, or portions of it, exist in English.

1048. Chapter and verse divisions in the Bible were not determined by those who wrote the words we read. These divisions were added to the text hundreds of years after the authors died. The original writers neither planned nor anticipated these divisions.

1049. Chapter and verse numbers in the apostles' letters, for example, would appear as strange to them as the following does to us:

Dear Aunt Sue,
Chapter One
Last week we went to town and learned that . . .

1050. "Divided on horseback" was the criticism of Robert Estienne, a French publisher and convert to Protestantism who decided to number the verses in the New Testament in order to make it easier to study and memorize. While Stephen Langton had divided the text into chapters, Estienne then broke each chapter into numbered verses. According to his son, he did much of the work while on horseback—leading critics ever since to suggest the reason some verses' divisions are short and others are long was because of the bumpy ride between his office in Paris and his home in southern France.

1051. The Bible was designed more for the ear than the eye. In antiquity people passed history and genealogy from generation to generation by oral tradition—through storytelling or by reading aloud. Those who wrote the Bible did so knowing that their words would be read aloud. So puns, acrostics, and cryptograms are all used widely throughout the Hebrew Scriptures.

1052. Mgn rdng ths bk wtht vwls. Myb ftr whl y cld fll n sm f th blnks nd fgr t mst f t. Ftr ll, t's smpl nglsh. Bt nw, mgn t s prt f n ncnt lngg tht hs flln nt dss vr svrl cntrs. Tht s hw th Bbl nc pprd. Imagine reading this book without vowels. Maybe after a while you could fill in some of the blanks and figure out most of it. After all, it's simple English. But now, imagine it as part of an ancient language that has fallen into disuse over several centuries. That is how the Bible once appeared.

1053. Hieroglyphics—derived from two Greek words that mean "sacred carvings," since the signs were at first chiseled on stone—were the basic writing system in Egypt at the time of Moses. Since young Moses was educated in the Egyptian sciences and arts, he no doubt learned to read and write Egyptian hieroglyphics. About 750 pictures were used at first in hieroglyphics. At least twenty-two signs existed for various birds, such as the curved neck of the Egyptian vulture, the flat face of an owl, and the tail feathers of the pintail duck.

1054. The alphabet's origin. A few hundred years after the time of Moses, the Phoenicians invented an alphabet. They took the Egyptian syllabic signs and used each to represent a single sound. The Phoenicians and the Hebrews used only twenty-two symbols and had no letters for vowels.

1055. The alphabet quickly spread throughout the Mediterranean world colonized by the Phoenicians. About 800 BC it was transmitted to the Greeks, who improved it by adding vowels. This is the alphabet that spread to the Romans, who passed it on to us almost in its present form.

1056. The Hebrew alphabet has twenty-two letters, all of them consonants. In fact Semitic languages like Hebrew, Aramaic, and Arabic are still generally written without any vowels, although a system of dots and dashes above and below the line of writing has been added in recent times to aid in knowing what vowels are needed. Readers of classical Hebrew were and are versed in its oral traditions and provide the vowel sounds from memory.

1057. When the Old Testament writers completed their scrolls, they depended on scribes, men who patiently copied the Scriptures by hand when extra copies were needed and when the original scrolls became too worn to use any longer. By the time Jesus was born, the books of Moses had been copied and recopied over a span of more than fourteen hundred years!

1058. Before beginning his work each day, a scribe would test his reed pen by dipping it in ink and writing the word *Amalek* and then crossing it out (cf. Deut. 25:19). Then he would say, "I am writing the Torah in the name of its sanctity and the name of God in its sanctity."

1059. The scribe would read a sentence in the manuscript he was copying, repeat it aloud, and then write it. Each time he came to the name of God, he would say, "I am writing in the name of God for the holiness of his name." If he made an error in writing God's name, the scribe had to destroy the entire sheet of papyrus or vellum that he was using.

1060. After the scribe finished copying a particular book, he would count all the words and letters it contained. Then he checked this tally against the count for the manuscript that he was copying. He counted the number of times a particular word occurred in the book, and he noted the middle word and the middle letter in the book, comparing all of these with the original. By making these careful checks, he hoped to avoid any scribal errors.

1061. The Bible was written in several languages. Most of the Old Testament books are in Hebrew, but parts of Daniel are in Aramaic. The New Testament books are written in *koine* ("common") Greek, though they contain Latin, Aramaic, and Hebrew phrases.

1062. The Masoretes were a group of Jewish scholars who wanted to ensure that the Old Testament documents would not become corrupted over time. Since the Hebrew language has no vowels, they created a system of inserting "vowel points" into the text to help priests and readers know how to pronounce the words properly. Their careful work has led to almost no changes in Old Testament wording for more than a millennium. Translators today still refer to the "Masoretic" text.

1063. The Hebrew language slowly changed, as languages do, throughout the centuries after the Old Testament writers passed away. The language of Moses would seem strange to a modern Israeli, just as the language of Chaucer or even Shakespeare is difficult for us to discern.

1064. The Greeks, who borrowed the basic twenty-two-letter alphabet used in Hebrew and Phoenician, added five new letters at the end of their alphabet. These five additional letters are the reason why the Greeks are credited for inventing the vowel system.

1065. Approximately two thousand years of history pass within the Bible's pages. Great empires came and went around the ancient Near East: Sumer, Akkadia, Babylon, Egypt, Assyria, Persia, and Greece. Along with those rising and falling empires and cultures, Hebrew and Aramaic fell into disuse and were eventually replaced by Greek. Sometime around 250 BC someone decided to preserve those writings in a complete Greek translation of Hebrew Scripture.

1066. At least three or four centuries elapsed between the close of the Old Testament writings and the opening of the New Testament. This silent period is called the intertestamental period and was comparable in length to the time that the judges ruled, or about the same number of years kings ruled Israel.

32

The Missing
Part—the Apocrypha

1067. The word *apocrypha* originates from a Greek word that means "hidden." There are a number of books of Scripture that were not included in the Protestant Bible because their origins were not believed authentic. The apocrypha includes in particular the Old Testament books that are included in Roman Catholic versions of the Bible.

1068. The Greek word *apocrypha* refers to a small group of ancient writings whose "divinely inspired" status has long been the subject of debate and controversy. Some of these books may have originally been written in Hebrew but were only known to exist in their Greek versions—one of the reasons the rabbis rejected them as part of Hebrew Scripture. They were included in the Septuagint, the Greek translation of the Hebrew Bible that was used by the early Christian church.

1069. The Apocrypha was accepted as part of the Bible by Augustine in the late fourth century. Since much Roman Catholic theology is based on the writings of Augustine, Catholics accept the Apocrypha as part of the Word of God. However, neither the Jews nor Christians in Palestine ever accepted it as Scripture. Protestants during the Reformation rejected it as part of the Canon, and it does not appear in Protestant Bibles.

1070. Pseudepigrapha is the term for the many other Old and New Testament apocryphal books that have been rejected and are considered of doubtful authenticity. The apocryphal books are considered those "hidden" books of the Old Testament that are found in Roman Catholic versions, but excluded from Protestant Bibles. The following books are included.

1071. First Esdras gives the same historic account as the Books of Chronicles, Ezra, and Nehemiah. An additional story is added in, called the "Debate of the Three Youths." The story is Persian and involves King Darius and Zerubbabel, a governor.

1072. Second Esdras comes from a Hebrew source, but it has changed and expanded with various Christian additions. The book is also called "the Apocalypse of Ezra." The book explains seven different visions involving Ezra speaking on the people's behalf, salvation, Jerusalem and Rome, and a final vision concerning the sacred books Ezra is supposed to restore.

1073. Tobit is a blind Jew in captivity in Nineveh. Tobit sends his son, Tobias, to collect a debt. Tobias falls in love with his cousin, Sara, along the way and has to defeat the demon Asmodeus in order to escape death unlike Sara's seven previous bridegrooms. Raphael helps him to do this. Tobias catches a fish in the Tigris River that eventually restores his father's sight.

1074. Judith is a book about a beautiful Jewish widow of Bethulia. She plays the heroine of her book by saving her city from Nebuchadnezzar's forces. Beautiful Judith entices the general, Holofernes, into a drunken stupor after going to see him on the pretense of sharing military secrets. When he is asleep, she cuts off his head and brings it back to her city. The people pursue the fleeing enemy.

1075. Additions to Esther may be more authentic than the other books as many scholars regard these passages as true additions to the original Hebrew. Some even consider the real Book of Esther an abbreviated work. The apocryphal version includes much of the same story line as the canonical Book of Esther.

1076. Wisdom of Solomon, though named after the wisest man who ever lived, was not written by him or even about him. It is believed to have been composed originally in Greek, and there is evidence of Greek philosophy and Platonic terminology. It is a historical account of how the Jews have been helped by wisdom.

1077. Ecclesiasticus was written around 180 BC and is held in high esteem by both Jews and early Christians. It contains the sayings of Joshua ben Sira, who recommended observing the law carefully and maintaining a healthy, pious fear of God. The book also gives practical advice for daily living.

1078. Baruch may have more than one author, but it is likely that Baruch, a scribe of the prophet Jeremiah, was involved. The book offers encouragement to the Jews in light of their exile to Babylon. It serves as a historical guideline for that time period as well.

1079. Additions to Daniel comes out of the Septuagint. The book includes stories regarding falsely accused people and an even more in-depth writing of the three Christians' prayers and praises from the fiery furnace. Daniel is a prominent figure in this apocryphal book.

1080. The Prayer of Manasseh is just what the title says it is—King Manasseh's prayer to God while he was in captivity, as described in 2 Chronicles 13. God allowed him to be captured because he had worshiped idols and been an evil king. The book is thought to be Jewish in origin.

1081. First and Second Maccabees trace Jewish history between 175 and 134 BC. The books describe the hero Judas Maccabeus and his family, the Maccabees. The first book was translated from a Hebrew work in about 100 BC. The second book is thought to have been taken from a work by Jason of Cyrene, a man little is known of. The first book is thought to be more accurate, though there are discrepancies between the two.

33

The Bible
into Translation

1082. The Vulgate was written by Jerome (340–420) in AD 382. It was a translation in Latin from the original Old and New Testaments' original languages (Hebrew and Greek). The Vulgate has long been the Roman Catholic Church's authorized version.

1083. The Synod of Toulouse in 1229 forbade everyone except priests from possessing a copy of the Scriptures. At that gathering Pope Gregory IX asked Dominican friars to question suspects and prosecute heretics, making the friars a powerful force and keeping the Bible out of the hands of laypeople.

1084. John Wycliffe (ca. 1328–1384) was a reformer who wanted to make the Christian Scriptures accessible to common people. In the Middle Ages it was common for only officials in the church to be able to read or even have access to the Scriptures. Wycliffe's work is considered the most historically significant in the effort to make the Bible available to all people.

1085. The Wycliffe Bible was translated from the Vulgate Bible into English by John Wycliffe in 1384. The Vulgate Bible was a Latin translation composed by Jerome. The Catholic church denounced Wycliffe as heretical for doing this as it was a forbidden act to translate the Bible into English at that time.

1086. The invention of movable type by Johannes Gutenberg was recently hailed as the most important technical advancement of the last millennium. Gutenberg, a printer in Mainz, found a way to make many copies of a page by using letters made of lead. By 1456 he and his fellow printers had created nearly two hundred copies of Jerome's Vulgate Bible. Prior to that time, all books were hand printed on papyrus sheets or animal skin, making them expensive, time intensive, and rare. Consequently, few people could read, and even fewer owned any books. Within twenty years of Gutenberg's first printed Bible, the printers of Mainz had created more Bibles than had been produced by hand in the previous fourteen hundred years.

1087. The printing press not only allowed for the dissemination of the Scriptures but also for the spread of critical, sometimes satirical, examinations of the church's excesses. These writings fit the growing mood in Europe that the Roman church was out of touch with common people's lives.

1088. The first copy of the Gutenberg Bible took three years of constant printing to complete. It was finished in 1455. It was done in two volumes, with 1,284 pages total. Nearly two hundred original Gutenberg Bibles were printed, and forty-eight still exist.

1089. William Tyndale (ca. 1494–1536) believed the Bible should be read by everyone, not just the few who understood Latin, the language of the church. So he set out to translate the Bible into English.

1090. Accused of perverting the Scriptures, Tyndale was forced to leave England, and his New Testament was burned as an "untrue translation." Arrested and imprisoned as a heretic, Tyndale was executed in Antwerp by strangling. His body was then burned at the stake in October 1536. William Tyndale is now honored as the "father of the English Bible." The Tyndale New Testament was published in 1526 from the ancient Hebrew and Greek texts. This version, too, was condemned by the church.

1091. An English Bible was prepared by Miles Coverdale at the same time the Tyndale Bible was being written. The English Bible was published in 1535, though it was translated by a man who was not versed in Hebrew or Greek. Coverdale drew from the Vulgate, some early German versions, and partly from the Tyndale Bible. This was the first Bible that placed the Apocrypha in a separate section, under the title of "noncanonical."

1092. The Matthew Bible was published in 1537 as an English Bible. It claimed to be "truly and purely translated into English by Thomas Matthew." In fact John Rogers wrote the Bible, which was a compilation of the English Bible and the Tyndale Bible.

1093. The Taverner Bible was written just two years after Coverdale finished the English Bible. In reality it was only a revision of the Matthew Bible.

1094. The Great Bible (1539) was the first widely popular English translation of the Scriptures to be owned and read by the common people. Produced by Miles Coverdale and John Rogers, it was based on translations from the Latin Vulgate, with additional notes from the writings of Martin Luther and Ulrich Zwingli. It was a significant improvement over the earlier Coverdale and Matthew Bibles due to its readability and understanding of poetry.

1095. The Geneva Bible (1560) was a product of the Calvinist movement in northern Europe. Rather than simply relying on Roman Catholic translations, the English exiles in Geneva created prologues to each book of Scripture, added marginal notes to aid understanding, and spent considerable time recrafting the poetic elements of the various books. One outstanding feature that the translators developed was the numbering of chapters and verses—something that not only made it a popular Bible but that has been copied by translators ever since.

1096. The Bishops' Bible appeared in 1568 at the order of the Archbishop of Canterbury, Matthew Parker. The Geneva Bible was not given official endorsement by Queen Elizabeth. As a result a new edition was started shortly after the Geneva Bible was printed.

1097. The Rheims-Douay Version was completed in 1610 by Roman Catholics who had escaped from England during Queen Elizabeth's reign. They settled in France and published the New Testament in Rheims in 1582 and the Old Testament in Douay in 1610. It is mainly a translation of the Latin Vulgate.

1098. While Gutenberg's Bible was the first printed Bible, it was done in Latin, so was limited to a scholarly audience. But in 1522 the church in Spain produced the Complutensian Polyglot, the first Bible with the Old Testament in Hebrew and the New Testament in Greek.

1099. In 1603, James VI of Scotland became King James I of England and began a program of peacemaking between hostile religious factions of Great Britain. That same year Dr. John Reynolds, the Puritan spokesman at a meeting of religious leaders at Hampton Court, proposed that a new English translation of the Bible be issued in honor of the new king. The 1768 revision is what most people now know as the King James Bible.

1100. The King James Bible, which was originally named the Authorized Version, was first suggested by the Puritans in 1604. James, who disagreed with the Calvinist leanings of the Geneva Bible, wanted a version that supported the right of kings to rule over people. He appointed fifty-four scholars, divided into eight teams, and demanded they examine all earlier English versions to aid in translation. Produced in 1611, the translation is marked by beautiful language, an accurate translation, and modesty when faced with embarrassing language and situations.

1101. The first Native American translation of the Bible, completed in 1663, was made into the language of the Algonquin tribe, whom the Puritan colonists then promptly wiped out.

1102. Stephen Langton, who was archbishop of Canterbury in the thirteenth century, created chapter divisions for the Bible. He died in 1228, and his work remains visible in the Bibles of today.

1103. The Aitken Bible was the first Bible printed in the United States. Congress authorized its publishing in 1781.

1104. The Revised Version was begun in 1870 in order to update the King James Version. The effort included both English scholars as well as American ones, and also included various denominations of believers. The English version was completed in 1885.

1105. The American Standard Version grew out of the Revised Version, which was worked on by Americans and the English. The English advisors had the decisive vote on differences in translation. The Americans agreed not to publish any editions for fourteen years. After that time period was over, the American Revision Committee produced an edition with the American preferences in 1901.

1106. The Red Letter Bible first appeared in 1928, when an American printer decided to put the direct quotations of Jesus in red ink. The idea caught on, particularly with Catholic printers, who still rely on red letters to note things of importance. The practice led directly to the phrase "red-letter day" to denote an important day in someone's life.

1107. The Revised Standard Version came out in 1952 and deserves mention because it was a modernization of the King James Version using current biblical scholarship to determine the underlying Greek and Hebrew texts.

1108. The Jerusalem Bible (1966), popular among Roman Catholics, contains about a dozen books that Jews and Protestants don't consider part of the Holy Scriptures.

1109. The Good News Bible of 1976 became a best-selling version quickly and remains a popular modern version throughout churches today.

1110. The New International Bible came out in 1978 and remains one of the most popular versions used today.

1111. There are complete Bibles in more than forty European languages and 125 Asian and Pacific Island languages. There are also Bible translations in more than one hundred African languages, with another five hundred African-language versions of some portion of the Bible. At least fifteen complete Native American Bibles have been produced.

Funny
and Fresh Takes

34

1112. The Gothic Bible did not contain the Books of 1 Kings or 2 Kings. The reason was that Ulfilas, the missionary who brought the gospel to the Goths of northern Europe in the mid-300s, didn't think the war-loving Gothic people should be reading about all the wars perpetrated by the Jewish kings. It's important to note, however, that the Goths had no written language at the time. In translating the Bible into the Gothic language, Ulfilas invented a Gothic alphabet so that the people could read the Good News for themselves.

1113. The Bug Bible was published in 1535 and was known more by its real name, the Coverdale Bible. It was dubbed the "Bug Bible" because of its rendering of Psalm 91:5: "Thou shalt not need to be afrayd for eny bugges by night."

1114. The Breeches Bible, or the Geneva Bible as it was better known, appeared in 1560. Genesis 3:7 reads that Adam and Eve "sowed figge-tree leaves together and made themselves breeches."

1115. The Placemakers Bible was the 1562 edition of the Geneva Bible. The word "peacemakers" in Matthew 5:9 was changed to "placemakers" to read: "Blessed are the placemakers."

1116. The Tryacle Bible came out in 1568 and was officially called the Bishops' Bible. The word "tryacle" was used in place of the word "balm" in Jeremiah. One instance can be found in Jeremiah 8:22: "Is there no tryacle in Gilead?" (*Tryacle* is a bit of a double entendre. It means "an antidote to poison," "a sweet dessert," and is sometimes used as a perjorative for anything cloyingly sweet.)

1117. The King James Version (first edition) was completed by Robert Barker, the official printer of King James I, as early as 1611. Scholars call this a "He" Bible because it renders Ruth 3:15 as ". . . He went into the city" instead of ". . . She went into the city." Different copies of the KJV published between 1611 and 1614 contain either he or she, indicating that two presses were producing the Bible at that time. Later editions accepted "she" as the proper wording.

1118. The Wicked Bible, or Adulterous Bible, was printed in 1632. The word "not" was accidentally left out of the seventh commandment: "You shall commit adultery" (Exod. 20:14).

1119. The Unrighteous Bible was the Cambridge edition of 1653. The word "not" was left out of 1 Corinthians 6:9, which made it appear as: "The unrighteous shall inherit the kingdom of God." Another mistake from this version was found in Romans 6:13—the word "righteousness" was substituted for "unrighteousness"— "Neither yield ye your members as instruments of righteousness unto sin."

1120. The Vinegar Bible was an Oxford edition from 1717. The heading for the segment of Luke 20 now known as the "parable of the tenants" was known in editions of that time period as "the parable of the vineyard." The word *vinegar* was mistakenly used in place of *vineyard*.

1121. The Printers' Bible came out in the early eighteenth century, but an exact date is unknown. Psalm 119:161 reads, "printers have persecuted me without cause." The word *printers* should read as *princes*.

1122. The Murderers' Bible was printed in 1801. The word *murmurers* was replaced with *murderers* in Jude 16: "These are murderers, complainers. . . ."

1123. The To Remain Bible was printed in Cambridge in 1805. A well-meaning proofreader was unsure about a comma in the manuscript and queried it. The editor penciled in the words "to remain"; thus Galatians 4:29 reads "he that was born after the flesh persecuted him that was born after the spirit *to remain*, even so it is now."

1124. The Standing Fishes Bible was printed in 1806, and mistakenly used the word *fishes* for *fishers* in Ezekiel 47:10: "And it shall come to pass that the fishes shall stand on it."

1125. The Discharge Bible also appeared in 1806. In 1 Timothy 5:21, the apostle says, "I discharge thee . . . that thou observe these things." The correct wording would have been "I charge thee . . ."

1126. The Idle Shepherd Bible appeared in 1809. This edition mistook the "idol shepherd" of Zechariah 11:17 and made it read "idle shepherd."

1127. The Ears to Ear Bible was published in 1810. Matthew 13:43 reads, "Who hath ears to ear, let him hear" instead of "Who hath ears to hear, let him hear."

1128. The Wife-hater Bible was printed in 1810. The word "life" was changed to "wife" in Luke 14:26: "If any man comes to me, and hates not his father . . . and his own wife also. . . ." It should read, "If any man comes to me, and hates not his father . . . and his own life also. . . ."

1129. Rebekah's Camels Bible is an 1823 edition that gives Rebekah "camels" instead of "damsels" in Genesis 24:61: "Rebekah arose, and her camels . . ."

Famous Words and Phrases

35

1130. "Raising Cain" means to act with abandonment or wildly. As a phrase, it is most likely descended from the Genesis character Cain who killed his brother, Abel, and was forever marked as a violent man.

1131. "Jezebel" or "Delilah" is the name often given to a woman of cunning and deceit. Both Bible characters were beautiful, though calculating in nature. Delilah was a seductress; Jezebel was a queen.

1132. A "Judas" can only refer to one personality trait: betrayal. Judas Iscariot betrayed his relationship to the Lord for thirty pieces of silver.

1133. "Doubting Thomas" didn't believe Jesus had truly risen from the dead. He insisted on touching the nail marks in the Lord's hands and side before he would believe. Today we call a person with doubts a doubting Thomas.

1134. "Jonah" is considered an unlucky name. The prophet Jonah tried unsuccessfully to run from God's calling. He took refuge on a boat and brought nothing but trouble to the other passengers, because God would not forget Jonah. Someone who brings bad luck or misfortune is considered a Jonah.

1135. The word *beautiful* was first used in the English language by William Tyndale when he produced his English translation of the New Testament in 1526. Some scholars considered it an outrage that a translator would use a new, fashionable word in his interpretation of Scripture.

1136. "The salt of the earth." Many of the words we use in our culture come from the Lord Jesus. In describing his disciples with these words in Matthew 5:13, Christ was saying that they were valuable—salt being the preferred method of payment in those days. The phrase is still used to describe people we find valuable or important.

1137. "Seek and ye shall find." These oft-quoted words of Jesus come from his Sermon on the Mount in Matthew 7:7. It is still generally used as advice or encouragement to those who need to be seeking.

1138. "A wolf in sheep's clothing." Jesus created this phrase in Matthew 7:15 to describe religious leaders who appear righteous on the outside but are actually evil on the inside. We still use it to describe hypocrites or those who portray goodness while intending evil.

1139. "The faith to move mountains." Although not currently used quite as often as it was in the twentieth century, the phrase refers to the power of belief. The words were first said by the Lord

Jesus in Matthew 17:20 when he was talking to his disciples about healing the sick and the demon possessed.

1140. "The blind leading the blind." Jesus coined this phrase in Matthew 15:14 when describing false teachers who insist they know the truth but do not, therefore leading innocent people astray. In our culture we generally use it as a negative descriptor for the self-important and self-deluded.

1141. "Do not throw pearls before swine." Jesus' words in Matthew 7:6 urge believers to take care with their message; it is not necessary to teach to those who are openly hostile to the gospel. A person wouldn't throw precious pearls to pigs, and Christians shouldn't throw the gift of salvation to those who will only turn around and attack them.

1142. "Eat, drink, and be merry" was a phrase created by Jesus in Luke 12 while telling a cautionary tale about a rich fool who thought the rest of his life was set. The fool died that very night. The words are still generally used in the sarcastic or pejorative sense.

1143. "The straight and narrow." Following the small, less-traveled path leads to the narrow gate of life. In Matthew 7:14, Jesus cautioned his followers against following the more glamorous, broad, and well-traveled path that led to a wide gate full of destruction.

1144. "A good Samaritan." Someone who goes out of the way to help another can be likened to the famed character of Jesus' parable in Luke 10:30–37. The hero acts for the good of another with no thought to his own situation.

1145. "Sweating blood" is a phrase used to describe someone going through a very difficult time. The etymology of the word relates back to Luke 22:44, when Christ's anguish in the Garden of Gethsemane caused him to sweat blood—something physicians say is, in fact, possible for those enduring great duress.

1146. "The forbidden fruit" is one of many Old Testament phrases still used regularly in the English language. The original "forbidden fruit" was the fruit from the tree of the knowledge of good and evil. Adam and Eve were instructed to stay away from it in Genesis 2:17, but when the Serpent tempted them to eat of it, the couple disobeyed God and chose to sin. Now we use the phrase to refer to partaking in an activity we know to be wrong or sensual.

1147. "Fire and brimstone" were the tools God used to destroy the cities of Sodom and Gomorrah, according to Genesis 19:24. The apostle John used those same words to describe the ultimate end of Satan in Revelation 21:8. Due to its colorful imagery, the phrase is generally used to describe preachers who focus on the punishment aspects of the biblical story, or for any fiery speaker who makes reference to a bad end for wrongdoers.

1148. "Taking a sabbatical" comes from the old Jewish notion of "taking time off." Leviticus 25 commands the people to allow the ground to lie fallow every seventh year in order to refresh itself—an action that was referred to as the "sabbatical year."

1149. "An eye for an eye" is a phrase that first appears in Leviticus 24:20. Rather than being a vindictive call for revenge, it actually limited the damage one person could do to another when taking retribution. Human nature encourages an individual to hurt others, but the Old Testament law wanted to limit that hurt to equivalent damage.

1150. "A land flowing with milk and honey" were the words God used to describe Palestine to Moses in Exodus 3:8. It's now generally used to describe a fine or pleasant place.

1151. "The apple of my eye" is a phrase first created in Deuteronomy 32:10 to describe God's perspective of Israel. The Hebrew words literally mean "center" or "pupil" of the eye, but in the poetic sense they refer to someone or something highly valued by another. The poet David asks God in Psalm 17:8, "Keep me as the apple of your eye."

1152. "Scapegoat." On the Day of Atonement, the high priest would lay his hands on one goat, symbolically transferring the sins of the people onto it. However, instead of being killed, that goat was driven into the wilderness as a symbol of the sins being "gone." The goat, which took the blame for the sins of others, was known as the "scapegoat."

1153. "Spare the rod and spoil the child." This bit of homely wisdom (generally quoted by senior citizens when somebody else's kids are acting up) is based on the wisdom of King Solomon, who says in Proverbs 13:24 that a parent "who spares the rod hates his son."

1154. "Pride goes before a fall," one of the most commonly quoted phrases in American history, were the words of King Solomon in Proverbs 16:18, referring to the fact that a prideful attitude can blind us and lead us into trouble.

1155. "A fly in the ointment" is a phrase commonly used to describe something that has gone wrong with a system or procedure. It comes from Ecclesiastes 10:1, which states that "dead flies spoil the perfumer's ointment."

1156. "Woe is me!" This phrase, once common in nineteenth-century literature, was first used in Isaiah 6:5 when the prophet came face-to-face with God. It also appears in the Book of Jeremiah as an expression of sorrow.

1157. "A drop in the bucket." Generally used to refer to "a small amount" or "a meaningless portion," the words are lifted in their entirety from Isaiah 40:15, in which we are told that to the Lord "the nations are a drop in the bucket."

1158. "Holier than thou." These words, which in our modern culture are generally used to describe a self-righteous person, were used in that same sense by the Lord in Isaiah 65:5 to criticize those who felt themselves better than others.

1159. "Like a lamb to the slaughter" were words first used in Isaiah 53:7 to describe the coming Messiah's willingness to accept his fate. It's now generally used in reference to an innocent victim or someone who is bound to lose in his or her circumstances.

1160. "The skin of our teeth." Generally used to mean "just barely," the imagery comes from Job 19:20. The phrase was popularized when made the title of a wildly successful play by American playwright Thornton Wilder.

1161. "Can a leopard change its spots?" This rhetorical question, which suggests people cannot change what they are inherently, was coined by the prophet Jeremiah in 13:23 of his book.

1162. "Feet of clay," an expression that has come to mean a personal flaw in an individual, was first used by the prophet Daniel when describing the statue he had seen in King Nebuchadnezzar's dream. The feet of the statue were made of clay mixed with iron—a weak base for such a big, heavy monument.

1163. "The handwriting on the wall" is a phrase that comes from Daniel chapter 5. The carnal King Belshazzar had seen a hand appear and write a mysterious message. Calling upon Daniel to interpret the message, the king learned that God had weighed Belshazzar on an eternal scale and found him wanting. His kingdom was to be taken away that very night—leading to our use of the phrase as "something inevitable that we can all see happening."

1164. "We reap what we sow." Generally accepted as cultural wisdom that means "you get what you earn," the phrase is lifted from Paul's letter to the Galatians in chapter 6, verse 7.

1165. "The powers that be," a phrase first created by Bible translator William Tyndale, is usually used to refer to "the government" or "those in charge." It means those in positions of authority are there by God's choice and therefore exist only because he wishes them to. The phrase was used by the apostle Paul in Romans 13:1 when, as the King James Version reads, he noted, "the powers that be are ordained of God."

1166. "A thorn in the side." The apostle Paul first used this phrase in 2 Corinthians 12:7 to describe some sort of physical ailment. Though he pleaded with God to take it away, the problem continued, thus keeping Paul humble. We still use the phrase to refer to an ongoing problem.

1167. "Money is the root of all evil." This popular phrase is actually a bit of a mistranslation from 1 Timothy 6:10. The actual words of Paul stated that "the *love* of money is the root of all kinds of evil" (emphasis added). Still the fact remains that lusting after money can get us into all sorts of trouble.

1168. "Nothing new under the sun." This statement by Solomon demonstrates the author's realization that despite temporary changes from one day to the next, there is nothing truly new or unexpected under the rising and falling of the sun each day. The phrase comes from Ecclesiastes 1:9.

1169. "The fat of the land." Pharaoh spoke these words to Joseph in Genesis 45:18. Joseph was to pass them on in turn to his brothers, who were hungry and in need of a place to live due to the famine affecting the land of Israel. The Egyptian king promised Joseph the best land of Egypt and that he and his brothers would be well provided for and able to eat "the fat of the land."

1170. "All things to all men." Paul is speaking in 1 Corinthians 9:22 of how he has become all things to everyone in order to win some to Christ. The phrase now is often seen as a "sellout" point, as it is difficult to be everything to everyone and keep sight of one's own welfare.

36

Strange
and Amazing Facts

1171. A stack of scrolls was the form of the Bible until the fourth century AD. Then it was compiled into one volume, though it was hardly complete at that point!

1172. It wasn't until the sixteenth century, many, many years after the Bible was first printed, that it was divided into the chapters and verses we are accustomed to today.

1173. No mention! There are two books of the Bible that never state the name of God: Esther and Song of Solomon.

1174. There are twenty-four books in the Hebrew Bible. Generally the books are categorized within three sections: the Law (Torah), Prophets, and Writings. The Hebrew Bible has only what Protestants would call the "Old Testament."

1175. The Protestant version of the Old Testament contains thirty-nine books. This is different from both the Hebrew Bible and the Catholic Bible. The New Testament of the Protestant version contains twenty-seven books.

1176. The Catholic Bible's Old Testament contains the thirty-nine books of the Protestant version's Old Testament but also includes seven books of the Apocrypha.

1177. How many chapters? There are 929 chapters in the Old Testament and 260 in the New Testament, making a grand total of 1,189 chapters in all!

1178. How many letters? With 3,566,480 letters in the Bible, and a word count between 773,692 and 773,746, depending on how the hyphenated words are counted, this book is quite large.

1179. The shortest book in the New Testament is 3 John, which contains only 294 words in its fourteen verses! John's second book has one less verse but four more words.

1180. The shortest book in the Old Testament is Obadiah.

1181. The longest book in the Bible is the Book of Psalms. It has 150 psalms.

1182. The longest verse in the Bible (King James Version) is Esther 8:9, which has ninety words total. The shortest verse, John 11:35, includes only two words: "Jesus wept."

1183. The Book of Isaiah is the most-often quoted Old Testament book, with 419 references made to it in the New Testament. The Book of Psalms is second and referred to in the New Testament 414 times.

1184. The oldest verses in the Bible are believed to be fragments from "the Song of Deborah."

1185. The newest verses in the Bible are thought to be found in the Gospel of John, which dates from around AD 100.

1186. Job was written when? Job, the book that appears before the Psalms, is actually a much older book than the books it is located near. Job and Genesis are actually on similar timelines!

1187. The most press? David receives second place for being mentioned a whopping 1,118 times in the Bible. He is second only to Jesus in this regard. Sarah, the wife of Abraham, receives the most references as a woman—fifty-six!

1188. The name *Jesus* appears seven hundred times in the Gospels and Acts, and less than seventy times in the Epistles. The name *Christ* can be found sixty times throughout the Gospels and Acts, but 240 times in the Epistles and the Book of Revelation.

1189. The most press for an animal? Sheep win the prize with mention of this very necessary animal occurring over four hundred different times.

1190. Who was the oldest? Methuselah is believed to have lived 969 years on earth before he died (Gen. 5:27), making him the longest-lived person. Prior to the flood, people lived very long lives, but afterward, only a few (the patriarchs and Moses among them) lived beyond the expected seventy- or eighty-year life span.

1191. The longest-reigning king in the Bible was Manasseh, who oversaw the kingdom of Judah for fifty-five years (2 Kings 21:1). The shortest-reigning king was Zimri, who wore the crown of Israel for only seven days (1 Kings 16:15).

1192. Weddings galore. King Solomon, the son of David, is the most-often married man in the whole Bible. This king had seven hundred wives (all of royal birth!) along with an additional three hundred concubines (1 Kings 11:3).

1193. A longer name can't be found in the Bible than that of Maher-Shalal-Hash-Baz. The Lord told Isaiah, in 8:3, to give his child, born of a prophetess, this name, which means "quick to the plunder, swift to the spoil."

1194. Though God is invisible and has no body parts, the Bible always refers to him with masculine pronouns, and we are said to be made "in his image" according to Genesis.

1195. Shakespeare honored?! William Shakespeare is perhaps the only man not of Bible times who is honored in the Bible. How? In honor of his forty-sixth birthday, which happened to be the year the King James Version was being printed for the first time, the scholars took the forty-sixth psalm and made sure that forty-six words into the psalm appeared the word *shake* and forty-six words from the end of the psalm appeared the word *spear.*

37

Famous Quotes

1196. **"The book of books,** the storehouse and magazine of life and comfort, the holy Scriptures."—George Herbert

1197. **"Prosperity is the blessing of the Old Testament,** adversity is the blessing of the New."—Francis Bacon

1198. **"Most people are bothered** by those passages in Scripture which they cannot understand; but as for me . . . the passages which trouble me most are those that I do understand."—Mark Twain

1199. "**The English Bible,** a book which, if everything else in our language should perish, would alone suffice to show the whole extent of its beauty and power."—Thomas Babington Macaulay

1200. "**The Bible is a window** in this prison of hope, through which we look into eternity."—John Sullivan Dwight

1201. "**If you believe those four words,** 'In the beginning God,' you have no problem believing all of the Bible."—Raymond Barber

1202. "**Unless I am convicted of error** by the testimony of Scripture or by manifest reasoning, I stand convicted by the Scriptures to which I have appealed, and my conscience is taken captive by God's word."—Martin Luther

1203. "**A young man who wishes** to remain a sound Atheist cannot be too careful of his reading. There are traps everywhere— 'Bibles laid open, millions of surprises'—. . . God is, if I may say it, very unscrupulous."—C. S. Lewis

1204. "**Either the Bible will keep you away from sin,** or sin will keep you away from the Bible!"—Author Unknown

1205. "**The Bible is literature, not dogma.**"—George Santayana

1206. "**The Bible is no mere book,** but a living creature, with a power that conquers all that oppose it."—Napoleon Bonaparte

1207. "**In the twentieth century our highest praise** has been to call the Bible 'the world's best-seller.' And it has come to be more and more difficult to say whether we think it is a best-seller because it is great, or vice versa."—Daniel Boorstin

1208. "**There are no songs comparable to the songs of Zion,** no orations equal to those of the prophets, and no politics like those which the Scriptures teach."—John Milton

1209. "**When you read God's Word,** you must constantly be saying to yourself, it is talking to me, and about me."—Søren Kierkegaard

1210. "**You can learn more about human nature** by reading the Bible than by living in New York."—William Lyon Phelps

1211. **"The New Testament is the very best book** that ever was or ever will be known in the world."—Charles Dickens

1212. **"What you bring away from the Bible** depends to some extent on what you carry to it."—Oliver Wendell Holmes

1213. **"The Bible is alive,** it speaks to me; it has feet, it runs after me; it has hands, it lays hold on me."—Martin Luther

1214. **"The Bible tells us to love our neighbors,** and also to love our enemies; probably because they are generally the same people."—G. K. Chesterton

1215. **"Intense study of the Bible** will keep any man from being vulgar in point of style."—Samuel Taylor Coleridge

1216. **"'The Bible,' we are told sometimes, 'gives us such a beautiful picture of what we should be.'** Nonsense! It gives us no picture at all. It reveals to us a fact: It tells us what we really are; it says, This is the form in which God created you, to which He has restored you; this is the work which the Eternal Son, the God of Truth and Love, is continually carrying on within you."—F. D. Maurice

1217. **"Read the whole Bible, and read it in order;** two chapters in the Old Testament and one in the New, daily if you can possibly spare the time; and you will have more time than you are aware of; if you retrench all needless visits, and save the hours spent in useless or unimportant conversation."—Adam Clarke, a Methodist circuit preacher of the nineteenth century, believed that only through regular Bible reading would Christians grow wise in their salvation.

1218. **"You may as well quit reading** and hearing the Word of God, and give in to the devil, if you do not desire to live according to it."—Martin Luther

The Old Testament Books

38

1219. The Books of Moses. Otherwise known as the Pentateuch, the first five books of the Bible attributed to Moses are the cornerstone of the books contributed by later generations. These books include Genesis, Exodus, Leviticus, Numbers, and Deuteronomy.

1220. Genesis. *Genesis* comes from a word meaning "to be born." From that same word we also get words like *genetic*, *congenital*, and *genealogy*. Though it marks the beginning, the best way to look at Genesis is not merely to begin and look forward, but to stand at Exodus and look back. Moses is writing for his fellow Israelite slaves. As they struggle with Egypt's oppression, Moses answers the question, "How did we get in this mess?" Genesis is the answer to that question. It tells the story of the Israelites' ancestors—all the way back to the first human beings.

1221. Exodus. This book opens several hundred years after the close of Genesis. Jacob and some seventy family members had grown into hundreds of thousands. God's promise of descendants to Abraham also included a promise of land on which the descendants would live. This land had already been settled and was called Canaan, after its original settlers. It is now the area of Palestine or Israel. *Exodus* means "the going out of." It is the story of the Hebrew people being led by Moses out of Egyptian captivity into the wilderness for forty years.

1222. Leviticus. The Levites were descended from Jacob's son Levi. Moses and Aaron were Levites. The Levites were to keep the tabernacle and all its services for the rest of the nation, and the priests were to have the most essential parts of that service. This book is somewhat of an appendix to Exodus as it is a log of the laws and guidelines for the Israelites.

1223. Numbers. The English title of this book refers to the census of the twelve tribes that opens the book. The Hebrew title, Ba-Midbar ("in the wilderness"), is more accurately descriptive because the book begins with the decision to leave Sinai and cross the desert toward the Promised Land.

1224. Deuteronomy. This book is essentially Moses' farewell address—actually three addresses—in which he restates the acts of God. Solemnly Moses warns of the temptations of Canaan and its evil ways. Moses pleads for loyalty to and love of God as the main condition for life in the Promised Land. A central message in Deuteronomy is that the worship of God is to be centralized in one place, so that the paganism of local shrines may be eliminated.

1225. The books of history. If the books of Moses can be considered the cornerstone of the Bible, then the next twelve books can be thought of as the first story of the building. The historical record of ancient Israel that began with Genesis through Deuteronomy is continued with these next twelve books. While the first five books brought Israel to the edge of the Promised Land, these next twelve tell what happened once Israel took up residence there.

1226. Joshua. Moses and Aaron were not allowed to enter the Promised Land, and neither were any of the people who came out of Egypt because of the Israelites' griping in the wilderness. Permission came at last for the Israelites to "conquer" the Promised Land after forty years of waiting. The Book of Joshua tells this story. As in many war stories, it gets pretty gory.

1227. Judges recounts the history of Israel from the death of Joshua to the time just before the birth of the Hebrew prophet Samuel, roughly a two-hundred-year span. The judges were warriorlike rulers over the tribes of Israel.

1228. Ruth. The short Book of Ruth—shortest of all the historical books—provides a welcome respite from the harsh times described at the end of Judges. The opening verses tell of the Moabites, Ruth's marriage to a Hebrew man during a time of famine, and how she chose to return to Judah with her mother-in-law after her husband's death. Her loyalty and kindness were rewarded and forever remembered by the Jewish people because she became the great-grandmother of King David.

1229. 1 and 2 Samuel and 1 and 2 Kings. Originally the two Books of Samuel and the two Books of Kings were each a single book in the Hebrew Canon of the Bible, telling the history of the kingdom of Israel. Once they were translated into Greek in the Septuagint, they no longer fit on single scrolls and were expanded into four books. Samuel contains the history of the prophet Samuel—the last judge of Israel—and the stormy tale of Israel's first two kings, Saul and David.

1230. The division of Kings occurred when the Book of Samuel was divided into 1 Samuel and 2 Samuel, the Book of Kings was divided into 1 Kings and 2 Kings, and the Book of Chronicles was divided into 1 Chronicles and 2 Chronicles. The motivation was not spiritual but practical—the books were simply too long to keep on one scroll.

1231. 1 and 2 Chronicles is the ancient *Reader's Digest* version of everything that had already taken place in the Bible from Genesis forward. It is abridged and simplified, with many of the nasty parts taken out. The first nine chapters contain long tables of "begats," showing the descendants of the Hebrew tribes, from Adam through the time of King David. The rest of 1 Chronicles and most of 2 Chronicles deal with the reigns of David and Solomon and the subsequent history of the kingdom of Judah until the Babylonian exile. Since these books are placed last in the Hebrew Canon, the Hebrew Scriptures end on a liberating note, with echoes of the Exodus.

1232. Ezra opens with a decree of Cyrus, the king of Persia, following his capture of Babylon in 539 BC, that those who want to may leave Babylon and return to Jerusalem to rebuild the temple. Founder of an extensive empire that lasted more than two hundred years, Cyrus was an extraordinary leader. Under Cyrus and his successors, much of the ancient Near East, from India to Egypt and the border of Greece, was brought under one ruler. Unlike other ancient conquerors who enforced their own religions on conquered peoples, Cyrus permitted the captive nations to preserve and restore their own institutions.

1233. Nehemiah. Jerusalem was constantly raided by various marauders. Nehemiah's particular concern was the security of Jerusalem, so he returned from exile specifically to help. He organized the people and rebuilt the city walls in fifty-five days. While Ezra's role was that of a priest, Nehemiah's was that of governor. When the rebuilding was completed, Ezra was invited to rededicate the city by reading from the book of Moses. Ezra-Nehemiah make a distinctive pair of books, together recording the rebuilding of Jerusalem after the exile.

1234. Esther (Hadassah in Hebrew). While Ezra-Nehemiah deal with events in Jerusalem, Esther tells of events far away. As Ruth was a vignette sketched in the period of the judges, Esther is a vignette sketched in the time of the exile. As one of the exiles, Esther finds herself in the service of the king of Persia. The king sets out to select a new queen, and the beautiful Jewish woman, Esther, is chosen. Haman, the king's right-hand man, plans to rid his country of the Jews. Through a fascinating sequence of events involving Esther, Haman's rampage against the Jews backfires. Esther retains the favor of the king and the Jewish people are saved.

1235. The books of poetry. Job, Psalms, Proverbs, Ecclesiastes, and Song of Solomon make up the Bible's books of poetry. Hebrew poetry is picturesque and vivid. There is a rhythm or cadence to Hebrew poetry that is lost to some degree in the translation. It is filled with concrete images and deep emotion. It touches the soul. The books of poetry aren't just a change in style from previous books; the subject matter shifts as well. Wisdom takes center stage in these five books; therefore, they are called the "wisdom literature" of the Bible.

1236. Job. Whenever the troubling question "Why do bad things happen to good people?" comes up, Job is first to come to mind. But few people ever really tackle this book that reads like the script for a play. The central characters are Job, three of his friends, a bystander, and God. The supporting cast includes Job's wife and children, the angels, and Satan as chief of the angels. The first two chapters and the last two chapters are prose, and the thirty-nine chapters in between consist of poetic dialogue between the central characters.

1237. Psalms. While Jews and Christians share the entire Hebrew Scriptures, or Old Testament, Psalms is the most emotionally and intensely shared book of Hebrew Scripture. Jews know many of the Psalms and individual verses by heart. Jesus often quoted or referred to the Psalms. Martin Luther called the Book of Psalms "a Bible in Miniature." The 150 "rosaries" later instituted by the Roman Catholic Church are in honor of the 150 psalms.

1238. Proverbs. Some proverbs are strung together in a meaningful sequence, while others are independent of each other and need to be "unpacked" by the reader. The opening chapters of Proverbs carry extended proverbs that progress with each verse. And mostly one-liner bits of wisdom form chapters 10 and following. Proverbs leaves no ambiguity over the contrast between the righteous and the wicked.

1239. Ecclesiastes. If Job reads like a play, and Psalms like poetry, and Proverbs like a book of maxims, then Ecclesiastes reads like an essay, or the thoughts of an old man thinking out loud. Its subject is the vanity of life. The book approaches Job's question, but from the opposite side: If this universe is governed by a moral God, why doesn't everything make sense? The conclusion of this book's search is that regardless of any apparent vanity, fearing God and keeping his commandments is the wisest course of action.

1240. Song of Solomon. Plain and simple, this book is an erotic love poem. The writing resembles Egyptian love poetry and Arabic wedding songs that praise the charm and beauty of the bride. The traditional interpretation, both in Judaism and Christianity, is that these love poems represent Yahweh's love for Israel while also establishing God's high regard for male-female love and sexuality.

1241. Isaiah opens by dating himself according to the reign of a particular king in Israel's history and then describing his visions in the form of poetry. Throughout his book, Isaiah made key references to historical markers, which keep his writings in context with the historical books. The other prophets often followed this form. Isaiah's ministry spread over the reigns of four of Judah's kings. Isaiah is quoted in the New Testament more often than any other book of prophecy.

1242. Jeremiah was another firebrand prophet of the declining years of Judah. Jeremiah, whose name meant "God hurled," was born in a tiny village northeast of Jerusalem, and before long, perhaps while he was still in his teens, he was thrown into the midst of his nation's most terrifying crisis. He was a faithful prophet to God but unpopular among the people. The young Jeremiah declared that the Babylonians would destroy the nation because the children of Israel had forgotten their God.

1243. Lamentations is a brief book of sorrowful poems, some in the form of alphabetic acrostics, which recall the grim fate of Jerusalem following its destruction by the Babylonians in 587/586 BC. The title is derived from the Hebrew word *qinoth* ("dirges" or "laments"). In Christian Old Testaments, the book is placed after Jeremiah, but it is found in the third part of the Hebrew Canon Writings. The poems are bitterly sad elegies for the "dead" city, but they express hope that God will restore a humbled and repentant Israel.

1244. Ezekiel is one of the hardest books to read in the Bible. It is long, with a somber tone like Jeremiah. Its images are complex and hard to understand. Babylon besieged Israel before the capital,

Jerusalem, finally fell. During those years of siege, captives were taken from the land and shipped to Babylon. Ezekiel was one of the captives. Ezekiel dealt first with the problems that caused Israel to lose her land. Second, he wanted his people to maintain hope for the future.

1245. Daniel. Like Ezekiel, the Book of Daniel has some complicated images. These images add to the glorious picture of the future of Israel. The central figure in that future was the Messiah, the Jews' image of hope. The first half of the book is straightforward narrative and is the source of some of the Bible's most loved stories: Shadrach, Meshach, and Abednego in the fiery furnace; Daniel in the lions' den; and the story that gave rise to the saying, "You could see the handwriting on the wall."

1246. Hosea is a prophet of love. Hosea's own experiences with his wayward wife, Gomer, are used as a symbol to illustrate God's pain in dealing with Israel. Like Gomer's sin, Israel's sin would be punished before there could be restoration. In the Book of Hosea, the sins of Israel are spelled out, and she is described as a "harlot." God is portrayed as a faithful and loving husband and Israel as an adulterous wife.

1247. Joel's theme is "This is the day of the Lord." The day of the Lord shows up in other prophetic books as well and means a day of reckoning—a day of judgment. It refers to a time when God brings down the wicked and haughty and lifts up the humble. The day of the Lord meant destruction for some and deliverance for others. Joel spoke of a day of the Lord approaching for Israel by describing a ravaging plague of locusts.

1248. Amos prophesied at about the same time as Hosea and Joel. Amos was a sheepherder from a Judean village who left his flocks to denounce the sins of his people during the time of the northern King Jeroboam II (786–744 BC), a prosperous time in Israel. Though a herdsman, Amos used some of the purest and most classical Hebrew in the entire Old Testament. In a style of informal satire, Amos attacked the oppression of the poor by the rich, as well as the latter's empty piety and immoral religious practices. If the people did not mend their corrupt ways, Amos warned, they would be destroyed.

1249. Obadiah is the shortest book in the Old Testament—only one chapter. Like Joel, he emphasized the coming day of the Lord. He said that since all nations have a day of reckoning, it does not pay to gloat when another nation encounters misfortune. He also emphasized the often-used words of wisdom, "As you have done it, so it will be done to you."

1250. Jonah. This book marks a distinct change of pace. Jonah's story is told in narrative form about how he first refused to deliver a message of warning to the great city of Nineveh, capital of Assyria. Israel's prophets often had words to deliver to surrounding nations, but Jonah had no desire to deliver a message of repentance to the enemies of his people. Jonah attempted to run away, booking passage on a ship going to Tarshish in southern Spain, the farthest-known earthly point to which a man could then travel. In the end Jonah learned a great lesson in the depth of God's mercy.

1251. Micah returns to the normal poetic style of the prophets. His writings are structured in three stages: reproof, threat, and promise. Micah reminded the people of all that God had done for them in the past. He called them to obedience in the present and hopefulness for the future. He spoke to both the people of the Northern Kingdom and the Southern Kingdom.

1252. Nahum. Like Jonah, Nahum was concerned with the city of Nineveh. Here there is no narrative story, but where Jonah gave us just the overview, Nahum spells out the full indictment of the city's wrongdoings. Descriptive words are piled on one another, creating rapidly moving pictures. Nahum lived long after Jonah. Nineveh's embrace of morality had ended, and Nahum warned them of their final fall.

1253. Habakkuk foresaw the assault on Israel by Babylon. He admitted Israel's sin but asked why an unrighteous nation like Babylon was so worthy to conquer. There is no lengthy answer in this short book. God's response is only that the righteous will live by faith. That is, he or she will trust that all accounts are eventually settled. Once again the people were instructed to live righteously.

1254. Zephaniah was a contemporary of Jeremiah. Zephaniah's prophecy came in the years immediately preceding the fall of Jerusalem. He talked of the coming day of the Lord, which for

Jerusalem was right around the corner. Yet he, too, spoke of the glorious long-term future God had in mind for his people—that a remnant of God's people would survive the day of judgment.

1255. Haggai and the next two prophets did their work after the remnant of Israelites returned from exile in Babylon. Haggai is specifically mentioned in the Book of Ezra as being among the returning exiles. Haggai's style is compact, forceful, and at times stern. Yet he encouraged the leaders and the people not to grieve over the brokenness of the nation they were rebuilding.

1256. Zechariah was a co-worker with Haggai. He, too, is mentioned in the Book of Ezra. His writing is considerably longer and more complex than Haggai's. This book can be divided into four sections (the first three are dated, but the last is not). He described visions, some of which are as complex as those found in Ezekiel and Daniel.

1257. Malachi. The twelfth and last of the minor prophets is more proselike than poetic, with a definite plan of argument. Malachi was concerned with the morality of the priesthood in his time. You would think that with all the warning the prophets had given before the fall of Jerusalem and all the chastening Israel had experienced that the priests would be diligent about keeping up their duties. But they weren't. Malachi warned the priests who thought they would get a "free ride" that they were in for a rude awakening.

39

In the Beginning

1258. God began it all. "In the beginning God . . ." is how the first verse of the first chapter of the first book of the Bible begins. The beginning of the history of the world is chronicled with those words!

1259. Elohim, which originates from the Hebrew word *el*, is translated as "god." The Hebrew word *el* actually is used for reference to all general gods. Another title of God, *el elyon*, is also a derivation of this and means "the most high God" (Gen. 14:18).

1260. Yahweh is the only name for God that is personal in nature. A Hebrew word, it is commonly translated into English versions as "Jehovah," or "the LORD" (Exod. 6:3).

1261. When creation began. Relying on biblical sources such as the chronologies and genealogies in Genesis, numerous people have attempted to pinpoint a time and date for the precise moment of creation. Ancient Hebrew scholars placed the moment as 3761 BC. Perhaps the most famous creation date was the one produced by Irish bishop James Ussher (1581–1656). Using Genesis, Ussher dated the moment of creation to the early morning of the twenty-third of October in 4004 BC (Ussher actually used the Julian calendar year of 710). Ussher's calculation was widely accepted by European Christians for centuries and was included in the margins of many editions of the King James Bible, giving it nearly divine "authority."

1262. Eden, which means "a place of delight," is believed by some scholars to have been located at the eastern end of the Fertile Crescent, near where the Tigris and Euphrates Rivers meet the Persian Gulf.

1263. The name "Adam" is a pun on the similar Hebrew words for "soil" and for "man." The word *Adam* is derived from the Hebrew word for "man" in the collective sense, as in humanity or humankind. It is also related to the Hebrew word *adamah*, which means "ground" or "earth." The author of Genesis used a wordplay. *Adam*, man, came from *adamah*, the ground.

1264. Not an apple. Though legend has it that the forbidden fruit of the tree of knowledge that Eve was tempted by the serpent to taste was an apple, nowhere does the Bible identify it as one. In fact most scholars agree that the one fruit it definitely could not have been was the apple. Apples were not likely to have grown in the Bible lands in Old Testament times. However, apples were cultivated by the Egyptians, and the Romans at the time of Christ had more than twenty varieties.

1265. The legend that the apple was the fruit on the tree of knowledge arose in the Middle Ages when artists painted pictures of Eve tasting the apple. Another source of confusion was the medieval custom of calling many different kinds of fruits "apples."

Lemons were known as "Persian apples," dates as "finger apples," and pomegranates as "apples of Carthage."

1266. Apples or apricots? The fruit meant by the Hebrew word commonly translated as "apple" was probably the apricot, which flourishes all over the Bible lands. A clue comes from Solomon, who used the same word to describe a tree: "I delight to sit in his shade, and his fruit is sweet to my taste" (Song of Sol. 2:3). Solomon seems to be describing the apricot, for even today nomads pitch their tents under its branches for shade, and it is the fruit with the sweetest taste in the Holy Land.

1267. "Apples of gold in settings of silver." Proverbs appears to describe the apricot in this way (25:11). Not only is this a lovely poetic description of an apricot tree, it is also remarkably accurate. Its fruit is golden and the pale undersides of the leaves look silver when they turn in the breeze.

1268. Adam and Eve. The story of creation is one of continuing wonder to believers and nonbelievers alike. Humankind *had* to come from somewhere, and the story told in Genesis 1 and 2 reveals how a creative, organized God spoke the world into existence.

1269. The fall of man. Though Adam and Eve lived in a perfect world, they chose to disobey God and eat the forbidden fruit. Scripture is clear that such a choice led to our current situation—humankind is sinful and separated from God yet still desires peace with him.

1270. The fig tree is the second tree named in the Bible. After eating the forbidden apricot, Adam and Eve "sewed fig leaves together and made coverings for themselves" (Gen. 3:7). The large, tough leaves of the fig tree would certainly have made adequate clothing. Fig leaves are still sewn together in the Near East to make baskets, dishes, and even umbrellas.

1271. Adam and Eve were banished from Eden into what the Bible describes as a land of thorns and thistles. Thorns and spines grow on many different kinds of plants, but they are especially common on plants of the desert and semiarid regions of the world. Many kinds of thistles grow abundantly in the Bible lands.

1272. Adam and Eve's firstborn son, Cain, is remembered as the first murderer for killing his brother, Abel. When God sentenced Cain to wander the earth, Cain begged for mercy and, in fear, thought that someone would kill him. So God marked him. Widely viewed as a sign of guilt, the so-called "mark of Cain" is actually a symbol of divine mercy. Opponents of the death penalty point to this first murder and God's merciful sentence on the murderer as a biblical rejection of capital punishment. For his crime Cain received a life sentence of hard labor.

1273. Who were the Nephilim? Squeezed between the generation after Adam and the time of Noah is a curious story (Gen. 6:1–4) about the mysterious "Nephilim," briefly described as the offspring of the "sons of God." Echoing tales of Greek gods who mated with mortal women, the biblical passage calls the offspring of the angelic-human marriages "heroes of old, men of renown." They are only mentioned once more in Hebrew Scriptures, where Nephilim literally translates as "the fallen ones." Many believe they were giants possessing superhuman powers.

1274. Some early theologians thought the Nephilim were fallen angels who were responsible for sin in the world. Whoever these "sons of God" and their children were, God was not happy with the situation. He limited human life spans to 120 years. People became so wicked that God was sorry he had made humankind on the earth, and it grieved him. "So the Lord said, 'I will wipe mankind, whom I have created, from the face of the earth—men and animals, and creatures that move along the ground and birds of the air—for I am grieved that I have made them.' But Noah found favor in the eyes of the Lord" (Gen. 6:5–8).

1275. Noah and the ark. Genesis chapters 6 through 9 tell the story of people becoming thoroughly evil and God's judgment against them by sending forty days and nights of continual rainfall. At the same time, he worked through one faithful man, Noah, to build an ark and preserve a faithful remnant so that humankind could continue. The story of judgment and mercy resonates through the ages.

1276. Famous Renaissance artist and inventor Leonardo da Vinci (1452–1519) was surprised to discover the fossilized remains of sea creatures while walking in the Alps, and he asked how they got there. The conventional wisdom of his day simply said it was proof that a flood once covered the earth.

1277. Almost every ancient culture has some sort of flood or deluge myth that shares much in common with the biblical flood. In most of them the gods send a catastrophic flood to destroy the world, but one good man is told of the coming disaster and his family is saved to continue human existence. The one most like Noah's story comes from the Babylonian Gilgamesh epic. In this story, the hero, Utnapishtim, also survives the flood by building a boat, which comes to rest on Mount Nisir, which is in the same region as Noah's "mountains of Ararat."

1278. Noah made his ark of "gopher wood" (Gen. 6:14), which probably meant the cypress tree. This wood is extremely durable. The doors of Saint Peter's in Rome are made from it and after twelve hundred years they still show no signs of decay.

1279. The Bible does not list all of the animals that took refuge on the ark. However, those animals that survived the flood must have been the ones that were best known to the Hebrews and also those mentioned most often in the Bible through symbolism or otherwise.

1280. The first bird Noah released was a raven, a powerful flier able to slice through the air or soar with the ease of a hawk on wings that span up to four feet. Its habitat is the mountain wilderness, and so it was just the bird to scout out any crags that might have emerged from the flooded earth. The raven is noted for its remarkable memory, so this scout would not forget the location of the ark.

1281. When the raven failed to give Noah any sign of land, Noah sent out a dove. ("Doves" and "pigeons," by the way, refer to the same birds.) The rock dove was one of the earliest of all animals to be domesticated. There are Egyptian records, dating back five thousand years, of people rearing them in captivity for food and probably also as carrier pigeons.

1282. Very fast fliers, the strong wings of doves make them capable of powerful flight in a straight line, despite storms and high winds.

After at least five thousand years of using doves and pigeons to carry messages, we are still not certain how a pigeon "homes"—finds its way back to its roost—as the biblical dove found its way back to the ark.

1283. The second time Noah sent out the dove, it returned before evening with an olive leaf. This was evidence that the waters had subsided enough to expose the valleys where olive trees grow. The olive was the most important tree cultivated in the Holy Land. It is native only to the lands bordering the Mediterranean Sea.

1284. The story of Noah and the ark yields some interesting analysis as a type of Christ. The ark itself is a type of Christ! God gave Noah every detail of how it was to be built, from its dimensions to its purpose in protecting Noah and his family from the judgment that awaited the rest of the world. Likewise, God planned every minute detail of how Jesus would redeem God's people; not a single detail was left to man. As the big boat brought earthly salvation for Noah, so Christ brings eternal salvation for all who believe in him. As the ark had but one door, so Christ is the door to God—he is the only way we can gain forgiveness for our sins and come to the Father.

1285. The families of Noah's sons "had one language and a common speech" (Gen. 11:1). Babel was the original name for Babylon, which in Hebrew means "gate of God." Situated on the southern part of the floodplain between the Tigris and Euphrates rivers, Babylon was the site where builders attempted to erect a tower "that reaches to the heavens" (Gen. 11:4). The builders never completed the tower because their language became confused and they could no longer understand one another.

1286. With the destruction of the tower of Babel, the Bible's story of the early history of humankind ends. Abraham, the great patriarch of the Hebrews, is a descendant of Noah's son Shem. Abraham was the man to whom God promised, "I will make you into a great nation and I will bless you; I will make your name great" (Gen. 12:2).

40

Early Israel

1287. Abram is the earliest biblical character who can be connected, rather remotely and speculatively, to recorded world history. There is still no specific proof of this individual outside of the Bible, but these are the first clues that the biblical world he lived in was the world as history knows it.

1288. In the biblical list of Abraham's ancestors (Gen. 11:10–26), many family names are the same as those of several towns around Haran. Abraham's relatives either took their names from the towns where they lived or were important enough to give their names to these towns. Abraham's father, Terah, who is said to have worshiped idols for several years (Josh. 24:2), moved his family from Ur to Haran. Terah lived there until he died at the age of 205.

1289. *Habiru* **(or "Hebrew")** was a word of disparagement, probably meaning "the dusty ones." It did not refer to the Hebrew people in particular but rather to all the land-hungry Semites who led a nomadic life. In the Book of Genesis (14:13), Abraham is called "the Hebrew," and so this general name was finally limited to his descendants.

1290. Abraham's journey southward from Haran led through the entire length of Canaan, through the Negeb Desert to Egypt, and finally northward again to the Promised Land. His caravans were not like the camel caravans seen today in the deserts of the Near East. It is possible that until he reached Egypt he traveled on foot, with no beasts of burden except perhaps a few donkeys.

1291. Abram was given his new name, Abraham, when God came to him in his ninety-ninth year. At that time he had one son. The new name meant "father of many nations." Abraham must have been puzzled over how God would bring him into a full understanding of his new name with but one child when he was already quite old.

1292. After Lot chose to travel to the lower Jordan Valley, he settled near the wicked cities of Sodom and Gomorrah. These cities were destroyed by what the Bible calls "brimstone and fire" (Gen. 19:24 KJV). No one knows for sure when the last volcanic eruption took place in the Holy Land, but it may have been as recently as the Middle Ages. Geologists can see clear evidence that the Jordan Valley has been a center of volcanism in the past.

1293. The remains of the Twin Cities of Sin have never been found. Myth has it that they lie buried beneath the Dead Sea. This theory may provide an explanation of why the Dead Sea area is rich in bitumen, or tar, supposedly left after the destructive "fire and brimstone." Bitumen was used in the Egyptian mummification process. Bitumen was also used for "tarring" houses and was one of the key trade items in this area.

1294. The Sodom and Gomorrah story has always been useful as a moral tale of God destroying evil. But a subtext to the story has been even more influential. It is all about the sin to which the name Sodom is attached. This story has always been cited as one of the basic biblical injunctions against homosexuality.

1295. Abraham was given a covenant child as was promised to him by the three angels who visited and prophesied of the event. Sarah delivered a healthy infant son and they called him Isaac. He was a miracle—his mother was in her nineties and his father was one hundred!

1296. Hagar was the servant of Sarah, Abraham's wife. She had become pregnant by Abraham and bore Ishmael. Sarah was jealous and treated her poorly and eventually Hagar was sent into the wilderness of Beersheba when Isaac was born. But God protected Hagar and her son and raised them up to be their own people. They were under Abraham's covenant, but Ishmael was not the promised son who would continue the lineage of the Hebrews.

1297. The sacrifice of Isaac. God called Abraham to follow him to a far land and promised to make his family a great nation. Yet when Abraham finally had a son in his old age, the Lord asked him to sacrifice the boy on Mount Moriah. Instead of a pagan practice, it was a test of faith—God intervened to stop the sacrifice and provided a ram to sacrifice in the boy's place. Then, praising Abraham's faith, God promised to bless all nations through his offspring.

1298. The story of Abraham's unshakable faith while offering Isaac is a central moment in the Bible. To many people it seems an unnecessarily cruel test of faith. Abraham doesn't even make the arguments for his own son that he made for the citizens of Sodom. His wife, Sarah, is silent in this episode, and Isaac's thoughts are not available to us either.

1299. When God stays Abraham's hand. The passage says that Abraham "fears" God. The "fear of God" is a commonly used expression today. The Hebrew verb for "fear" can be understood two ways. Occasionally it meant being afraid, but very often the biblical "fear" meant awe or reverence for someone of exalted position. Abraham was not necessarily "afraid" of God as much as he held God in profound respect.

1300. The Bible notes that Abraham was "very rich in cattle" (Gen. 13:2 KJV), and he is often described as having flocks and herds. In the early books of the Bible, however, the word cattle is believed to usually refer to sheep and goats rather than to cows.

1301. Throughout the history of the Hebrews, even after they became a mighty nation under kings as in the glittering court of Solomon, the simple life of the shepherd was remembered and upheld as the most desirable existence.

1302. After Sarah died at age 127, Abraham buried her in a cave in Hebron. He purchased the burial land from the local people, the Hittites, and the verses elaborately explain the great measures Abraham took to stake a legal claim to this land. This passage is one of the oldest recorded real estate deals, a legal confirmation of possession of land that had already been divinely promised.

1303. After Sarah died, Abraham decided to marry again and took another wife, Keturah. She birthed six more of Abraham's children. These were the ancestors of other Arabic tribes including the Midianites, who play a role in the story of Moses. When Abraham died at age 175, he was buried alongside Sarah in the cave on the site he had purchased at Hebron.

1304. Isaac's name meant "laughter." He was the second patriarch. Isaac married Rebekah and they had two sons, Jacob and Esau, who were twins. They were never close brothers and had few similar interests. Esau was the older of the two and was a hunter. Jacob was closer to his mother and appeared crafty and the smarter of the two.

1305. The classic story of how Jacob gained the birthright, the right to all the blessings of the firstborn son, is a story of true deceit, yet it was prophetic that Jacob gained the upper hand. God had said the "older will serve the younger." Both were ultimately blessed by God, but Jacob did use trickery to con his aged father into giving him the blessing by pretending to be Esau after getting Esau to sell his birthright for a bowl of stew.

1306. Wrestling with God. The life of Jacob contains a number of interesting stories that make him appear more a scoundrel than a patriarch. He cheated his brother Esau and tricked his father.

However, one of the strangest stories occurs in Genesis 32. While preparing to meet Esau, Jacob met God (appearing as a man) and wrestled with him all night. After having his hip torn from his socket, Jacob told the man that he would continue wrestling until he was blessed. With that God changed Jacob's name to Israel, which means "wrestles with God."

1307. Jacob married two sisters, Rachel and Leah. Through deceit on the girls' father's part, Jacob ended up being tricked on his wedding night. Jacob served Laban for seven years for Laban's younger daughter, Rachel. The morning after the wedding, Jacob found he had married Leah, Laban's older daughter, instead! Laban agreed to give him Rachel, too, in exchange for another seven years of service.

1308. Eventually the two sisters and their two maids produced twelve sons, who would become the twelve tribes of Israel. They were Reuben, Simeon, Levi, Judah, Dan, Naphtali, Gad, Asher, Issachar, Zebulun, Joseph, and Benjamin. Throughout the story of Jacob's life, God was with him. As long as Jacob remained obedient to God, he was blessed. The history of Israel would go on (and on!) all the way through the New Testament and the birth of a Savior from these early roots.

1309. Before leaving the place of her birth, Rachel stole her father's "household gods." These small "household gods" were idols, typical of the cults in Canaan and elsewhere in Mesopotamia. Small statues of fertility symbols, they were placed in the homes. Laban caught up to Jacob's caravan and began to search for the idols. When Laban came to search Rachel's tent, she sat on a saddlebag, which held her father's gods, telling them she was menstruating and couldn't get up. This story would have been told by the Israelites with derisive mockery as Rachel sat on the idols in her time of "uncleanness."

1310. The story of Joseph's "coat of many colors" remains a favorite of many people. Joseph was the gifted son, the one who had found favor with God. He was also his father's favorite son, much to the chagrin of most of the other brothers. Jacob made Joseph the heir, even though he was the second to the youngest! He was a bold young man and his brothers eventually sold him into slavery in Egypt.

1311. God never forgot Joseph, however. Eventually this young man who saw visions and could interpret dreams would make himself useful to Pharaoh himself! He would become a chief minister of Egypt and would be reunited with his family in their time of need during a drought affecting the whole land.

1312. Elaborate court records survive of many of the pharaohs before and after the presumed time of Joseph. But none of them mentions a Semite slave becoming a high official who had helped save Egypt in a time of extraordinary famine. Periodic drought and famine were not unusual in ancient times, and several were recorded, although none exactly match the biblical scenario. So we do not know who Joseph's pharaoh was.

1313. Joseph had two sons: Manasseh and Ephraim. The brothers were born in Egypt and would eventually be blessed by Jacob. As had happened in Joseph's own experience, God blessed the younger, Ephraim, more than the older brother, Manasseh. God's blessing continued to fall on those who were not expecting the bulk of it.

1314. They all remained in Egypt and lived happily there until the whole generation of Joseph and his brothers passed away. Then they were oppressed by the Egyptians and used as slaves. The Egyptians feared the great numbers of Hebrew people being born and even demanded that the midwives kill the newborn males.

1315. Moses was another miracle. He should have been killed as many of the other male infants were, but he was saved by God for a special purpose. His mother floated him down the Nile in a basket made of reeds, and he was eventually taken into the palace by the royalty of Egypt. Moses would grow up to be a great man of God and the hero of the early Israelites.

1316. Egyptian texts confirm that about the time Moses became angered at seeing an Egyptian overseer beating a Hebrew worker, the Hebrews were engaged in dragging stones for temples built by Pharaoh Ramses II. The Bible says Moses killed the overseer and fled into the desert wilderness of the Sinai Peninsula where he would later see the bush that "burned with fire."

1317. Moses—or *Moshe* in Hebrew—is the central human figure in the Hebrew Bible, the great lawbringer, and for Christians, the symbolic model for Jesus. Moses was saved after a king ordered the Jewish babies killed; Jesus was saved after a king ordered Jewish babies to be killed. Moses parted the waters; Jesus walked on the waters. Moses spent forty years in the wilderness; Jesus spent forty days in the wilderness. Moses went to a mountain and gave a sermon; Jesus gave a sermon on the mount. Moses delivered the covenant; Jesus delivered the new covenant.

1318. Aaron was Moses' older brother. He was a good speaker (Moses was not) and was sent by God to help Moses ask Pharoah to let the Israelites go. He served as the first high priest of Israel. He and Moses were the leaders of the exile from Egypt.

1319. The escape from Egypt. Moses went before Pharaoh and demanded that his people be set free. The story of Moses—who was miraculously saved and raised as royalty, then lost his position due to immature violence, only to be called by God to greatness—is a wonderful riches-to-rags-to-riches story. The plagues, the escape, and the parting of the Red Sea make it one of the most-told stories of all time.

1320. "The Song of Miriam," a victory chant led by the sister of Moses after the Israelites crossed the Red Sea, is thought to be one of the oldest poetic verses in Hebrew Scriptures:

> I will sing to the Lord,
>   for he is highly exalted.
> The horse and its rider
>   he has hurled into the sea.

Exodus 15:21

1321. The "Aaronic benediction" was given by God to Aaron. This extremely ancient blessing is still widely used in temples and churches today among both Jews and Christians:

> The Lord bless you
>   and keep you;
> the Lord make his face shine upon you
>   and be gracious to you;
> the Lord turn his face toward you
>   and give you peace.

Numbers 6:24–26

1322. God brought his people out of Egypt and they settled in the desert. The Israelites, as they had come to be called, didn't always trust God as they should. They constantly forgot what a miracle their escape from Egypt was. As a result they suffered some difficult times and were eventually forbidden to go into the Promised Land God had for them until the entire first generation of people died off.

1323. A flakelike stuff as fine as frost, called *manna*, appeared each morning on the surface of the ground in the desert. When the ancient Israelites first encountered this miraculous provision of food from God in the desert, they asked, "What is it?!" And the name stuck. So "manna," the word the Israelites used to call the stuff on the ground, meant "whatchamacallit."

1324. The Great Commandment. "Hear, O Israel: The LORD our God, the LORD is one. Love the LORD your God with all your heart and with all your soul and with all your strength" (Deut. 6:4–5). This is the Shema, the most commonly spoken prayer in Judaism, also traditionally called the "Great Commandment." Many Christians know it in the form that Jesus used in Mark 12:29.

1325. From out of Canaan. As the Israelites approached the borders of the Promised Land, Moses sent out scouts who reported giants in the land. The scouts were frightened, and they returned to the camp carrying clusters of grapes and pomegranates as proof that they had at least entered the land of Canaan.

The Israelite Adventure

41

1326. **Freed at last, the Israelites set about making a temple in which to worship God.** The tabernacle was their first place of worship. Very explicit instructions were given for how it was to be built (Exodus 26). Inside the tabernacle, which was a giant tent, were several rooms, including the Most Holy Place and the curtain separating that section from the Holy Place. The tabernacle was 75 feet by 150 feet in diameter.

1327. The tent of the tabernacle was covered with badger skins. These skins are mentioned several times in the Old Testament. They were highly valued and were listed along with gold, jewels, and other precious objects. Most badger pelts were extremely durable and tough, making excellent waterproofing material for the tabernacle.

1328. The ark of the covenant was the single most important object in the history of ancient Israel, though it disappeared from the Bible without mention. It was first housed in the tabernacle. After Jerusalem was destroyed in 586 BC, the fate of the ark was never discussed. It was a huge chest that contained the stone tablets of the Ten Commandments. Above the chest stretched the wings of two cherubim.

1329. Offerings of all sorts were an important part of worshiping as an Israelite. Leviticus details the necessary sacrifices for the burnt offering, sin offering, grain offering, fellowship offering, guilt offering, and others.

1330. The Israelites had many hostile enemies on all sides— Philistines, Assyrians, Babylonians, Moabites, and so on. These enemies were given over at times into the Israelites' hands, but at other times God allowed them to overrun the Israelites. Throughout their history they experienced peace and prosperity as well as hardship and exile.

1331. Out of the mouth of donkeys. Threatened by the Israelites, the king of Moab asked a magician named Balaam to come to Moab and put a curse on the Israelites. So the Mesopotamian wizard saddled up his donkey and went to help King Balak. As Balaam was riding down the road, the donkey saw an angel of the Lord and refused to move. Unable to see the angel, Balaam struck the donkey. Finally the donkey turned around and asked the magician, "What have I done to you that you have struck me three times?" God then opened Balaam's eyes and he saw the angel blocking the road. The heavenly messenger then gave Balaam specific instructions. Instead of cursing Israel, the magician gave his blessing (Numbers 22–23).

1332. Sihon was a king of the Amorites. He refused the Israelites access to the Promised Land (it would have taken them through his land) and even marched against God's people. God allowed the Israelites to defeat Sihon and then take his territory. Throughout history God delivered many enemies into their hands.

1333. Rahab is a famous woman of the Bible. Though a prostitute in the city of Jericho, she understood the power of the Israelites and rightly attributed it to God. When two spies came to study the city, she protected them by hiding them in her home. They escaped through her window, promising not to harm her and her family if she would leave a scarlet cord tied in her window (Joshua 2). Later she would be taken into the Israelites' people and even marry and become part of the lineage of Jesus Christ!

1334. At least six cities west of the Jordan were destroyed approximately thirty-two hundred years ago, when the invasion under Joshua was taking place. Even a written record from Egypt exists dating from that time that tells of a pharaoh's dealings with "the people of Israel" in Canaan.

1335. After the crossing of the Jordan, twelve river stones were set in a pile at Gilgal. The first Passover in the Promised Land was celebrated there and a mass circumcision was performed with flint knives because all the men born in the wilderness had not been circumcised. That is why Gilgal means "Hill of the Foreskins" (Joshua 5).

1336. Joshua became the leader of the Israelites after Moses died. It was under his authority that the people at last crossed over into Canaan. He served God and was revered by the people, but he too failed at times and disobeyed God. He is perhaps most remembered for his part in the battle of Jericho.

1337. The battle of Jericho is one of the most miraculous demonstrations of God's power to the Israelites as they became a new nation. The Israelites were instructed to march around Jericho one time each day for six days. The priests were to carry rams' horns at the front of the army. On the seventh day the priests were instructed to blow the trumpets. Then the people were all to shout. God promised Joshua that the walls would then collapse and the men would be able to go inside the city walls and take the city. And it happened just as the angel promised Joshua it would (Joshua 6).

1338. Some of the Israelites continued to disobey God in spite of the intensity of his miracles. Achan was one such case. During the battle of Jericho, he took some of the prized gold and other precious items that belonged to God and kept them for himself. As a result the Israelites lost their next battle (Joshua 7). God punished his people repeatedly for disobeying his commands. He is ever the faithful Father, yet he is a righteous God who demands obedience.

1339. Once the Israelites were established in Canaan, they were governed by judges, people who had usually been warriors first. God gave his people strong leaders to follow, but they didn't always do so. The Book of Judges tells of the difficulties they suffered when they did not obey God.

1340. After Joshua died, it wasn't long before the Israelites "did what was evil in the sight of the Lord." The Israelites were soon mesmerized by the Canaanite gods: Baal, Astarte, and Asherah. It is believed that the Torah laws relating to lewd and perverse sexual practices were in response to Canaanite sexual practices.

1341. Othniel was the first judge. When the Israelites began worshiping these Canaanite gods, God allowed Cushan-Rishathaim, a Syrian king, to overcome them. They were ruled over by the Syrians for eight years. As soon as Israel repented of their sins, God led Othniel to raise up an army to defend Israel. They defeated the Syrians handily. Othniel ruled Israel for forty years after that (Judg. 3:9–11).

1342. Ehud is perhaps the most famous left-handed warrior in history. The Israelites had been ruled by the Moabites for some time. When Ehud, a Benjamite judge, went to pay taxes to King Eglon, he hid a sword under his cloak. Since Ehud was left-handed, and few if any people (evidently) drew swords with that hand, the king didn't suspect anything when Ehud drew his sword. He swiftly killed the king and then defeated the other Moabites. Then he continued to rule as a judge, and the Israelites lived in peace for many years (Judg. 3:15–30).

1343. Shamgar was made judge after Ehud died. By then Israel had turned again from God and was under the power of the Canaanites and the Philistines. It was a difficult time in the history of Israel. The people were under Jabin's rule, and he was a harsh Canaanite king. Shamgar fought back and killed six hundred Philistines with a single metal-tipped stick called an oxgoad (Judg. 3:31). He could not stop Jabin, however.

1344. The two most famous military heroines mentioned in the Old Testament are Deborah and Jael, and they both had a hand in the same victory. God spoke through Deborah to tell the general, Barak, how to defeat the Canaanites, including their king, Jabin. Barak agreed to attack, but wanted Deborah to go with him into the battle. She did and the enemies were defeated.

1345. Sisera was a king of Canaan. He fought hard against Israel, but his nine hundred iron chariots were no match for the rain God sent. As a result the chariots were stuck in the mud and God gave Sisera and his people over to the Israelites.

1346. Jael became a hero of the Israelites, though she herself was a Kenite. Hers was a peaceful tribe that lived comfortably near the Israelites, thanks to her ties to Moses' father-in-law, Jethro. Jael would eventually kill Sisera when he sought refuge with her family. She lulled him to sleep in a tent and then hammered a peg through his head (Judges 4).

1347. Barak and Deborah ruled over Israel in peace for forty years. Deborah is also famous for her victory song, a portion of which is here:

> When the princes in Israel take the lead,
>   when the people willingly offer themselves—
>   praise the LORD! . . .
> So may all your enemies perish, O LORD!
>   But may they who love you be like the sun
>   when it rises in its strength.
>
> Judges 5:2, 31

1348. Gideon is one of the most famous judges. His victory over the Midianites was a testimony to his faith in God and his obedience to what God had ordered him to do. God told Gideon to send away all of the men who were planning to fight except for three hundred in order to show that God would take care of the people. Gideon obeyed, and God delivered the Midianites into the Israelites' hands. Later young Gideon became a judge. He was faithful to God almost to the very end. He was blessed with seventy sons (Judges 6–8).

1349. Hardly the image of a judge, and the illegitimate son of a prostitute, Jephthah was an outcast from his father's family and became an outlaw, an ancient Hebrew "Robin Hood." He is known as the one who, after asking for God's help, made a terrible vow: He promised to sacrifice whoever greeted him if he was victorious. After he won the battle against the Ammonites, he was greeted by his own daughter, who was then sacrificed (Judges 10–11).

1350. The Philistines, the so-called "Sea Peoples" of the Mediterranean, eventually settled on the southern coast of Canaan, in what is now the area around Gaza. From this coastal base, the Philistines pressed inland and collided with the Israelite tribes who were spreading themselves down from the hill country toward the coast. The well-organized military force of the Philistines and their considerable use of iron were a major threat to the Israelites.

1351. Samson is perhaps the most famous judge of all time. He was not the most faithful of all judges; he was proud and did not heed God's word. He was lured into trusting Delilah, a woman paid by the Philistines to find out the secret of his immense strength. Samson would routinely kill large numbers of Philistines, thereby protecting the Israelites. Delilah easily charmed the secret out of him, using her wiles, and Samson's hair was cut. He was taken captive, blinded, and forced to stay in chains in a Philistine dungeon (Judges 13–16).

1352. Yet God heard Samson's final request: Samson prayed for one last chance to serve God and punish the Philistines. God granted his wish with a miracle of amazing proportions. Samson was led into the Philistine temple to be mocked by many Philistines one night. The Philistines put him between two pillars of the temple. Samson pushed with the strength that God had granted him. The temple toppled over and killed the Philistines as well as himself (Judg. 16:23–30).

1353. Also living during the time of the judges were Ruth and Boaz. Ruth was a Moabite, but she moved to Bethlehem to be with her mother-in-law after they both lost their husbands. Ruth was accepted and married Boaz, a good and faithful man, and they were blessed with children and a happy life. Their story is yet another demonstration of how God works to bring people into his plan and to further their joy. Ruth and Boaz were the great-grandparents of King David.

1354. Samuel was the last judge of Israel and also served as a prophet. He was born to childless parents after his mother, Hannah, promised to dedicate a child to God to serve him in the temple. God heard her prayer. Samuel was a mighty figure of Israel and helped put the first kings of the nation on the throne.

1355. Saul was the first king of Israel. He was anointed by the prophet Samuel. He was known to be very tall and majestic of frame. God blessed Saul as long as he was obedient to God and listened to Samuel. But Saul fell away from God and suffered an unhappy ending. He became proud and jealous of David, a young man who was loyal to him and served him in battle and also on a personal level. God did not allow Saul's sins to go unpunished. During a battle, Saul and many of his family were lost; Saul killed himself in order to avoid being captured.

1356. On witches. God told Moses, "Do not allow a sorceress (female witch) to live." King Saul visited a medium at Endor, disregarding the forbidden practice. She summoned up the spirit of the dead Samuel, who had bad news for Saul: He and his sons and the Israelites would fall to the Philistines in battle. The predictions came true as Jonathan and two of Saul's other sons were killed. Saul fell on his sword with the help of his armor-bearer.

1357. David, the youngest son of Jesse, was anointed by Samuel to be the second king of Israel when he was only a shepherd boy. He was a faithful witness to God's amazing love and found much joy and happiness as both a warrior and a king. Yet he, too, sinned and was punished. But he came back to God and was forgiven. David was also a famous poet—many of the Psalms were written by him.

1358. David's defeat of Goliath was his first step toward the throne and away from the fields of sheep he normally watched over. The battle pitted the underdog (a shepherd boy named David) against a mighty warrior (the Philistine Goliath). Though trained soldiers were afraid to fight the giant, David's simple faith made him courageously step forward and kill the giant using a stone thrown from a sling. The stone hit Goliath in the forehead, knocking him down. David then cut the giant's head off with his own sword. The Philistine armies fled, and David's career as a leader of Israel was born (1 Samuel 17).

Poetry of Kings

42

1359. Job is never identified as a Jew, and he wasn't a king, but his book fits with the poetic books of both King David and King Solomon. Job is thought to have lived in the Arabian Desert, somewhere between Babylon and the Holy Land. Interestingly, he was the great naturalist of the Old Testament, and he displayed a deep knowledge and an observant eye for the world around him. "Speak to the earth and it shall teach thee," he advises (Job 12:8 KJV). He followed his own advice because he describes precisely the habits of mammals, the way of birds, the patterns in the skies, the rains, and the floods. He speaks knowingly of the various trees that grow along the streams, from the papyrus in the marshes to the thorny shrubs of the desert.

1360. A keen watcher of the skies. In chapter 9 Job refers to "Arcturus, Orion, and Pleiades, and the chambers of the south" (KJV). He was aware that the stars are not scattered at random in the night sky but are fixed in unchanging patterns, one of which is the Zodiac. The Zodiac is an imaginary belt across the sky consisting of twelve groups of stars—constellations, or "chambers," as Job called them—through which the sun and moon seem to pass. Each constellation appeared to the ancients to represent the figure of some animal or a mythical being usually associated with animals.

1361. "Oh that I had wings like a dove! for then would I fly away, and be at rest" (KJV). David, weighed down by his duties, must have wished he could take flight from his tasks. He might have selected almost any bird to express this wish in Psalm 55, yet he chose the dove for a particular reason. The former shepherd knew that while most birds can fly, only doves can take off with a sudden burst of speed and sustain their powerful flight for a long distance.

1362. David was more than a great warrior. He was a musician who played the eight-stringed harplike instrument known as the lyre. He was also a great poet who composed about half of the Psalms. David used many descriptions of animals, birds, and plant life in the Psalms to portray poetic images.

1363. Was he a lover or a fighter? David's eye for beauty included a passion for women as well as nature. As was the custom, many of David's wives and concubines were the result of political maneuvers that expanded and secured David's kingdom territory.

1364. The habits of the Palestinian house sparrow were so well known that Psalm 102 uses it as a symbol of desolation: "I watch, and am as a sparrow alone upon the house top" (KJV). Here is an intentional contradiction, for it is difficult to visualize a lone sparrow. House sparrows are highly gregarious birds; they seek food in large flocks and at night they group in protected places, such as under the roof eaves of buildings. This psalm's unlikely picture of a single sparrow evokes a feeling of utter loneliness and abandonment.

1365. "I am like a pelican of the wilderness" (KJV). Also found in Psalm 102, this too is David's lament. The white pelican is abundant around the inland lakes and rivers of Africa and Eurasia where it preys on fish, but many Bible readers have wondered what the pelican was doing in the wilderness. In the Bible the word wilderness refers to any unpopulated place, such as a mountain, desert, or marsh. Pelicans are often found living in the deserts of the Bible lands, so long as there is an inland lake within flying distance.

1366. The shortest psalm (117) has just two verses and the longest psalm is just two psalms later (119). It is also the longest chapter in the Bible, and longer than some whole Bible books—such as Obadiah, Philemon, and Jude.

1367. It appears that this collection was begun as something of a hymnbook for temple worship in Jerusalem. Words such as *selah, maskil,* and *miktam* are found throughout the book to give direction to those who would speak or chant these psalms in public worship.

1368. The Book of Psalms is really five different books of songs and poems; all connect our relationship to God. Book 1 includes Psalms 1–41; book 2 is Psalms 42–72; book 3 includes Psalms 73–89; book 4 has Psalms 90–106; and book 5 has Psalms 107–50.

1369. Acrostic poems are found throughout Jewish literature. Psalm 119, the longest chapter in the Bible, is an acrostic poem—every new stanza begins with the successive letter of the Hebrew alphabet. Psalm 112 is similar, with each line beginning with the next letter of the alphabet. This was not only poetic but also aided in the memorization of the psalm.

1370. The Penitential Psalms is the title given to seven psalms that express deep repentance over sin: Psalms 7, 32, 38, 51, 102, 130, and 143. All but two are attributed to King David—most notably Psalm 51, which is his lament over committing adultery with Bathsheba.

1371. The Messianic Psalms are Old Testament psalms that relate information about the coming Messiah. They were generally quoted by the Lord Jesus or the New Testament writers in reference to him. These include Psalms 22, 40, 41, 45, 69, 72, and 118.

1372. The Psalms of Ascent are the songs that were sung by Jewish pilgrims as they traveled upward from the surrounding areas of Palestine to the city of Jerusalem for festivals. The songs tell of looking up to the hills, seeing the walls of Jerusalem, and observing the many people gathering together to worship. They end with a joyous shout of praise as the pilgrims finally arrive at the gates of the temple.

1373. The Philistines held a monopoly on the manufacture of iron, and in this way they exerted control over the Israelites. The Philistines jealously guarded the secrets of the complicated smelting process, and they prevented the Israelites from stocking up on iron swords and shields by not allowing them to have smiths in their territory. Only after the first two kings of Israel, Saul and David, defeated the Philistines did the metal come into common use. The Israelites then learned the techniques of iron-making. Even the Hebrew words for "knife" and "helmet" came from the Philistines.

1374. The conquest of the city of Jebus was one of David's victories. He changed the name to Jerusalem, which means "City of Peace." Jerusalem is situated on a limestone ridge about twenty-five hundred feet above sea level. To the south and west is the valley of Hinnom (or Gehenna), which was used to burn refuse. By New Testament times Gehenna had become a symbol for hell, probably because of the fires constantly burning there.

1375. Solomon became king in the year 961 BC and reigned for thirty-nine years. The name Solomon is derived from the Hebrew word for "peace," and Solomon indeed lived up to his name. Under his reign Jerusalem became one of the most important cities in the Near East.

1376. Solomon was the wisest man who ever lived; he was "wiser than all men" (1 Kings 4:31 KJV). God had asked him what he wanted more than anything, and Solomon asked for wisdom in order to better rule the people of Israel. His wisdom was unsurpassed, and the people lived very well under his rule. A beautiful temple was even built, but sadly many of the Israelites, including Solomon, eventually began sacrificing to other gods. God raised up armies to fight against him and his people, but he made a decision not to take the nation from Solomon's rule . . . he would spare

Solomon that for his father's sake. Instead Israel would be lost during the reign of Solomon's son, Rehoboam.

1377. Knowing it all. Not only did Solomon speak over three thousand proverbs and write more than a thousand songs, some of which come down to us in the Books of Proverbs and the Song of Solomon, he could also speak knowingly on any subject. And he was obviously an authority on natural history. The Bible says that he could lecture on "trees, from the cedar tree that is in Lebanon even unto the hyssop that springeth out of the wall: he spake also of beasts, and of fowl, and of creeping things, and of fishes" (1 Kings 4:33 KJV).

1378. The cedar was the largest tree that Solomon could have known, and the little fragrant herb, the hyssop, was among the smallest. Unlike modern hyssop, the plant Solomon spoke of is believed to have been one of the marjorams, members of the mint family that grow clusters of white flowers among rocks and in crevices in walls. Under these conditions it is among the smallest flowering plants in the Holy Land.

1379. The cedar of Lebanon was the largest and most noble tree growing in the Bible lands. It was once abundant in the regions of Lebanon, Syria, and Turkey. It towered as high as 120 feet, and the diameter of its trunk sometimes reached eight feet. It had a fragrant gum that made walking in a cedar grove a delight. Its wood not only was a beautiful reddish color, but it also resisted decay and attack by insects.

1380. A gardener on a grand scale. The Bible describes Solomon as a gardener (Eccles. 2:4–6). No one has yet found the exact location of Solomon's gardens, but they must have been quite close to the palace. A few miles outside of Jerusalem are three large reservoirs that have traditionally been called the Pools of Solomon, and they may be the reservoirs he built to provide water for his gardens.

1381. The most unusual of Solomon's gardens must have been the one devoted to spices, for Solomon's far-flung trade with Arabia and India brought him many exotic plants. One of the prizes of the spice garden was spikenard, which was found in the Himalaya Mountains of Asia. The dried stems became an important trade item in the ancient world.

1382. Dried spikenard was transported across Asia by camels and stored in alabaster boxes to preserve its fragrance. That is the reason spikenard was extraordinarily expensive, as John points out when he states that Mary anointed the feet of Jesus with "a pound of ointment of spikenard" (John 12:3 KJV).

1383. Acacia, the "shittim wood" referred to often in the Bible, has many uses. Fine grained and durable, its wood was suitable for beautiful things like the ark of the covenant, the altar of the tabernacle, and the mummy coffins of the Egyptians. Various species of acacia also provide perfumes, gum arabic, medicine, food for cattle, and firewood.

1384. An alliance with the Phoenicians was one of the most enterprising of Solomon's many ventures. The Bible never refers to the Phoenicians by name but instead calls them the people of Tyre, Sidon, or Gebal, the three main cities from which the Phoenicians sent out trading voyages to all parts of the ancient world. The word *Phoenicians* comes from the Greek word for "reddish-purple," which refers to the dye the Phoenicians prepared from species of murex, a marine snail. The murex has a gland that secretes a milky white fluid as a defense against predators, but when exposed to light and air, the fluid turns purple and is a permanent dye on fabric.

1385. "Tarshish ships." This biblical reference to the ships of Solomon refers to those that were built via an agreement Solomon negotiated with his Phoenician neighbor, King Hiram of Tyre. Together they obtained skilled workmen to build him a fleet of merchant ships. No one knows exactly what the ships looked like, but they were probably a mix between the Phoenician battleships and merchant ships. Solomon's fleet was based near his smelters, at Eziongeber on the Gulf of Aqaba. From there his ships sailed with metal and other items to a place known as Ophir.

1386. After Solomon's death between 930 and 925 BC, political and religious differences quickly shattered the kingdom built by David and Solomon. The ten tribes in the north broke away from the southern tribes of Judah and Benjamin, and two weaker kingdoms were left: Judah in the south and Israel in the north.

1387. The call of wisdom is made throughout the first ten chapters of Proverbs. Solomon, who was given great wisdom from God, says in Proverbs 8:22 that wisdom was the first creation of God. It's interesting that Solomon always refers to wisdom in the feminine sense: "She calls out . . ."

1388. Canticles or the Song of Songs is a set of love poems shared between a man and a woman. Some of the images are so mature that Jewish boys were not allowed to read it until they reached adulthood. Many people have questioned its place in Scripture, but Jewish leaders decided in ancient times that the book is allegorical—the man chasing a woman is a depiction of God pursuing sinful Israel. In medieval times Christian scholars suggested that the book also represented Christ pursuing the church.

1389. "Solomon's sword" is the phrase used to describe a wise choice. It comes from the time two women, both claiming to be the mother of an infant, approached King Solomon and asked him to settle their dispute. Solomon asked for a sword, announcing he would cut the child in half. With that the real mother insisted that the baby not be harmed and instead be given to the other woman. The king, recognizing that the true mother would intervene for the baby's welfare, awarded the child to her.

1390. "Turn, Turn, Turn." During the 1960s, there may have been no more widely quoted Bible verses than the words from Ecclesiastes. They provided Pete Seeger with the lyrics that eventually became a hit single for the Byrds. Americans of that era may recall that President Kennedy admired these verses so much that they were read at his funeral.

Prophets Speak

43

1391. Prophets and priests played an important role in early Israel, though many of the prophets do not have books named after them. The purpose of these godly men was to serve as messengers from God to the people. The prophets and priests received orders from God and acted upon them.

1392. Moses said God would raise up prophets like him in the generations to follow. And God did. Generally keeping a low profile, the prophets did not possess administrative power like the kings. And they had no place in the tabernacle or temple rituals like the priests. They simply spoke the mind of God as it was given to them. Unlike the kingship and the priesthood, the position of prophet could not be passed on to one's descendants. God individually chose each one.

1393. Nathan served as a prophet in the time of David and Solomon. It was his responsibility to confront David after David stole a soldier's wife, made her pregnant, and then had the soldier killed in order to cover up his deceitful behavior. When Nathan confronted David for his behavior, David repented, but God took the child born of the woman, Bathsheba, as a punishment. However, the next child David and Bathsheba conceived was Solomon, who would be king.

1394. Elijah trusted God completely, so much so that when King Ahab appointed prophets to worship the false god Baal, Elijah told him no more rain would fall. Three years after the drought began, when Israel was literally starving, Elijah had a contest with the Baal prophets to see which deity would answer their prayers—God or the false god Baal. The people were brought to their senses by the sign of a soaked altar bursting into flame, and they came back to God.

1395. As one of only two men who never died, Elijah was truly a special prophet of God. Enoch, a man who walked with God, was the other. Elijah was taken up to heaven in a chariot of fire, but before he was taken he appointed Elisha, his servant, to succeed him.

1396. Even though Elijah and Elisha were two of the most prominent prophets in the days of the northern kingdom, no book is named after them. Because of this we can assume that the seventeen books of prophecy in the Bible are just a sampling of all that the prophets spoke.

1397. The books of prophecy. This section of the Bible is composed of seventeen books beginning with Isaiah and ending with Malachi, closing out the Old Testament. Like the books of poetry, these books don't extend the time line of Israel's history; rather, they fill in the one laid down by the books of history. Apart from Job, most of the books of poetry were associated with the kings of Israel's glory days. By contrast the books of prophecy were associated mainly with the period of Israel's decline and fall.

1398. Prophecy in the Old Testament was not so much a telling of the future as it was an urgent statement made on behalf of God to his people. Certain elements of Hebrew prophecy spoke of the future in terms that human behavior could not change, but most of it offered God's people a choice and often stated the harsh consequences if the Israelites chose to disobey.

1399. Both the major and minor prophets are organized in historical order. This doesn't mean the minor prophets followed the majors in history, however. They coexisted with them. Hosea, for example, was a contemporary of Isaiah. Since the fall of Jerusalem is dated by historians at 586 BC, all the books of prophecy—major and minor—can be dated within a century or two of that date.

1400. Majors and Minors, part 1. The distinction is made by the length of each book. Isaiah, for example, is longer than all twelve of the minor prophets put together. Although Lamentations is short, Jeremiah was a major prophet, and the full title is "The Lamentations of Jeremiah."

1401. Majors and Minors, part 2. Israel's prophets were not the type of people to include on your invitation list to a party. The Hebrew prophets denounced evil, corruption, and immorality. The three longest prophetic books, Isaiah, Jeremiah, and Ezekiel, along with Daniel and Lamentations, have traditionally been labeled the "Major Prophets." The other twelve books are called the "Minor Prophets."

1402. Jonah was cast into the sea by the sailors around him in order to stop the raging sea. The prophet knew God had sent the storm after he refused to go and minister to Nineveh, the capital of the Assyrian Empire. When he was thrown overboard, the sea calmed, but Jonah was swallowed by a big fish. Many believe the fish was a whale, but it is also possible that it was a shark that "saved" Jonah. He returned to Nineveh after spending three days in the belly of the big fish.

1403. The plant that God appointed to grow and shade Jonah after he finished preaching at Nineveh is sometimes translated a "gourd plant" and sometimes simply a "plant." It is believed that the writer meant for his readers to imagine the castor bean. In hot climates it grows very fast and often seems like a tree, with huge umbrella-like leaves that make wonderful shade. The Hebrews valued the oil of its beanlike seeds and used it widely in lamps and ceremonial rites.

1404. Nineveh's demise in 612 BC brought the city to its end. Nineveh fell after a two-month siege carried out by an alliance among Medes, Babylonians, and Scythians. The attackers destroyed Nineveh by releasing the Khoser River into the city, where it dissolved the buildings' sun-dried bricks. This was a remarkable fulfillment of Nahum's prophecy: "The gates of the rivers shall be opened, and the palace shall be dissolved" (Nah. 2:6). Nineveh was lost for well over two thousand years.

1405. At the forefront. In the period of the divided kingdom, the focus of the Bible books moves away from the kings to the ministries of a series of "prophets," those who spoke on the behalf of God after receiving divine messages through dreams or visions. Prophets tried to counsel—usually with little success—the rulers and people of Israel and Judah. The prophets became crucial biblical characters who overshadowed the kings and took their message to the entire nation.

1406. Hosea suffered greatly as a prophet. His name means "Save, oh God!" His was a unique task: to marry a prostitute and live as a faithful husband to her. Their relationship paralleled what Israel was doing to God—God was a faithful husband to a harlot nation. Hosea thus could speak from experience and feel personally what great pain God must suffer when his people abandon him repeatedly.

1407. Gomer was the wife Hosea was sent to marry. She bore three children to Hosea, though none of them were likely his own children. God provided names for each of the children, but they were not names to rejoice over. Rather they were fateful reminders of what Israel had become. Their names were Jezreel (in honor of a massacre that took place in Jezreel for which God was going to punish the Israelites); Lo-Ruhamah, which means "not loved"; and Lo-Ammi, which means "not my people."

1408. God's chosen people. One of the most significant lines in Amos is the prophet's message to Israel from God: "You only have I chosen of all the families of the earth; therefore I will punish you for all your sins" (3:2). This is the essence of the Jews' designation as the "chosen people." God's covenant with the people did not entitle them to special favors; rather, being chosen increased their responsibility.

1409. Amos was the first prophet to have his words written down. One of the more interesting facts about his book is that he used the lion to emphasize that his mission was to bring the Hebrews back to righteousness. No other wild animal is mentioned so often in the Bible as the lion. It appears in thirty-one of the sixty-six books of the Old and New Testaments.

1410. Lions were still abundant in the Bible lands when Amos lived, and they ranged from Africa across the Near East to India. In the Holy Land itself, the lion was exterminated by about the time of the Crusades in the Middle Ages. It vanished from Egypt in the last century, and the last wild lion seen in the Near East was captured in Iran in 1923. Hunting lions was an ancient sport in the Bible lands, and many pictures show them being captured in nets and pits. Like many other Near Eastern monarchs, King Darius of Persia kept a den of lions—into which Daniel was cast.

1411. Micah lived after Amos and Hosea. He prophesied of a future king who would be born in Bethlehem. He looked forward to that time as the current kings he suffered with consistently led the people toward idol worship and other forms of sin.

1412. Jehoiada and his wife saved the line of kings from the wrath of King Ahaziah's mother, Athaliah, who tried to seize the throne by killing the entire family. Jehoiada was chief priest at the time. They stole Ahaziah's baby, Joash, and hid him for six years. Then they overthrew Athaliah and put Joash on the throne to reinstate his lineage.

1413. Following the reign of Manasseh, a notorious king of Judah who reintroduced idol worship, a crucial moment in biblical history occurred in 621 BC. During the reign of King Josiah, an ideal king who reigned for thirty-one years after taking the throne at age eight, a scroll that was about to be removed from the temple was discovered by a priest. When Josiah read the scroll, he tore his clothes in anguish because he knew how far the people had fallen from God. He began vigorous reforms and removed all pagan items from Jerusalem.

1414. Hilkiah was the high priest who found the scroll that brought King Josiah to his knees. Together he and the young king tried to bring the people back to God.

1415. The longest prophetic book in Hebrew Scripture, Isaiah has had a remarkable impact on our language. Perhaps more than any other book of Hebrew prophecy, Isaiah has played a central role for Christians and has even been called the "the fifth Gospel" because so many of the book's prophecies were fulfilled in the life of Jesus.

1416. The Book of Isaiah has two distinct halves. The first thirty-nine chapters seem to have been written before the Babylonian conquest of Israel, but the rest of the book was clearly written after that event. That has led scholars to suggest there were two authors or possibly even two different prophets named Isaiah.

1417. Many well-worn phrases were born in Isaiah. Besides providing Handel with wonderful lyrics, Isaiah has yielded phrases commonly used even today:

> "White as snow"
> "Neither shall they learn war any more"
> "The people that walked in darkness"
> "And a little child shall lead them"
> "They shall mount up with wings as eagles"
> "Be of good courage"
> "Like a lamb to the slaughter"

1418. The Servant Songs is the name given to the passages of Scripture in Isaiah 42, 49, 50, 52, and 53 describing an innocent man who endures great pain. Many Jewish scholars did not know what to do with these passages and could not reconcile them to the images of the Messiah coming as a mighty king. But Christians from earliest times have applied them to Jesus Christ, who suffered greatly for the sins of all humankind.

1419. Christians and Jews disagree on a key portion of Isaiah's prophecies found scattered throughout Isaiah chapters 42, 49, 50, 52, and 53 in songs that speak of a "suffering servant of God." When Isaiah speaks of a despised, rejected man of suffering who is led like a lamb to slaughter, Christians see another symbolic prophecy of Jesus. Jewish readers, on the other hand, prefer to view this as either a reference to Isaiah himself, the prophet who suffered because his words were unpopular, or to the people of Israel, who suffer for the nation's sins.

1420. Huldah, the wife of Shallum, is one of the most noteworthy Hebrew prophetesses. She was active in ministry during the days of King Josiah. When the Book of the Law was found in the temple, the religious leaders came to her and asked what God wanted the nation to do. This "Book of the Law" is generally thought to be an early version of Deuteronomy, which places special emphasis on removing any trace of idolatry from the worship of God. For the first time since the time of the judges, before the rise of the monarchy in Israel, the Passover was properly celebrated.

1421. The prophet Jeremiah warned of the oncoming destruction by hostile empires, and he said that sinful people would become "meat for the fowls of the heaven, and for the beasts of the earth" (Jer. 7:33 KJV). By "fowls" that would feast on the slain, Jeremiah undoubtedly meant vultures, because they feed on dead animals. The griffon is a huge vulture in the Holy Land, particularly in the mountainous areas. Although it is large and powerful, it never kills its own prey, and it will not feed on any animal that still shows signs of life. It is a remarkably clean bird in its habits, bathing almost as often as it finds water.

1422. The Babylonians came. They laid waste to the countryside and were on the verge of capturing Jerusalem just as Jeremiah had foretold. Yet on the eve of destruction, Jeremiah did a strange thing. He bought a piece of real estate, a field near his home village. He paid seventeen shekels of silver for it, had the deed signed, sealed, and witnessed, and then instructed Baruch to put the deed in a clay jar so that it could be preserved for a long time. For just as he believed that God would surely destroy the nation of Judah, Jeremiah also believed that God would build it up again. "Is there no balm in Gilead?" Jeremiah cried out and answered his own question by refusing to despair. God would not forsake his people, no matter how faithless they had been.

1423. Jeremiah is believed to be the author of the Book of Lamentations. In chapter three, the writer cries out:

I am the man who has seen affliction
    by the rod of his wrath.
He has driven me away and made me walk
    in darkness rather than light;
indeed he has turned his hand against me
    again and again, all day long.
He pierced my heart
    with arrows from his quiver.
I became the laughingstock of all my people;
    they mock me in song all day long.
He has filled me with bitter herbs,
    and sated me with gall.

                                        verses 1–3, 13–15

1424. Origin of the term *Jews*. In the year 587BC the holy city
lay in ruins, and its people were led off to captivity in Babylon after
the armies of King Nebuchadnezzar overran Judah and conquered
Jerusalem. Their name changed to "Jews" (from the Hebrew *Yehudi*,
which means "belonging to the tribe of Judah"). They kept alive
their faith and their way of life during the years of exile.

1425. Habakkuk is thought to have been a prophet around the
time of Jeremiah. He struggled with how God would want his
people, despite how badly they were behaving, to come under the
influence of an even more ungodly people—the Babylonians. God
was faithful to his prophet and assured Habakkuk to trust him for
the answer.

1426. Ezekiel spoke knowingly about the land and its life. Scholars
disputed for a long time about what animal he meant by "the great
dragon" (Ezek. 29:3 KJV), until archaeologists excavated ancient
Babylon and discovered the remains of an enormous gate that was
ordered to be built by Nebuchadnezzar. The ruins of the Ishtar Gate
showed decorations with rows of animal sculptures—at least 575
figures in all. One of the animals is a fantastic beast: the Sirrush or
Dragon of Babylon.

1427. Why a dragon? No one knows for certain why the image of
the Sirrush was placed on the gates, but Nebuchadnezzar ordered
these words inscribed on it: "Fierce bulls and grim dragons I put
and thus supplied the gates with such overflowing rich splendor
that all humanity may view it with wonderment." It is possible that

the figures were intended to impress or even frighten the Medes and Persians. So although actual dragons never existed, sculptured figures of them must have been seen by Ezekiel during the exile in Babylon.

1428. The valley of dry bones was a graveyard to which the prophet Ezekiel was commanded to preach. As he did so Ezekiel watched the bones reattach to one another and come to life—an image of the spiritually dead nation of Israel coming back to life by the power of God's Word. This event, recorded in Ezekiel 37, is one of several strange visions of the prophet.

1429. The period of the exile in Babylon, lasting approximately from 586 to 538 BC, deeply impacted Judaism and the Bible. Without the temple in Jerusalem as the focal point of Yahweh worship, the Jews were forced to create a new form of communal ritual with the earliest beginnings of the synagogue as their center for prayer, Torah study, and teaching.

1430. The spirit of hope to return to Jerusalem and restore the temple gave many exiled Jews a purpose. They began to look for a Messiah, a new leader or savior. However, only a minority of the Jews took advantage of the offer to return to Judah and rebuild Jerusalem. Many of these people had lived in Babylon for two generations and intermarriage had become common.

1431. The Hebrew Bible gained much of its present shape during the exiled years in Babylon. The Pentateuch, or Torah, approached the form it now holds, and the history of Israel, from Joshua through 1 and 2 Kings, and the earliest prophetic writings, were all most likely composed during the exile.

1432. Jeshua was allowed to return to Jerusalem after nearly fifty years of captivity by King Cyrus of Persia. This young man, whose name means "the Lord is salvation," led the way for Jews to begin worshiping once again. He served as chief priest and helped to lead the effort to rebuild the temple.

1433. The beginnings of the diaspora, the great dispersal of Jews throughout the Mediterranean world and eventually into Europe, is marked by the period of exile and return. While in Babylon some Jews had entered official government service, such as Nehemiah, "a cupbearer" to one Persian king, and Mordecai, who also served a Persian king in the Book of Esther.

1434. Daniel was a statesman, not a prophet. As a result, Jewish scholars do not place this book among the prophetic books. However, because Daniel had the gift of prediction, the New Testament calls him a "prophet" (Matt. 24:15). Daniel saw many symbols in his prophetic visions, and he often recorded them without attempting to interpret what they meant.

1435. Starting in 538 BC, about seventy years after the destruction of Jerusalem, Jews began returning to their holy city. The Book of Ezra describes the exiles' return. Ezra was a priest who led a group of Jews to their homeland. He was accompanied by some seventeen hundred Babylonian Jews, including some Levites. A census was recorded of who returned to the Promised Land. Much of this book deals with temple worship and its responsibilities. Ezra taught the details of the Law of Moses so that Jews could reinstate the practices in the Promised Land.

1436. In Jewish history, law, and theology, Ezra is a character of great significance. Some Hebrew scholars rank him second only to Moses as a lawgiver and prophet, and he's considered by many as the second founder (after Moses) of the Jewish nation. Not only did Ezra reinstate the law and temple worship practices, he required that all Jewish men get rid of their foreign wives and children. Ezra ends poignantly with the words, "All these had married foreign women, and some of them had children by these wives."

1437. Around 520 BC, Haggai came onto the scene. The work of rebuilding the temple had nearly stopped. Haggai cheered the people on to continue the effort. He also gave great comfort to the other two priests who were hard at work. Within four years the work was done and the temple was rebuilt.

1438. The Judah of the return from Babylon was a far cry from Solomon's empire, and the second temple, completed in 516 BC, was modest, despite the fact that Cyrus provided funding for the rebuilding of the temple. All the gold and silver vessels that had been salvaged from the original temple and taken to Babylon were returned to Jerusalem. But never again in Scripture is the fate of Judaism's most sacred object, the ark of the covenant, mentioned.

1439. At the rededication of the city of Jerusalem in 445 BC, all the Jewish people and all who could hear with understanding gathered at the square in front of the Water Gate. Ezra began to read the Book of Moses before the assembly, "which was made up of men and women and all who were able to understand. And all the people listened attentively to the Book of the Law" (Neh. 8:3). This verse refers to the fact that most Jews no longer understood Hebrew. By the time of the return, Aramaic, a related Semitic language, had replaced Hebrew as the common language.

The New
Testament Writings

44

1440. The four Gospels follow closely in the tradition of the books of history we saw in the Old Testament—words spoken and deeds done. Little is told of the inward thoughts and motivations of the various people in the stories. The Gospels tell how Jesus was a descendant of David, which was an essential requirement of the Messiah, according to the prophecies of Scripture.

1441. Matthew was written by a former tax collector named Matthew. His book covers the lineage of Jesus and also tells the story of much of his ministry, including the Beatitudes.

1442. The Beatitudes are a well-known portion of Scripture from Christ's Sermon on the Mount in which he blessed certain types of people. Matthew 5 records that Jesus blessed the poor in spirit, those who mourn, the meek, those who hunger and thirst for righteousness, the merciful, the pure in heart, the peacemakers, and those who are persecuted for righteousness' sake—all of which describe the people who would populate the kingdom of God. However, the actual word *beatitude* doesn't appear in Scripture. It's from the Latin word for "blessed" and was made popular by the Vulgate.

1443. The parables are the stories Jesus used to convey spiritual truth. They were essentially comparisons—"The kingdom of heaven is like a treasure hidden in a field" or "Everyone who hears these words and puts them into practice is like a wise man who built a house." While his concrete images made the parables memorable, they also puzzled people who could not always follow Christ's meaning.

1444. Mark is a Gospel that details Jesus' service to those he called and preached to. Jesus' portrayal as the great servant can be found in this Gospel, which was written by someone we know very little about.

1445. Luke opens his Gospel by saying that "many" had attempted to write an account of Jesus' life and ministry, but that he himself is doing so because God has given him "perfect understanding of all things from the very first" (Luke 1:3 KJV). God not only gave the Gospel writers firsthand exposure as eyewitnesses to the events of Jesus' ministry but also perfect understanding. Luke is especially forthright about Christ the man.

1446. John, perhaps the most famous book of the whole Bible in terms of its saving message, is a description of both Christ's deity and his redeeming work for sinners. The Gospel was written by the "disciple whom Jesus loved," John.

1447. John was compelled to address the question of how a flesh-and-blood man could also be a divine being as Jesus was. The notion of gods having sex with humans was commonplace in many pagan traditions, especially among the Greeks. But to make it clear that the birth of Jesus was of God in the flesh, the Gospels described the virgin birth. Other pagan writings did not.

1448. The four Gospels therefore tell of all aspects of Jesus: Matthew of his right to be called "King," Mark of his title as "Greatest Servant," Luke of his completely human nature, and John of his being the Savior of the world—God's only Son.

1449. The Book of Acts was written by Luke, also the author of the Gospel of Luke. He begins with a salutation to Theophilus and makes reference to the "first account I composed" (the Gospel of Luke). Luke's two books could be titled, "The Acts of Jesus" and "The Acts of the Apostles." They comprise a two-volume history of New Testament times. The events in Acts take place over several decades. As the books of Moses established the historical framework for the Old Testament, so the Gospels and Acts establish the framework for the New Testament.

1450. The apostles' letters are sometimes called Epistles. The word *epistle* helps convey that there was a formal or public element to these letters. These last twenty-two books of the Bible were personal letters in that they often specify the names of both the sender and the recipient(s). The fact that no point is made of the authors' identities implies how unimportant the issue is. The apostles were charged with the responsibility of spreading Jesus' message faithfully, and that in and of itself gave the writings authority in the eyes of Christ's followers.

1451. Romans. In this letter Paul writes to the disciples in Rome. Normally he wrote to communities of disciples that he himself had established. Romans is an exception, for in this case he wrote in advance of his first visit. Misunderstandings about the message of Jesus were complex, so Paul gives an extended explanation of his understanding of the message. He also deals with the complexities of Jewish versus Gentile perspectives.

1452. First Corinthians. Corinth was a city in southern Greece. Acts 18 describes how Paul spent eighteen months there. This letter is written some time after that. Parts of this letter are difficult to follow because Paul goes straight into his answers to the Corinthians' problems without restating what they were. First Corinthians 13, the famous love passage, is timeless and universal.

1453. Second Corinthians. By the time this letter was written, Paul had to make a defense of his ministry. Recurring problems at

Corinth and the infusion of false teachings had sullied his reputation. In this wonderfully moving letter, Paul states that the purpose of the defense is not to protect his reputation but to defend the truth for those he had taught.

1454. Galatians begins a series of shorter letters. Galatia was a region situated on the eastern side of Asia Minor. The letter was therefore addressed more broadly than the letters to Rome and Corinth. The Epistle of Galatians was to be read by various gatherings of disciples in various cities of Galatia. The purpose of the letter was straightforward: to protest and refute false teaching that had taken root in that region.

1455. Ephesians. Ephesus was a seaport on the western coast of Asia Minor. In New Testament times this region was called Asia. This letter was very general in nature and served as an explanation of God's design, followed by specific instructions for everyday living. It was intended for communities beyond Ephesus as well.

1456. Philippians. This letter is as specific as Ephesians is broad. Philippi was a city in northern Greece. Paul preached there on his second major journey. The people in Philippi held Paul in high esteem. He was sending words of encouragement to them during a time of persecution. Ironically Paul seems to be writing from jail. Sharing his hope, he writes of his intent to return to them at some future time.

1457. Colossians. Colosse was a city located due east of Ephesus. This letter is very similar to Ephesians, except much shorter. As the letter ends, it gives instructions to send it on to Laodicea, another nearby city.

1458. First Thessalonians. Thessalonica was a city in northern Greece. It was just down the road from Philippi. Paul's first visit there was recorded in Acts 17. As usual he was met with two different responses: enthusiastic acceptance and severe resistance. Paul wrote this letter to strengthen and encourage the believers there. Above all he urges them to look for "the day of the Lord" when everything will be made right.

1459. Second Thessalonians. Sometime after the disciples at Thessalonica got Paul's first letter, they began to wonder whether "the day of the Lord" might have come and gone. Paul quickly assured them that indeed it had not. He urged them to continue imitating Jesus and loving the people around them.

1460. The Pastoral Letters are the instructions of Paul to two young Christian ministers. Detailing useful advice about church leadership, particularly the importance of setting high moral standards, the Books of 1 Timothy, 2 Timothy, and Titus have a fatherly tone as Paul writes to his young protégés.

1461. First Timothy. Timothy was Paul's best-known helper. He is first mentioned in Acts 16. Paul met him on one of his journeys, and the two later agreed to work together. Paul writes to Timothy as a father would to a son, so there was likely a significant age difference between them, as well as a bond of love. The message of this book can be summed up with the words "The goal of this command is love, which comes from a pure heart and a good conscience and a sincere faith" (1 Tim. 1:5).

1462. Second Timothy. Paul's second letter to Timothy was written when Paul was facing imminent death. Though the Scriptures don't record it, modern historians generally agree that Paul was beheaded in Rome for continuing to preach the gospel. This letter to Timothy was apparently written in anticipation of that event and is extremely moving. Paul charges Timothy to continue the good fight of faith.

1463. Titus. Though Titus comes after 2 Timothy in the Bible, it was obviously written sometime before it because it contains none of Paul's immediate anticipation of death. Titus was another helper and co-worker of Paul's. This letter is structured much like 1 Timothy. Paul reminds Titus to give attention to instruction and to the appointment of others who could help spread the message.

1464. Philemon barely takes up a page in most Bibles. Though the title is "Philemon," it is also addressed to Apphia, Archippus, and the group of disciples that met in their house. The subject of the letter was a runaway slave of Philemon's named Onesimus. Paul ran across Onesimus and urged him to return home. At the same time, Paul encouraged Philemon not only to forgive Onesimus but to treat him as a brother rather than a slave.

1465. Hebrews. Though the King James Version of the Bible attributes this letter to Paul, most modern English versions do not. The uncertainty stems from the fact that if Paul did write this letter, he failed to specify such a fact in the text as he had in all his other letters. Regardless of who wrote this epistle, it is distinctly different from any of the other letters in the Bible.

1466. The Book of Hebrews is the only anonymous letter in the New Testament. It is placed at the end of Paul's letters in our New Testament specifically because the collectors of the Canon were not sure if it was written by Paul or not. We're also not sure of the intended recipients, though it was widely circulated in the early church. Still, the focus of the letter is clear: Jesus is our Great High Priest, the mediator between holy God and sinful man.

1467. The Christian Hall of Fame is the title often given to Hebrews 11, which begins with Abel and proceeds to list the key figures of the Old Testament. Since it was probably intended for Jewish Christians, the list emphasizes Abraham and Moses but goes on to include the many believers who suffered persecution and martyrdom for the cause of the faith.

1468. James. It is believed the author of this book was James, the brother of Jesus and leader of the Jerusalem council. James was written most likely for Jewish Christians, as it is addressed to the "twelve tribes scattered among the nations." James wrote to instruct and encourage Christians in the midst of persecution and personal trials. James is especially marked by its emphasis on a faith accompanied by good works and a lifestyle that is consistent in its faithfulness to Christ.

1469. First Peter. This is the first of two letters from Peter written in Rome. He addressed it to the Gentiles of Asia Minor who were enduring severe persecution. It appears to be a letter meant to circulate; it deals with practical subjects of faith, hope, and love for everyday living. Although certain aspects of his style are rough, others are quite elegant and similar to classical Greek. This leads scholars to believe that Peter may have had a Greek amanuensis (someone to take dictation) named Silvanus (1 Peter 5:12).

1470. Second Peter. In Peter's second letter (less elegantly written than 1 Peter) he began by pointing out that he did not have long to live and wanted to lay down the things most essential for his disciples to remember, urging them to grow in the knowledge of the truth. Near the end of this epistle, Peter made reference to some of Paul's letters.

1471. First John is the first of three letters written by John. These three letters have notable similarities to his Gospel and the Book of Revelation. These letters speak out against the heresy of Gnosticism. The Gnostics taught that the body and this world are evil and that salvation came through special knowledge.

1472. Second John. In this short but personal letter, John dealt with the problem of false teachers. He appeared to be counseling a particular congregation not to receive visiting teachers who proclaimed false teachings.

1473. Third John. Ironically this letter dealt with the flip side of the problem covered in 2 John. In this case John wrote to a congregation that had been rejecting visiting teachers. Only here, the visiting teacher in question was true. Second and Third John are the two shortest books in the entire Bible.

1474. Jude, like James, was a sibling of Jesus. His letter seemed to be written at a time when many of the apostles had already been martyred. He made references to their warnings about false teachers and Peter's and Paul's predictions. Jude made the point that these teachings had indeed reached projected proportions. Jude's writing sets the stage for the final book of the Bible.

1475. The Epistle of Jude quotes from 1 Enoch 1:9 and the Assumption of Moses. Many Christians have not heard of these books because they were written before the time of the New Testament and were not accepted into the Canon of inspired Scripture by the Jewish or Christian communities. Yet Jude used them to make a point in his epistle.

1476. Apocalyptic writing was a kind of code, a way of communicating that unbelieving enemies would not understand. A person who wrote such literature could encourage his readers to stand against the pagan state and predict its downfall under divine judgment, without fear of official reprisal. Modern readers often miss this aspect of the apocalyptic genre, just as the ancient pagans did. It was designed to reveal its message to insiders in terms that an outsider could not understand.

1477. Revelation. The longest of all the New Testament letters, "The Revelation to John" was addressed to seven specific communities, all of them located in Asia. Like Hebrews, this book was built upon quotations and allusions to Old Testament passages (hundreds of references). The line of the book is as follows: Goodness and evil wage a cataclysmic battle in which goodness wins the decisive victory. The practice of using bizarre conflicting images was a practiced style in ancient times. It was called "apocalyptic," so the book is sometimes called the Apocalypse instead of Revelation. The meaning is actually the same, only *apocalypse* comes from a Greek root, while revelation comes from a Latin root word.

1478. The identity and meaning of the beast numbered 666 has deeply concerned Christians throughout history. Its symbolism has been assigned to Satanism in popular culture and to such notorious figures as Napoleon and Hitler. Some scholars believe that while Satan is a major player in Revelation, the meaning 666 was clear to the people of the time of its writing. In both Greek and Hebrew, letters doubled as numerals. One solution to the 666 puzzle? The number is produced by adding up the Hebrew letters of "Kaisar Neron," or Emperor Nero, which reaches an equivalent of the number 666.

1479. The extraordinary prophetic vision of the second coming of Jesus and the last judgment were given while John was exiled on Patmos, an Aegean island used as a Roman penal colony. The author had been banished there for his preaching most likely during the reign of Roman Emperor Domitian (AD 81–96).

1480. Apocalypse is the Greek name for the Book of Revelation. The word literally means "to unveil" or "to reveal something that has been hidden." The early church had numerous books claiming to reveal future events, and it wasn't until the fourth century that John's apocalypse was recognized as the one inspired version.

A Savior, Which Is Christ the Lord

45

1481. Jesus Christ, more than any other figure or historical happening mentioned, is the most important figure in the Bible. The Old Testament prophesies about his coming and his death; the New Testament sees him be born, establish a ministry, and eventually sacrifice himself for all who believe in him.

1482. Many incidences in the Old Testament point to Christ: Abel's lamb was a type of Christ. So was Abraham's willing offering of his son, Isaac, for sacrifice. The Passover lamb in Egypt was a type of Christ. Even the scarlet cord the prostitute Rahab hung in her window was a symbol of Christ!

1483. "To him give all the prophets witness." Truly, God had been telling his people about the coming Savior long before Jesus was ever born. Micah foretold Jesus' birth; Zechariah told of how he will eventually reign as King over all the earth. Joel described the day of judgment and what part Jesus will play in it.

1484. The New Testament is the unraveling of all those prophecies and foretellings of the Old Testament. Jesus' birth is recorded in two Gospel books: Matthew and Luke.

1485. The Christmas story reveals the depth of God's love to all humankind. Matthew's and Luke's Gospels tell the story of the virgin birth, the humble beginnings of Jesus, and the joyous celebration set off in heaven when Christ was born. Though missed by many, God allowed both great (the magi) and humble (the shepherds) to join in the celebration.

1486. The number of magi who followed the star of Bethlehem is unknown. The Bible doesn't tell much about them. The Christian tradition that there were three kings did not arise until about seven hundred years after the event took place. Their legendary names— Balthasar, Melchior, and Caspar, in Western traditions—emerged much later. So did the story that one of them was black. Medieval Christians reasoned that the three kings must have come from the three continents, so one must have been African.

1487. The magi did not come to the actual stable where Jesus was born. Their trip is thought to have taken place when Jesus was closer to two years old.

1488. Because Herod ordered the slaughter of young Jewish children, Mary and Joseph fled to Egypt with the child Jesus. The Egypt in which Jesus found shelter was much different from the proud and mighty nation that his ancestors Abraham and Moses had known. The glory that had been Egypt was gone. The flourishing cities through which pharaohs once rode in pomp were decaying and the great pyramids and temples were crumbling.

1489. Symbolically the announcement of the angel to the shepherds provides a counterpoint to the homage paid by the wealthy wise men. In New Testament times shepherds ranked low on the social register. The shepherds also served as a reminder that Jesus was coming as both the shepherd to the flock of Israel and as the sacrificial lamb that would take away the sins of the world.

1490. Joseph and Mary returned from Egypt some time after the death of Herod in 4 BC and made their home in Nazareth, a town in Galilee. The name Nazareth is derived from Hebrew words that mean "consecrated people," because this town was noted for clinging to the ancient laws and customs of the Hebrews. Jesus' birthday is celebrated on December 25 now, but that wasn't always the case. For centuries a different calendar was used, and the date was in the spring.

1491. The baby Jesus was like any other baby—he was human and had the same needs as babies do today. He cried to be held and fed, needed his diapers changed, and learned to talk like any other baby does.

1492. Though nativity scenes tell the story differently, there were likely no animals present at Jesus' birth. The Bible makes no mention of camels, donkeys, cattle, or sheep. All these are cultural additions to the story that have been added through the ages.

1493. The shepherds weren't given a miraculous sign to follow like the magi were two years later. The "star of the East" did not guide them. The angels told the shepherds to look for a baby wrapped in cloths and lying in a manger. Presumably this was an unusual sign in itself and the shepherds found Jesus with little difficulty.

1494. The Christmas story has undergone cultural interpretation to such an extent that many people believe the Bible tells of Joseph asking the innkeeper if the baby can be born there. There is, however, no record of such a conversation occurring. Luke 2:7 simply states: "She wrapped him in cloths and placed him in a manger, because there was no room for them in the inn."

1495. Jesus did not receive his name, which means "the Messiah" or "the Christ," until his eighth day when he was circumcised. The name had been given to Mary by the angel before she conceived, but the practice was to officially name the child when he was circumcised.

1496. At twelve years of age, Jesus already demonstrated that he was aware of his lifework. His parents had taken him to the Passover feast in Jerusalem. When they left, they thought he was with them, but he had stayed behind in order to speak with the teachers at the temple.

1497. His ministry began when he was about thirty years of age. John the Baptist was serving as a "voice in the wilderness" and calling the people to remember that their Savior was coming, that the time had come to repent. Jesus was baptized by John at the Jordan River.

1498. Satan tempted Christ and tried to weaken the Savior's resolve, but Jesus stood firm in his mission. Christ's ministry would ultimately lead to his death, and though Satan's temptations would have saved him great pain, he was faithful to his heavenly Father.

1499. The Lord's preaching took him all over the area for three years. He traveled throughout Galilee, Judea, and Samaria. He healed the sick and brought hope to many through miracles. He often spoke in parables to the people to help them better understand what his ministry was all about.

1500. Jesus spent much of his ministry life in and around the Sea of Galilee. Galileans in Bible times were considered country hicks to the more cosmopolitan residents of Jerusalem. Jesus spoke primarily to the humble people who labored on the land and were familiar with the animals and plants around them. His parables are filled with images of the natural world.

1501. Jesus met all manner of people—and accepted them all if they repented of their sins. Harlots, tax collectors, liars, cheats, the infirmed, and the diseased all received kind words, healing, and a message of hope. One such man was especially memorable.

1502. A rich tax collector called Zacchaeus wanted to catch a glimpse of Jesus, but he had to climb a sycamore tree (Luke 19:4).

This is an inferior kind of fig tree that has traditionally been a food of impoverished people in the Near East. Thus the rich man was forced to rely on the tree that was a symbol of poverty. Jesus did not harbor any love, however, for the proud and often conniving leaders of the Jewish faith who consistently misled the people.

1503. Obedience to laws without a sense of mercy is an action empty of spiritual value. Several times Jesus quoted the prophets who had said, "God desires mercy more than sacrifice." He reserved a special anger for the scribes and Pharisees, who might loosely be called "lawyers." Matthew's term for Pharisees is hypocrites, a term in Greek that applied to actors or people who were pretenders. They were people who said one thing but did another.

1504. The Pharisees were a group of Jewish clerics who felt that their strict obedience to Jewish traditions set them apart from the rest of the pagan culture. Their name means "the separated ones." They were intolerant of anyone considered ritually unclean and persecuted many people. Their reliance on rules made them appear pious to the masses, but Jesus criticized them for having an outward show of piety while neglecting the fact that inwardly they were proud, pompous sinners.

1505. The Sadducees were the Jewish artistocracy who rather enjoyed the artistic and political advantages that came from being allied to the Roman Empire. During Christ's life they controlled the high Jewish council, called the Sanhedrin, but they were haughty and pompous and generally disliked by the common people.

1506. Jesus called special helpers to his aid in order to preach and teach and minister to the people. There were twelve helpers in all—Simon Peter, Andrew, James, John, Philip, Bartholomew, Thomas, Matthew, James, Thaddaeus, Simon the Zealot, and Judas Iscariot.

1507. The words *disciple* **and** *apostle* are often used interchangeably but mean quite different things. The word *disciples* means "learners" or "students." The disciples of Jesus were those who listened to Jesus, followed him, and even taught what Jesus taught. An apostle, from the Greek *apostolos,* for "one who is sent out," generally means a messenger of the gospel. The author of Luke used the word *apostle* specifically for the twelve disciples who had been companions of Jesus, were witnesses of the resurrection, and eventually became leaders of the church.

1508. The name Mary, derived from the Greek form of the common Hebrew *Miriam*, the name of the sister of Moses, is the name of three different women in the life of Jesus. His mother, Mary, only made a few appearances in the Gospel accounts, but she was at the foot of the cross with John. Mary the sister of Martha and Lazarus was a close friend of Jesus. Jesus healed Mary Magdalene (or Mary of Magdala, a town near Tiberias) by casting out the demons within her. She then became a devoted follower of Christ.

1509. To the devout Jews who accepted Jesus, he was the promised Savior who fulfilled the word expressed in their Scriptures of a coming "Messiah" or "anointed one" from the line of David who would deliver the children of Israel and usher in a new age of peace under God's rule. Though he was later called the "Christ," this is not a name but a title. *Christos* comes from the Greek meaning "anointed one" or "Messiah."

1510. Hebrew was still the language of the places of worship, but outside of them the people spoke a dialect known as Aramaic. They also carried on conversations in Greek. It was not the classical language of Homer and the heroes but a dialect known as *koine*, the language in which the bulk of the New Testament was written. Undoubtedly Jesus learned to speak all three languages.

1511. The "eye of a needle" was the phrase Jesus used in Mark 10:25 when he said, "It is easier for a camel to go through the eye of a needle than for a rich man to enter the kingdom of God." Those words must have shocked his original audience, who had thought that prosperity was a sign of God's blessing. In recent years some people have tried to identify a particular gate into Jerusalem as "the eye of the needle," thereby missing Christ's main point: Someone committed to worldly wealth is probably not as interested in heavenly gain.

1512. Jesus was not alone in works of healing. Just as other men claimed messiahship to attract political followers, numerous wonder-workers and healers wandered the Roman Empire in that day. Jesus even referred to others who were healing in his time. The Jewish Talmud discusses several wonder-working rabbis of Jesus' time. But none made the claim that Jesus' followers made—that he had the ability to raise the dead and had done so on three occasions with witnesses.

1513. Jesus was well received by the people as long as he was performing miracles and teaching, but they did not look to him as the King of Kings. Sadly they were looking for an earthly king instead of a heavenly one. As a result their love for Jesus was short-lived.

1514. Jesus took three of his most trusted disciples up on a mountain, where they experienced an extraordinary event. While the disciples watched, Jesus was miraculously "transfigured." His physical being was transformed, and the figures of Moses and Elijah, the two great prophets of Judaism, stood beside him. The disciples also heard the voice of God saying Jesus was God's beloved Son. The accounts all say Jesus' face shone as Moses' did when he encountered God on Mount Sinai in Exodus.

1515. As Christ rode a donkey into Jerusalem, he was hailed by the people with palm leaves and shouts of "Hosanna!" The people celebrated him as their king. They did not want the greatest gift that Christ offered and that they needed most. They wanted freedom from the Romans and a nation of their own instead, and thought Christ brought that, despite the many warnings and explanations given of his ministry.

1516. Satan provoked Judas to betray Jesus, as it is stated in the Gospel of John. The treachery of Judas has provoked some speculation over motives, including the notion that he might have been an anti-Roman zealot who was disappointed that Jesus had not proved to be the rebel leader many were expecting. The Gospel of Mark tells how Judas went to the chief priests to betray Jesus before being offered a bribe, suggesting that he had some other motive besides money. Matthew specifically states that Judas asked how much he would be given, and he was paid "thirty pieces of silver" in fulfillment of ancient Hebrew prophecy.

1517. The Last Supper was a preparation for Jesus himself as he readied himself for the end, which he knew was near. Judas Iscariot was even confronted by Christ at the table. The Lord celebrated a final supper with his disciples, his most trusted companions. This special dinner was given to Christians in order to remember the sacrifice Jesus made for his people.

1518. The words "Take and eat: this is my body," and "This is my blood of the covenant, which is poured out for many for the forgiveness of sins" (Matt. 26:26, 28) are part of a sacrament of the Christian church that originated with the Last Supper. Communion is based on the events of the Last Supper and serves as one of two main sacraments in the Christian church to this day.

1519. After the Last Supper, Jesus spent his last night of freedom in the Garden of Gethsemane on the slopes of the Mount of Olives. The name means "olive presses." In Jesus' time the Mount of Olives was covered with a luxuriant growth of these trees, and the inhabitants of Jerusalem often rested there to seek relief from the sun.

1520. "Today—yes, tonight—before the rooster crows twice you yourself will disown me three times" (Mark 14:30). On the way to Gethsemane, Jesus told his disciple Peter this prophecy. The roosters first crowed about midnight, and they were so punctual that Roman soldiers used the sound as a signal for changing the guard. The roosters crowed a second time about three o'clock in the morning, which awakened the second watch of soldiers.

1521. Many first-century Jews died, just like Jesus, on a cross. Some estimates for the number of Jews crucified in this time for a variety of crimes run as high as one hundred thousand. But this was not at the hand of other Jews. Crucifixion was exclusive to the Romans, and it was an extreme penalty generally reserved for cases of runaway slaves or rebellion against Rome. An uprising of slaves against Rome led by the gladiator-slave Spartacus in 71 BC resulted in some six thousand crucifixions. Bodies were left to decompose as a grim warning.

1522. Gall is mentioned several times in the Bible. It refers to the juice of a poisonous and bitter plant, but there is no way of knowing exactly which plant. The best guess is the poison hemlock, the plant that poisoned Socrates and served medicinally as a sedative. Hemlock was considered a plant of ill omen and associated with witches and evil spirits.

1523. The Seven Last Utterances are the final words spoken by Christ while on the cross. The four Gospels reveal different phrases, but grouped together they include: (1) "Today you will be with me in paradise" (spoken to the thief next to him). (2) "My God, my God, why have you forsaken me?" (3) "Father, forgive them, for they know not what they do." (4) "I thirst." (5) "Woman, behold your son. Son, behold your mother" (spoken to Mary and the disciple John). (6) "It is finished." (7) "Into your hands I commit my spirit."

1524. "A mixture of myrrh and aloes, about a hundred pound weight" was brought after the crucifixion. "Then took they the body of Jesus, and wound it in linen clothes with the spices, as the manner of the Jews is to bury" (John 19:39–40 KJV). Myrrh was one of the main ingredients used in the purification of the dead.

1525. The linen in which Jesus' body was wound was made from flax, the oldest textile fiber known. In the ancient world there were different grades of linen. Fine linen was used in the cloths of the rich, for curtain hangings in the temple, and even for sails of Phoenician trading ships. The poor people, however, wore only ordinary coarse linen. The Bible did not specify what type of linen Jesus was wound in.

1526. The death of Jesus at Golgotha must have had no more significance to the Romans than the deaths of the thousands of other Jews they crucified at that time. Yet soon the whole ancient world heard about Jesus. His disciples carried his teaching to the farthest outpost of the Roman Empire.

1527. Yet to one Roman, Christ's death did have significance. The Roman centurion who watched Christ die said, "Surely this man was the Son of God!" when he saw the sun darken and felt the earth quake at Jesus' death.

1528. The resurrection of Jesus is the central story to all Christianity. After dying on the cross, being wrapped in a burial shroud, and being interred in a sealed tomb, Jesus rose from the dead—conquering death and offering the hope of eternal life to all who believe in him.

1529. After Jesus was resurrected, he appeared several times to various disciples. His resurrection fulfilled every prophecy he and all the early prophets had made concerning the Savior of the world. Though some doubted, many believed and were brought to a saving understanding that Jesus was truly their Savior and the King of Kings.

1530. Jesus commissioned his followers to preach the gospel to all people. His call to them brought the disciples and other faithful followers to the beginning of the church. And through a history of almost two thousand years, the church has experienced persecution, misery, and separation. Yet never has it died and never will it fall, despite what might happen, for Christ is the head of his church. And his kingdom cannot fail!

1531. Christ ascended into heaven, on a cloud, to be with the Father and to "sit at the right hand of God" until the time of his second coming. He will come again at "the last days" as the Bible writers prophesied. His message remains today for all who will believe in him and trust him as their personal Savior.

Miracles of Amazing Proportions

46

1532. Biblical miracles are found in both the Old and New Testaments. Many show God's power over nature while other miracles are a sign of his mercy and love for those who fear him. These events are supernatural and can only be the work of God.

1533. Miracles demonstrate God's hand intervening in earthly affairs in extraordinary ways. New Testament miracles tend to be "personal" miracles, as opposed to miracles affecting the entire nation, such as the plagues on Egypt or the crossing of the Red

Sea. Apart from his own miraculous birth, resurrection, and the transfiguration, Jesus performed more than thirty-five miracles in the Gospels.

OLD TESTAMENT MIRACLES

1534. The flood is an example of a miracle of nature. Certainly it was a judgment against the world, but it was no less than a sign of God's power and dominion. He caused it to rain so hard and so fast and so long (forty days) that every living thing on the whole earth was swallowed up in a gigantic flood.

1535. Noah's surviving in the ark during the flood is an example of God's provision and mercy for the one man and his family who did not die in the flood. That this man was able to build the ark and then fill it with animals and find food for all of them is an amazing feat—too amazing to be possible without divine intervention.

1536. Sarah delivered a healthy baby boy when she was well past her childbearing years. Her husband, Abraham, was already a centenarian, and she had given up hope of having a child. Yet God had promised them a son to fulfill the covenant.

1537. The burning bush. The first clear miracle recorded in the Bible is Moses' encounter with God, described in Exodus 3. That passage describes Moses, who was living as a shepherd in Midian, seeing a bush that was on fire but did not burn up. As Moses approached, God called him by name, told him that he was standing on holy ground, and announced that he would be sent to free the Israelite slaves in Egypt. While earlier passages describe things like the miraculous growth of Jacob's herd of sheep or the hand of God on Joseph's life, this is the first recorded instance of a clearly supernatural act.

1538. Aaron's staff becomes a snake. When Moses and Aaron approached Pharaoh in Exodus 7, they threw a wooden staff to the floor, and it miraculously turned into a snake. After Pharaoh's magicians appeared to duplicate that feat, Aaron's staff/snake swallowed all the magicians' snakes—a sign of God's supernatural power being greater than that of man's magical power.

1539. The ten plagues. In an attempt to free his people from slavery, Moses revealed to Pharaoh that ten plagues would hit Egypt: water turning to blood, frogs, gnats, flies, cattle disease, boils, hail, locusts, darkness, and the death of all firstborn males. While there are natural explanations for all ten, the occurrence of them all together, along with the fact that Moses predicted them, certainly categorize them as a special act of God.

1540. The pillar of fire and the parting of the Red Sea. Exodus 14 describes the flight of the Israelites from Egypt. Pharaoh's armies, chasing them, were kept from approaching the Israelite camp by a protective pillar of fire. The Red Sea then opened up, allowing the Israelites to cross the sea "on dry land." When the Egyptians tried to follow, the sea closed over them, killing them all. The pillar then guided the Israelites through the wilderness—a cloud by day, and fire by night.

1541. Manna from heaven. While the Israelites lived in the wilderness, God miraculously provided them with bread from heaven that would appear on the ground each morning like dew. Exodus 16:31 describes it as tasting "like wafers made with honey," and the Jews referred to it as manna, which literally means, "What is it?"

1542. Water from the rock. When the people in the wilderness were thirsty, Moses was instructed by God to strike a rock with his stick. Exodus 17 records that Moses did this in full view of the elders, and water poured forth from the rock, quenching the thirst of the Israelites.

1543. The budding of Aaron's staff. In an attempt to prove that Aaron had a special place of leadership, Moses gathered the walking staffs of each tribal leader and placed them in a tent before the Lord. The next morning Aaron's staff had sprouted, budded, blossomed, and produced almonds, according to Numbers 17:8. The staff was kept in front of the people, as a sign of God's choice of leaders.

1544. The bronze snake. Numbers 21 tells how God sent venomous snakes among the people as a discipline for complaining. After many Israelites died, God told Moses to make a bronze snake and put it on a high pole. Anyone who was bitten could simply turn and look at the snake, and they would be saved. Just as the bronze snake was lifted up and offered life to those who would believe and turn toward it, Christ was lifted up and offers the free gift of salvation to all who believe.

1545. The walls of Jericho. While most Old Testament miracles were confined to the lives of Moses, Elijah, Elisha, and Daniel, one of the few other supernatural events occurs in Joshua 5–6. Rather than attacking the city of Jericho, the armies of Israel followed God's command to march around the city walls and blow trumpets. After doing this for a week, they gave a great shout and the walls of Jericho simply fell down in front of them. Recent archaeology of the site has shown that the walls did, indeed, fall outward—a strange occurrence, since walls were generally pushed inward by invading armies.

1546. Gideon's fleece. Another Old Testament miracle is recorded in Judges 6. Gideon, chosen by God to lead Israel's armies, needed a sign that God was really on his side. He laid a fleece on the ground one night and asked the Lord to let it be wet with dew the next morning, even though the ground was dry. God did just that. The next night Gideon laid the fleece and asked that it would be dry while the ground was wet. Again God acted. This miracle has led to people talking about "laying out a fleece" when they want to test something or someone.

1547. Fed by ravens. The prophet Elijah, after proclaiming a drought, hid in the Kerith Ravine. First Kings 17 records that God sent ravens with bread and meat to him every morning and evening, sustaining him through the difficult times.

1548. Multiplying flour and oil. When Elijah asked the widow of Zarephath to make him a cake during the drought, she replied that she and her son were about to die of starvation. However, Elijah told her that if she made him a meal, her jar of flour would never run out and her jar of oil would never run dry. First Kings 17:15–16 records that the widow's jars were miraculously filled each day.

1549. Raising the widow's son. When the widow of Zarephath's son died, Elijah took the boy in his arms, went into an upper room, and cried out to the Lord, "O LORD my God, let this boy's life return to him!" (1 Kings 17:21). God raised the boy to life—presaging a miracle Jesus Christ would perform hundreds of years later.

1550. Fire on Mount Carmel. One of the best stories in Scripture takes place in 1 Kings 18, when Elijah did battle with 450 prophets of Baal. Placing a bull on an altar on top of Mount Carmel, he challenged the prophets to make fire come down and consume the sacrifice. When they failed, he taunted them, suggesting that their god must be asleep or away on a trip. Elijah then had water poured on the bull, stepped forward, and said a short prayer: "Let it be known today that you are God in Israel and that I am your servant." Fire suddenly came from heaven and burned up the sacrifice—leading the crowd watching to prostrate themselves before God, then turn and slaughter the false priests.

1551. Chariots of fire. Second Kings 2 records that Elijah did not die but was taken up to heaven in a chariot of fire pulled by horses of fire. Those same chariots appeared later in Elisha's life, when the Aramean armies came to capture him. Though Elisha's servant was afraid for his life, God opened his eyes and helped him to see that they were surrounded by chariots of fire sent by God. In response to that vision, Elisha struck the entire Aramean army blind.

1552. Oil aplenty. When a widow asked Elisha for help to pay her creditors, the prophet instructed her to ask neighbors for their empty jars. After collecting the jars, she was to pour oil from her small oil pot into the jars. She kept pouring and pouring, miraculously multiplying her oil until all the jars were filled. The widow then sold the oil and paid her debts.

1553. Raising the Shunammite's son. When a childless woman invited Elisha to stay with her, then prepared his room and all his meals, the prophet announced she would soon become pregnant and have a son. She did, but the boy died from an internal problem a few years later. Second Kings 4 reveals that Elisha went to see the body, lay down on top of him, and raised the boy to life.

1554. Feeding the multitudes. Elisha took twenty loaves of barley bread and divided them among a hundred men. According to 2 Kings 4:42–44, the Lord multiplied the bread so that everyone had their fill, and there was bread left over. Jesus would later do a similar miracle, feeding five thousand, recorded in Matthew 14.

1555. Naaman healed of leprosy. When the commander of Syria's armies came down with leprosy, his wife encouraged him to visit

Elisha. The prophet told Naaman to wash seven times in the Jordan River. Though he was skeptical, Naaman did as he was told and was miraculously cured of his disease. Second Kings 5:15 records his response: "Now I know that there is no God in all the world except in Israel."

1556. An axhead floats. Second Kings 6 tells the story of a workman with a borrowed ax cutting some trees, when the axhead fell into some water. Elisha cut a stick, threw it into the water, and the iron axhead floated to the top.

1557. Nebuchadnezzar's dream. The king of Babylon, who conquered Jerusalem and carried off its citizenry into exile, had a strange dream that none of his wise men could interpret. But the prophet Daniel, a young Jew selected to serve in Nebuchadnezzar's court, asked God to help him understand the dream. Not only did God reveal the dream to Daniel, but the Lord gave him the meaning of the dream—which accurately revealed what would happen to future kingdoms.

1558. The fiery furnace. When Daniel's three friends—Shadrach, Meshach, and Abednigo—refused to bow down to an idol, the king of Babylon had them thrown into a fiery furnace. The furnace was so hot that even the soldiers leading them toward it were killed, but the three followers of God were miraculously saved. When the king looked into the furnace, he saw not only the three men but a fourth man, who looked like "the Son of God." Recognizing it as a miracle, he issued a decree that no one was to slander the God of Israel.

1559. The writing is on the wall. Daniel 5 records that when the loathsome King Belshazzar threw a drunken party and used sacred cups that had been brought from the temple in Jerusalem, the fingers of a human hand suddenly appeared and wrote a message on a wall: "Numbered. Weighed. Divided." Though none of the king's astrologers could divine the meaning, Daniel could. He told the king that God had judged Belshazzar and found him wanting, so his kingdom would be taken away that very night. That is exactly what happened.

1560. Daniel in the lions' den. When King Darius decreed that anyone found praying to God would be killed, Daniel went into his room, opened the shutters, and prayed loudly to the Lord. Darius reluctantly had Daniel thrown into a lions' den, but God shut the mouths of the lions and he was preserved without a scratch. The court members who had plotted against Daniel were then thrown into the den and devoured.

1561. Jonah and the whale. The last miracle recorded in the Old Testament involves the reluctant prophet Jonah who, while attempting to run away from God, was caught in a horrible storm and thrown into the sea in the sailors' attempt to pacify their gods. He was swallowed by a great fish, survived for three days, then was coughed up onto the shore. Upon reaching the intended city of Nineveh, Jonah preached repentance, and the pagans there turned to God (much to Jonah's disgust).

NEW TESTAMENT MIRACLES

1562. The virgin birth. No doubt the first miraculous event recorded in the New Testament is the birth of Jesus Christ. Mary, a virgin, was "found to be with child through the Holy Spirit," according to Matthew 1:18. Several other miracles surrounded that birth, including the striking dumb of Zechariah in Luke 1, the angels' appearance to the shepherds in Luke 2, and the star that led the magi to visit in Matthew 2.

1563. Water into wine. The first recorded miracle of Jesus occurs in John 2, when Christ was attending a wedding in the city of Cana and the hosts ran out of wine. Jesus requested six large jars to be filled with water, and they then miraculously turned into fine wine. As John records, "He thus revealed his glory, and his disciples put their faith in him."

1564. Healing. One of the things Christ was most known for was his ability to heal the sick. Matthew 4:23–24 records that "Jesus went throughout Galilee . . . healing every disease and sickness among the people. News about him spread all over Syria, and people brought to him all who were ill with various diseases, those suffering severe pain, the demon-possessed, those having seizures, and the paralyzed, and he healed them." The sick included lepers, paralytics, and those with internal bleeding.

1565. A man born blind. Certainly one of the most amazing miracles of Jesus was the healing of a man born blind in John 9. Christ made some mud with his saliva, rubbed it on the man's eyes, and instructed him to wash in a nearby pool. Upon doing so the man received his sight. Jewish leaders denounced him as a fraud, but when questioned, the man responded, "One thing I do know. I was blind and now I see!"

1566. The centurion's servant. Since Roman conquerors were hated by most Jewish citizens, it was generally forbidden for a Jew to enter a Roman's home. Thus when a God-fearing Roman centurion told Jesus that his servant was ill, he informed the Lord that Jesus didn't have to enter his home to perform the healing. Instead Christ could do it from a distance. Marveling at the man's faith, Jesus replied, "I have not found anyone in Israel with such great faith" (Matt. 8:10). Before the centurion could get home, the servant was healed.

1567. Jesus calms the storm. Matthew 8 relates the story of Jesus asleep in a boat when a violent storm arose. When the disciples, fearing they would drown, awakened the Lord, he simply rebuked the winds and the waves, making them calm.

1568. Raising the dead. In Matthew 9, Jesus tells a crowd of mourners that a ruler's young daughter is not dead but asleep. Though the mourners laughed at him, Jesus proceeds to raise her from the dead. Luke 7 also tells of Jesus raising the dead, this time a widow's son. And John 11 records the raising of Lazarus, which was witnessed by a crowd of people.

1569. Feeding the multitudes. After preaching to a large crowd, the disciples encouraged Christ to send the people away so that they could find something to eat. Instead the Lord had them gather their food—five loaves of bread and two fish—and proceeded to feed five thousand people.

1570. Walking on water. After his disciples had sailed off in a boat to the other side of a lake, the disciples watched Jesus walk out to them on the waves. Peter asked to join him, and also walked on water for a short time. But Matthew notes that as soon as Peter took his eyes off the Lord and began to look at the waves, he began to sink. Christ helped Peter back into the boat—prompting the disciples to say, "Truly you are the Son of God."

1571. The transfiguration. A few days before his death, Jesus took Peter, James, and John up to a high mountain. There he was "transfigured" before them. His face "shone like the sun, and his clothes became as white as the light." Moses and Elijah, two of the handful of miracle workers in Scripture, then appeared with Jesus, and the voice of God announced, "This is my Son, whom I love; with him I am well pleased" (Matt. 17:5).

1572. The tearing of the veil. Matthew 27:51 records an important miracle that took place during Christ's death on the cross: "At that moment the curtain of the temple was torn in two from top to bottom." The tearing of that curtain, which created a barrier between the worship area and the Holy of Holies where God dwelt, meant that man was no longer to be separated from God.

1573. The resurrection. The greatest of all miracles in the Christian faith is the fact that Jesus rose from the dead, conquering death and sin. The evidence for the resurrection as a historical fact (the empty tomb, the Roman guard, the eyewitness reports of those who were there, the lack of any other explanation) is overwhelming.

1574. Apostles heal a cripple. In the apostolic age some of the followers of Christ had the power to do miracles. Acts 3 records Peter and John healing a beggar who had been crippled since birth, and Acts 5:12 notes that "the apostles performed many miraculous signs and wonders among the people."

1575. Ananias and Sapphira. The early church encouraged members to take care of one another. One couple, Ananias and Sapphira, schemed to sell some property and give some of the money away but then deceive the church by keeping some of it for themselves. When they stood before the leadership, God struck both Ananias and Sapphira dead.

1576. Peter's escape from prison. When Peter was arrested for preaching the gospel, he was held in prison, bound to a soldier on either side. But Acts 12 relates that late one night Peter was awakened by an angel, his chains simply fell off, and the gates before him miraculously opened by themselves. He walked to freedom . . . while the guards who were supposed to be keeping watch over him were later executed.

47

Speaking
in Pictures

1577. The parable of the sower, found in Matthew 13, likens sharing the gospel to a farmer scattering seed. Seed sown on the path is eaten by birds—which the Lord explains is similar to what occurs when a hearer doesn't understand the message. Satan snatches it away, so that it cannot have an impact on the hearer's life. Seed scattered on rocky soil sprouts, but it dies because it cannot set its roots—this is likened to someone who initially believes the gospel but falls away from the faith due to persecution. Some seeds grow but are choked out by thorns—a depiction of the person whose belief is undermined by worldly concerns. But the good seed that grows is like the individual who hears the gospel, understands it, and chooses to follow Christ.

1578. The parable of the weeds also tells the story of a farmer sowing seeds, but an enemy sows weeds among the wheat. When it sprouts, a servant asks the farmer if he should pull them up. The farmer replies, "No, because while you are pulling the weeds, you may root up the wheat with them. Let both grow together until the harvest" (Matt. 13:29). Jesus later explains that he is the good seed, the weeds are the sons of evil, spread by the enemy Satan, and the field is the world. The harvest represents the end of time, when God will bring his people into his house, but send those who reject him to judgment.

1579. The parable of the new wine in old wineskins, found in Matthew 9:16–17, describes the new life Jesus brings. This new life cannot be confined by old forms—or by hardened hearts. Jesus' meaning was clear: to embrace the special gift he brought, a person had to be born again, to become a new form, because the old one would burst and be ruined by the message of Jesus.

1580. The parable of the wise and wicked servants discusses what faithful servants (believers) should be doing while their master (Jesus) is away. A wise servant who is left in charge of the other servants will make sure they are being taken care of and doing their work. The foolish servant will assume he can do as he likes since the master will be staying away a long time. He will beat the other laborers and become drunk. Yet the master will return unexpectedly and find out who has acted wisely and who has acted foolishly. The foolish servant will be cast into a dreadful place for not honoring the master while he is away.

1581. The parable of the sheep and the goats is a picture of what will happen when Christ returns. Sheep symbolize believers; goats symbolize unbelievers. The sheep will be parted from the goats with a final destination of heaven. The goats will be sent to hell, the place of eternal punishment.

1582. The parable of the growing seed is only found in one of the Gospels of the New Testament—Mark. The parable describes how the kingdom of God is like a seed that is scattered into the ground and eventually sprouts and grows and produces grain. It does this with no help or direction. The seed's power to grow itself is likened to the power of the gospel message: It has its own mysterious power.

1583. The parable of the watchful porter is a reminder that no one knows the exact return of Christ. Believers are to be ready, to stand at attention like an attentive porter would at the door of a building, to not let down their guard as they wait for Christ's return.

1584. The parable of the two debtors likens debtors to sinners. In this very short parable from Luke, there are two debtors. One owes a small amount of money to a lender, the other ten times the amount of the first debtor. If the lender forgives both of them, Jesus asks, who will be more thankful? The obvious answer is the debtor with the larger amount of debt. The same concept holds true for sinners. Whether large or small, Christ forgives, but those with more to be forgiven will be more thankful. This parable was told after Jesus' feet were anointed by a former prostitute. The Pharisee sitting at the table was convinced Jesus wouldn't let such a sinner touch him if he only knew her past. Jesus' parable speaks directly to the heart issue.

1585. The parable of the good samaritan tells the story of a man who was beaten by robbers and left for dead. Though a passing priest and temple worker refused to help the victim, a despised Samaritan stopped, assisted the man, and agreed to pay for all costs in his recuperation. The story shows that God's love moves beyond social prejudice.

1586. The parable of the barren fig tree is a picture of how eternity will not wait forever for nonbelievers to make up their minds. In the story the owner of a vineyard tells the steward to cut down a fig tree that hasn't yielded fruit in three years. Thinking he has allowed an ample amount of time, the owner is frustrated and sees no point in using up soil to nourish it. Yet the steward asks for one more year to fertilize the fig—perhaps the steward is Christ interceding on our behalf!

1587. The parable of the lowest seat at the feast likens the seating arrangement to how Christians are to behave on earth.

They are to humble themselves now in order to be exalted later. At a feast it is wise to take a seat in a lower position and then be asked to move up to a more exalted position rather than exalting oneself first and then being asked to move down by the host. This is an often-repeated theme in the Bible: Believers are to be humble and not seek out positions of exaltation.

1588. The parable of the great banquet is a reminder that not everyone will enter the kingdom of heaven. Though all are invited, many will reject the invitation and be lost. The story describes a gracious host who plans a large banquet and sends invitations to many people. But on the day of the banquet, those who are invited make excuses and don't come. The owner then sends for the poor, the lame, those who are in need. He will not force anyone to come into the banquet hall. Rather it is a matter of accepting an invitation.

1589. The parable of the mustard seed likens the kingdom of heaven to the smallest seed known in that part of the world. Though the seed is tiny, it grows to a great height. In the same way, though the church started small, it would grow rapidly and become a worldwide force throughout the rest of history.

1590. In the parable of the yeast, Jesus describes the kingdom of heaven as being like a small amount of yeast that gets mixed into a large amount of flour, permeating all the dough. Once the process of leavening begins, it cannot be stopped. Similarly once the good news of the gospel took hold in the world, there would be no stopping it. (In a later passage, Christ would warn against the evil yeast of the Pharisees, which could also permeate lives.)

1591. The parables of the hidden treasure and the pearl both compare the gospel message to something of great value. Just as a man sells all he has in order to purchase the field with hidden treasure or the fine pearl, Jesus would give all he had—even his own life—in order to provide redemption for his people.

1592. The parable of the net states that the kingdom of God is like a net that catches all kinds of fish. When the net is full, it is pulled on shore and the good fish are separated from the bad fish. Jesus explains that the net and sorting represent the action that will take place at the end of time, when Christ will remove the righteous from the unrighteous, sending believers to heaven and unbelievers to hell.

1593. The parable of the lost sheep, in Matthew 18, is one of the sweetest stories of Jesus. In it he tells of a loving shepherd caring for one hundred sheep. If one gets lost, he will leave the ninety-nine to go find the one that is missing. In the same way, God is concerned about each person and he doesn't want anyone to be lost.

1594. The parable of the lost coin likens a poor woman's rejoicing when finding a lost coin to the rejoicing in heaven when a sinner repents and turns to God. This parable can be found in Luke 15.

1595. The parable of the unmerciful servant relates the story of a man who owes a great debt to his master. Falling on his knees, he pleads for mercy and it is granted. But moments later the servant sees a man who owes him a small amount and has him thrown into debtors' prison. When the master hears of this, he is outraged and has the servant arrested and punished until he can pay back his entire debt. Forgiveness should be in direct proportion to the amount forgiven—since the servant had been forgiven much, he should in turn forgive others. Since Christians have been forgiven for all their sins, they should in turn be willing to forgive the failings of others.

1596. The parable of the workers in the vineyard, found in Matthew 20, tells the story of a landowner hiring workers to help in his fields. Some are hired in the morning, some at noon, and others near the end of the day, but they are all paid the same amount. Jesus used the parable to explain that rewards are under the sovereign control of God. Some prominent people will be demoted while some lowly people are exalted. The Lord's evaluation is all that matters in the final accounting of our lives.

1597. The parable of two sons is about a father asking two boys to work in a vineyard. One says he will, but fails to go. The other says he won't, but does anyway. The one who eventually obeyed was righteous—a point Christ used to explain why prostitutes and tax collectors who turn to God will make it into heaven, while the Pharisees and religious leaders will not because they have not repented and believed.

1598. The parable of the tenants may have been Christ's most powerful story. In Matthew 21 he tells of a careful landowner who rents out his vineyard. When he sends servants to collect the rent, the tenants beat them. Then he sends his own son, whom the tenants kill. Jesus used this illustration to depict a loving God caring for Israel yet being rejected by them. Eventually God sent his own Son, whom they would crucify. The result is that the kingdom of God would be taken from Israel. The religious leaders of the day, completely misunderstanding Christ's meaning, were enraged by the parable.

1599. The parable of the wise and foolish builders contrasts a wise man who builds his house on a rock foundation with a foolish man who builds his house on sand. When a storm comes, the house on sand falls apart, while the house built on rock stands firm. In other words, the quality of the foundation determines the strength of the building. The firm foundation represents Christ's work of transforming lives from the inside out, contrasted with the Pharisees' religion, which relies on a merely outward appearance of righteousness. This parable, following a story about choosing which fruit to eat and which road to walk, reveals that there is always a wise choice that leads to God and a foolish choice that leads away from him.

1600. The parable of the wedding banquet tells the story of a king trying to invite people to his son's celebration. Since the invitations are ignored or rejected by most, he angrily sends his army to punish those who snubbed him and invite people off the street to fill the wedding hall. The parable illustrates that Israel had rejected their Messiah, so Gentiles would be welcomed into the kingdom of God. An interesting detail is that one guest is expelled for not wearing wedding clothes that were given by the king—an illustration that we must not only respond to God outwardly, but inwardly by appropriating what God provides.

1601. The parable of the ten virgins, found in Matthew 25, pictures Israel as ten virgins awaiting the return of the bridegroom. The wedding custom of the day called for the groom to return to his home leading a procession, and the image is that of Christ returning from heaven with his bride, the church. Preparation for the banquet is necessary, but five of the virgins have failed to prepare by bringing enough oil. They leave to shop for oil, and by the time they get back, the feast is in progress and they are denied admission. The image is that Israel is unprepared, though they should know that the Messiah is coming.

1602. The parable of the talents is the story of a master entrusting three servants with various amounts of money to invest while he is away. Upon his return two have invested wisely and are praised. The third has hidden his money and is rebuked. His words and actions reveal a lack of faith in the master. The point of the parable is that God's people must serve him while he is away.

1603. The parable of the lamp reminds us that no one lights a lamp and then hides it. Instead we use a lamp to illuminate the darkness. In the same way, we have not been given the truth of the gospel in order to keep it a secret but to share it with others.

1604. The parable of the prodigal son is one of the most well-told stories in Scripture. A father has two sons, one of whom demands his inheritance, leaves town, and wastes the money on foolish pleasures. The other son stays at home, working with his father. When the profligate son decides to return, the father rejoices, while his brother grouses about his father's response. Christ's point in telling the story was that not only is everyone welcome in God's family, but we should all rejoice when a lost soul repents and enters into fellowship with God.

1605. The parable of the rich fool, related in Luke 12, tells of a wealthy man who builds bigger and bigger barns, promising himself that he will soon be able to take life easy. God's response is clear: "You fool! This very night your life will be demanded from you." Life is more important than hoarding material things. The rich fool's wealth would do him no good in eternity.

1606. The parable of the shrewd manager is one of the more difficult parables to understand. A financial manager, in danger of losing his job, does favors for some of the people who owe money to his master. The master then praises the manager for acting shrewdly. The point is not that it's good to be dishonest but that it was good the manager had planned ahead—in essence, he had used material goods for future benefits.

1607. The parable of the rich man and Lazarus, in Luke 16, relates a story of a wealthy man dying and going to hell, while a poor man dies and goes to heaven. The initial point Christ was making was that material wealth has nothing to do with spiritual righteousness. But there is more to the story. When the rich man asks to go back and warn his living brothers, his request is rejected—a suggestion from the Lord that people will always be asking for more signs, even though they've already been given more than enough information that Jesus is the Christ.

1608. The parable of the persistent widow tells of a woman seeking justice from an unjust judge. Though he routinely refuses to hear her case, the woman's persistence finally wears him down, and she gains justice. Jesus interpreted the parable by saying, "Listen to what the unjust judge says. And will not God bring about justice for his chosen ones, who cry out to him day and night?" (Luke 18:6–7).

1609. The parable of the Pharisee and the tax collector is perhaps the most touching story Christ told. A self-righteous priest stands before God and offers a prayer of thanks that he is not like the tax collector. But the tax collector is too humbled to even look up to God and pleads with the Lord to forgive him for his sins. Jesus' point is that we dare not trust in our own righteousness or compare ourselves to others in order to be justified. Instead we must humble ourselves before God in order to find forgiveness and gain his righteousness.

A Church Begins

48

1610. Until the Book of Acts, the Bible primarily belonged to the Jewish people. Of the many radical elements of Jesus' message, one of the most radical was that he meant for it to apply to Gentiles (non-Jews) as well as Jews. When Jesus told his apostles to go to the ends of the world, he really meant it. This brisk narrative begins in Jerusalem and ends in Rome, symbolizing how Jesus took the faith of ancient Israel and opened it up to the whole world.

1611. The lists of disciples differ slightly from one book to another. The Gospel of Matthew lists Simon, Andrew (Simon's brother), James and John (the Sons of Zebedee), Philip, Bartholomew, Thomas, Matthew the tax collector, James the son of Alphaeus,

Thaddaeus, Simon the Cananite, and Judas Iscariot. Luke refers to Simon as "the zealot" (a brand of political protestors) and mentions "Judas son of James" instead of Thaddaeus. Many of these men were pillars of the early church.

1612. Peter, who was called Simon before Jesus renamed him, was the first leader of the early church. Peter had a long history with the Lord; he denied Christ three times before the cock crowed but went on in faith following Christ's death and resurrection to become exactly what his new name meant—"the rock."

1613. James and John, both sons of Zebedee, were brothers. They both were active in the early church. Both had been especially close to Jesus, being present at the transfiguration. It is strongly believed that John went on to write the Gospel of John.

1614. Acts introduces the New Testament's second most influential figure (Jesus was the first!), an educated, pious Jew and tent-maker named Saul. Born in what is now Turkey, Saul went to Jerusalem to learn from the esteemed rabbi Gamaliel, grandson of the legendary rabbi Hillel, the most prominent Pharisaic rabbi of the first century. Given authority by the high priest to arrest followers of Christ in Damascus for blasphemy, Saul vigorously persecuted early Christians. His name was changed to Paul after he experienced a transforming vision and conversion.

1615. Paul developed a strategy for his traveling ministry that he followed through all his journeys. He generally moved farther westward from Israel with each mission. When he entered a city for the first time, he would look for a synagogue or other place where he could find the Jews of the city. In the first century AD, Jews were dispersed throughout the world. Hardly a city didn't have Jews who met together regularly. Sometimes synagogues were receptive to his message; at other times hearers were extremely hostile.

1616. When Paul was arrested in Jerusalem for his "heretical" views, he demanded a trial in Rome before the emperor, his right as a Roman citizen—the equivalent of an American traveler demanding a hearing with the U.S. president.

1617. Many other missionaries preached the gospel in the early years of the church. Their mission was to spread the Word to all parts of the known earth, as they had been commissioned to do by Jesus before he returned to heaven. Thanks to their efforts, Christianity gained a foothold quickly in nearly every part of the known world.

1618. Barnabas was one of the earliest converts to Christianity and a close friend of Paul's. A Greek-speaking Jew from Cyprus, Barnabas's real name was Joseph, but because he was an excellent teacher, his friends called him Barnabas, which means "Son of encouragement." He accompanied Paul on the first missionary journey through Asia Minor.

1619. Timothy was one of Paul's main helpers. Paul mentored the younger man through two letters (1 and 2 Timothy) and called him his "true son in the faith." Timothy also traveled on his own.

1620. Philip became a missionary and was the first to preach the gospel to those living in Samaria. He is especially remembered for how he helped an Ethiopian read a passage from Isaiah. An angel directed him to go to the Ethiopian. Upon arriving they read the passage together. The foreigner asked to be baptized and became the first Ethiopian Christian.

1621. Silas traveled as a missionary with Paul and Peter. He sang hymns joyously to Christ when he was imprisoned with Paul during the earthquake in Philippi. The jailer became a Christian because he was so moved by their display of faith. He was to Paul a "faithful brother."

1622. Phoebe is one of the few women missionary figures of the New Testament. History indicates that it was not uncommon for women to be in leadership roles in the early church, though it was certainly not typical in Jewish synagogues. Phoebe traveled to Rome, most likely to bring Paul's letter (what we know as the Book of Romans) to the Christians there.

1623. Apollos was a Jew from Alexandria. He was actually a missionary before he met Paul. John the Baptist had mentored him and helped Apollos become a powerful preacher. He found help for his questions about Jesus in Corinth when he spoke with Priscilla and Aquila.

1624. Roman subjects incorporated emperor worship into the local religion throughout the empire. In the provinces, leading citizens became priests in the imperial cult to cement their ties with Rome. (Augustus, however, exempted the Jews from the imperial cult.) Emperor worship continued as the official pagan religion of the empire until Christianity was recognized under the Emperor Constantine (AD 305–337).

1625. Paul stayed longer in some cities than others. Some larger cities, such as Ephesus, became teaching centers through which he could reach outlying areas of the surrounding regions. Paul's goal was to teach his followers well enough so they could teach others. Those who were able to accept this role were called elders, overseers, and pastors. The focus, however, was not on building an organization but on preaching the Word.

1626. The excellent highway system constructed throughout the Mediterranean world by the Romans was traveled frequently by Paul. Built so Roman armies could move swiftly and their traders could deliver goods efficiently, the Roman roads also contributed to the spread of the Christian message.

1627. Since many Jews traveled to Jerusalem for annual feasts, and since many apostles were on the road with Christ's message, Paul sometimes found that the gospel message had reached a town before he did. This was the case with Rome, the center of the world in its day. There were many disciples in this metropolis long before Paul reached it.

1628. The gospel of Christ spread primarily by word of mouth. Sometimes the apostles would move on to another city only to receive a request for more teaching from the city they had recently left. So they would write letters to be read aloud to groups of individuals who met for teaching and encouragement. They also wrote letters while confined in prison.

1629. The *agrapha* is a phrase meaning "things not written." It was used in the early church to refer to sayings of Jesus that his followers remembered, but which were not written down in any of the Gospels. For example, in Acts 20:35, Paul quotes the Lord Jesus as saying, "It is more blessed to give than to receive." Those words can't be found in any of the Gospels, so apparently that is one of the things the Lord's followers remembered him saying, and would cite him as the source, even though it was never written down as such.

1630. How do you tell the world the "Good News" if you don't speak their language? The disciples were gathered in an upper room when all of a sudden "tongues of fire" touched the followers. They began to speak in other languages. Some people who saw them thought they were drunk. This was the arrival of the Holy Spirit that Jesus had promised. The disciples could now go and spread the Word of God everywhere.

1631. The early church grew as a "communistic" society in which everyone shared, according to the reports in Acts. There was a utopian state of harmony depicted in these first days of the Christian community, although they were not yet called "Christians." A young man named Matthias was elected to replace Judas as one of the Twelve. The group prospered, made collective decisions, and enjoyed common ownership of goods, making the early Christians in Jerusalem a practical model for the kibbutz.

1632. In Acts 6, we see that seven young men were appointed to see to the needs of the church people, in order to free up the time of the disciples and eventual apostles. Stephen, a gifted speaker, was one of these men. He was a skilled debater and angered many who could not argue well with him or win him over. Eventually these men became so angry that Stephen was arrested and tried before the Sanhedrin.

1633. The first martyr of the church was Stephen. A young Pharisee named Saul was present. Eventually Saul would be converted and receive the name Paul. His conversion is a sign of the wondrous grace God has in store for those who believe in him. When Stephen was stoned, he died with a vision of Jesus in sight. He was at peace and thus incensed his captors even more. Before he died Stephen said, "Lord, do not hold this sin against them."

1634. The early church was not a perfect organization. Early Christians were as sinful then as they can be now. One of the earliest instances of this appears in Acts 5. Ananias and his wife, Sapphira, lied about the amount of compensation they received after selling a field. Had they not pretended to sell it for less, it wouldn't have mattered, but since they did lie in order to keep back money for themselves, God took them both. As Peter told them, "You have lied to the Holy Spirit."

1635. Another famous Ananias was Ananias of Damascus. When Paul was converted, he became blind. Ananias was told to go to the house where Paul was staying. He did so, though he knew that the man Saul was coming to arrest Christians. He prayed and the newly converted Paul received his sight back.

1636. Dorcas, who was also called Tabitha, also received a miracle during the early days of the church. She lived in Joppa. She fell ill and then died. Her distressed friends sent for Peter, the "rock" of the church. He prayed for her even as she was dead! She was given her life back and sat up. Many of her friends became believers as a result of this miracle.

1637. Cornelius was actually a Roman soldier and was stationed at Caesarea. He was a Gentile who had joined a synagogue in order to seek God. He was a "God fearer." An angel appeared to him one day and told Cornelius to send for Peter. When Peter came, Cornelius and his entire family learned about Jesus. They were baptized immediately and praised God.

1638. Eutychus had been named well. His name means "lucky." While he was listening to Paul preach, he fell out of a third-story window (he fell asleep) and was lying still and believed to be dead when they reached him. Paul embraced him and he was healed. He had been blessed, not lucky, but his name seems appropriate!

1639. Philemon had an interesting conversion experience. He was a wealthy Christian from Colosse, and he was converted by his slave, Onesimus. Onesimus had run away and eventually met the apostle Paul and became a believer. Paul sent him back to his master, Philemon, and urged Philemon to receive him as a "beloved brother." Philemon did so and was also saved!

1640. Lydia is one of the few women mentioned in the early church. She was a seller of purple cloth and a Gentile, but sought God by going to a Jewish prayer center. She then met Paul and his fellow missionaries. She became converted, and eventually she and her family and even their workers were baptized. Paul and his friends stayed in her home.

1641. Stephanas and his entire household were the first Christians to convert during Paul's ministry in Achaia. As the church grew in that area, Stephanas took a more active role in caring for other new Christians. Paul was fond of him and his family and he especially enjoyed Stephanas's visit with him in Ephesus.

1642. Aquila and Priscilla were a tent-making couple from Corinth. They became Christians after listening to Paul preach. They were dear friends of Paul and supported him to the very end, even risking their lives for him. They were loved and known in many churches in Greece and Asia Minor.

1643. Acts closes with Paul incarcerated and under a mild form of house arrest in the imperial capital. He continued preaching the gospel and writing letters to the churches he had established. Acts says nothing more about Paul's appeal or ultimate fate, or that of Peter. Both eventually disappear from the biblical account without any specific word about what happened to them. According to well-established tradition, both apostles were martyred during Emperor Nero's persecution of Christians after the great fire in Rome in AD 64.

The Bible Lands

49

1644. The Bible lands ceased to be the focal point for the ancient world in the five centuries between the rebuilding of the temple at Jerusalem and the birth of Jesus. New empires rose, this time in Europe. First the Greeks and then the Romans overran the Bible lands. The Near Eastern peoples watched their land become ravaged of trees and precious metals to supply their conquerors. What forests had survived were cut down. The wilderness gave way to fields, and wild beasts were largely replaced by domesticated animals.

1645. Most rivers in the Bible lands dry up during the rainless summer, but not the Nile. Heavy rains and melting snow feed the tributaries that form the Nile River. The torrent of water reaches Egypt during the late summer and it overflows the banks, leaving a fresh layer of fertile moist soil along its banks.

1646. The Holy Land is so small that a soaring eagle can see almost all of it at once on a clear day. From Dan to Beersheba is little more than 150 miles, roughly the same distance as from New York City to Albany. From east to west, the Holy Land is even narrower. At its widest point, a hundred miles lie between the Mediterranean coast and the Arabian Desert on the east. The land in which such great events took place is only a little larger than the state of New Jersey and smaller than Belgium.

1647. This land that gave birth to our civilization is inconspicuous on a map of the world. But no other part of the world, square foot for square foot, has played such a historic role in human history.

1648. The Holy Land's position at the crossroads of three continents makes it a meeting ground for species of plants and animals of different origins. Almost every kind of bird, for example, that inhabits northern Africa, southern Europe, and western Asia has been seen at one time or another in the Bible lands. The fauna comes from as far away as Central Asia (the horse), equatorial Africa (the crocodile), and western Europe (the stork).

1649. The great variety of deserts, mountains, forests, grasslands, lakes, and seashores provides nearly every possible habitat in which plants and animals can find the exact living conditions they need. About 2,250 species of trees and shrubs and annual and perennial plants grow in the Holy Land; Egypt, although much larger, has only fifteen hundred. About seven hundred species of mammals, birds, and reptiles are found in the Holy Land.

1650. The contrasts in the landscape are remarkable. Mount Hermon rises to 9,400 feet, and its summit is arctic in climate. A little over a hundred miles away, at the Dead Sea, the climate is tropical. In the same glance you can see snow-capped mountains and sun-baked deserts. Alongside cultivated fields are stark deserts that afford scarcely enough pasture for flocks.

1651. The road from Jerusalem to Jericho drops three thousand feet in only fifteen miles, and while fruit is growing on the farms around Jericho, it may be snowing in Jerusalem. The varied animals and plants, the many different landscapes, the abrupt changes in climate—all these realities were observed by the Bible's writers. And they put them to use to illustrate spiritual teachings.

1652. The Jordan Valley is part of the Great Rift that extends from Turkey deep into Africa for four thousand miles. The Great Rift is the deepest chasm on the face of the globe. Unlike the Grand Canyon, which was formed by the process of erosion, great swells and cracking of the earth's crust caused huge blocks of land to collapse, leaving deep valleys that were flooded. In the Holy Land this formed the Jordan River, Lake Huleh, the Sea of Galilee, and the Dead Sea.

1653. The Jordan River is among the most rapid of any rivers in the world. In approximately two hundred winding miles, it drops from almost two thousand feet *above* sea level to the surface of the Dead Sea, which is nearly thirteen hundred feet *below* sea level.

1654. The shore of the Dead Sea is the lowest place on the land surface of the earth. This sea is also the saltiest body of water in the world, and nine times saltier than the oceans! It is so salty that it is impossible for a human swimmer to sink in it. During the Roman siege of Jerusalem in AD 70, a Roman commander sentenced some prisoners to death by having them thrown into the Dead Sea. The condemned men were thrown in from a hill, but they did not drown. Several times they were pulled out and tossed in again, yet each time they bobbed to the surface. The commander was impressed by this seeming miracle, since he did not understand its cause, and he pardoned the prisoners.

1655. Ancient Hebrews had an unlimited supply of salt. They formed brine pits called "salt pans" along the Dead Sea's flat coastal area. The sun evaporated the water in the pits, leaving behind an abundant supply of mineral salts.

1656. Salt was the chief economic product of the ancient world, and the Hebrews used it in a variety of ways: for flavoring foods, preserving fish, curing meat, and pickling olives and vegetables. Infants were rubbed in salt to ensure good health before swaddling.

Salt was also believed to have been an antidote for tooth decay. Salt was an ingredient in the sacred anointing oil and ritual sacrifices symbolizing God's perpetual covenant with Israel (Num. 18:19).

1657. Cool streams, luxuriant pastures, and mountains shaggy with trees are often described in the Bible. Yet visitors today usually see a bleak and barren landscape with waterless flatlands and bare hills. Almost everywhere the rocky bones of the earth show through the soil. An ancient Hebrew legend states that God had two bags of rocks when he made the world. He scattered the contents of one bag over the entire earth—but all the other rocks in the other bag he dropped on the small area of the Holy Land.

1658. The face of the land looked very different than it does today. The first step toward agriculture was the cutting down of the forests. That is what Joshua told the tribes of Ephraim and Manasseh to do when they complained about the lack of farmland in the areas assigned to them: "But the forested hill country [shall be yours] as well. Clear it, and its farthest limits will be yours" (Josh. 17:18).

1659. Mount Sinai, a solid block of reddish granite that rises steeply out of the desert, is only about three thousand feet high, not much in comparison to other mountains. It looms so dramatically out of the surrounding land, however, that the Israelites must have found it a fitting place for God to dwell.

1660. Mari, dating back to the eighteenth century BC, was unveiled as one of the great cities of the ancient world. A ziggurat was unearthed, and so were twenty thousand clay tablets of writing. Among other things, these clay tablets preserve ancient police records that refer constantly to threats of Semitic nomads who lived on the frontiers of the kingdom and raided the towns of Mari.

1661. Haran, a little mud-brick settlement, is one of the most important cities in the Near East. It was a key city connected by ancient trade routes to Ur. Nearly four thousand years ago, Abraham, his wife, Sarah, and his household set off with their herds and flocks on a historic journey to a Promised Land. Abraham's travels correspond to known migratory and commercial routes before Ur was conquered and abandoned in 1740 BC.

1662. The city of Corinth was one of the most important cities in the Roman Empire during Paul's lifetime. A commercial bridge between East and West, it attracted merchants, traders, and visitors from all around the Mediterranean area, making it something like the "Times Square" of its day.

1663. Solomon's ships sailed with metal and other items of trade from Eziongeber on the Gulf of Aqaba to a place known as "Ophir." Its location has been heavily disputed, and it was even believed to be a legendary land until a discovery was made near the ancient port of Joppa (Jaffa) in Israel of a Phoenician storage jar inscribed with the words "gold of Ophir."

1664. Ophir very well may have been located in India or Ceylon, because the Bible states that the round-trip voyage took three years and that the ships brought back "gold, and silver, ivory, and apes, and peacocks" (1 Kings 10:22 KJV).

1665. The ancient cities of the Near East were usually walled, and at night the gates were closed for protection against invaders. In case any of the citizens were unable to return before nightfall, one small opening was left in the gate, an opening known as "the needle's eye." It was so low and so narrow that a camel laden with riches could never fit through. Only when the owner unloaded the camel and left the load outside the gate could the camel, with its head bent low, squeeze through.

1666. Jesus' teaching in Matthew 19 seized on the analogy of the camel making its way through "the needle's eye" and compared it to a rich man trying to leave the earth with riches to get into heaven. A rich man can enter the kingdom of heaven—but only if he first casts off his worldly goods and, like the camel squeezing through the needle's eye, bows his head in humility.

1667. The civilization of the Egyptians was already an ancient one by the time Joseph arrived there some 3,650 years ago. The first pyramid was built about five thousand years ago. It is known as the Step Pyramid because it rises in a series of steps or terraces to a height of 250 feet, much like the ziggurats of Babylon.

1668. The Great Pyramid of Cheops at Giza, built only a few hundred years after the Step Pyramid, was the tallest structure ever erected until the nineteenth century. It rises to a height of 481 feet, and its base is 756 blocks of stone, many blocks weighing as much as five thousand pounds. This pyramid was built with no other mechanical equipment than the lever and the roller, because at that time the Egyptians had not yet learned the use of the wheel.

1669. More than thirty major pyramids were built during the thousand years before Joseph. Each one guarded the body of a pharaoh entombed in a chamber deep inside the pile of stone blocks. However, no pyramids are mentioned in the Bible. Despite the fact that these structures would have certainly been the talk of the ancient world, the authors of the Bible didn't consider them worthy of note. They did not play a part in the unfolding of the biblical narrative.

50

Festivals
and Holidays

1670. Within the Hebrew calendar, there are twelve months of the year, just like our modern calendar. However, the Hebrew calendar starts in Tishri (September). The other months of the year are Heshvan, Kislev, Tevet, Shevat, Adar, Nisan, Iyar, Sivan, Tammuz, Av, and Elul.

1671. Rosh Hashanah is the first day of the Hebrew year and is celebrated as we celebrate New Year's Day. Numbers 29:1 and

Leviticus 23:24 explain the celebration in detail; typically the holiday falls in mid-September.

1672. Yom Kippur is the Day of Atonement and comes on the tenth day of Tishri (Lev. 16:29; 23:27). The day falls toward the end of September.

1673. Succoth, or the Feast of Tabernacles or Booths, is celebrated the week of the fifteenth to the twenty-second of Tishri, concluding with a solemn assembly (Lev. 23:34–36).

1674. Solemn assembly comes on the twenty-second day of Tishri (Lev. 23:36) and falls in our month of October.

1675. Dedication (Hanukkah) is celebrated in the month of Kislev, on the twenty-fifth day (John 10:22).

1676. Purim is celebrated in the month of Adar on the fourteenth and fifteenth days. The month falls between February and March. Purim commemorates the events of the Book of Esther (Esther 9:18–22). Therefore, it is not mentioned in Leviticus.

1677. Esther's triumph is celebrated in the Jewish festival of Purim, a joyous festival to commemorate the Jews' deliverance from Haman while they lived under Persian rule. Since the time of the exile, Jews have observed this feast in recognition of God's continued deliverance of his people. As the Book of Esther is being read, each time the name of Haman is read, the listeners yell out, "Let his name be blotted out!" The names of Haman's sons are all read in one breath, to emphasize the fact that they were all hanged at the same time.

1678. The bitter herbs for the celebration of the Passover mentioned in Numbers 9:11 may have included chicory, wild lettuce, and several plants whose leaves were gathered for use in salads; but they were most likely dandelions. Though we find them invading lawns in many parts of the world, the dandelion's original home was in the lands bordering the Mediterranean.

1679. Pesach, or Passover, is celebrated on the fourteenth day of Nisan, which falls on our Palm Sunday, and can be in March or April depending on the year. Exodus 12 and Leviticus 23 explain the commemorative reasons in more detail.

1680. The Feast of Unleavened Bread comes between the fifteenth and twenty-first days of the month of Nisan. This commemorates the Israelites' time in the desert and the food they were to eat—unleavened bread (Lev. 23:6).

1681. The Waving of the Sheaf of Firstfruits celebrates the firstfruits of harvest (Lev. 23:10) and falls on the seventeenth day of Nisan, somewhere between March and April of our calendar year. It is just two days past the celebration called the Passover.

1682. Shavuoth, or Pentecost, is held in the month of Sivan, on the sixth day. It is also known as the Feast of Weeks (Lev. 23:15).

Family Life

51

1683. In the East, every company of travelers, every tribe, every community, every family must have "a father," who is head of the group. Jabal "was the father of all such as handle the harp and organ." Jabal was the "father of such as dwell in tents and . . . have cattle" (Gen. 4:20–21 KJV). Easterners would not conceive of any band or group without somebody being "the father" of it.

1684. Under the patriarchal system, the father is supreme in command. The authority of the father extends to his wife, his children, his children's children, his servants, and all his household. Many of the bedouin Arabs of today are under no government other than this patriarchal rule. When Abraham, Isaac, and Jacob lived in tents in the Land of Promise, they were ruled by this same system.

1685. Reverence of the children for their parents and especially the father is almost universal in the Bible lands. It is quite customary for a child to greet the father in the morning by kissing his hand and standing before him in an attitude of humility, ready to receive any order, or waiting for permission to leave. After this the child is often pulled up onto the lap of the father.

1686. Women were confined to different roles than men. They never ate with the men, and the husband and brothers were served first. While walking, women followed at a respectful distance. The woman was closely confined and watched with jealousy; and when she went out she was veiled from head to foot.

1687. The ancient Hebrew women did not have unrestrained freedom, but they did have power in their role and influences within the family. A woman had tremendous influence for good or ill over her husband, and in most cases he showed her great respect. Sarah was treated like a queen by Abraham, and in matters of the household, she ruled in many ways.

1688. The tribute to the wife and mother in the Book of Proverbs indicates she was a person of great influence: "Her husband has full confidence in her and lacks nothing of value" (31:11). "She speaks with wisdom, and faithful instruction is on her tongue" (31:26). "Her children arise and call her blessed; her husband also, and he praises her" (31:28).

1689. Several cities mentioned in the Old Testament were built above underground springs. Megiddo and Hazor were two of these cities. In Hazor a woman would walk through the streets to a deep shaft. Then she descended thirty feet on five flights of stairs to the water tunnel, along which she proceeded to the water level to fill her large water jug. She needed considerable strength to climb back out of the water shaft with a heavy water jug. Gathering water was also a time for the women to socialize.

1690. The hum of the hand mill grinding grain would be one of the first sounds heard in the early morning of an Israelite village.

For those who live in the Holy Lands, this sound is associated with home, comfort, and plenty. This task belonged to the women and began in the early morning because it would often take half the day to finish. When Jeremiah foretold judgment upon Israel for her sins, he said that God would "banish from them the sounds of joy and gladness, the voices of bride and bridegroom, *the sound of millstones* and the light of the lamp" (Jer. 25:10, emphasis added).

1691. Making clothes for the family from the wool of their flocks was one of the responsibilities of Jewish women. Another task was the washing of clothing. The ancient women of Israel washed·their clothes by going to nearby sources of water such as streams, pools, or watering troughs. Like Arab women, they dipped the clothes in and out of the water and then placed them on flat stones to beat them with a club. They carried the water in goatskins and had a vessel for rinsing.

1692. Collecting water from a well or spring is another household task of the women. The same practice is used today in many places in the East just as it was done in Genesis: "it was toward evening, the time the women go out to draw water" (24:11). It is customary for Syrian women to carry the pitcher of water on their shoulders, although sometimes it is carried on their hip. Most Arabs of Palestine carry it on their heads. Scripture says that Rebekah carried her pitcher on her shoulder (Gen. 24:15).

1693. "A man carrying a jar of water . . ." Carrying water was universally done by women. So when Jesus instructed two of his disciples, "Go into the city, and a man carrying a jar of water will meet you. Follow him" (Mark 14:13), it was an easy way of identifying the man. However when larger supplies of water were needed, men used large skins of sheep or goats for carrying it.

1694. The hard leather portable bucket with a rope is brought to the well in addition to the pitcher in order to let down the bucket to the level of the water. The Samaritan woman whom Jesus met at Jacob's well had brought all this with her, but Jesus did not have anything with him. This is why she said to him, "Sir, you have no bucket, and the well is deep" (John 4:11 NRSV).

BEARING CHILDREN

1695. Levirate marriage. The Israelites believed that it was very important for a man to have an heir. To preserve the property inheritance that God had given them, they had to convey it through family lines (Exod. 15:17–18). If a woman's husband died before she had borne an heir, the practice of levirate marriage (which was part of the Law of Moses) began. According to the law, when a woman was widowed, her dead husband's brother would marry her and the children of this marriage became heirs to the deceased brother. If a man refused to marry his widowed sister-in-law, he was publicly disgraced (Deut. 25:7–10).

1696. Many Israelite couples were unable to bear children. Today we know that couples may be childless due to either the husband's or wife's sterility, but in Bible times only the wife was blamed for the problem. Barrenness was more than a physical or social problem. Deep religious meanings were attached to the problem as well. Moses promised the people that if they obeyed the Lord, blessing would follow: "Thou shalt be blessed above all people: there shall not be male or female barren among you, or among your cattle" (Deut. 7:14 KJV). So barrenness was believed to be a result of disobeying God.

1697. A barren couple spent a good deal of time examining their past failures to see if any sin had been unconfessed. Childlessness became the main theme of the couple's prayers. Isaac begged the Lord to let his wife bear a child (Gen. 25:21). Hannah sobbed before the Lord and promised that if God would give her a son, she would dedicate him to the Lord's service (1 Sam. 1:11). When sin was ruled out as the cause of the problem, the wife would then inquire about different kinds of remedies.

1698. Modern excavations in Israel have produced many clay fertility figures. These were supposed to help a woman get pregnant by "sympathetic magic." Each figurine was molded to look like a pregnant woman. As the barren woman handled it and kept it near her, she hoped to take on the likeness of the pregnant figure. Women also wore amulets, an ornament or gem worn against the body, to ensure fertility.

1699. Adoption practices were common in ancient times. Adoption solved many problems. The adopted son would care for the couple in their old age, provide them a proper burial, and inherit the family property. However, if the couple had a natural son after one had been adopted, he would become the rightful heir. After Bilhah's baby was born, it was placed in Rachel's lap. This act was a central part of the adoption ceremony. Other biblical adoptions include Moses adopted by Pharaoh's daughter and Esther adopted by Mordecai.

1700. Another ancient custom that continues in the East is the care for an infant child. Instead of allowing the baby the free use of his arms and legs, it is bound hand and foot by swaddling bands, quite like a mummy. At birth the child is washed and rubbed with salt, and with its legs together and its arms at its side, it is wound around tightly with linen or cotton strips, four to five inches wide and five or six yards long. The band is also placed under the chin and over the forehead. Not only does the Bible describe the baby Jesus as swaddled, but Ezekiel also mentions the custom of swaddling (Ezek. 16:4).

1701. It was considered a privilege and a duty for the Jewish mother to breastfeed her infant. But sometimes a mother was not physically able to do so. For these women, a wet nurse was secured. This wet nurse (usually unrelated to the baby) fed the baby her own breast milk. When Pharaoh's daughter found Moses floating among the reeds of the Nile, one of her first orders was to get a Hebrew woman who could nurse him.

1702. The weaning of a child is an important event in the domestic life of the East. In many places it is celebrated by a festive gathering of friends, by feasting, religious ceremonies, and sometimes the formal presentation of rice to the child. Hebrew babies are often nursed for two years and sometimes for four or five. It was probably after age three that Hannah weaned Samuel and brought him to be presented to the Lord. A scriptural example of the weaning feast is found in Genesis 21:8, when Isaac was weaned and dedicated to the Lord.

1703. Names were very important in the world of the Old Testament. Hebrew names usually carried meaning about the person's character, praise to God, or the location or circumstances surrounding the child's birth. Jewish people believed that they must first know a person's name before they could know the person. The name Jesus is a Greek form of the Hebrew name Joshua, which means "salvation of Yahweh." The name was given by one or both parents. Scripture indicates that the mother usually named the infant.

1704. Many cultures in the world today practice circumcision for hygienic reasons. Some primitive tribes perform the operation on infants and young boys, while others wait until the boys reach puberty or are ready for marriage. These traditions have remained unchanged for centuries. For the Israelites, circumcision signified that the infant was being taken into the covenant community. This ritual remains a hallmark of Judaism today. Flint knives were used until New Testament times when they were finally replaced by metal. Jewish boys were circumcised on the eighth day.

1705. Recent studies have confirmed that the safest time to perform circumcision is on the eighth day of life. Vitamin K, which causes blood to coagulate, is not produced in sufficient amounts until the fifth to seventh day. On the eighth day the body contains 10 percent more prothrombin than normal; prothrombin is also important in the clotting of blood.

1706. Since all firstborns were God's possession, it was necessary for the Israelite family to redeem, or buy back, the firstborn infant from God. The redemption price was five shekels of silver, given to the priests when the child was one month old—possibly an amount of time to be certain the child would live (Num. 18:15–16). Scripture doesn't tell us about the redemption ceremony itself.

1707. By rabbinic times the redemption ceremony took place in the child's home with a priest and other guests present. The rite began when the father presented the child to the priest. The priest would then ask the father, "Do you wish to redeem the child or do you want to leave him with me?" The father answered that he would redeem the child and handed the priest five silver coins. The priest would then declare, "Your son is redeemed!" After the priest pronounced a blessing on the child, he joined the invited guests at a banquet table.

Manners and Customs

52

1708. Knowing the manners and customs of the East (those living in countries east of Europe) is necessary for a thorough understanding of the Bible. Westerners can easily misunderstand the motives and meanings of why our ancient Israelite forefathers and mothers did and said what they did in the Scriptures.

CLOTHING AND ACCESSORIES

1709. The manner of dress in the Eastern countries is largely the same as it was centuries ago. There is a prevalent view in the

Bible lands that it is morally wrong to change anything that is ancient.

1710. The inner garment. The tunic was a shirt worn next to the skin. It was made of leather, haircloth, wool, linen, or in modern times, usually cotton. The simplest style was without sleeves and reached to the knees or ankles. The well-to-do wore it with sleeves and it extended to the ankles. Both men and women wore this garment, although there was no doubt a difference in style and pattern in what was worn. The garment of Jesus for which the Roman soldiers cast lots was a tunic without seams.

1711. The garment Jacob gave to Joseph (Gen. 37:3), translated in the Septuagint and Vulgate Bible as the "coat of many colors," is the same expression used for the garment worn by Tamar, the daughter of King David. It is translated in Greek and Latin as "a sleeved tunic" (2 Sam. 13:18). For this reason, many Bible scholars believe it was a long undergarment with sleeves. The working classes usually wore a short tunic, whereas the aristocracy wore a long tunic with sleeves.

1712. The girdle. If the tunic was ungirded (or untied), it would interfere with a person's ability to walk freely, and so a girdle was always worn when leaving home (2 Kings 4:29; Acts 12:8). There were and still are two types. A common variety is made of leather, usually six inches wide, with clasps. This was the kind worn by Elijah (2 Kings 1:8), and by John the Baptist (Matt. 3:4). The other, a more valuable type, is made of linen or sometimes silk or embroidered material. The girdle served as a pouch to carry money and other things, as well as to fasten a man's sword to his body.

1713. The outer garment or "mantle." The outer garment that a Palestinian villager wears is a large cloak that serves as an overcoat. It is made of wool or goat's hair and serves as a shelter from the wind and rain, as well as a blanket at night. It was this outer garment or mantle with which Elijah smote the waters of the Jordan and crossed over. When Elijah was taken up to heaven, this mantle was thrown down to Elisha (2 Kings 2:8–13).

1714. Because the outer garment was a man's covering by night, the law did not allow anybody to take this as pledge or security on a loan because it would deprive him of his means of keeping warm while sleeping. When a garment was taken, it had to be returned by sunset (Exod. 22:26–27).

1715. Hair. The Jews of the Bible gave much attention to the care of their hair. The young people loved to wear it long and curled (Song of Sol. 5:11), and they were proud to have thick hair (2 Sam. 14:25–26). Middle-aged men and priests would occasionally cut their hair, but not very often.

1716. Baldness was scarce, and suspicion of leprosy was often attached to the condition. When the youth said to Elisha, "Go on up, you baldhead!" (2 Kings 2:23), he was using an extreme curse.

1717. Baldness disqualified a man from the priesthood, as is demonstrated by Leviticus 21:5. Priests were not allowed to shave their heads or rip their clothes, or even to mourn a mother's or father's death (Lev. 21:10–11).

1718. Men allowed their beards to grow long and rarely if ever cut them.

1719. Jews always wore a turban in public. At certain seasons of the year, it is dangerous to expose the head to the rays of the sun. This turban was made of thick material that was wound several times around the head. Both Job and the prophet Isaiah mention the use of the turban as a headdress (Job 29:14).

1720. Wearing what is appropriate. The Law of Moses forbade men to wear women's clothing or women to wear men's clothing (Deut. 22:5).

1721. The dress of women was different in detail from men's clothing rather than in style. They too wore a tunic and cloak, but in every case their dress was a little more elaborate. The veil was the distinctive female apparel. All females, with the exception of maidservants, women of low status, and prostitutes, wore a veil.

1722. The headgear of Bethlehem women shed light on biblical customs. The headgear included a high cap on the front of which might have been sewn rows of gold and silver coins. There was also a veil, perhaps six feet long and four feet wide that covered the cap but left the coins showing. Some had embroidery work and some were nearly covered with needlework.

1723. Jewish men did not wear jewelry as a rule. They often carried a cane or staff with some ornamentation at the top. Certain men wore a ring on their right hand, or on a chain around their neck. This was the signet ring or seal and served as the personal signature of its owner.

1724. Jewish women did use ornaments, such as in elaborate braiding of their hair (which Peter and Paul spoke against in 1 Peter and 1 Timothy). Earrings were worn by women of Jacob's family (Gen. 35:4), and the gold earrings of the Israelite women contributed to the gold in Aaron's golden calf (Exod. 32:2). Abraham's servant had two bracelets ready to give Rebekah, and in the third chapter of his prophecy, Isaiah lists many feminine ornaments (Isa. 3:18–20).

1725. Each society has its own standards of physical beauty. It is difficult to know just what the ancient Hebrews found beautiful. Most of the attractive women mentioned in the Bible are not described in detail. The writer usually notes simply that a woman was "beautiful." Some of the most important women in the Old Testament were said to be beauties: Sarah, Rebekah, Rachel, Bathsheba, Tamar, Abishag, and Esther.

1726. What did Jesus wear? He must have worn the turban, worn by both the rich and poor alike. Under his turban his hair would be rather long and his beard uncut. His tunic, the undergarment, was one piece without a seam. It was therefore of some value and had probably been given to him by one of the wealthier women who ministered to him. Over this he wore the mantle, loose and flowing. This cloak probably was not white, because we're told it turned white during the transfiguration. It was most likely a common blue or it may have been white with brown stripes. Jesus did have at the four corners of this mantle the tsitsith (fringe).

1727. In Old Testament times practically all clothing was made from sheep's wool. We are accustomed to seeing sheep that have been bred for their white wool, but in biblical times most sheep had brown coats or were black and white.

1728. The hair clipped from goats was woven into coarse cloth to make the black tents in which the nomads lived. The size of the tent depended on the wealth of the owner, but even the simplest tent was divided by curtains into a front room for entertaining and another room for cooking and housing the children.

TENTS

1729. Tents are one of the earliest family shelters mentioned in the Bible. The first reference to tent life in the Scriptures is found in Genesis 4:20, when Jabal is described as "the father of such as dwell in tents." Following the flood Japheth was said to have lived "in the tents of Shem" (Gen. 9:27 KJV). The patriarchs, Abraham, Isaac, and Jacob, lived most of their lives in tents, in and around the land of Canaan. The children of Israel lived in tents during their forty years in the wilderness and for many years after entering the Promised Land. Hundreds of years later, in the days of David, it was said to the king, "The ark, and Israel, and Judah, abide in tents" (2 Sam. 11:11).

1730. The bedouin's home is his tent, which is made of black goat hair. This is the same material as the sackcloth of Bible times. The main overhead portion is a large awning that is held up by poles. The ends of the tent are drawn out by cords tied to pegs and driven into the ground. It was one of these tent pegs that Jael used to drive into Sisera's head while he slept (Judg. 4:21).

1731. The tent is usually oblong and divided into two and sometimes three rooms by goat-hair curtains. The entrance leads into the men's quarters where guests are received. Beyond this is the area for the women and children. Sometimes a third section is used for servants or cattle. The women in the inner section are screened from the view of those in the reception room, but they can hear what goes on. Remember Sarah overheard the angel and laughed (Gen. 18:10–15).

1732. Bible time nomads were constantly on the move so their furnishings included only the necessities. Rugs covered the ground and bedding was brought out at night. They laid on mats or carpets and covered themselves with their outer garments worn during the day. In a nomad tent you would find bags of grain and a hand mill and mortar with which to pound the grain. Hanging from the poles would be skin bags or bottles for water and other liquids; a leather bucket to draw water up from any well available; an earthen pitcher used by women to carry water; and a few pots, kettles, and pans. Serving dishes included mats, platters or larger dishes, and cups for drinking. For some, a primitive lamp was used at night. If the family had a camel, then the camel bags or saddle would have been used as seats.

1733. Seeing new tents is and was out of the ordinary. Even today goat clippings are accumulated over the course of the year, and with these, the women make new strips to repair the old tent. The section that is most worn is ripped out and a new piece is sewn in. The old piece is then used for a side curtain. Each year new strips of cloth replace the old ones and the "house of hair" is handed down from father to son without it being completely old or new at any one time.

1734. As the tent-dweller's family grows larger or he becomes richer, he adds on another section to his old tent. Isaiah had this process in mind when he compared the prophetic prosperity of Israel to a bedouin tent.

> Enlarge the place of your tent,
>   stretch your tent curtains wide,
>   do not hold back;
> lengthen your cords,
>   strengthen your stakes.
>
> Isaiah 54:2

HOUSES

1735. A life of agriculture took the place of the wandering life of nomads after Israel had been in the land of Canaan for many years and settled in. Houses began to take the place of tents. The average home of the common people was a one-room shelter. In Bible times, people spent as much time as possible in God's outdoors. The Hebrew word for house is *bayith* and means shelter. It served only as a place to rest after a day outside. The sacred writers referred to God as a "shelter" or a "refuge" (Ps. 61:3; Isa. 4:6).

1736. **The one-room houses** were usually made of clay bricks dried in the sun (similar to adobe houses in Mexico), but sometimes they were made of rough, local sandstone and set with a mud mortar. Only the palaces or houses of the wealthy were constructed of hewn stones, like the palaces of Solomon (1 Kings 7:9).

1737. **The roofs** of these humble houses were made by laying beams across from wall to wall, then putting down a mat of reeds or thornbushes and over it a coating of clay or mud. Sand and pebbles were then scattered over this and a stone roller was used to make it smooth enough to shed rain.

1738. **Earthy homes** create challenges unfamiliar to westerners. It is not uncommon to see grass growing on the tops of the houses, as the Bible even references, "May they be like grass on the roof, which withers before it can grow" (Ps. 129:6; see also 2 Kings 19:26; Isa. 37:27). With a dirt roof, leaks often soak through after a heavy rain. The Book of Proverbs compares this dripping to a quarrelsome wife (Prov. 19:13; 27:15). Not only did dripping cause trouble, but snakes often crawled in through cracks, and thieves could dig through and get into the house. Job said, "In the dark they dig through houses, which they had marked for themselves in the daytime" (Job 24:16 KJV).

1739. **The houses with one room** were in the villages and those with more than one room were in the cities. If a house with two rooms was to be built, the rooms weren't placed side by side. Rather the breadth of another room was left between the two rooms, and a wall was constructed between the ends to make an open court. If there were three or more rooms, a room would be substituted for the wall at the end of the court and there would be more rooms around the courtyard, making a secluded area from the street.

1740. **Cisterns** were often built in the courtyards for water, and fires were built for warmth, as described by Simon Peter's experience in the courtyard of the high priest's house where Jesus was being tried (John 18:18). The courtyard was a place to eat and also a place to bathe. When David looked down from his palace rooftop and saw the beautiful Bathsheba bathing (2 Sam. 11:2), she was in the courtyard of her house, a protected place not visible to ordinary observation.

1741. The roof of an Arab's house was and is used today for a large variety of purposes, much like it was used in the days of the prophets and the apostles. It is used for storage (Josh. 2:6), as a place to sleep (1 Sam. 9:26), a spot for gathering in times of excitement to see down the streets (Isa. 22:1), a place of public proclamations (Matt. 10:27), a place of worship and prayer (Zeph. 1:5; Acts 10:9), and as a way of escape in time of danger (Matt. 24:17; Mark 13:15; Luke 17:31).

1742. Candles weren't a part of Bible life. The King James Version of the Bible frequently uses the word *candle* because candles were so widely used at the time that version was written. However, a literal translation of the original words would use *lamp* or *light*. Bible characters knew nothing about candles.

1743. A lamp was considered to be the Palestinian peasant's one luxury that was a necessity. When the sun set, the door of his house was shut, and then the lamp was lit. To sleep without a light was considered by most villages to be a sign of extreme poverty. When a late traveler saw a light in a house, he knew there was life there. To wish a man's light be put out was to wish on him a terrible curse.

1744. Fuel is so scarce in the Holy Lands that peasants often burn dried dung and sell sticks that they gather. Dried grass and withered flowers are also carefully gathered into bundles and used for making a fire. This was done in the days of old as well. As Jesus said, "The grass of the field, which today is, and tomorrow is cast into the oven" (Matt. 6:30 KJV; Luke 12:28). Another popular fuel is thorns or thorny shrubs. The widow of Zarephath gathered sticks to build a fire (1 Kings 17:10), but the fire built in the courtyard of the high priest where Simon Peter warmed himself was built with charcoal (John 18:18 KJV).

GUESTS AND HOSPITALITY

1745. A custom of sending double invitations to a special event has been observed in some parts of the East. Several examples of this custom are found in the Bible. At some time before the feast is to be served, an invitation is sent forth; then when the appointed time draws near, a servant is sent again to announce that everything is now ready. One example of this is in the parable of the great supper: "A certain man was preparing a great banquet and invited many guests. At the time of the banquet he sent his servant to tell those who had been invited, 'Come, for everything is now ready'" (Luke 14:16–17).

1746. "Then the master told his servant, 'Go out to the roads and country lanes and make them come in, so that my house will be full'" (Luke 14:23). In the East the one invited is expected to reject an invitation upon the first invite. He must be urged to accept. All the while he expects to attend, but he must allow the one inviting him the privilege of "compelling him" to accept.

1747. Ancient banquets were usually held at night in brilliantly lighted rooms, and anybody who was excluded from the feast was said to be cast out of the lighted room into "the outer darkness" of the night. In the teaching of Jesus, the day of judgment is likened to being excluded from the banquet (Matt. 8:12). In the East a lamp is usually kept burning all night. Because of people's fear of the darkness, the Savior could have chosen no more appropriate words than "outer darkness" for the future punishment of the unrighteous.

1748. Seats were uncommon in early Bible times, except in the king's circle or at other times of ceremony. The prophet Amos was the first of the biblical writers to refer to the custom of "stretch[ing] themselves upon their couches" when eating (Amos 6:4). By the time of Jesus the Romans were accustomed to reclining on couches at supper.

1749. A triclinium was a common dining setup of the Romans. It included a short square table with three couches to surround three sides of the perimeter. The fourth side was left open so the servant could reach the table easily.

1750. Guests of honor were held in special esteem when they were assigned to a room with a higher floor than the rest of the house. Many houses had such a room for special company.

1751. Guests were also honored by being seated at the right of the host during meals. The next highest place was at the left of the host. Jesus condemned the Pharisees for their insistence on having the highest places of distinction when they were invited to a banquet.

1752. Dancing was often part of the entertainment at feasts. When the prodigal son returned home, there was music and dancing (Luke 15:24–25). Mainly the women and girls danced, although sometimes men did, too, as David did when the ark was brought into Jerusalem (2 Sam. 6:14). But there is no scriptural record that Jewish men danced with the women.

1753. Sharing hospitality with others was an integral part of Israelite life. Men of the East believed guests were sent by God. Therefore providing for their hospitality became a sacred duty. When Abraham entertained three strangers who proved to be angels, his enthusiasm seemed to indicate this same belief (Gen. 18:2–7). We typically think of guests as friends or business acquaintances. But in the East there are three types of guests: friends, strangers, and enemies.

1754. Strangers as guests. An old Eastern proverb says, "Every stranger is an invited guest." Like Abraham, the bedouin Arab of today will sit in the entrance of his tent in order to be on the watch for a stranger and guest (Gen. 18:1). In the New Testament, when Paul taught the Roman believers to be "given to hospitality" (Rom. 12:13 KJV), he was referring to the same thing. The Greek word he used for hospitality is pronounced "fil-ox-en-ee-ah," which means "love to strangers."

1755. Enemies as guests. One remarkable aspect of Eastern hospitality is that an enemy can be received as a guest. As long as he remains in that relationship, he is perfectly safe and is treated as a friend. Certain tribes of tent-dwellers live by the rule that an enemy who has "once dismounted and touched the rope of a single tent is safe."

1756. Customs of hospitality and honor for guests are very important in the East. When a guest first enters a home, bowing between the guest and host will take place. An expressive custom is that of saluting with the head erect and the body inclined forward by raising the hand to the heart, mouth, and forehead. The symbolic meaning of this is to say, "My heart, my voice, and my brain are all at your service." On many occasions those who are used to this custom enter into a more complete bow afterward.

1757. The greetings upon entering an Arab house or a bedouin tent go something like this: The host will say, "Salam alakum," which means "Peace be on you." The guest will then respond with the words "Wa alakum es-salam," meaning "And on you peace." The greeting is then followed with a kiss. The men will place their right hand on the other's left shoulder and kiss his right cheek, and then reverse the action. Scriptural examples of the kiss are found when Jacob kissed his father; Esau kissed Jacob; Joseph kissed his brothers; Aaron kissed Moses; Moses kissed Jethro; David and Jonathan kissed each other; and the father of the prodigal son kissed him when he returned home.

1758. Guests take off their shoes before entering the main room of a house. This is necessary because they will sit on a mat, rug, or divan, with their feet beneath them. Shoes would soil the couch and their clothes. This led to the custom of removing shoes upon entering sacred places. At the burning bush the Lord told Moses, "Take off your sandals, for the place where you are standing is holy ground" (Exod. 3:5).

1759. The Eastern guest is offered water for washing his feet after the bowing, greeting, and kissing are completed. A servant will assist the guest by pouring water over the guest's feet above a copper basin, rubbing them with his hands, and wiping them on a towel. When Jesus was with his disciples, he took the place of the servant and washed their feet.

1760. The custom of anointing guests is an ancient one among nations of the East. Olive oil is often used by itself, but sometimes it is mixed with spices. Simon the Pharisee was accused of being inhospitable because he didn't anoint Jesus (Luke 7:46). David memorialized this custom when he wrote in his shepherd psalm, "You anoint my head with oil" (Ps. 23:5).

1761. Many accounts of anointing are found in the Bible, each carrying different meanings of the custom as a way of showing courtesy, respect, and devotion; for healing purposes; and as a symbol of the pouring out of God's Spirit.

1762. One of the first beverages a guest is offered is a drink of water. This is to recognize him as a person worthy of peaceful reception. To give a drink of water is the simplest way to pledge friendship with a person. The words of Jesus in the Gospel of Mark (9:41) demonstrate this custom, "Anyone who gives you a cup of water in my name because you belong to Christ will certainly not lose his reward."

1763. The sharing of food in Eastern cultures is a very special act of hospitality. It is a way of making a covenant of peace and fidelity. When Abimelech wanted a permanent covenant with Isaac, the confirmation of that covenant came when Isaac "made a feast for them, and they ate and drank" (Gen. 26:30).

1764. "The guest while in the house is its lord." This is a true statement of the spirit of Eastern hospitality. One of the first greetings a Palestinian host will give his guest is to say, "Hadtha beitak," meaning "This is your house." This phrase is repeated many times during the guest's stay. There was a similar attitude between Lot and his guests when he said, "My lords, please turn aside to your servant's house" (Gen. 19:2).

1765. Defending to the death. In the lands of the East, when a host accepts a man as his guest he agrees to defend the guest from all possible enemies during the time of his stay, whatever the cost. The psalmist felt utterly secure, though he had enemies close to him, when he knew that God was his host. "You prepare a table before me in the presence of my enemies" (Ps. 23:5).

1766. Eastern people make mention of God in daily conversation. An astonished person will exclaim, "Mashallah," or "See what God has done!" which is the exact expression used by Balaam centuries ago (Num. 23:23). If a person is asked if he expects to do a certain thing, he will answer, "If God wills." Such an answer was recommended by James in his epistle (James 4:15).

1767. The Eastern manner of speaking often includes picturing what is meant with figurative language and exaggerated expressions or even by demonstrating a concept. If John the Baptist had spoken like a westerner, he might have said, "Your pretense of virtue and good birth far exceed your actual practice of virtue." But being an easterner he said, "You brood of vipers! Who warned you to flee from the coming wrath? Produce fruit in keeping with repentance. And do not think you can say to yourselves, 'We have Abraham as our father.' I tell you that out of these stones God can raise up children for Abraham" (Matt. 3:7–9).

WORSHIP

1768. Canaanites and Phoenicians worshiped many nature gods. Baal, who was regarded as master of the earth, had an arm that hurled bolts of lightning, and his voice caused thunder. The Israelites referred to Baal as Baal-zebul or Beelzebub, which means "lord of the flies," no doubt referring to the hordes of flies that buzzed around the animals sacrificed to this god. By New Testament times Beelzebub had become a title for Satan.

1769. Mutual gods. Just as the Israelites were attracted to Canaanite gods, so were the Philistines. Their deities—Dagon, Ashtaroth, and Baal-zebub—were all related to Canaanite gods.

1770. The father was the priest of the whole family in the days of the early patriarchs. This honor and responsibility was then passed down to the firstborn son after the father's death. This practice continued until the Law of Moses transferred the right to the tribe of Levi, who became the priests of the Hebrew nation.

1771. The altar. Throughout the Old Testament many altars were built and described. After Abraham pitched his tent in the vicinity of Bethel, the Scripture says, "There he built an altar to the Lord and called on the name of the Lord" (Gen. 12:8). Altars served as monuments of holiness and provided an approach to God through sacrifice.

1772. Clay figures called teraphim were household gods that served as guardian angels of the home in Babylonia. At the death of a father they were passed down to the eldest son. When Jacob left the home of Laban in Haran, Rachel stole the teraphim that belonged to her father (Gen. 31:19). This made Laban very upset, so he pursued Jacob's caravan. Even though Jacob told his family to get rid of the foreign gods and purify themselves, the teraphim appeared several times in later history of the Israelites.

1773. Religious education in the family became a special mark of Judaism. The Law of Moses was very specific in its requirements that parents must train their children in the knowledge of God and his laws. The emphasis on this education in the family has contributed largely to the permanence of the Jews in history.

1774. The pilgrimage made to the place of sanctuary was a very important part of Hebrew life. "Three times a year all your men are to appear before the Sovereign Lord, the God of Israel" (Exod. 34:23). The whole family could go, but the men and boys were required to go. Remember Joseph and Mary traveled a day's journey on their return from Jerusalem before discovering that Jesus was missing. Because clans traveled together, parents could go for hours without seeing their sons.

1775. Jewish boys had to be able to recite "the Shema," a prayer, by the age of twelve. The prayer was the quotation of three passages from the Pentateuch that was repeated morning and evening by Jewish men. The three passages were from Deuteronomy 6:4–9; 11:13–21; and Numbers 15:37–41.

1776. The idea of *minyan* is central to the spiritual life of Jewish people. While anyone can pray at any time, before an official prayer service can be held there must be at least ten men present. This group of ten men is called a *minyan*. It was stated in the law that whenever ten adult men were gathered together in the name of God, the Lord himself would actually be present in the room with them. Any room then became consecrated ground, a holy place where men could perform their religious rituals and worship God.

1777 The early gathering place for Christian worship was in people's homes. The earliest excavation of a church by archaeologists, where a date has been assigned (dating back to the third century AD), is of a room within a house that was set apart for worship and furnished as a chapel. In the days of the apostles, believers also took seriously their responsibility to care for believers who came to their town. In a time of persecution, this refuge was very important to those who traveled to spread the gospel.

Food

1778. A single large olive tree in biblical times provided an entire family with all of the oil it needed for food and lamps, as much as half a ton of it a year. The tree gave a year-round crop because both the unripe and the ripe fruit are edible. So the olive leaf in the dove's beak promised a rebirth of life to Noah and his family.

1779. The ordinary food of the average Hebrew of Bible times was bread, olives, oil, buttermilk, and cheese from their flocks, fruits and vegetables from their orchards and gardens, and meat on rare occasions.

1780. The eating of raw grain is a modern custom in Palestine that dates back to very ancient days. Contemporary Arabs often pick the heads of grain, rub them in their hands, and eat them. Some Pharisees approached Jesus and his disciples as they ate raw grain in the fields. "One Sabbath Jesus was going through the grainfields, and his disciples began to pick some heads of grain, rub them in their hands and eat the kernels" (Luke 6:1).

1781. When grain in the wheat field has passed the "milk stage" and begun to harden, it is called "fereek" and is considered delicious eaten raw. For centuries the unwritten law of hospitality has been that wayfarers may eat some of the wheat as they pass by or through a field, but they must not carry any away with them. The law of God allowed this same privilege in Deuteronomy 23:35.

1782. Parched grain is another common food eaten in Bible times. It is prepared with grains of wheat that are not fully ripe. They are roasted in a pan or on an iron plate. The grain is eaten either with or without bread. Jesse sent some of it with David to his older sons in the army (1 Sam. 17:17). Abigail included some in her gift to David (1 Sam. 25:18), and David received some from friends after he had fled from Absalom (2 Sam. 17:28).

1783. Besides wheat and barley, millet and spelt ("rie" in some translations) were also grown. Wheat was the first choice of people, with barley reserved for the poor. Spelt is actually a weak strain of wheat.

1784. Bread is unquestionably the principal food of the East and is considered sacred. In some places of Palestine, there is such a reverence for bread that people will not rise to greet a guest if they are in the midst of breaking bread together. The guest will have to wait until they are finished. Everything about bread, from the sowing of grain to the baking, is done in the name of God.

1785. The sacredness of the bread. There is a universal Eastern custom of *breaking* bread and not cutting it. To cut bread would be thought of as cutting life itself. Because Christ broke bread when he instituted the ordinance of the Lord's Supper, the expression "breaking of bread" came to refer to the practice of taking communion.

1786. The expression "eating bread" is often used in the Bible to mean eating a whole meal. When the Bible says, "The Egyptians might not eat bread with the Hebrews" (Gen. 43:32 KJV), it means that they would likely not eat a meal with them. In Lamentations 4:4 we read: "The young children ask bread, and no man breaketh it unto them" (KJV). The expression "breaking of bread" means the taking of a meal.

1787. The Israelite's Egyptian diet included leeks, onion, and garlic, and the prophet Isaiah mentions a "garden of cucumber" (Isa. 1:8 KJV). Gourds were also used (2 Kings 4:39).

1788. The two most widely used vegetables in Bible times, however, were beans and lentils. The most famous biblical use of lentils was, of course, the selling of Esau's birthright for a meal of lentil stew with bread (Gen. 25:34).

1789. Fruits included olives and grapes, which were eaten fresh and also dried as raisins (1 Sam. 25:18) or made into wine. Pomegranates were grown for their juice, and it is possible, though not likely, that apples were grown as well. Both of the latter fruits are mentioned in Song of Songs.

1790. Figs, though mentioned often enough and thought of largely as food by contemporary sources, were grown for medicinal purposes as well as general consumption in Bible times.

1791. Wine was the most common alcoholic drink. It is mentioned throughout the Bible. The vineyard and the process of making wine are common examples in Jesus' teachings, most likely because they were familiar analogies for people since the beverage was so common.

1792. Beer was brewed in Egypt and Mesopotamia, and perhaps the Israelites were familiar with this beverage also. Also brewed in these two areas was a wine made of figs.

1793. Milk was considered a substantial food for all ages in Bible times. The Promised Land was often called "a land flowing with milk and honey" (Exod. 3:8; 13:5; Josh. 5:6; Jer.11:5). A form of milk that is commonly used among the Arabs today is called "leben," which means "white." It is like our sour milk curds. It was probably this that Abraham gave to his guests (Gen. 18:8) and also that Jael gave to Sisera (Judg. 4:19; 5:25).

1794. Butter and cheese were made from the rich cream and curds (Prov. 30:33; Job 10:10). As the Hebrews didn't eat meat often, these would have served as a protein source for the people.

1795. Meat was only eaten on special occasions, such as when a stranger or guest was entertained, or when a feast was made. Kings and wealthy men, on the other hand, ate meat often. The daily menu of four kinds of meat for King Solomon's court is given in Scripture: beef, mutton, game, and fowl (1 Kings 4:23).

1796. Nuts also count as a protein source, and though meat was rare, nuts weren't. Almonds and pistachios are mentioned in Genesis 43:11.

1797. Numerous references to honey and honeycomb in God's Word are proof that the Holy Land abounded with the sweet stuff. Many scriptural citations indicate that wild honey was very common, being found in cavities of trees, such as when Jonathan discovered and ate some honey (1 Sam. 14:25–27). It is also mentioned as being found in the holes of rock, where it was often extracted (Ps. 81:16), and even in the dried carcasses of animals, as when Samson ate honey from the carcass of the lion (Judg. 14:8–9).

1798. Honey is used in the poetic books of the Hebrew Bible to make many comparisons. The judgments of God are compared to it (Ps. 19:10). Pleasant words are likened to it (Prov. 16:24), as are knowledge and wisdom to the soul (Prov. 24:13–14). And the bride and bridegroom of Solomon's Song speak of honey (Song of Sol. 4:11; 5:1).

1799. Seasoning most often refers to salt (Job 6:6). However, other types of spice, such as dill ("anise" in the KJV), mint, cumin, and coriander are also mentioned.

1800. What is "kosher"? Many people, Jew and Gentile alike, commonly ask if something is kosher, loosely using the term to mean "permissible" or "okay." *Kosher* is a Yiddish word for "proper" that derives from the Hebrew word *kashrut*. Although in the modern sense we commonly associate "kosher" with only dietary laws, the notion of what is "proper" covers a broad range of items that must be done in accordance with the law.

1801. Hand washing was very important to the Israelites. They were careful to wash their hands before each meal. Water was poured (most often by a servant) over the hands to be washed as they were held over a basin. Because the Hebrew people did not eat with silverware, washing was a necessity. Elisha poured water over the hands of Elijah in 2 Kings 3:11. As Elijah's servant, this was an important part of Elisha's duties.

1802. Meals were eaten on a mat spread on the ground (like a picnic blanket), or at a low table when the diners were commoners. The Hebrew word pronounced "Shool-khawn," usually translated "table," has as its root meaning "a skin or leather mat spread on the ground." While eating, people would sit on the floor with their legs folded under them or in the position of kneeling.

1803. A blessing was said by each person after the master of the house said it, such as "In the name of God," or "God be praised." Only after all had said the blessing did they begin to eat by dipping or scooping with their bread in a common serving bowl. The only dishes used were those in which the food was placed on the table; there were no individual dishes for those dining. Gideon put the meat in a basket, and the broth in a pot (Judg. 6:19). Meat was generally eaten with the fingers.

1804. A prayer of thanks was said at the end of the meal. Deuteronomy 8:10 states: "When you have eaten and are satisfied, praise the LORD your God for the good land he has given you." It was customary for one of the guests to give the thanks in a loud voice, and for the rest to say, "Amen."

1805. The Hebrew families looked to the promise God originally gave to them about health for their bodies throughout their wilderness experiences and after they were in the Promised Land. "If you listen carefully to the voice of the LORD your God and do what is right in his eyes, if you pay attention to his commands and keep all his decrees, I will not bring on you any of the diseases I brought on the Egyptians, for I am the LORD, who heals you" (Exod. 15:26). Health was promised if they were obedient to the law of God.

SICKNESS AND DEATH

1806. Sickness could be expected when God's law was disobeyed, according to the law. The twenty-eighth chapter of Deuteronomy lists many curses that would come upon the children of Israel because of disobedience. Therefore the Israelites would grow up believing that health was a reward for obedience and sickness came as punishment. The ancient Hebrews did not go to physicians when they were ill. There are surprisingly few references to doctors in the Old Testament times, and it's possible that those mentioned were foreigners (2 Chron. 16:12; Job 13:4; Jer. 8:22).

1807. Multitudes of sick people in the land are described in the New Testament Gospel records. Many were brought to Jesus to be healed. In the days before the British occupied the land and before the modern Jews brought in scientific medical skills, the land of Israel was overrun with all kinds of afflicted people. While traveling through the land, one would hardly be out of sight of blind beggars, crippled people, or lepers.

1808. The Jews of the New Testament lacked knowledge of medicine, so they would seek help from the most pious man for healing power, rather than the most educated. They believed sickness was punishment for the sin of the sick person or a relative. Concerning the blind man, the disciples asked Jesus, "Rabbi, who sinned, this man or his parents, that he was born blind?" (John 9:2).

1809. Mark adds an interesting fact in his account of Christ healing the woman with an issue of blood. He says that she "had suffered a great deal under the care of many doctors and had spent all she had" (Mark 5:26). One scholar of the Talmud of Babylon suggests that some of the rabbis posed as physicians and some prescribed very queer remedies for a woman with this type of ailment. If one procedure didn't succeed, another one was suggested.

1810. As soon as a death took place, a wail was raised to announce to all the neighborhood what had happened. This was a sign for the relatives to begin their grieving. The death wail is described as a sharp, shrill, ear-piercing shriek. This shriek is followed by prolonged wails. This death wail was referred to in connection with the death of all the firstborn in Egypt. "Pharaoh and all his officials and all the Egyptians got up during the night, and there was loud wailing in Egypt, for there was not a house without someone dead" (Exod. 12:30).

1811. Relatives and friends continued their laments from the time the death wail was heard until the burial. The prophet Micah compared it to the cry of wild beasts or birds. During these lamentations, loved ones exclaimed their sorrow, repeating words over and over as David did when he mourned the death of Absalom: "O my son Absalom! My son, my son Absalom! If only I had died instead of you—O Absalom, my son, my son!" (2 Sam. 18:33).

1812. Professional mourners, who were called in at the time of sorrow to express mourning for the dead, are mentioned by the Hebrew prophets: "Call for the mourning women, that they may come; . . . And let them make haste, and take up a wailing for us (Jer. 9:17–18 KJV). Professional wailers were hired like singers would be for a Western funeral.

1813. Sackcloth was worn, and they often tore their garments in order to let people know the depth of their grief (2 Sam. 3:31). Even today mourners will cry freely and beat their breasts to express sorrow. It is interesting to note, however, that priests were not allowed to rip their clothes even to mourn a parent's death.

1814. Burial follows death quickly, usually the same day. The people of these regions have a primitive idea that the spirit of the one who dies hovers near the body for three days after death.

Mourners believe this spirit is able to hear the wailing calls of grief. Martha, no doubt, thought it would be hopeless to think of reviving her brother's body, because he had been dead four days (John 11:39).

1815. Three classes of Arabs are found in Palestine. The nomad or bedouin Arabs are shepherds who live in tents. The peasant or fellahin Arabs are farmers and usually live in villages in one-room houses. City or belladin Arabs do business in the larger cities. The belladin Arabs have come in contact with Western civilization and their manners and customs have undergone many changes. The peasant farmers, however, have changed customs very little and the bedouins have adopted almost no changes.

Culture Shock between the Ages

53

1816. The Bible speaks about miracles without making apology or even changing its tone. In other words, it doesn't anticipate skepticism. It considers the whole creation rather miraculous. Its writers show the same awe for a sunrise as for a day when the sun stands still.

1817. Male-female relationships in the Bible do—compared to our present-day standards—put women in a subordinate position to men. But when the Bible is compared to the standards of the day in which it was written, it continually gave women a better place in life than that culture allowed them.

1818. A modern atheist says that he or she doesn't believe in God—not gods. Antiquity knew no such atheists. Everyone and every nation had a god of their own, and usually more than one. The proclamation of monotheism must have sounded very strange to the surrounding cultures of that time.

1819. The issue of intermarriage is still a divisive and emotional question among contemporary Jews because it defines who is a Jew. According to Jewish law, a Jew is one who is born to a Jewish mother or is converted to Judaism.

1820. The Mosaic law allowed polygamy (more than one wife) among the Hebrew people. Wives were given certain protections against abuses and there were various regulations regarding these marriages. There was among the Israelites, however, a marked tendency toward monogamy (only one wife). The main reason may have been that the custom of having more than one wife was too expensive for most people.

1821. The Mosaic law did forbid multiple wives for the kings of Israel with the warning that the king's heart would be led astray (Deut. 17:17). The cause of much trouble in the lives of David and Solomon, as well as Ahab, was that they followed the example of the kings in their day of taking many heathen wives, rather than obeying God's law. Men like Adam, Noah, Isaac, Joseph, Moses, and Job had only one wife.

1822. In the East the custom of arranged marriages goes back to early Old Testament times. When Esau married against his parents' wishes, he caused Isaac and Rebekah grief. Why did parents insist on their right to select a bride for their son? The new bride became a member of the bridegroom's clan, and the whole family had a vested interested in knowing if she would be a good fit. There is evidence that sometimes the son or daughter was consulted, as in Rebekah's case when she was asked if she was willing to go and become the wife of Isaac (Gen. 24:58).

1823. What's love got to do with it? Eastern peoples consider love between husband and wife very much like westerners do between brother and sister. It is believed that husbands and wives should love one another because God chose them for each other through the selection of their parents. Love comes after marriage. There are some exceptions to the rule. The case of Jacob and Rachel is the most notable example. For Jacob it was love at first sight (Gen. 29:10–18).

1824. For centuries it has been possible for a husband in Arab lands to divorce his wife by a spoken word. When the wife is divorced, she is entitled to all her wearing apparel, and the husband cannot take anything from her that she has on her body. For this reason, coins on the headgear, rings, and necklaces became an important source of wealth in time of a woman's need. Such customs of divorce were no doubt prevalent in Gentile lands during Old Testament times. A woman was not allowed to divorce her husband.

1825. A husband must give a written certificate of divorce (Deut. 24:1) to his wife in order to divorce her. This is so that she may remarry. The prophet Malachi taught that God hated divorce and severely condemned any man who dealt treacherously with the wife of his covenant (Mal. 2:14–16).

1826. The sin of adultery did not have anything to do with divorce under the Jewish law. Adultery was punishable by death or stoning (Lev. 20:10). A man who was guilty of unfaithfulness was considered a criminal only in that he had invaded the rights of another man. Jesus swept away all grounds for divorce under the law, and made unfaithfulness the lone grounds for divorce for New Testament Christians (Matt. 5:31–32).

1827. Prostitutes often appear in the stories of the Bible. There were two kinds of prostitutes in the Hebrew Scriptures. There were "cultic prostitutes" of the Canaanite religion, but Rahab, the prostitute in Jericho, was a *zonah*, which is Hebrew for a common prostitute. Rahab was the prostitute who hid the Israelite spies and later dangled a red cord out her window to mark her house for protection during the conquest of Jericho. New Testament genealogy in Matthew lists Rahab as the mother of Boaz, who married Ruth and is an ancestor of David, as well as Jesus.

1828. Jesus took no public stand against slavery, racism, class warfare, state-sponsored terrorism, military occupation, or corruption in government in the Gospels. He spoke not a word against abortion or infanticide, homosexuality or the exploitation of women and children. Of all the social evils of his day, Jesus spoke out against the Pharisees and their spiritual corruption.

1829. One sacrifice that only the women gave to the Lord was offered after the birth of a child: "When the days of her purification for a son or daughter are over, she is to bring to the priest at the entrance to the Tent of Meeting a year-old lamb for a burnt offering and a young pigeon or a dove for a sin offering" (Lev. 12:6).

1830. Jewish women were perhaps less active in temple or synagogue worship than later in history. Although there was a special area at the temple known as the "court of women," women were not allowed to go into the inner court. Sources other than the Bible indicate that women did not read the Torah or recite prayers in the synagogue, but they could sit and listen in the special women's area.

1831. A different picture unfolds in the early Christian church. Luke 8:1–3 indicates that Jesus welcomed some women as traveling companions. He encouraged Martha and Mary to sit at his feet as disciples.

1832. After Jesus ascended into heaven, several women met with the other disciples in the upper room to pray. Both men and women gathered at the home of John Mark's mother to pray for the release of Peter; and both men and women prayed regularly in the church at Corinth (which is why Paul gave instructions to both men and women about how to pray in public).

54

Angels
in the Bible

1833. The word *angel* comes from the Greek word *aggelos* (pronounced angelos) and means "messenger." In the Bible this is the form used in almost every mention of angels except one—in Luke 20:36 (KJV) where the phrase reads "equal unto the angels," or the Greek word *isaggelos*, which means "like an angel" or "angelic."

1834. Angels are beings that are created as "intermediate" beings between God and man. They are created beings by God, making them lower, but Psalm 8:5 states that man was made a little lower than the angels.

1835. There are more than three hundred references to angels in the Bible. They play an important role and are seen in some of the most famous Bible stories, including the Christmas story.

1836. An angel is neither a god nor a human. Angels are spirits, as Hebrews says: "[they are] ministering spirits sent to serve those who will inherit salvation."

1837. The first mention of angels in the Bible is when Adam and Eve left the Garden after the fall. They are banished from Eden, and Eden is protected by cherubim, angels that are depicted elsewhere as winged bulls or lions with human heads.

1838. Cherubim are symbolic attendants to places of the Lord's "enthronement" on earth in the Old Testament. They guard the Garden of Eden and the ark of the covenant.

1839. People had forgotten what cherubim signified by Jesus' time, and the historian Josephus wrote in the first century AD that "no one can tell what they were like." Now archaeology has unearthed much of the forgotten past of the biblical world, and it is believed that a cherub was a small wing-bearing lion with a human head, in other words a sphinx. This was the winged creature most often portrayed in Canaanite art, and Canaanite kings are often shown seated on thrones supported by two cherubim. The Israelites may have adapted the cherubim to make a throne for the invisible presence of God.

1840. Angels have three important responsibilities: to attend God's holy throne, to protect people, and to serve as messengers carrying special news or tidings. They are worshipful beings that serve God by carrying out his wishes through these three main roles.

1841. Daniel gives a prophetic picture of what attending the throne of the Almighty God appears like:

> The Ancient of Days took his seat.
> His clothing was as white as snow;
>   the hair of his head was white like wool. . . .
> A river of fire was flowing,
>   coming out from before him.

Thousands upon thousands attended him;
ten thousand times ten thousand stood before him.

Daniel 7:9–10

Angels are all around God, worshiping him.

1842. Guardian angels are spoken of throughout the Bible. Abraham spoke of God sending his angel before his servant Elias as the steward went to seek out a wife for Abraham's son Isaac. Psalm 91:11–12 also speaks of watchful angels:

For he will command his angels concerning you
to guard you in all your ways;
they will lift you up in their hands,
so that you will not strike your foot against a stone.

1843. As messengers the angels communicate God's will to us. They serve as rescuers (such as when Lot was saved from Sodom); as bearers of great tidings (to Mary concerning the birth of Jesus); to instruct prophets (Daniel was given detailed direction from "the man Gabriel"). Angels are mediators who pass along messages God has for his people.

1844. Hebrews 1:14 says angels are "ministering spirits sent to serve those who will inherit salvation." As such they come to our aid and offer help where they can to make our lives better. They are spiritual beings that remain invisible.

1845. A "heavenly host" is not merely a bunch of angels. The term means an "angel army." The heavenly host that came upon the shepherds when Jesus was born was singing and praising God, but they were a "company" of God's army of angels nonetheless.

1846. Jacob's vision depicts the angels as being lined up on an immense ladder that stretches between the earth and the heavens (Gen. 28:12–15). God looks down and sees us and watches as the angels bring their messages from him.

1847. There is a hierarchical organization of angels, though it is uncertain exactly what that might look like. There are seven angels in God's presence that surround the throne. These angels are constantly worshiping their Creator.

1848. Saint Denis the Areopagite wrote a treatise called "De Coelesti Hierarchia" that claims there are defined levels and ranks of angels. However, his work was largely unaccepted except for that pertaining to choirs of angels. The church heartily accepts this idea but does not make believing in varying levels of angels a requirement.

1849. Gregory the Great demonstrated what the early church believed concerning angels with his comments: "There are nine orders of angels, viz., Angels, Archangels, Virtues, Powers, Principalities, Dominations, Throne, Cherubim, and Seraphim." He based this on the apostle Paul's findings as well as other Scriptures.

1850. The apostle Paul tells us four of the orders of angels in his letter to the Ephesians: "above all principality, and power, and might, and dominion" (KJV). He also writes to the Colossians concerning angels: "whether they be thrones, or dominions, or principalities, or powers."

1851. Saint Thomas, who was also from the early church, divided the angels into three hierarchies with three orders of angels in each. Where they are in terms of God himself is the main basis for the divisions. The seraphim, cherubim, and thrones are in the first one; the dominations, virtues, and powers in the second; and the principalities, archangels, and angels are in the third and final hierarchy.

1852. Only two personal names for angels are given in the Bible: Michael and Gabriel. Other angels with personal names are given in the Apocrypha, such as Uriel and Jeremiel.

1853. Gabriel makes appearances in both the Old and New Testaments. He interprets Daniel's visions in the Book of Daniel and also announces the births of John and Jesus to their respective parents.

1854. Michael is an archangel and a warrior in the angelic realm. He is the protector of Israel, according to several references in the Book of Daniel and one in the Book of Revelation.

1855. Fallen angels are angels who have rebelled against God and lost their standing in heaven. They have not been cast into hell, and they are under God's power, but they take orders from Satan (Rev. 12:7).

1856. The Nephilim are a people spoken of in Genesis 6. Some believe this people of great strength were the result of fallen angels marrying the daughters of men on earth to produce offspring of unusual size and strength. The Bible calls these people "the heroes of old, men of renown." God did not look with favor on the actions of these angels, and their offspring were eventually wiped out with the flood.

1857. Satan is perhaps the most famous angel of all time. He is a fallen angel, one who was cast out of heaven after rebelling against God. Paul speaks of how Satan "masquerades as an angel of light" (2 Cor. 11:14). In reality Satan is "the prince of darkness."

1858. A final battle between the good angels and the fallen angels is prophesied in Revelation 12:7–9: "And there was war in heaven. Michael [archangel] and his angels fought against the dragon, and the dragon and his angels fought back. But he was not strong enough, and they lost their place in heaven. The great dragon was hurled down—that ancient serpent called the devil, or Satan, who leads the whole world astray. He was hurled to the earth, and his angels with him."

1859. Christians will see angels on the last day. Matthew 24:31 states that God will "send his angels with a loud trumpet call, and they will gather his elect from the four winds, from one end of the heavens to the other." Angels will escort believers into heaven and to the holy throne!

The Animal Kingdom

55

1860. The Bible is full of animal references. About eighty species of mammals are named, about twenty-five kinds of birds, eight types of reptiles and amphibians, and a dozen insects. We now know that many other living things inhabit these lands besides those named in the Bible. Yet this knowledge of approximately 125 kinds of animals reveals how remarkably familiar these ancient people were with the living things around them.

1861. Sheep were the most important domestic animals of the Hebrews. Both goats and sheep provided meat, but the sheep was preferred for its wool and the goat furnished milk. Sheep were generally only eaten for sacrifices. The sheep is named more often in the Bible than any other animal—more than four hundred times.

1862. The goat may have been the earliest food animal to be domesticated by man, and that probably took place in the vicinity of Jericho about nine thousand years ago. The only animal domesticated earlier was the dog! The goat is mentioned nearly two hundred times. Goats were especially appreciated for their ability to live on rough land and forage in difficult areas.

1863. Cattle are actually descended from a wild breed of ox. They were used early on in the Bible for their milk, although the bulls were eventually prized even more for their abilities to carry heavy loads. Cows even carried the ark of the covenant back to Israel (1 Sam. 6:7)!

1864. Cows are much more difficult to keep than sheep and goats. Cattle require more care, as well as a constant food supply, when they are in permanent settlements. Because Abraham lived much of his life as a nomad, he may have maintained cows, but certainly not as many as his sheep and goats.

1865. The first mention of the donkey, or ass, in the Bible occurs when it is stated that the Pharaoh of Egypt presented Abraham with several donkeys as gifts (Gen. 12:16). To the Egyptian, as in Abraham's culture, the donkey was solely a means of transporting goods. Only later was it used for riding, pulling the plow, and turning millstones to grind grain.

1866. The domesticated donkey is one of the world's most useful animals. And it certainly was to the Hebrews. Numerous laws were given about their treatment, which testifies to the important place they held in the Hebrew economy. A donkey had to be rested on the Sabbath, and one that had fallen under the weight of its burden had to be helped.

1867. Abraham used donkeys in his caravans long before camels were on the scene.

1868. The Hebrews were the only people in the ancient world recorded as riding on donkeys. And only the common people did so. It was considered humiliating for a ruler to ride on one. Biblical kings such as David are recorded as riding on mules (the hybrid mix of a male donkey and a female horse) or in chariots pulled by horses, but never on donkeys. So when Jesus rode on a donkey, it was a symbol of his humility.

1869. Donkeys go long periods without water, work hard in hot climates, and survive on a minimum amount of food. Also a donkey's milk is extremely nutritious, closely resembling human milk in its chemical composition.

1870. Horses were used largely for battle purposes. They were a war symbol of power and strength. They weren't as strong or as capable as the donkeys, camels, and cattle to serve as beasts of burden.

1871. Jericho, an imposing fortress near where the Jordan enters the Dead Sea, stood in the way of the Israelites, but with the blasts of the ram's horn, or *shofar*, the walls tumbled down. Ancient breeds of sheep often grew huge horns from which musical instruments were made. The horn was heated with steam until it was soft enough for its natural curve to be straightened out. Then the wide end where the horn had been attached to the ram was bent at almost a right angle.

1872. The camel had not yet reached Egypt when Abraham visited, according to the findings of archaeologists. It was common in the Fertile Crescent where Abraham's servant was sent to find a bride for his son Isaac. In Genesis 24:12–21, the servant came upon Rebekah who, in offering to water the servant's camels, showed herself to be God's choice for Isaac.

1873. The biblical camel is the one-humped kind, often called a dromedary. Camels are desirable animals only to people who live in deserts because they are excellently adapted to the conditions there. But most of the ancient world preferred other beasts of burden such as donkeys, horses, and oxen. The camel has only one baby every three years, and sometimes fewer than that. Its ability to learn is meager, and it is impossible to train one to respond as well as a horse. It is so bad tempered (especially the males) that Roman soldiers kept them outside the walls of their posts.

1874. It is true that a thirsty camel can drink enormous amounts of water very fast, about twenty-five gallons in approximately ten minutes. It is also true that a camel can travel four days without taking a single drink of water. It is not true, however, that water is stored in its hump. The camel's hump actually stores food. It is a mass of muscle around which fat accumulates. A camel can be fed at the beginning of a trip and not again until the end. After a long, hard journey, the hump shrinks and it flops to one side.

1875. It is completely untrue that a camel has a special sense of direction in the trackless desert. In fact camels easily lose their way and often become separated from the rest of their caravans.

1876. Locusts are insects, the most-mentioned insect in the whole Bible. They destroy crops and plague people. They were one of the plagues sent upon Egypt by God before Pharaoh let the people go out of the land. Some think they were permitted as food, however, because John the Baptist ate locusts and honey while staying in the wilderness (Mark 1:6).

1877. Insects such as ants and honeybees were well respected in the Bible. Ants are busy animals and work hard to stay organized; Proverbs rewards the ant by giving it a place in Scripture. Honey was a special commodity in the Middle East, and honeybees were prized.

1878. Flies, fleas, and gnats (also translated "lice") were disliked strongly and could also carry disease. As in modern times, such insects were greatly unappreciated. They were a plague that descended on Egypt when Pharaoh remained stubborn about letting the Israelites leave.

1879. Lions were kept by royalty and remain a sign of wealth and power. The regal beasts were a common enough animal in the Old Testament, but they have since become extinct in the Middle East. Killing a lion was a sign of great strength, as evidenced by David and Samson when they slew the majestic beasts.

1880. The bear is given little mention in the Bible. However, they were perhaps feared more than lions (Amos 5:19). Researchers believe the references are to the Syrian brown bear, a species found today in certain parts of the Bible region. The young children who mocked Elisha because of his baldness were eaten by bears.

1881. Behemoth . . . or hippopotamus? In a long series of verses in chapter 40 of the Book of Job, the main character describes an animal he calls a "behemoth," but it is very likely a hippopotamus. Hippopotami may have inhabited the Jordan Valley in biblical times, although none are found there now. The Hebrews knew them in Egypt, and it is even possible that Job's behemoth is derived from the Egyptian name for this animal—*pehemau*, which means "ox of the water."

1882. An unknown beast. Job goes to great length (thirty-four verses in chapter 41) identifying the "leviathan." Commentators on the Bible disagree as to whether the leviathan was a crocodile, a whale, or even some mythical animal. Most likely Job had in mind a crocodile, although his description includes fire spouting from its mouth.

1883. The "beasts of the earth" that Jeremiah said would appear after the destruction of Judah probably referred to wild dogs and hyenas. Today dogs are known as "man's best friend," but during biblical times packs of snarling dogs foraged through the city streets and even dug up corpses to feed on them. When Jezebel's body was eaten by dogs after her death, it was a sign of utter humiliation.

1884. The striped hyena is found in the Holy Land and was the most feared and detested of the animal kingdom in the ancient world, due to its habit of digging up graves. The only people who did not hold this strong aversion to hyenas were the Egyptians, who domesticated them for a source of food. Young hyenas are easy to tame and quickly become attached to their masters.

1885. The red fox, an animal we regard as exceedingly clever, won no praise from Solomon. Every reference to it in the Bible is contemptuous. Because they scavenged like wild dogs and hyenas, in the Israelite cities foxes were killed quickly. They feed on almost anything: rodents, eggs, insects, and grass. They even eat fruit, which may explain Solomon's reference to "the little foxes that ruin the vineyards" (Song of Sol. 2:15).

1886. Pigs were unclean and not domesticated by the Hebrews. They are mentioned, but the references are always negative. Jesus drew demons into a herd of pigs, and the prodigal son who squanders everything and ends up tending to pigs has reached the very lowest level of employment.

1887. Ravens and crows were common birds. The raven was the first bird to leave the ark (Gen. 8:6–7). Elijah was fed by ravens while he was hiding from enemies (1 Kings 17:6).

1888. The ostrich was abundant in the Arabian Desert in Job's time, but it became extinct there during World War II. Job paints a vivid word picture of the ostrich in chapter 39 (vv. 14–17).

1889. The crane is tall and stately with a wingspread of about eight feet. It is the largest migrating bird to fly over the Holy Land. Its mass flights are dramatic because the birds number in the thousands, and also because they make a trumpeting sound that fills the air. One of the loudest sounds made by any bird, it is produced by the crane's extremely long windpipe, which is coiled like a French horn.

1890. The earliest statements about bird migrations came from Jeremiah. No one in the ancient world, however, seemed to know for sure where migrating birds came from, why they left, or where they flew next. "Even the stork in the sky knows her appointed seasons; and the dove, the swift and the thrush observe the time of their migration" (Jer. 8:7). The white stork is unmistakable in flight because of its sharply pointed head and extended neck, long dangling legs, and slowly flapping wings. Flocks of several thousand of them pass over the Holy Land at a time.

1891. Sparrows were eaten as food. They were carefully hunted and sold in the marketplace. Jesus spoke of two sparrows being sold for a farthing.

1892. Jonah was swallowed by "a great fish." There has been considerable dispute, however, about what sea creature is large enough to swallow anything the size of a human. A likely creature that swallowed Jonah is a true fish—the man-eating white shark, often found in the Mediterranean. This shark is extremely large, occasionally up to sixty feet in length, and it is quite capable of swallowing a human. It can also store food in its belly for many days without digesting it.

1893. Snakes, or serpents, are part of the reptile family and receive some mention in the Bible. Satan appeared as a serpent to Eve in the Garden of Eden. Moses held up a brass serpent figure to cure the bites of snakes on the people. Later it became a worshiped object. Interestingly most of the references found in the New Testament are metaphorical rather than literal.

1894. Lizards are the most common reptile in the Bible region. They were an unclean creeping animal as described in Leviticus 11:29–39, and though common, they were not appreciated as a food source.

1895. The Israelites knew about monkeys from their stay in Egypt, because the African baboon was sacred to the god Thoth and was sometimes even kept as a pet. The monkey brought back by Solomon's fleet possibly was the rhesus, the kind most often seen in zoos.

1896. Peacocks were the last of the precious cargo mentioned from Ophir, and although the common peacock is native only to southern India and Ceylon, people have spread it around the world. It is hardy and can endure a wide range of climates and living conditions.

1897. The Israelites were familiar with quail, for wall paintings in Egyptian tombs dating from the time of the exodus show that people caught the birds in nets for food. However, they had probably never seen so many of them at one time as when God sent them quail in the wilderness (Exod. 16:13).

1898. Migratory quail are short winged and have only weak powers of flight. They are often blown off course by strong winds and fall exhausted onto the nearest land. God used this very process to cause quail to fall on the Israelite camp. The Bible states that there was a wind that brought the quail from the sea and that the quail fell to earth in the evening.

1899. The rooster was little different from its wild-pheasant ancestor, the red jungle fowl. It was found from Pakistan to Java until recent decades, when new breeds of chickens were developed.

The red jungle fowl closely resembles the barnyard chicken both in appearance and in habits, except that it can still fly.

1900. The chicken may have been domesticated as early as fifty-two hundred years ago in India. The birds were raised at that time for the sport of cockfighting, and were not bred for food until several centuries before the time of Jesus.

The Plant Kingdom

56

1901. Almond trees were admired for their beautiful blossoms by the ancients. The pretty blooms were even used in artwork, such as on the ark (Exod. 25:33–34). The nuts and oil taken from the nuts were used for food. Almond blossoms had a special religious significance for the Hebrews, who in ancient times carved them on the golden candlesticks in the tabernacle, and who still carry them to this day to the synagogue for festivals.

1902. Apple trees are only mentioned in two books of the Bible: Proverbs and Song of Solomon. As a result it is not clear if the "apple" tree was in fact apple bearing or if perhaps the "apples" might have been apricots or even figs.

1903. Cedar trees came from Lebanon and were greatly prized for their height, strength, and the durability of the wood. The temples of early Israel utilized the mighty trees for their buildings.

Cedar wood is mentioned for use in cleansing rituals, but it is now believed that specific reference was actually to a different type of wood, Phoenician juniper.

1904. Solomon had the tall cedars felled by the thousands to supply timber for the temple and for his fabulous palace, which he named "the House of the Forest of Lebanon." He sent shifts of ten thousand Israelites a month to aid the native workers in cutting down the forests.

1905. Only barren slopes remain where the cedars used to be. Only a few scattered groves survived the axes of empire after empire. One small grove is preserved in a park about eighty miles north of Beirut, Lebanon.

1906. Cutting down an olive tree actually rejuvenates it. At the time of cutting, new and more vigorous sprouts grow up out of the roots. The roots are extremely long-lived, and it is almost impossible to kill an olive tree merely by chopping it down. The olive was the symbol of peace in the ancient world, and so it was fitting that it was associated with Jesus, who was known as the Prince of Peace.

1907. Solomon built smelters, a shipyard, and a port at Eziongeber (today known as Elath). His smelters were located in a seemingly unlikely place, an inhospitable desert where water was scarce. There was good reason for building them there, however. The smelters utilized some of the principles of the modern blast furnace. A constant and powerful wind roars down the valley where Solomon's smelters stood, and it acted as bellows that kept the furnace fires burning at high temperatures.

1908. Forest trees served as a symbol of holiness to the Israelites. The names of both the oak and the terebinth, the two most common forest trees of the Holy Land, were derived from Hebrew words meaning "God." David's son Solomon, in the fourth year of his reign, began work on the magnificent temple at Jerusalem. The walls of the temple were built of marble, but they were roofed and lined inside with wood from the cedar of Lebanon.

1909. Oak trees were used as burial places (Gen. 35:8; 1 Chron. 10:12). Three species of the oak tree grow in Palestine; it is believed the tabor oak is the one referred to in Scripture.

1910. Palm trees were especially abundant in the Jordan Valley, and Jericho was known as the city of palm trees. Symbolically the trees were used to depict grace. The date palm also symbolized rejoicing; when Jesus made his triumphal entry into Jerusalem, the crowds waved palm branches to celebrate and honor him.

1911. Sycamore trees vary from continent to continent. Those talked about in the Bible (Egypt and Palestine) are sturdy evergreen trees that bear figs. The Egyptians cultivated it for lumber as well as for its fruit, but in Israel it was mainly grown for the fruit. The sycamore tree is perhaps best remembered for its helping Zaccheus, a short man, see Jesus as he passed by.

1912. Willow trees generally grow near streams in the Middle East. Most Bible references to the trees associate them with water as a result—"the willow of the brook" for instance.

1913. The tree of the knowledge of good and evil is perhaps the most notorious tree in history. The only source of temptation for Adam and Eve in the Garden was the tree from which God had told them not to eat.

1914. The castor oil plant grows and withers quickly, especially when handled, and some believe it may be the "gourd" plant Jonah refers to in Jonah 4. The spiky, dark green leaves and reddish, yarn-ball blooms do not make gourds, however.

1915. The city of Ashkelon was famed in the ancient world for the profusion of fruits and vegetables that grew in its fertile soil. One vegetable was the small onion or scallion, for which the city became noted in Roman times. Our word *scallion* comes from the Latin *caepa Ascalonia*, which means "onion of Ashkelon."

1916. Hyssop is mentioned in the Bible on many occasions, but no plant we know of today by that name is a native species of the Middle East. It is thought that the plant referred to might be the herb marjoram, which is fragrant and comes from Syria.

1917. The lily, though mentioned often in the Bible, is most likely not the common flower that goes by that name.

1918. Mandrakes are a flowering herb that bears fruit in the spring. They are said to have powers and can serve as an aphrodisiac, which we know from Leah and Rachel's quarrel over their husband, Jacob, visiting their separate tents and whether it was worth sharing some mandrakes in order to promote conception.

1919. Myrtle has beautiful pink blossoms with a delicate fragrance; the leaves are also quite fragrant. The myrtle was used by Isaiah as a symbol of God's continuous care and provision of Israel (Isa. 41:19–20). The branches were used for festivals as well (Neh. 8:15–16).

1920. Roses are not native to the Bible lands, and so it is unlikely that the blooms we know as roses actually grew there. More likely other flowers were being referred to. Roses are mentioned several times in the apocryphal books and once in Song of Solomon.

1921. Wormwood is used to symbolize bitterness because it has a unique bitter taste. The plant has many species that grow in Palestine. It is almost more of a shrub, though it can grow quite tall. It is in the same plant family as mugwort and western sagebrush. These plants all have a bitter taste and a strong odor. The Hebrews thought of bitter things as poisonous and thus as symbols of calamity and sorrow, but they used wormwood as a seasoning, a tonic, and a worm medicine.

1922. Balm of Gilead refers to a fragrant resin that is obtained from cuts in the bark of trees. It is used for both perfumes and medicines. Several different plants produce such resins, and no one is sure which one Jeremiah meant. It might have been the Jericho balsam, but a more likely possibility is liquidambar, which produces the gum known as storax or stacte, which is still used in medicine. It is almost identical to the tree Americans call red gum or sweet gum.

1923. Compared to the desert, Canaan must have seemed like paradise, with its vineyards and its orchards of olives, figs, dates, and pomegranates. Next to the grape, the fig was the Israelites' most valued crop. It provided a large part of their daily food. Both figs and dates were eaten either fresh or dried. Fig fruits were also used medicinally; and the sheaths of date clusters provided a sap that was used to make a kind of wine as well as a syrup called "honey" in the Bible.

1924. Pomegranates grow wild as large shrubs or small trees in many parts of the Near East. So important was this "apple with grains," filled with many red-colored, juicy seeds, to the Israelites that it was used as a design to decorate the temple and also coins in Jerusalem.

1925. Along the Nile and throughout the ancient Near East, the most important grain crops were wheat and barley. Both grains have been cultivated in Egypt and the Near East since the earliest recorded times. The earliest evidence comes from near Mount Carmel, on the coast of northern Israel. It dates from about nine thousand years ago.

1926. In the Holy Land, barley was mainly used to feed animals because its protein content was less than wheat. It was also the chief grain of the poor people and so it became a symbol of poverty. Barley was such a staple grain of the Hebrews that it furnished them with units of measurement—three barley grains laid end to end were equal to an inch, about twenty-four to a "span," and forty-eight to a "cubit" (about seventeen inches).

1927. The tall and graceful papyrus reed or bulrush was one of the most abundant plants to grow along the banks of the Nile. At the top of its fifteen-foot stem is a plume of wispy stalks that resemble feathers. Papyrus furnished the world's first material for making paper. In fact our word *paper* is derived from it. The stem was pressed flat under heavy weights until it dried. It was then cut into sheets of suitable size, which were polished with ivory to make a smooth writing surface. Sometimes sheets were glued or sewn together to make long rolls of paper, usually about thirty feet long. One roll has been discovered that is 130 feet in length! Each end of the roll was attached to a handle to make winding easier.

1928. In Jesus' parable of the prodigal son, the younger of two sons squandered his half of the inheritance. He then became so poor that he would fill his belly with the husks that the swine ate (Luke 15:16). Husks came from the pods of the carob tree, also commonly called the locust, which were fed to farm animals.

1929. The carob tree grows beans in a pod that resemble our green peas. Today in the Near East the pods provide fodder for animals and food for very poor people, although in Jesus' time humans did not eat them unless they were as famished as the prodigal son.

1930. Some think that the "locust" (Matt. 3:4) John the Baptist ate in the wilderness was not the insect but rather the pod from the carob tree. For this reason the carob is sometimes called "Saint John's bread tree."

1931. Few plants in the Holy Land have seeds smaller than the mustard seed. As Jesus points out in his parable in Matthew 13, mustard often grows as large as a tree, reaching a height of about fifteen feet, with a stalk as thick as a man's arm. Mustard was widely cultivated in the Middle East for the flavor of its seed.

1932. References to the grapevine abound in Scripture. It is a plant so widely cultivated in the Holy Land that it was known to all. The grapevine is one of the very first plants mentioned in the Bible (one of Noah's first jobs after the flood was to plant a vineyard) and its image appears some two hundred times in both the Old and New Testaments. The grape has been cultivated for so long that its origin is shrouded in mystery.

1933. The date palm was a sign of majesty and fruitfulness to people of the Holy Land. The huge leaves were symbols of triumph and were often carried in ceremonies, but they were also used for roofing, fencing, and the making of mats, baskets, and dishes. Rope was made from the fibrous material in the crown of the trees. The trunk was used for timber, and the date fruit was food for animals as well as people. It is said that the date palm has more uses than the year has days.

1934. The shrub commonly known as "crown of thorns," grown in many European and American gardens, could not possibly be the one mentioned in the Bible. This plant is native to the island of Madagascar and it was unknown in the Holy Land in Jesus' time. Many scholars now believe that the crown was made from a straggly shrub often called the Jerusalem thorn. It grows abundantly around Jerusalem, and its twigs are flexible enough to be woven.

Music in the Bible 57

1935. Musical instruments as well as human melody are mentioned all through the Bible. The Hebrew culture included music; it was in fact an important part of their daily lives. Music was used for both sacred and secular occasions.

1936. "The father of all who play the harp and flute." Jubal was the son of Lamech and a descendant of Cain, but his main title was that of music patriarch (Gen. 4:21).

1937. Music was played at all occasions, such as at religious festivals and worship services, at funerals (Matt. 9:23), in battle (Exod. 15:20–21; 2 Chron. 20:28), and even just to pass the time while shepherds watched their sheep. David was a talented harpist. There are instances of music in royal settings as well as very humble ones in the Bible. It doesn't appear to be an aspect of culture that was truly only for one segment of society.

1938. Instruments ranged in types and styles, but the necessary elements for an orchestra were present: strings, wind instruments, and a percussion section. Though instruments could certainly be played alone, orchestras did exist. David was said to have four thousand instrumentalists organized for his musical needs and requests.

1939. The "pipe" instrument mentioned in Scripture was perhaps an oboe. The pipe would have been used in festivals and other times of rejoicing, as well as funerals and sad occasions. The prophet Jeremiah once compared the soulful, haunting sound to a sad heart (Jer. 48:36).

1940. The organ is another wind instrument from Bible times, though it may have been a generic term for all wind instruments (Gen. 4:21 KJV).

1941. Trumpets referred to a variety of different wind instruments—everything from a ram's horn to Moses' silver trumpet may correctly be classified within this instrument family. Another name used was "cornet."

1942. The flute is only mentioned once in the King James Version of the Bible, in Daniel 3:5, but it is mentioned more in other, newer translations, such as the NIV (three times). It very well may have referred to a reed flute or some other instrument that closely resembles a modern flute.

1943. The harp is perhaps the most-mentioned instrument in the Bible. It is believed that the instrument actually refers to the lyre, a similar stringed instrument of smaller proportions. The lyre was made of wood and had between eight and ten strings to pluck. The fingers or some sort of pick may have been used. The instrument may be of Syrian origin.

1944. Harps and heaven? Many people associate heaven and harps. Many people don't realize that this connection actually comes from the Bible. The apostle John describes this in his vision, seeing the heavenly throne in the Book of Revelation.

1945. A psaltery is another kind of harp, as is a viol. These were even smaller wooden-framed harps, and they would have been plucked with the fingers to make music. They may have been of Phoenician origin. The Bible mentions these in 1 Samuel 10:5 and Isaiah 5:12.

1946. The sackbut, despite the funny name, is a type of harp with a triangular shape. It has been mistranslated (Dan. 3:5) in various versions, but it is a harp.

1947. Cymbals are a percussion instrument. They were used both in celebration and at ceremonies such as the dedication of the wall of Jerusalem (Neh. 12:27). There were two kinds of cymbals. The first had flat metal plates that were struck together to make a clashing, crashing noise. The other kind had one cymbal that was held stationary while the other one was banged against it.

1948. Timbrels, or tambourines, are instruments still in use today. The bells and other "jingly" sounds come from light pieces of metal that shake and rattle together when the wood they are attached to is shaken or beat. The timbrel was used for happy occasions and to make music for singing and dancing.

58

Symbols

1949. **The cross** is perhaps the most recognized symbol of the Christian. Jesus was crucified on a cross between two criminals. His hands and feet were nailed into the cross, signs to forever remain that demonstrate the atoning work he performed on the cross for believers.

1950. **The hand of God** is perhaps the most ancient symbol of God the Father. Like most symbols, it is referenced from Scripture. The meaning of the symbol relates to the creative power of God. Through his handiwork came forth the genius of creation.

1951. A crown is a representation of the office Christ holds as King. The Scriptures teach that he is the "King of Kings." The Bible also refers to Jesus as the "Crown of Life," which all who believe may take for themselves.

1952. The lantern is a symbol of betrayal that comes directly from Scripture. When Judas came with the soldiers to arrest Jesus, the group carried torches and lanterns in order to find Jesus. Alternatively the lantern is a symbol of light.

1953. Jesus is the Light of the world, the source that brings life to a dead world. Furthermore Christ's two distinct natures, divine and human, are an important tenet of Christ being both God and man. The traditional symbol to display this doctrine is to light two candles during church services, with one on either side of a cross.

1954. The Good Shepherd is a biblical reference to Jesus' description of himself in the Gospel of John. As the redeemer of his people, the sheep, Jesus watches over them, protects them, and provides for their way into the shelter.

1955. The Holy Spirit is most often represented by a dove and recalls the story of Jesus' baptism from the Scriptures. After Jesus was baptized by John the Baptist, a dove descended and God spoke from heaven. This is one of very few symbols for the Third Person of the Trinity.

1956. The seven doves, seven lamps, and seven-pointed star all represent the seven gifts of the Holy Spirit stated in the Book of Revelation. The seven gifts are strength, honor, glory, blessing, power, riches, and wisdom.

Bias Trivia

59

1957. Though *Trinity* is a common Christian term, the Bible never mentions the Trinity as such. It was a doctrine developed much later when the church was more established.

1958. Dreams were often used as a means for God to speak to his prophets and other favored children. Items within the dreams symbolized real events or people or even future happenings. Joseph's dream about wheat sheaves foretold the time when he would be powerful in Egypt and lead that people through a drought and famine.

1959. The doctrine known as "Immaculate Conception," the belief that Mary herself was conceived without sin, has no biblical justification. This belief began early in Christian history and was officially accepted as dogma essential to Roman Catholic beliefs by Pope Pius IX in 1854.

1960. Knowing the basics. In a 1997 survey, the *London Sunday Times* found that only 34 percent of 220 Anglican priests could recite all of the Ten Commandments without help.

1961. Two separate creation stories are told in Genesis (Gen. 1:1–2:3 and Gen. 2:4–25), but there is no mention of an apple in the Garden of Eden story.

1962. The original Hebrew word for "ark" meant "box" or "chest" in English.

1963. Although the King James Version is often associated with Shakespearean English, neither Moses nor Jesus is ever quoted as saying "thee" or "thou."

1964. Place-names in the Bible often came from the person or persons who settled the area. They would give it a special name to commemorate the occasion.

1965. Jericho is the world's oldest city. It was founded about 3500 BC.

1966. Polytheism, the belief in more than one god, distinguishes our age from that of the Bible more than any other cultural issue.

1967. The name *Jesus* is the Greek version of the name Joshua.

1968. David, the shepherd, warrior, and king of Israel, broke half of the Ten Commandments, from what we are told in the Bible. More than likely he broke all ten!

1969. Frankincense and myrrh are both fragrant resins imported from India, Arabia, or Africa. They were therefore costly and precious in the Holy Land.

1970. The star. About the time of the birth of Jesus in Bethlehem, a phenomenon occurred in the night sky. There has been considerable dispute about what this bright star of Bethlehem may have been. Whatever the astronomical phenomenon was exactly, it did not go unobserved in the ancient home of astronomy, Mesopotamia. The wise men or magi who saw the star and believed that it heralded the birth of Jesus were probably astronomers.

1971. *Magus* **is a Persian word** that referred to the priests of Persia, and from *magus* we get our English word *magic.* In the ancient world the priests who could predict eclipses and the motions of the planets must have seemed to possess magical powers.

1972. Samaritans did not have a great reputation among Jews. They were not good neighbors. The Jews and Samaritans had a long and unhappy history. The Samaritans had first come into the land when the Assyrians conquered Israel. An offshoot sect, they followed the books of Moses but did not treat the rest of the Hebrew Scriptures as sacred. As a result bad blood grew between the groups.

1973. As archaeologists excavated the mound of the ancient city of Jericho (about a mile or so northwest of the modern city), they found not one ancient city but instead successive cities, each built atop the ruins of the previous ones. Jericho is the oldest known town in the world. Above the first signs of human habitation, five cities were built in antiquity—and the fourth of these appears to be the one that was conquered by Joshua.

1974. Double walls nearly thirty feet high, with each wall about six feet thick, were discovered by archaeologists at the Jericho site. It is clear that this city had a violent end. Sections of the wall crumbled, and there is evidence of fire so intense that it burned bricks and cracked stones.

1975. Shibboleth. Jephthah's men fought and defeated the tribesmen of Ephraim (another Israelite tribe who did not help Jephthah in his battle with the Ammonites). If an Ephraimite tried to cross the Jordan, Jephthah's men would ask him to say "Shibboleth," a word that means either "ear of corn" or "flood torrent." But due to regional dialects, these men couldn't pronounce the "sh" sound, and said "sibboleth" instead. Forty-two thousand men with this speech deficiency died at the Jordan. A contemporary story is told from World War II in which Dutch resistance fighters were able to cull out Nazi infiltrators who couldn't pronounce a particular Dutch name. "Shibboleth" has since come to mean a word or catchphrase that is distinctive to one group.

1976. Hammurabi (meaning "westerner") was an Amorite who conquered several Sumerian cities and developed a small empire, making him the first king to elevate Babylon from a small town to a major power. Some scholars believe that Hammurabi—generally dated as king of Babylon from 1792–1750 BC—might be the mysterious King Amraphel, king of Shinar, mentioned in Genesis 14.

1977. Hammurabi is best remembered for a code of law, set down toward the end of his reign on clay tables and on stelae, or stone pillars. Clear parallels as well as clear differences can be drawn between Hammurabi's code and the law Moses received from God on Mount Sinai. Sadly the tablets on which the Ten Commandments were written disappeared with the ark of the covenant, but Hammurabi's laws were uncovered by French archaeologists in the ancient city of Susa and remain on display in the Louvre in Paris.

1978. Towers known as ziggurats, which literally means "houses that lift up their heads," were erected throughout the Babylonian Empire and were probably intended as stairways for men to ascend and meet the gods. A ziggurat resembles a pyramid, but its sides are steplike. In constructing the tower, the builders "had brick for stone, and slime had they for morter" (Gen. 11:3 KJV). The bricks were made from mud and the "slime" was asphalt, found all over the Iranian oil fields even today.

1979. Pottery, made from clay and baked in a kiln, is one of the most durable materials ever made. Glass flakes away, metals corrode and rust, wood and fabrics are destroyed by dampness and insects. Pottery alone survives. Although a pottery jar can easily be shattered, the broken pieces or shards may last for centuries and give clues to when the pottery was made, who made it, and its relationship to pottery made by neighboring people.

1980. Archaeologists have studied the shards discovered in the Negeb that date from about the time Abraham crossed it. All the pottery made throughout this vast area was almost exactly the same, revealing that those were settled times and that the people of the Negeb traded peacefully with one another.

1981. The Shema is the central confession of the Jewish faith: "Hear, O Israel: The LORD our God, the LORD is one." It is originally found in Deuteronomy 6:4, and Jesus quoted it, saying that the verse that follows ("Love the LORD your God with all your heart and with all your soul and with all your strength") is the greatest commandment.

DEAD SEA SCROLLS

1982. Muhammed ed Dib was tending goats in the spring of 1947, while the British still controlled Palestine. In the arid hills that surround the northern Dead Sea shore, the young goatherd dropped a stone into a cave and heard it hit something. Investigating further, he found ancient clay pots filled with scrolls and scraps of old leather covered in mysterious writing. His accidental find was the beginning of one of the most momentous and controversial discoveries in history—the "Dead Sea Scrolls."

1983. Muhammed's find launched a wider search of the surrounding area, called Qumran, approximately ten miles south of Jericho, on a plateau overlooking the Dead Sea. Over the years many more scrolls and remnants of scrolls were uncovered. It was soon clear that these ancient scrolls included some of the oldest known texts of the Hebrew Bible ever found.

1984. More than two hundred biblical documents have been found, some almost complete, written in both Hebrew and Aramaic—a Syrian language closely related to Hebrew, and the language spoken by Jesus. The Dead Sea Scrolls contain at least a portion of every book of the Hebrew Bible, except the Book of Esther.

1985. Among the Dead Sea Scrolls is a complete "book" of Isaiah, composed of seventeen separate pieces of leather stitched together to form a roll nearly twenty-five feet long. Sophisticated dating techniques have proved that some of these scrolls were written nearly three hundred years before Jesus was born. Others came from Jesus' own lifetime.

1986. Copper scrolls were also discovered in the Dead Sea caves at Qumran, describing a treasure—twenty-six tons of gold and sixty-five tons of silver—hidden at sixty-four locations throughout Israel. Most scholars believe the treasure is a hoax or myth, although others hold that the treasure was indeed taken from the temple and hidden before the Roman legions arrived in AD 70. It is very rare to find a Hebrew text on thinly beaten sheets of copper such as these.

RELATIONSHIP BETWEEN THE SHEPHERD AND THE SHEEP

1987. Palestine has always been known for large flocks of sheep, and Arabs of the Bible lands have been largely dependent on sheep for their living throughout the centuries. The large number of sheep in the land can be understood when we read that Job had fourteen thousand sheep (Job 42:12), and that King Solomon, at the temple's dedication, sacrificed one hundred and twenty thousand sheep and goats (1 Kings 8:63).

1988. Fat-tailed sheep were the most common variety. The fat tail provides reserve strength for the sheep, much like the hump does on a camel. When the sheep is butchered, this fatty tail is quite valuable. People will buy the tail, or part of it, and use it for frying. The Pentateuch makes reference to the fat tail of the sheep in Exodus 29:22, "Take from this ram the fat, the fat tail . . ."

1989. The youngest boy in the family becomes the shepherd of the sheep. As the older son grows up, he begins to help the father with sowing, plowing, and harvesting the crops, so he passes the shepherd tasks down to the younger brother and on down until the youngest of all becomes the family shepherd. Such was the custom when Jesse raised his family of eight sons. David was the youngest.

1990. The shepherd's scrip is a leather bag. When he leaves home to tend the sheep, his mother will fill it with bread, cheese, dried fruit, and perhaps some olives. It was into a bag like this that David placed the five smooth stones when he went to battle with the giant Goliath.

1991. The Law of Moses speaks of tithing (giving 10 percent) from the flock. "The entire tithe of the herd and flock—every tenth animal that passes under the shepherd's rod—will be holy to the LORD" (Lev. 27:32). To do this Jewish writers tell us that the shepherd called the animals to him, and as they would pass under his rod at a narrow entrance, he would mark every tenth one with his rod, which had been dipped into a dye.

1992. More than a weapon. From the story of David, we are familiar with the sling, but in addition to using a sling against wild animals or robbers, the shepherd found it very handy for directing the sheep. A stone could be dropped close to a sheep that was lagging behind and startle the sheep into coming along with the rest of the flock.

1993. In selecting pasture for the flock, it is an absolute necessity that plenty of water is provided too. Flocks are often stationed near a stream of running water, but the sheep can be afraid of water that is running too quickly or that is roiled up with mud. The shepherd looks for pools of water or provides some quiet place where the sheep can quench their thirst.

1994. More than one flock may be kept in the same fold. Often flocks are even mixed while being watered at a well. No attempt is made to separate them. When it is time to separate the sheep, one shepherd after another will stand up and call out: "Tahhoo! Tahhoo!" or a similar call of his own choice. The sheep will lift their heads, and after a scramble each one will begin following his master.

1995. The Eastern shepherd has a personal relationship with his sheep that gives the figure of the Lord as the Shepherd of his people deep meaning. Not only does the shepherd often know his sheep by name; he never drives them but leads them instead. This does not mean that he is always in front of them. He may walk by their side or sometimes follow behind.

1996. The shepherd is so acutely aware of each of his sheep that often he doesn't even need to count them. He is able to feel the absence of any one of his sheep. When a shepherd of Lebanon was asked how he could keep track of his sheep if he didn't count, he replied, "If you were to put a cloth over my eyes, and bring me any sheep and only let me put hands on its face, I could tell in a moment if it was mine or not."

1997. The shepherd plays with the sheep to pass the hours. A shepherd does this by pretending to run away. The sheep will soon overtake him and completely surround him, jumping and twisting with delight. The sheep know their shepherd will not leave them or turn them away.

WEIGHTS AND MEASURES

1998. To measure length in the Old Testament, one would have used several units. From smallest to largest, the scale was finger-palm-span-cubit. The cubit was considered the most basic form of measurement, something like what Americans consider the "foot" measurement. The cubit was the length of the forearm measured to the tip of the middle finger. Generally this length varied between seventeen and eighteen inches in length.

1999. The span was the distance from the tip of the thumb to the tip of the little finger with the hand extended and the fingers held apart. It was roughly one-half of the standard cubit. The palm was approximately one-sixth of the common cubit and was initially measured as the breadth of the hand at the base of the fingers. The finger measurement was considered to be about one-quarter of a palm and was considered the smallest subdivision of the cubit.

2000. Weights in the Bible followed their own system of measure. The weights ascended from the smallest weight of a pim, beka, or gerah, to the larger shekel, mina, and talent (as Jesus mentioned in one of the parables). For the smaller weights, balances would have been used to measure properly.

2001. A shekel was .403 ounces. The pim, beka, and gerah were all smaller fractions of the shekel. In order for these weights to be effective, balances were used. As the cubit was the standard measure, so the shekel was the standard unit of weight. Shekel is descended from the word meaning "to weigh."

2002. The talent was by far the largest unit of weight used to measure. Each talent was worth three thousand shekels and weighed around seventy-five pounds. Minas were between fifty and sixty shekels, depending on whether the system was Israelite or Babylonian. Each mina weighed roughly 1.25 pounds.

Bibliography

The NIV Study Bible. © 1985 by The Zondervan Corporation. The Holy Bible, New International Version copyright © 1973, 1978, 1984 by International Bible Society.

Psalter Hymnal. Copyright ©1976 by the Board of Publications of the Christian Reformed Church, Inc., Grand Rapids.

Bancroft, Emery H. *Elemental Theology.* Grand Rapids: Zondervan, 1977.

Bloesch, Donald G. *God the Almighty: Power, Wisdom, Holiness, Love.* Downers Grove, Ill.: InterVarsity Press, 1995.

Bulkley, Ed. *How Big Is Your God? Finding a Faith That Really Works.* Eugene, Oreg.: Harvest House, 1997.

Caputo, Michael. *God Seen through the Eyes of the Greatest Minds.* West Monroe, La.: Howard Publishing, 2000.

Davis, Kenneth C. *Don't Know Much about the Bible: Everything You Need to Know about the Good Book but Never Learned.* New York: Eagle Brook, 1998.

DeHaan, M. R., M.D. *Portraits of Christ in Genesis.* Grand Rapids: Zondervan, 1966.

435

De Witt, John R. *What Is the Reformed Faith?* Carlisle, Pa.: Banner of Truth Trust, 1981.

Farb, Peter. *The Land, Wildlife, and Peoples of the Bible.* New York: Harper and Row, 1967.

Gantt, Michael. *A NonChurchgoer's Guide to the Bible.* Intercourse, Pa.: Good Books, 1977.

Glaspey, Terry W. *Pathway to the Heart of God: Inspired to Pray by the Great Christian Writers.* Eugene, Oreg.: Harvest House, 1998.

Kelly, Douglas, and Philip Rollinson. *The Westminster Shorter Catechism in Modern English.* Phillipsburg, N.J.: Presbyterian and Reformed, 1986.

Lang, Stephen. *1001 Things You Always Wanted to Know about the Bible but Never Thought to Ask.* Nashville: Thomas Nelson, 1999.

MacGregor, Jerry, and Marie Prys. *1001 Surprising Things You Should Know about the Bible.* Grand Rapids: Baker, 2002.

Mysteries of the Bible: The Enduring Questions of the Scriptures. Pleasantville, N.Y.: Reader's Digest Books, 1988.

Packer, J. I., Merrill C. Tenney, and William White Jr. *Nelson's Illustrated Encyclopedia of Bible Facts.* Nashville: Thomas Nelson, 1980.

Paterson, John and Katherine. *Consider the Lilies: Plants of the Bible.* New York: Thomas Y. Crowell, 1986.

Phillips, Bob. *In Pursuit of Bible Trivia.* Eugene, Oreg.: Harvest House, 1985.

Pink, Arthur W. *The Attributes of God.* Grand Rapids: Baker, 1975.

Roberts, Jenny. *Bible Facts.* New York: Barnes and Noble, 1990.

Shelley, Bruce. *Church History in Plain Language.* Dallas: Word, 1982.

Stafford, Thomas Albert. *Christian Symbolism in the Evangelical Churches.* New York: Abingdon-Cokesbury Press, 1942.

Tozer, A. W. *The Knowledge of the Holy.* San Francisco: HarperCollins, 1961.

Who's Who in the Bible: An Illustrated Guide. New York: DK Publishing, 1998.

Wight, Fred H. *Manners and Customs of Bible Lands.* Chicago: Moody, 1953.

Index

Jerry Chip MacGregor is an associate publisher with Time Warner Book Group and the author of several books. A former pastor and college professor, he lives in Tennessee with his wife.

Marie Prys, a graduate of Dordt College, is a freelance editor and writer who works with Christian authors and publishers. She lives in the Pacific Northwest with her husband and two children.

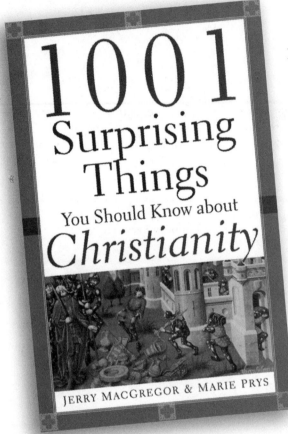